The Encyclopedia of
Jazz
Chords

Published by
Hal Leonard

Exclusive distributors:
Hal Leonard
7777 West Bluemound Road, Milwaukee, WI 53213
Email: info@halleonard.com

Hal Leonard Europe Limited
42 Wigmore Street Maryleborne, London, WIU 2 RY
Email: info@halleonardeurope.com

Hal Leonard Australia Pty. Ltd.
4 Lentara Court Cheltenham, Victoria, 9132 Australia
Email: info@halleonard.com.au

Order No. AM92591
ISBN 0-7119-4668-X

Cover design by Studio Twenty, Lonodn
Compiled and edited by Jack Long
Music processed by Woodrow Edition

Printed in EU.

www.halleonard.com

The C Collection
Page 6

The C♯ Collection
Page 12

The D♭ Collection
Page 13

The D Collection
Page 24

The D♯ Collection
Page 30

The E♭ Collection
Page 31

The E Collection
Page 42

The F Collection
Page 48

The F♯ Collection
Page 54

The G♭ Collection
Page 55

The G Collection
Page 66

The G♯ Collection
Page 72

The A♭ Collection
Page 73

The A Collection
Page 84

The B♭ Collection
Page 90

The B Collection
Page 96

Index
Page 108

INTRODUCTORY NOTES

1. The chords in this book are voiced in a way that makes them easy to find and play effectively. But that doesn't mean you can't play them differently if you want to.
   The notes contained in the right hand can be rearranged in any order you like, and will still represent the chord symbol shown, like this:

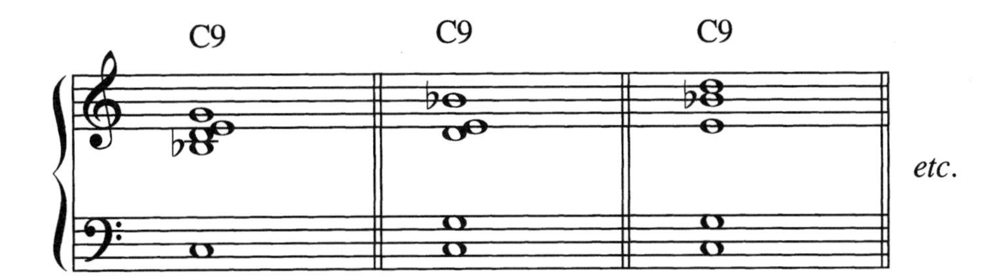

   The left hand can also be changed to alter the chord structure. Sometimes, when this is specifically required, the left hand alteration will be indicated by a 'cut' (or 'slash') chord, consisting of a chord symbol followed by a sloping line (the 'cut' or 'slash'), followed by the root, or bass note, that you need to play. C/E, for instance, means that a chord of C is to be played with an E root, or bass note.
   Here's one way of playing that:

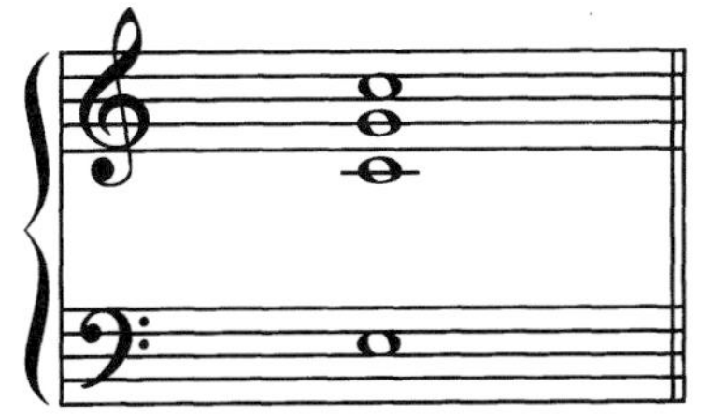

   In addition you will often see 'cut' chords containing a root not found in the chord itself. Am7/D, for instance, played like this:

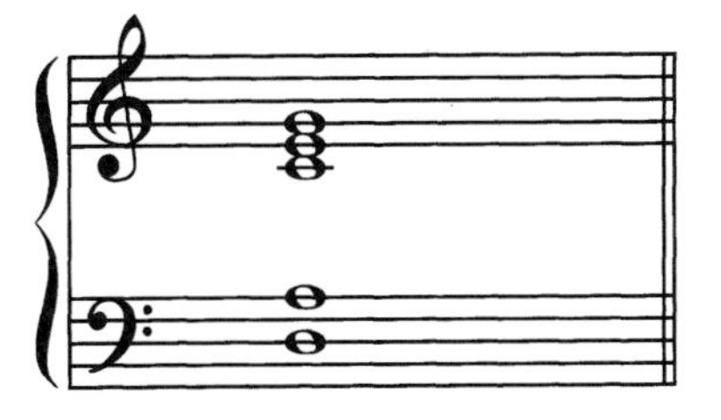

   is actually D11, described in a more commonly understood fashion for those who may not know what D11 means. Now, however, with the help of this book, you will never again have any trouble playing D11 – or, indeed, any other chords you're likely to be faced with!

2. All keys are covered here, except A♯. You will come across this key so rarely – if at all – that you only need to remember it's the same note as B♭, and any A♯ chords are played exactly the same way as their B♭ equivalents (e.g. A♯7 = B♭7, etc.).

3. 𝄫 is the sign for double flat, and means the note is to be lowered one tone.
   𝄪 is the sign for double sharp, and means the note is to be raised one tone.

The C Collection

C major - C

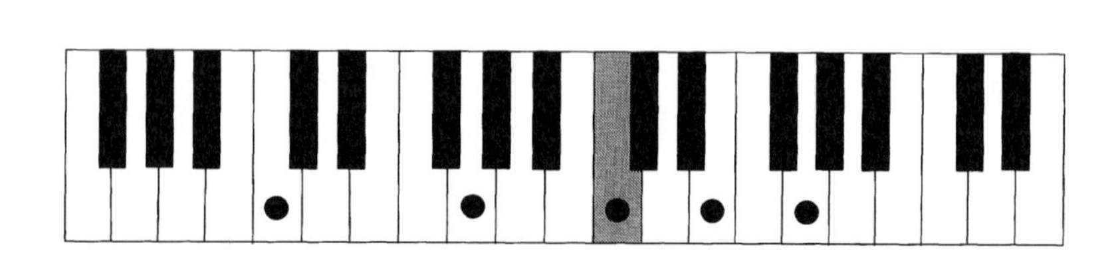

C suspended 4th - Csus or Csus4

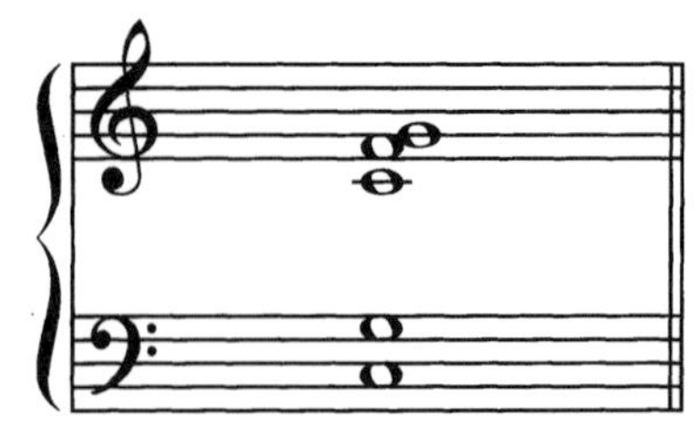

C augmented 5th - C+ or Caug

C added 6th - C6

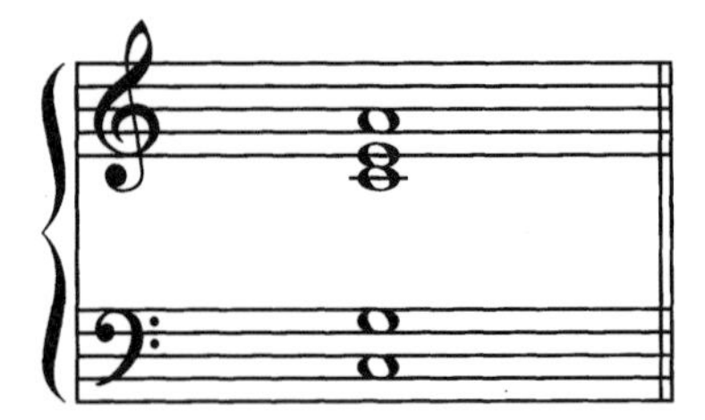

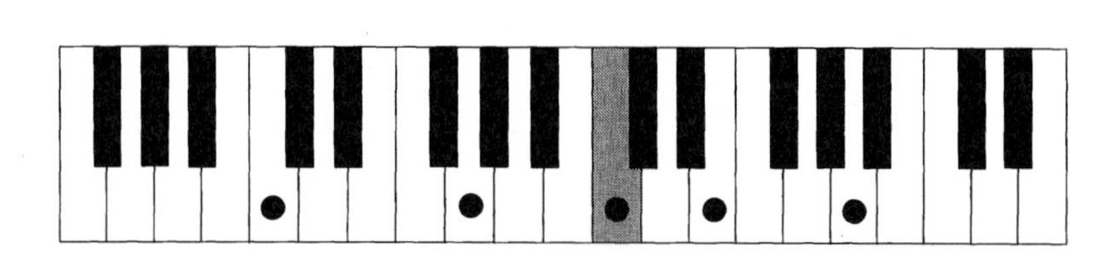

C added 6th and 9th - C6/9

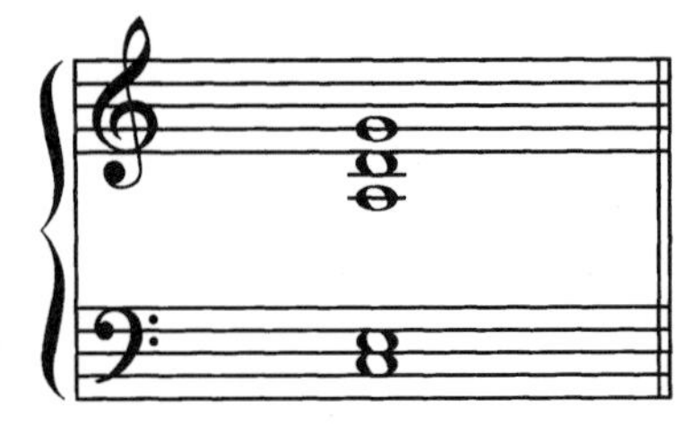

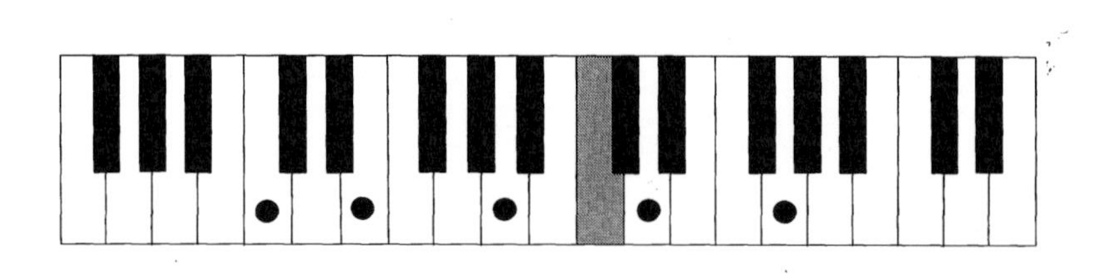

The C Collection

C major 7th - Cmaj7

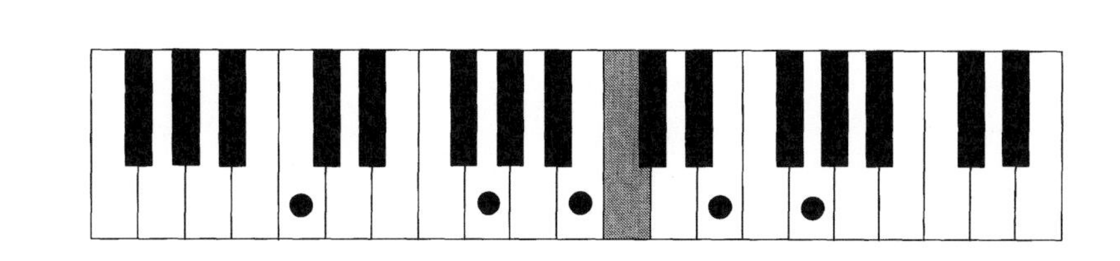

C dominant 7th - C7

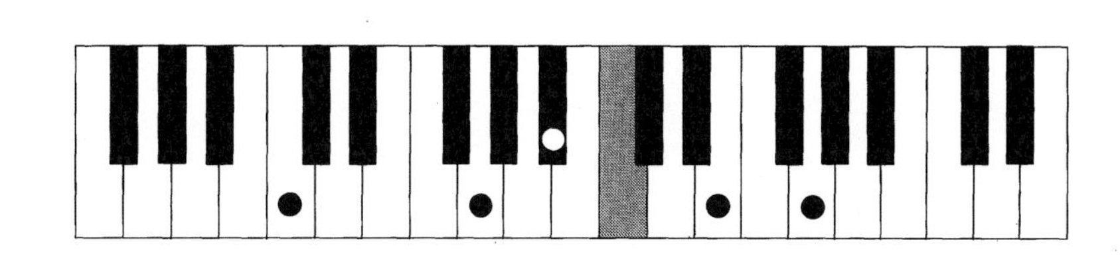

C dominant 7th with suspended 4th - C7sus or C7sus4

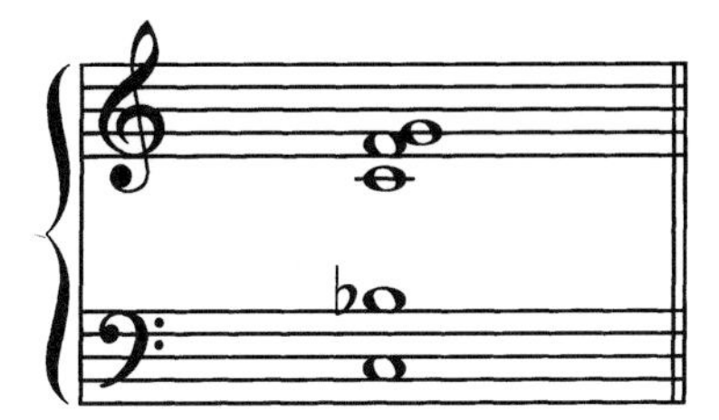

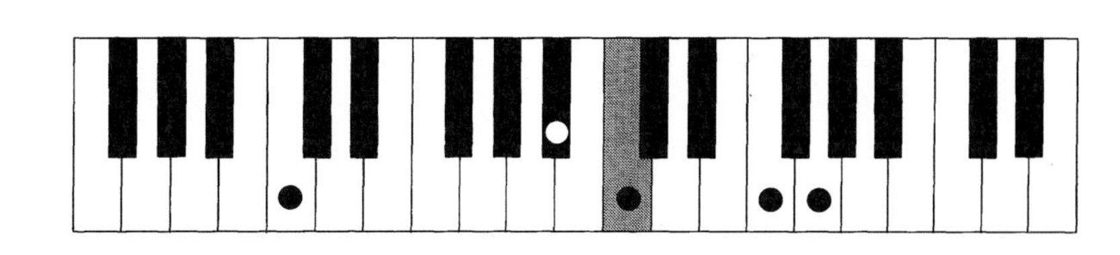

C dominant 7th with flattened 5th - C7(♭5)

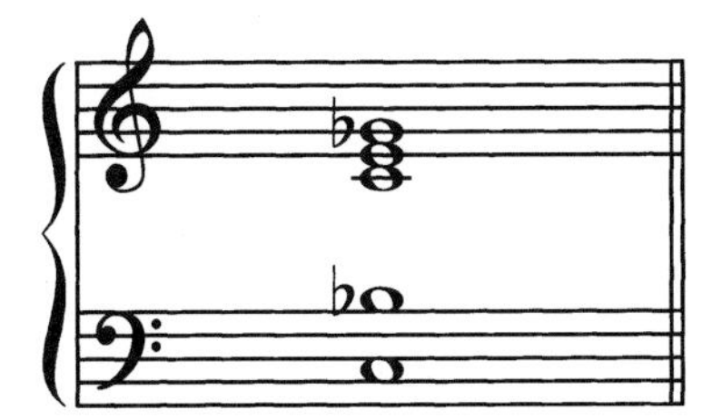

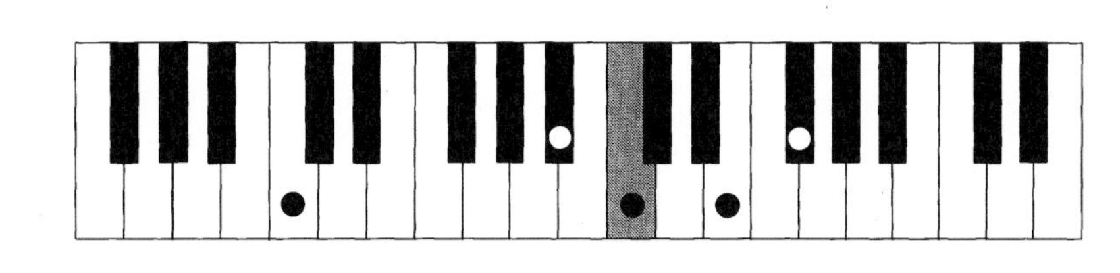

C dominant 7th with augmented 5th - C7+ or C7aug

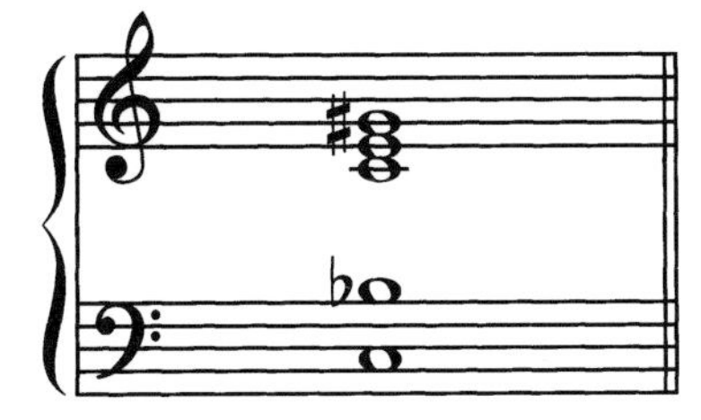

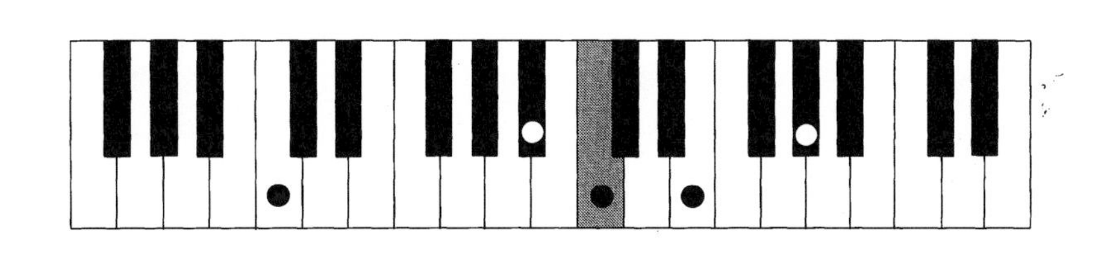

The C Collection

C dominant 7th with flattened 9th - C7(♭9)

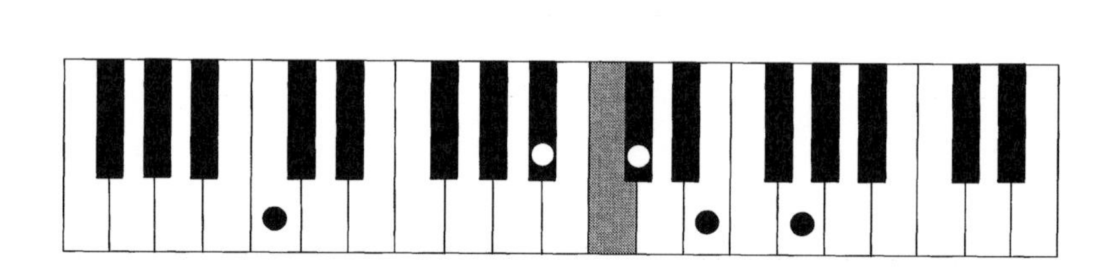

C dominant 7th with flattened 9th and 5th - C7(♭9/♭5)

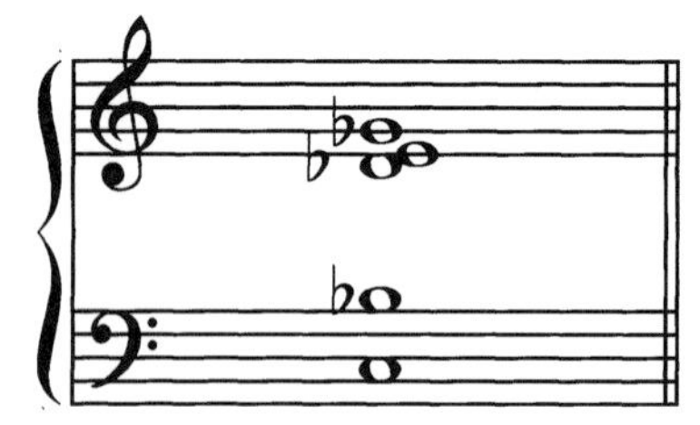

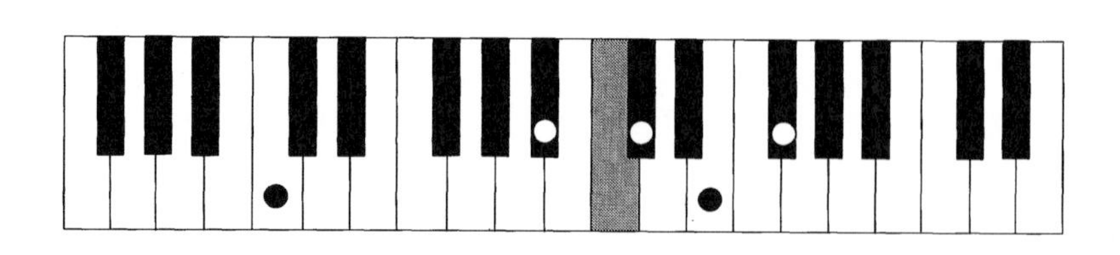

C dominant 7th with sharpened 9th - C7(♯9)

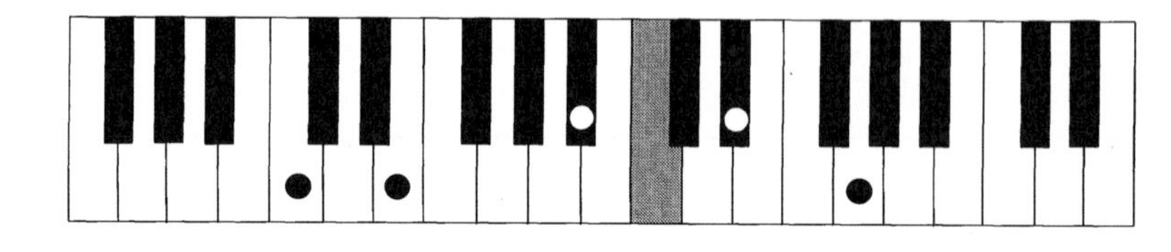

C added 9th - Cadd9

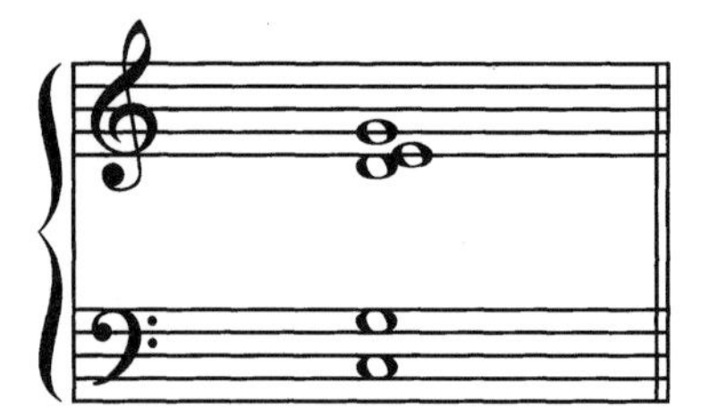

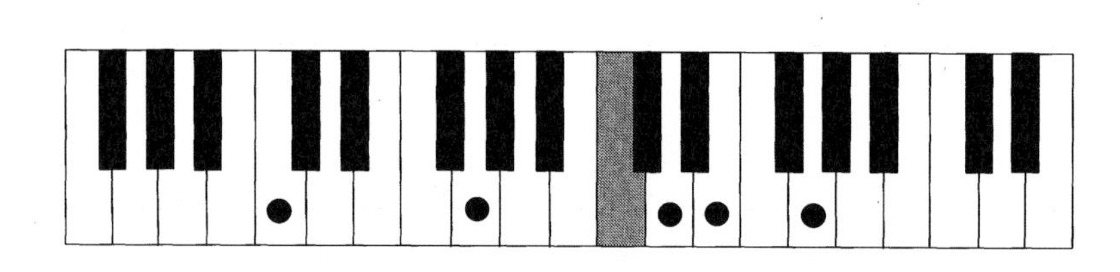

C major 9th - Cmaj9

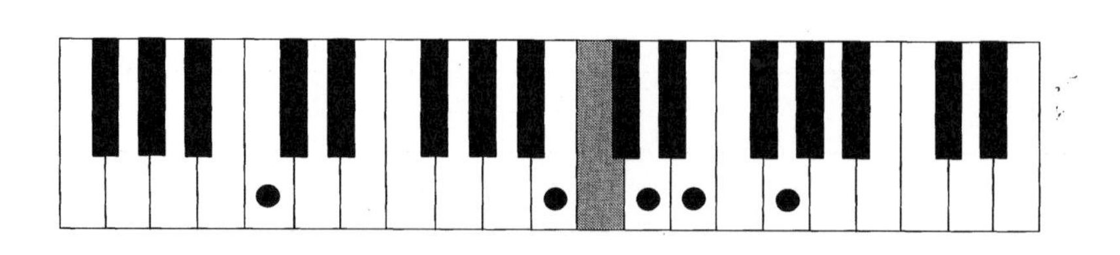

The C Collection

C dominant 9th - C9

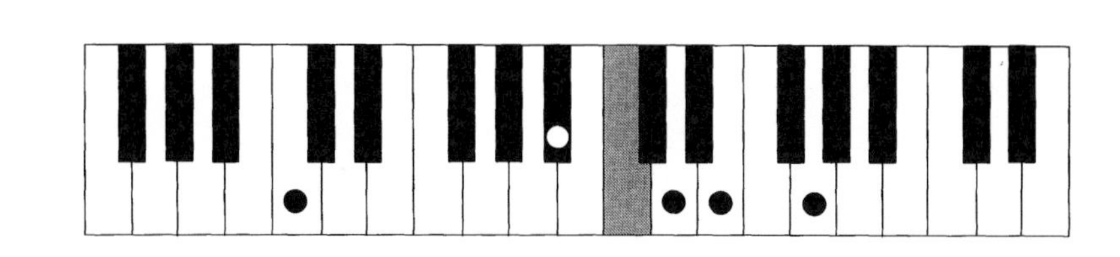

C dominant 9th with suspended 4th - C9sus or C9sus4

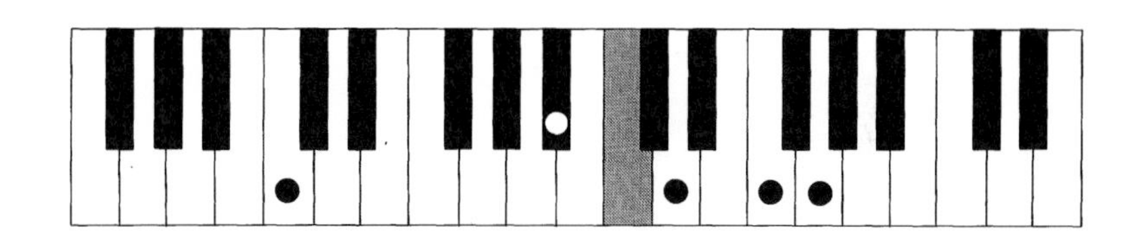

C dominant 9th with augmented 5th - C9+ or C9aug

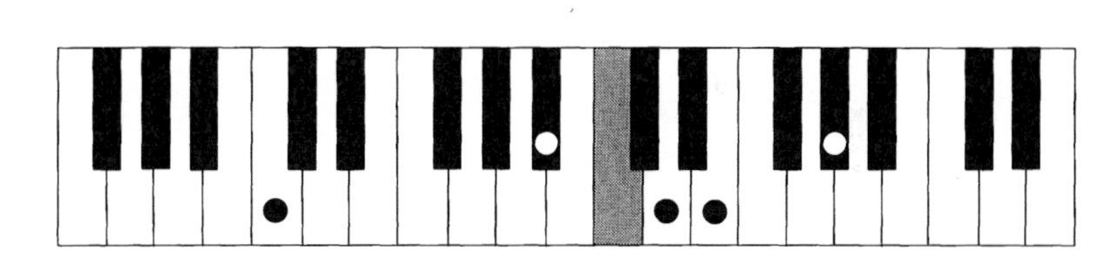

C dominant 9th with sharpened 11th - C9(♯11)
with flattened 5th - C9(♭5)

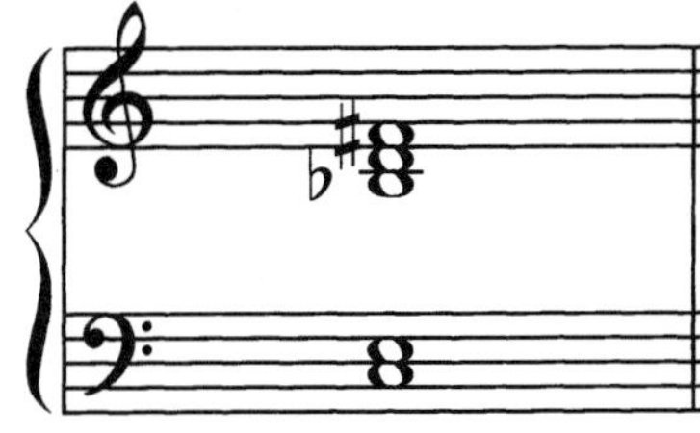

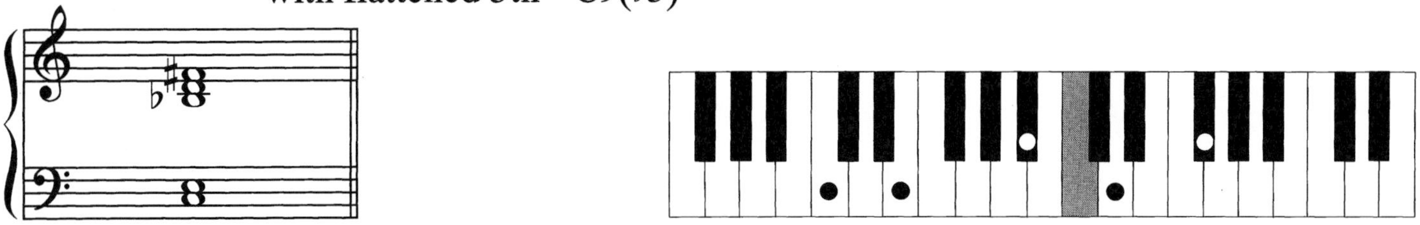

C dominant 11th - C11

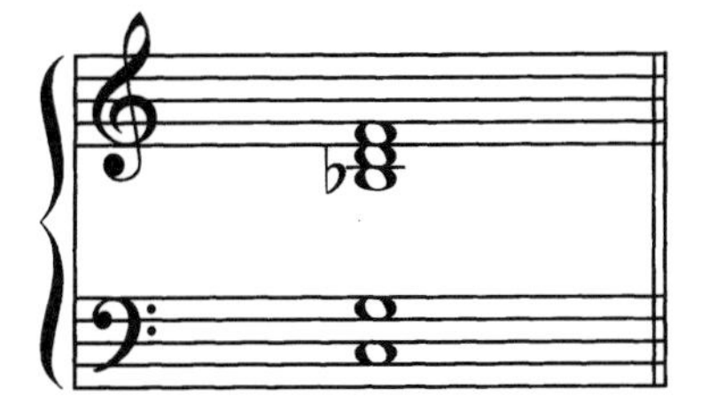

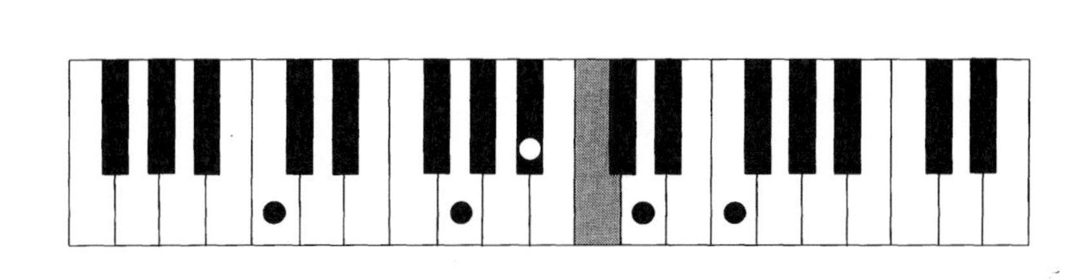

The C Collection

C dominant 11th with flattened 9th - C11(♭9)

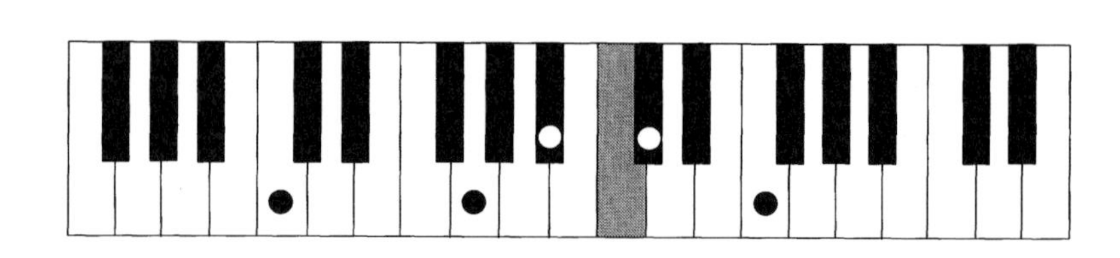

C dominant 13th - C13

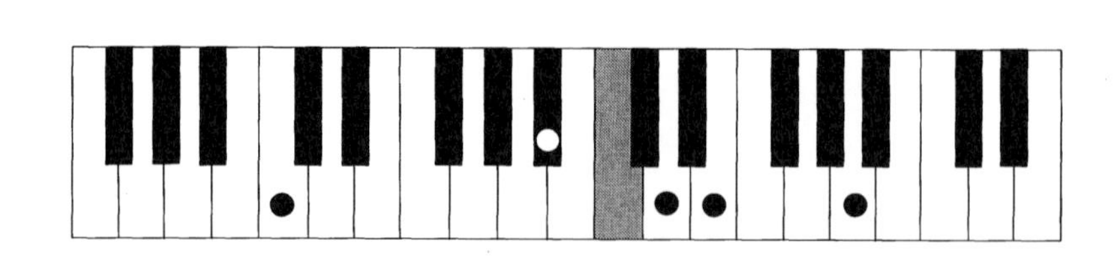

C dominant 13th with flattened 9th - C13(♭9)

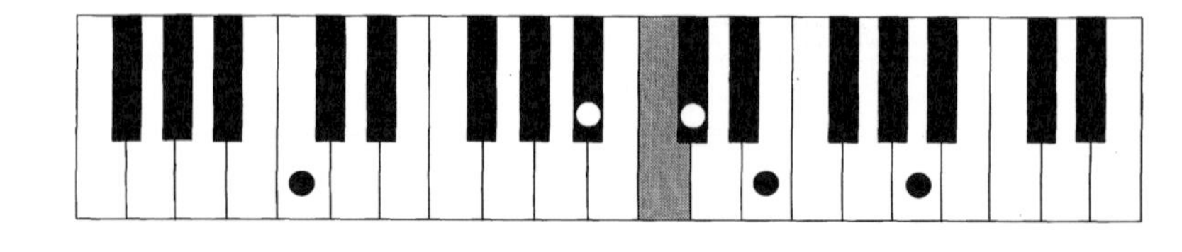

C minor - Cm

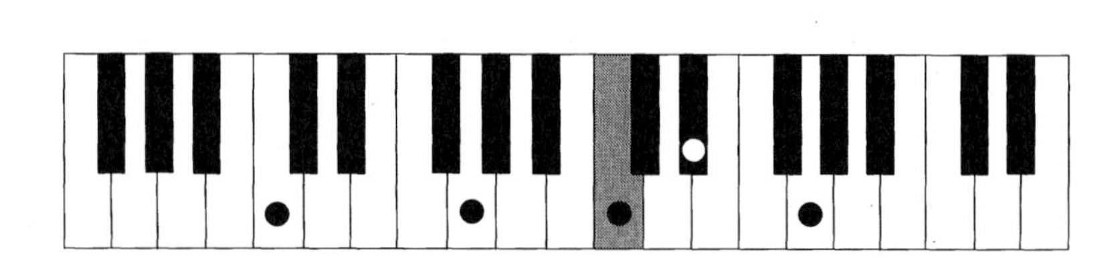

C diminished - C° or Cdim

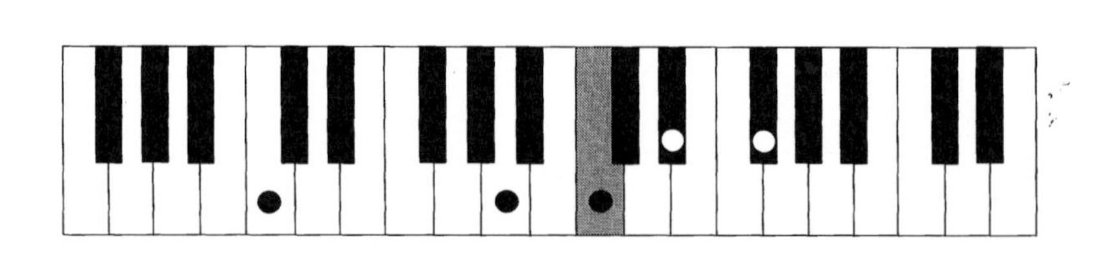

The C Collection

C minor added 6th - Cm6

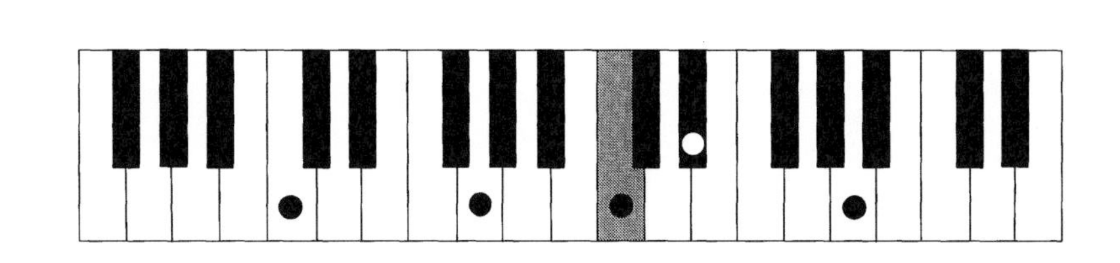

C minor 7th - Cm7

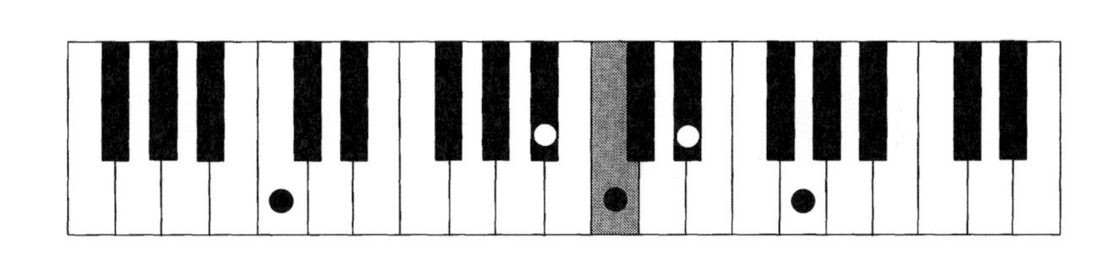

C minor 7th with flattened 5th - Cm7(♭5)

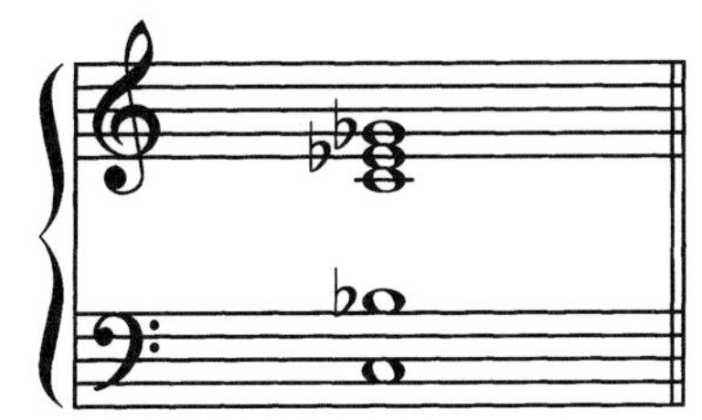

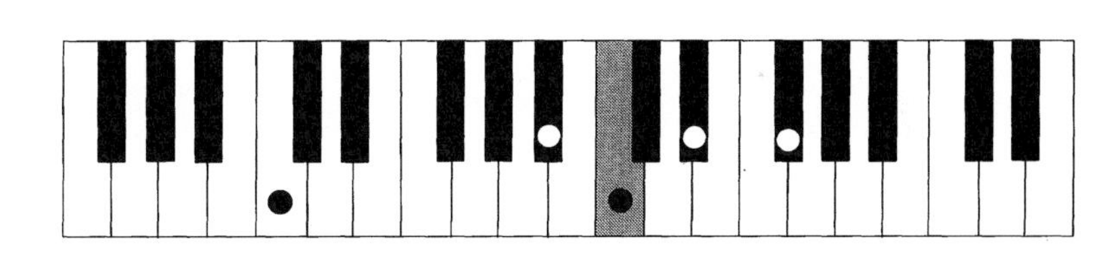

C minor added major 7th - Cm(maj7)

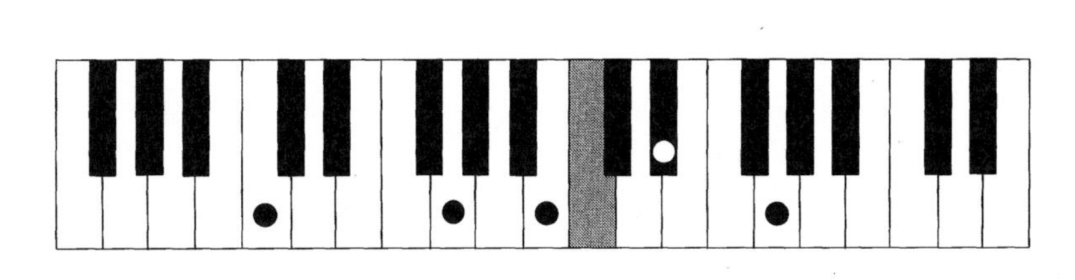

C minor 9th - Cm9

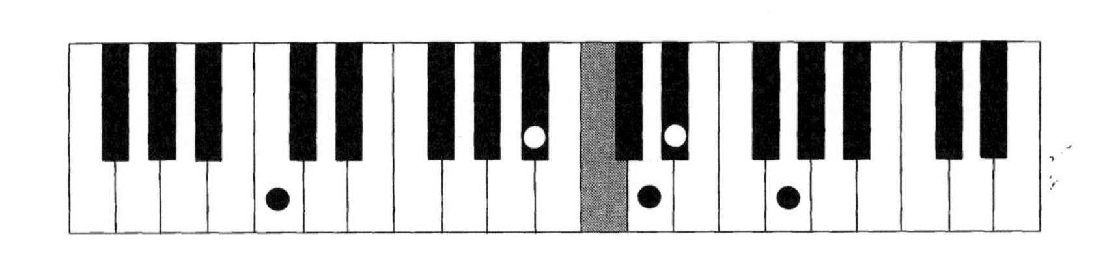

The C♯ Collection

C♯ major - C♯

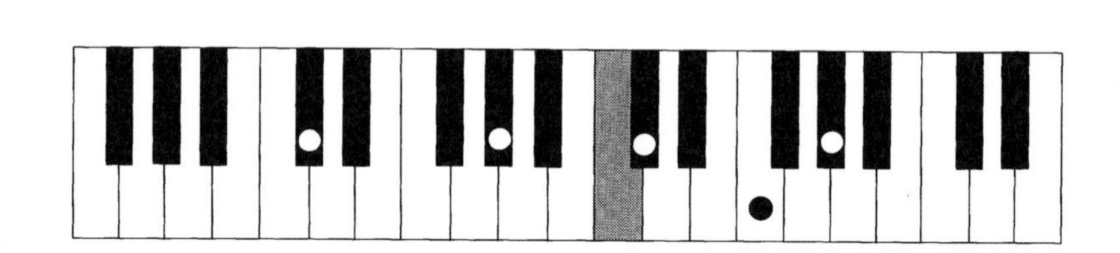

C♯ suspended 4th - C♯sus or C♯sus4

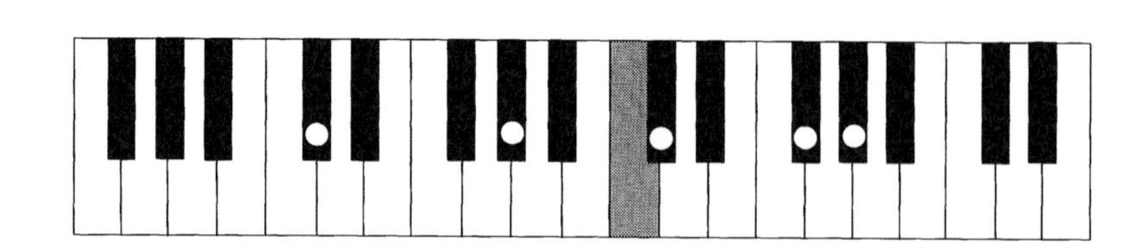

C♯ augmented 5th - C♯+ or C♯aug

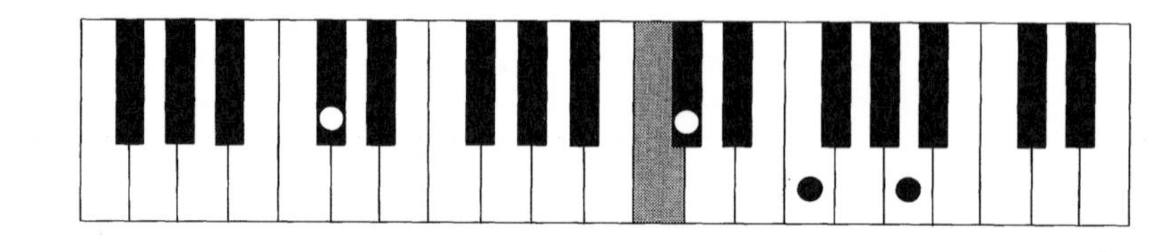

C♯ added 6th - C♯6

C♯ added 6th and 9th - C♯6/9

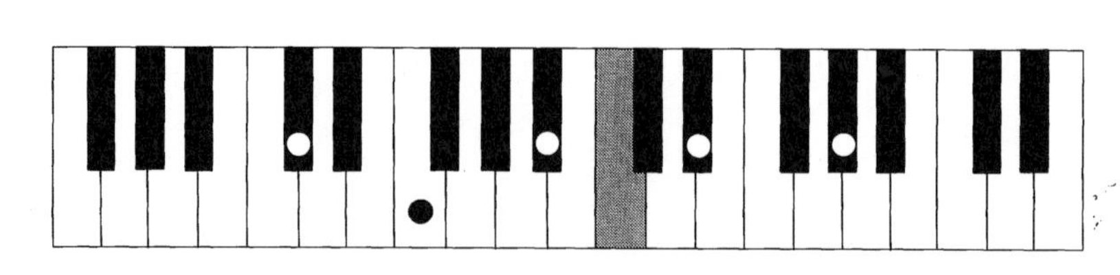

C♯ and D♭ are the same note spelled in different ways, depending on the key you are in.
For this reason, C♯ and D♭ chords are grouped together on facing pages.

The D♭ Collection

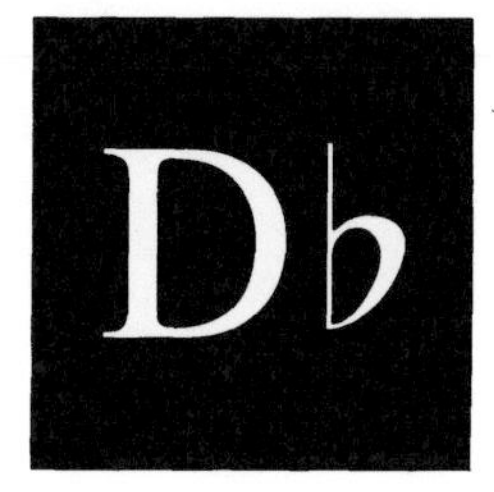

D♭ major - D♭

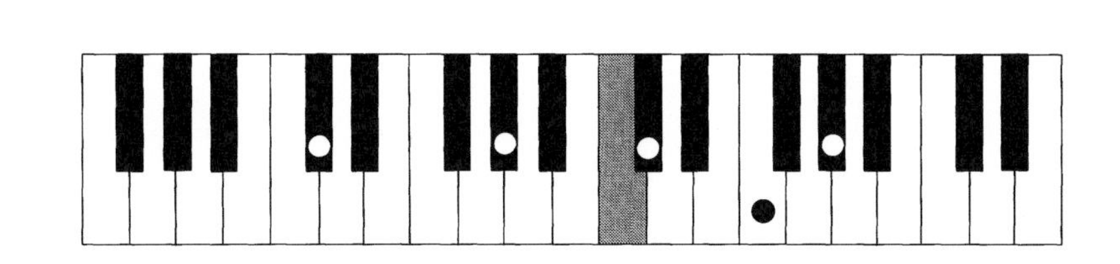

D♭ suspended 4th - D♭sus or D♭sus4

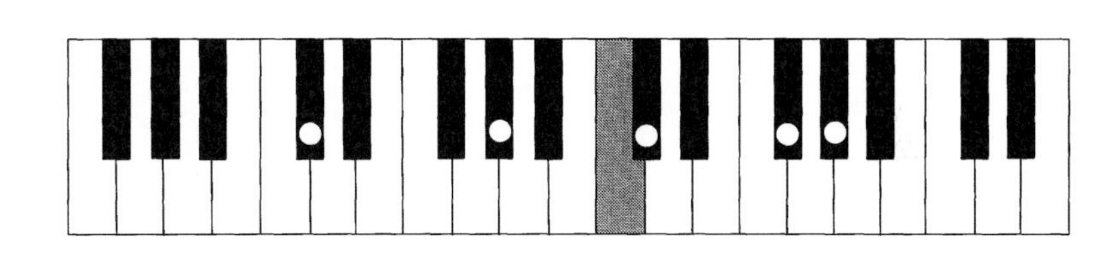

D♭ augmented 5th - D♭+ or D♭aug

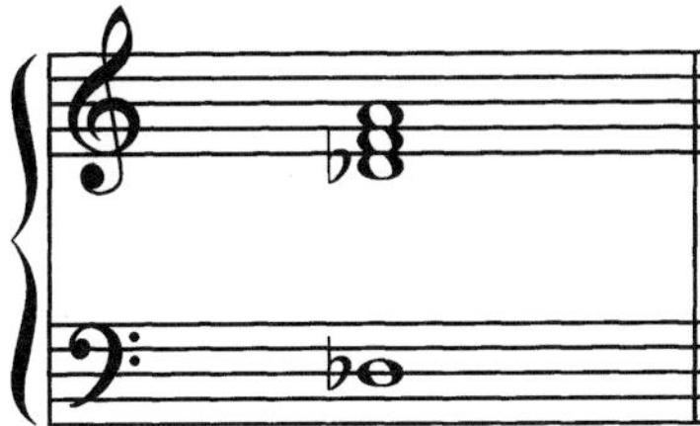

D♭ added 6th - D♭6

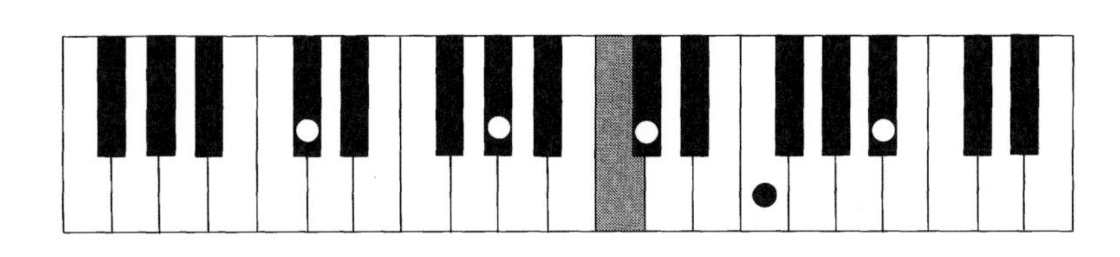

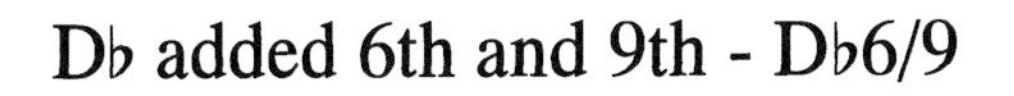

D♭ added 6th and 9th - D♭6/9

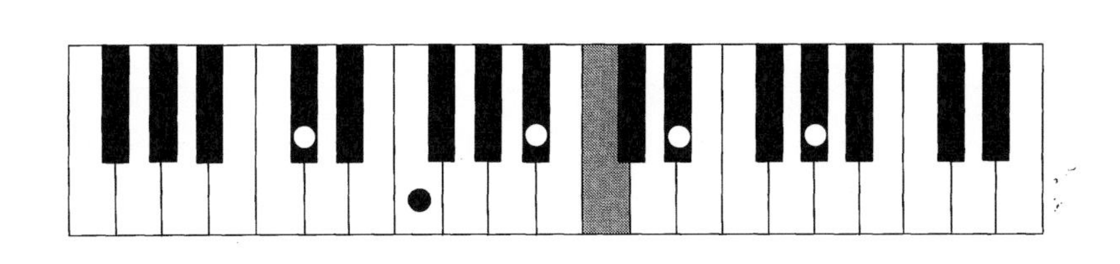

The C♯ Collection

C♯ major 7th - C♯maj7

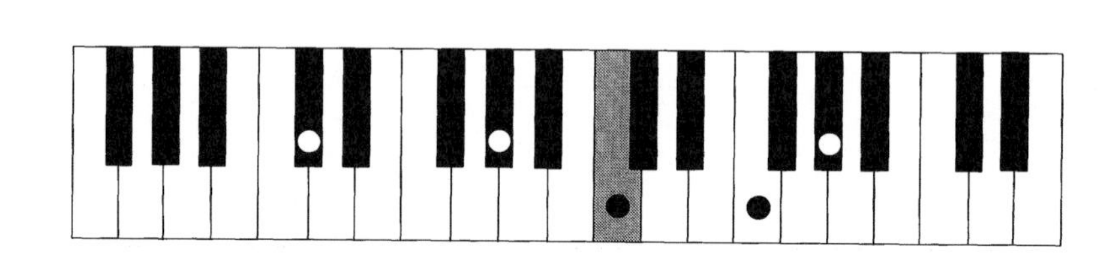

C♯ dominant 7th - C♯7

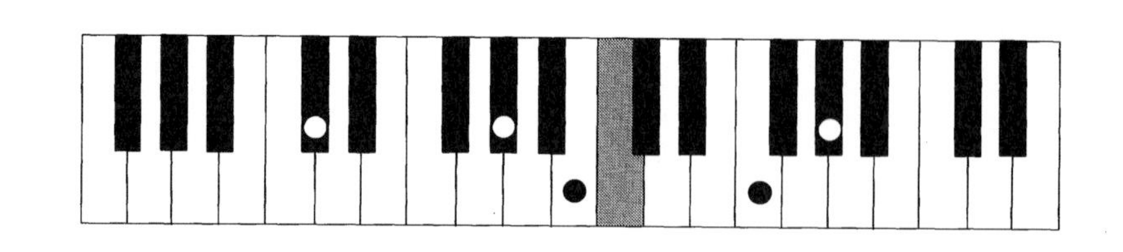

C♯ dominant 7th with suspended 4th - C♯7sus or C♯sus4

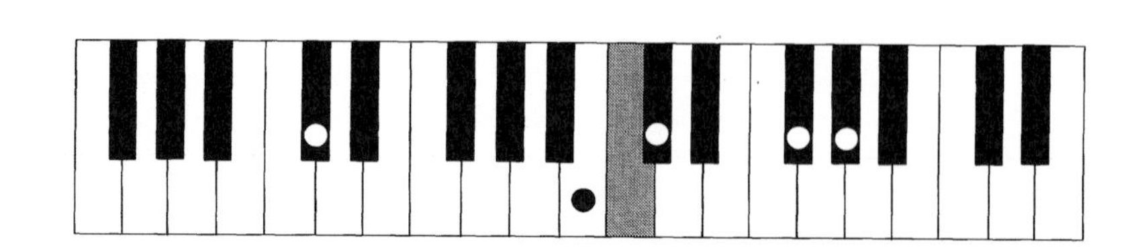

C♯ dominant 7th with flattened 5th - C♯7(♭5)

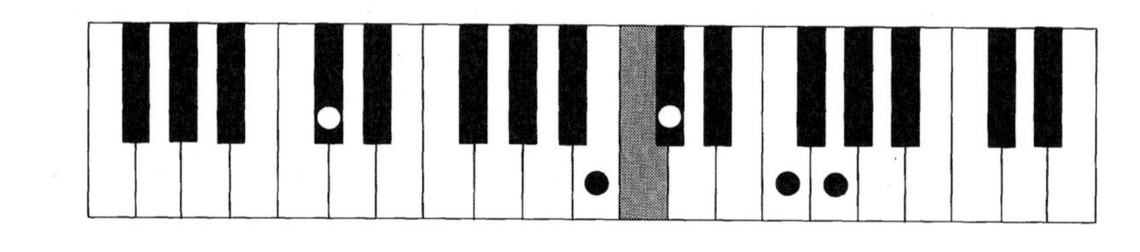

C♯ dominant 7th with augmented 5th - C♯7+ or C♯7aug

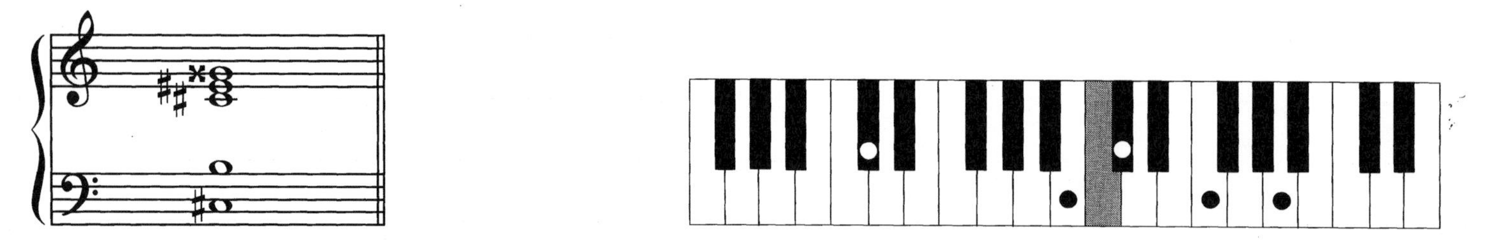

The D♭ Collection

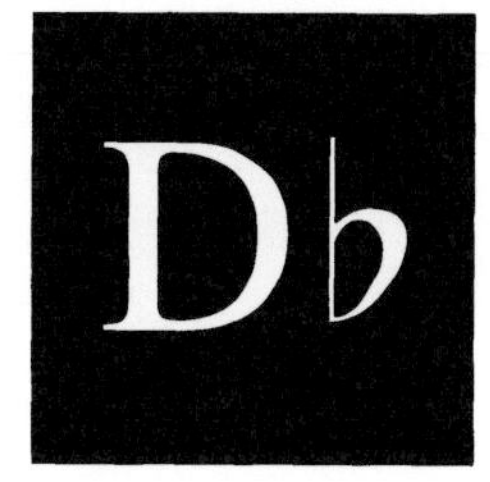

D♭ major 7th - D♭maj7

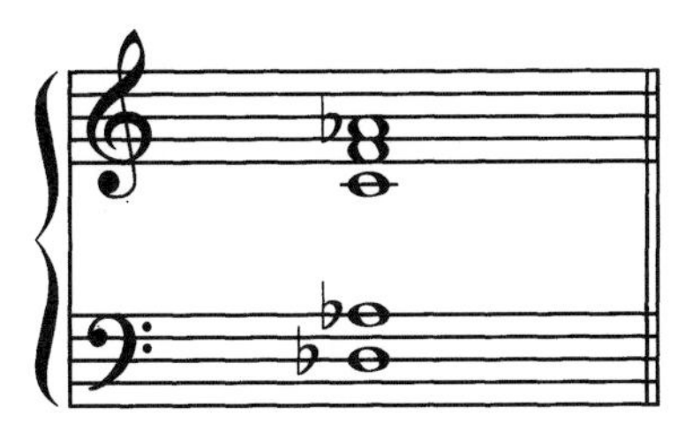

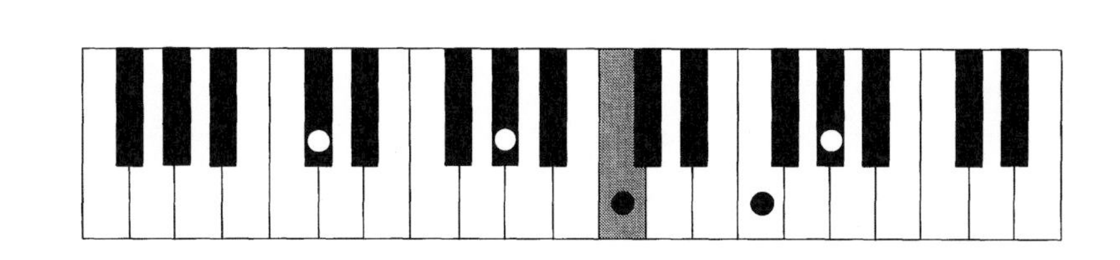

D♭ dominant 7th - D♭7

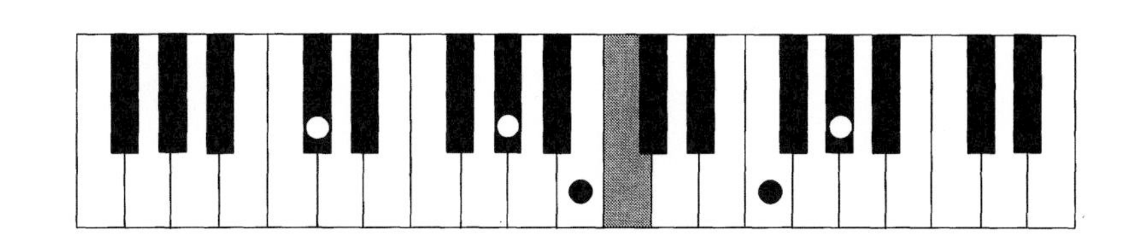

D♭ dominant 7th with suspended 4th - D♭7sus or D♭7sus4

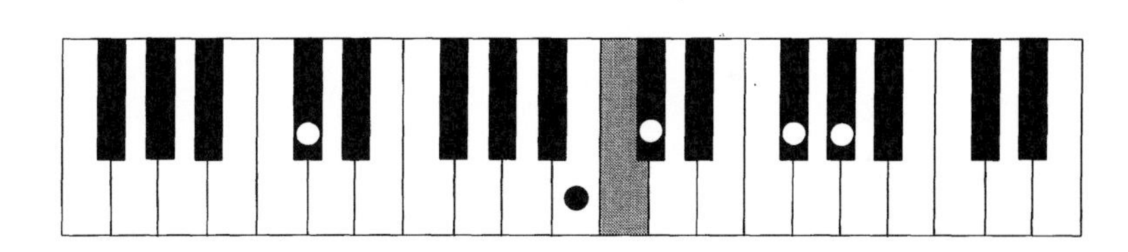

D♭ dominant 7th with flattened 5th - D♭7(♭5)

D♭ dominant 7th with augmented 5th - D♭7+ or D♭7aug

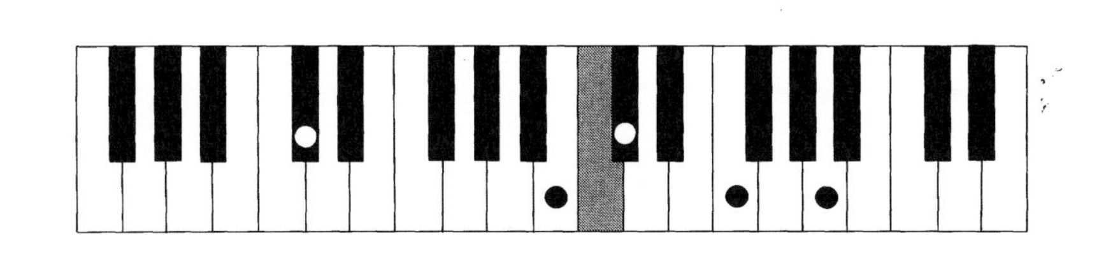

The C♯ Collection

C♯ dominant 7th with flattened 9th - C♯7(♭9)

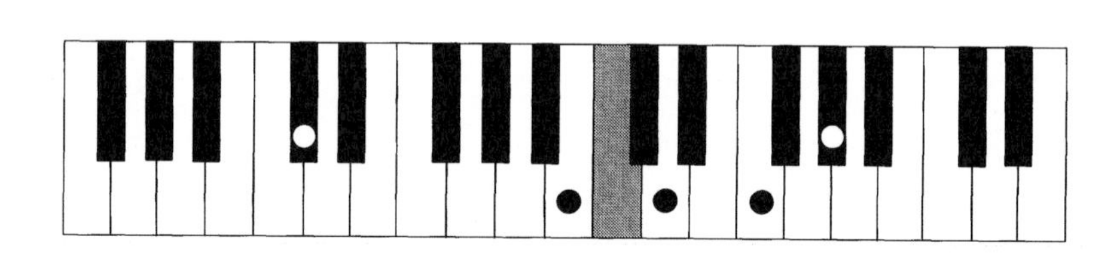

C♯ dominamt 7th with flattened 9th and 5th - C♯7 (♭9/♭5)

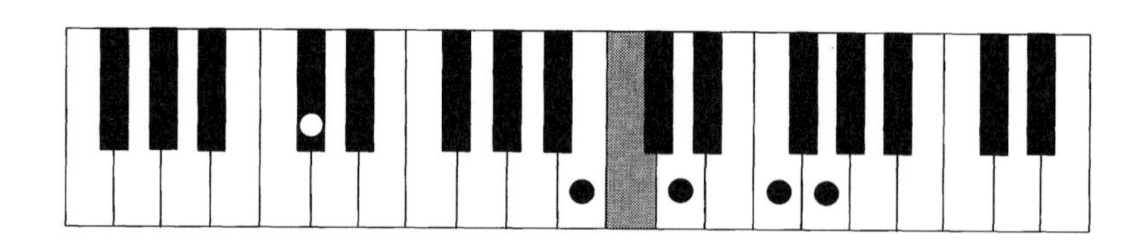

C♯ dominant 7th with sharpened 9th - C♯7(♯9)

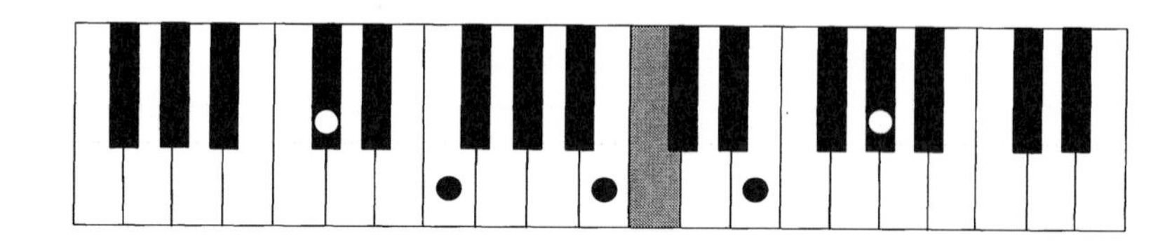

C♯ added 9th - C♯add9

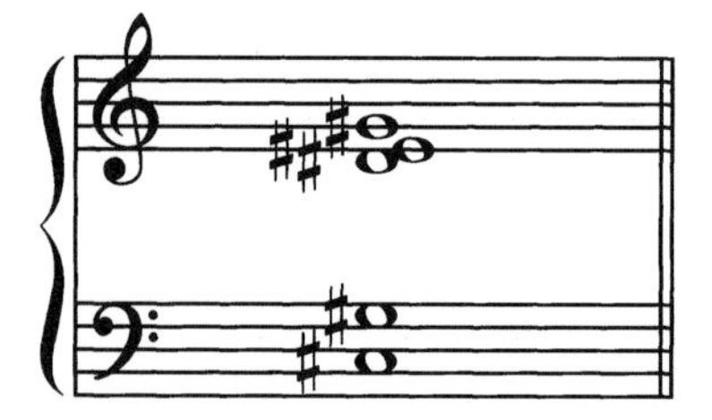

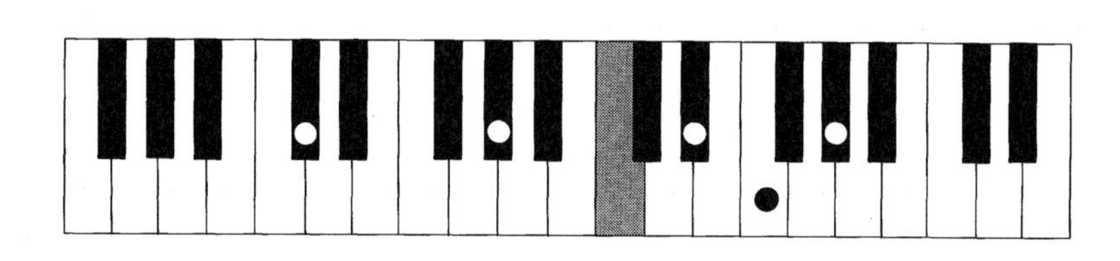

C♯ major 9th - C♯maj9

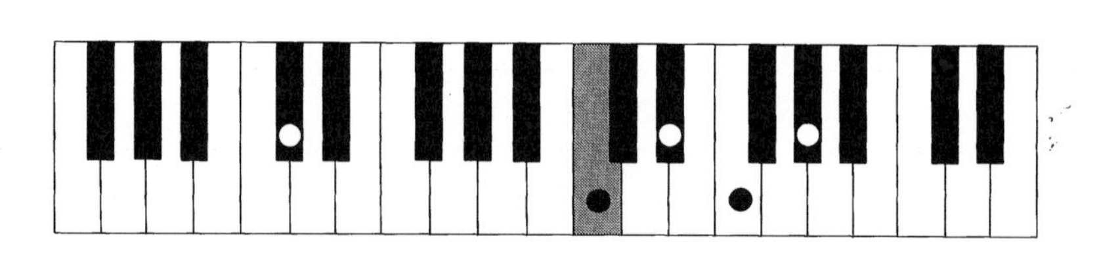

The D♭ Collection

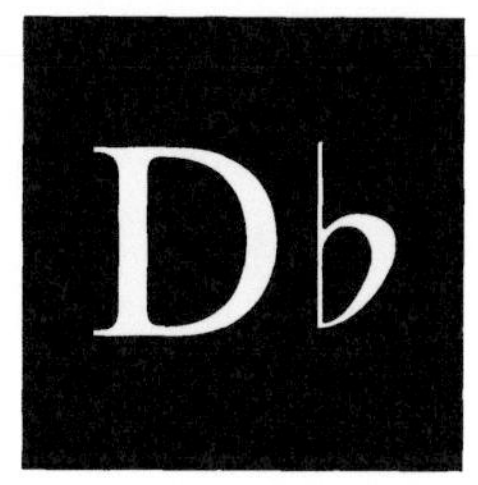

D♭ dominant 7th with flattened 9th - D♭7(♭9)

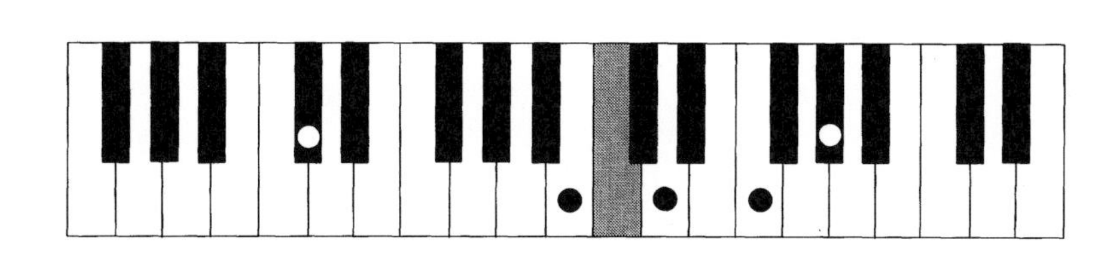

D♭ dominant 7th with flattened 9th and 5th - D♭7(♭9/♭5)

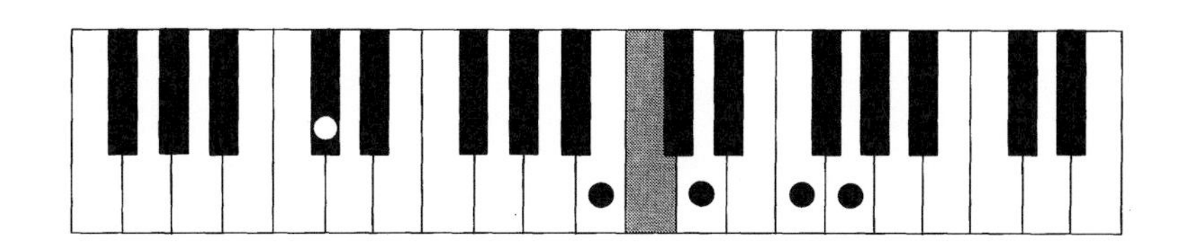

D♭ dominant 7th with sharpened 9th - D♭7(♯9)

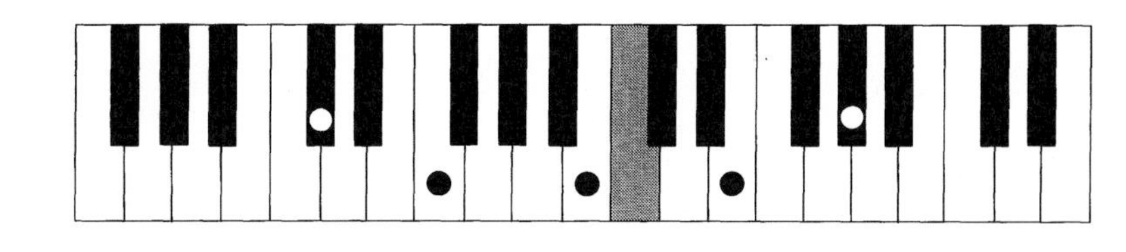

D♭ added 9th - D♭add9

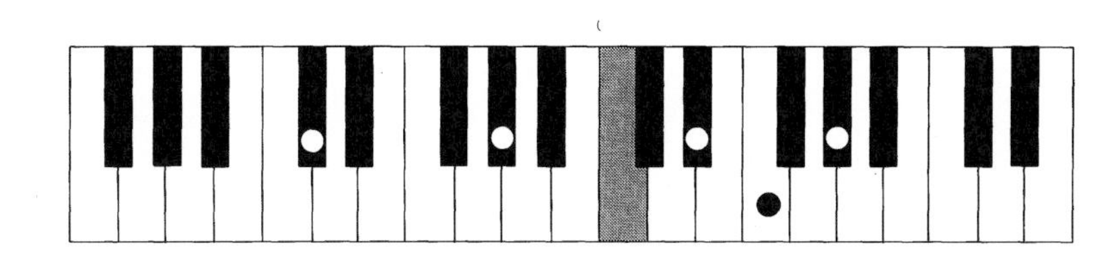

D♭ major 9th - D♭maj9

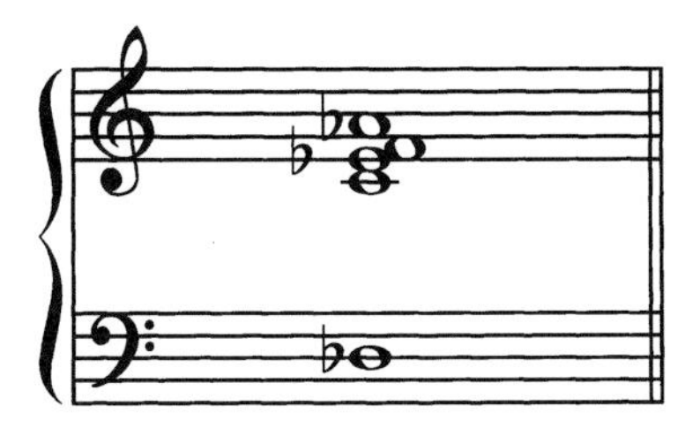

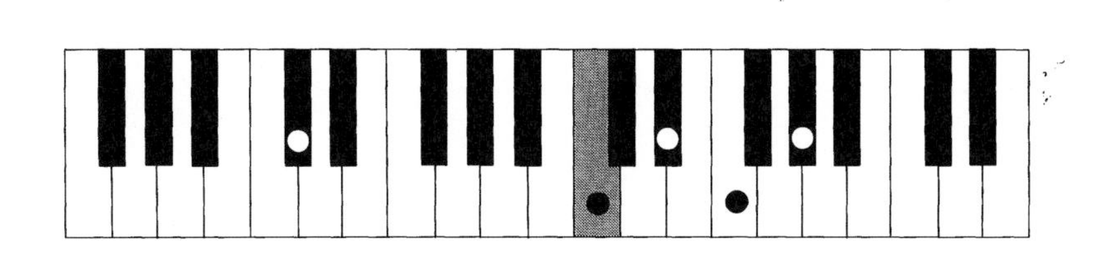

The C♯ Collection

C♯ dominant 9th - C♯9

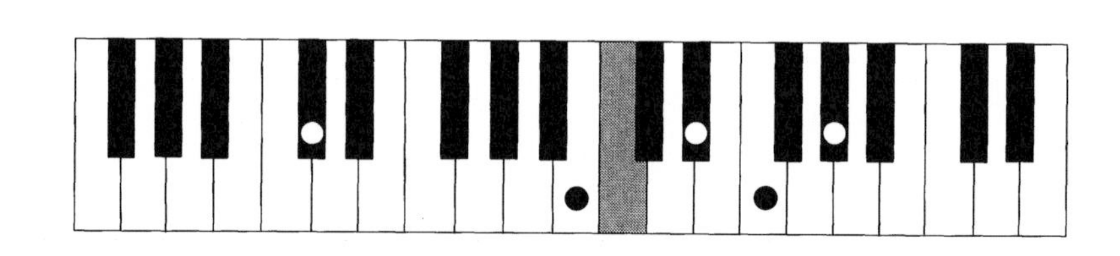

C♯ dominant 9th with suspended 4th - C♯9sus or C♯9sus4

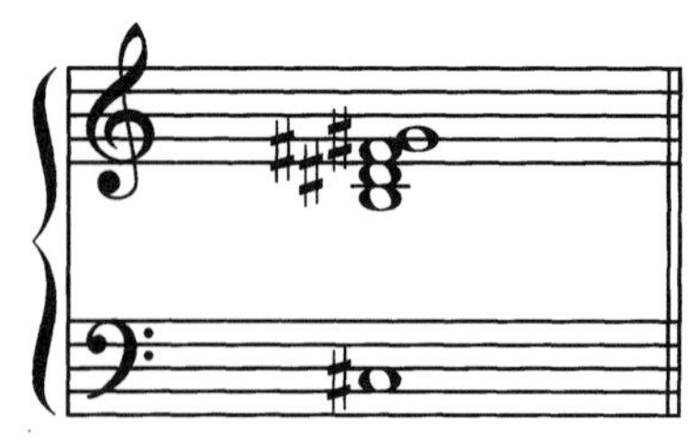

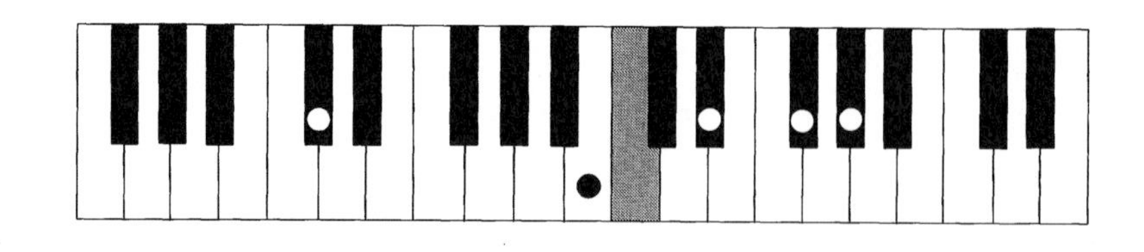

C♯ dominant 9th with augmented 5th - C♯9+ or C♯9aug

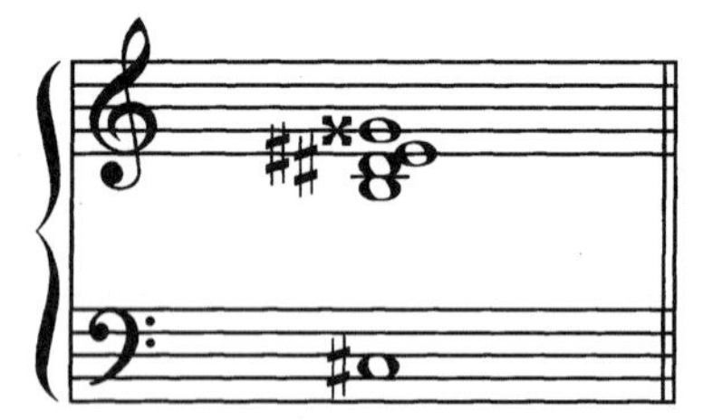

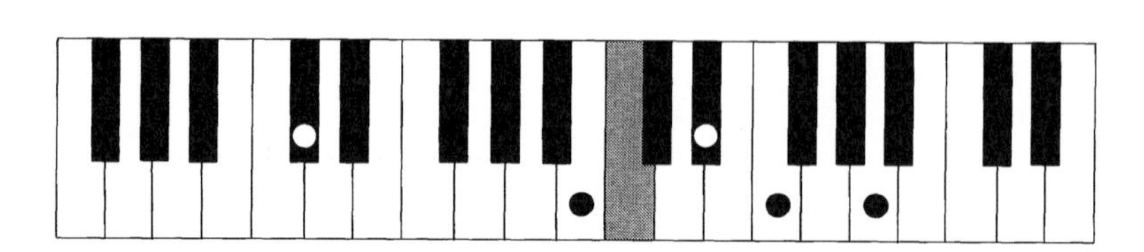

C♯ dominant 9th with sharpened 11th - C♯9(♯11)
with flattened 5th - C♯9(♭5)

C♯ dominant 11th - C♯11

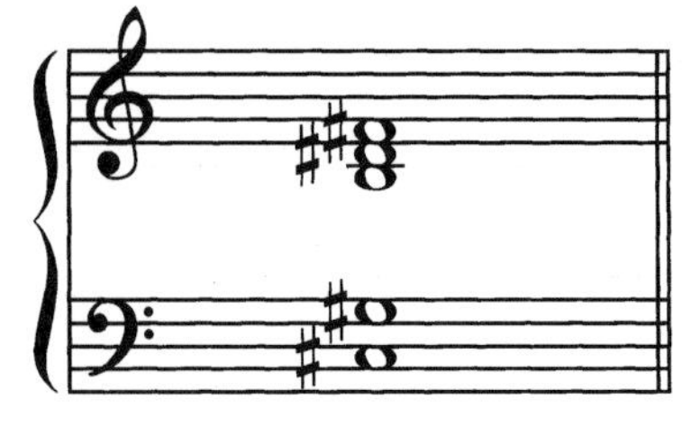

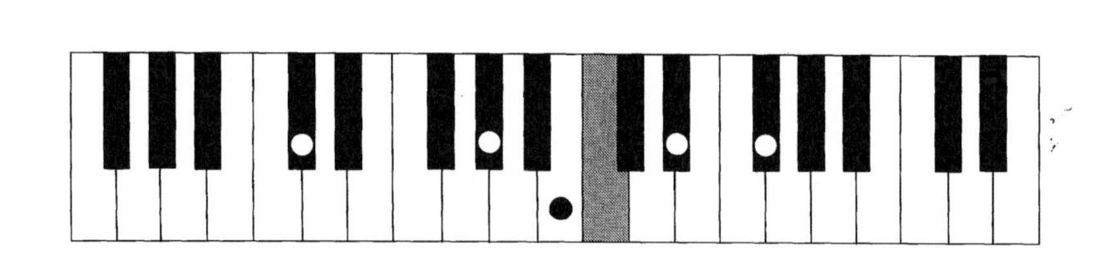

The D♭ Collection

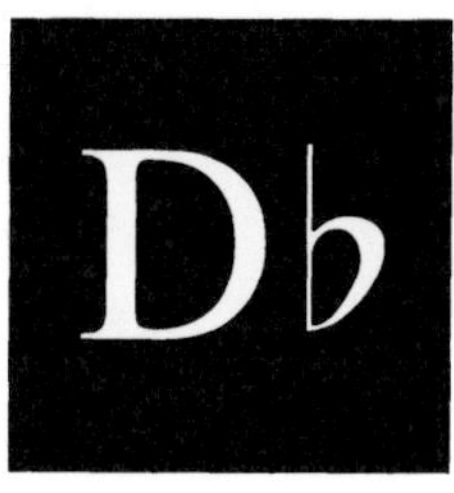

D♭ dominant 9th - D♭9

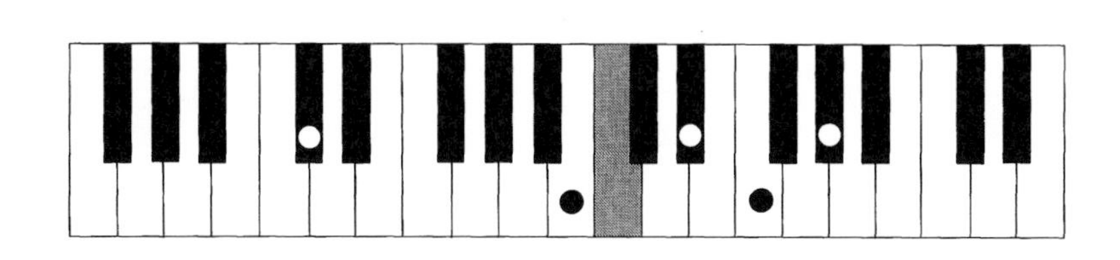

D♭ dominant 9th with suspended 4th - D♭9sus or D♭9sus4

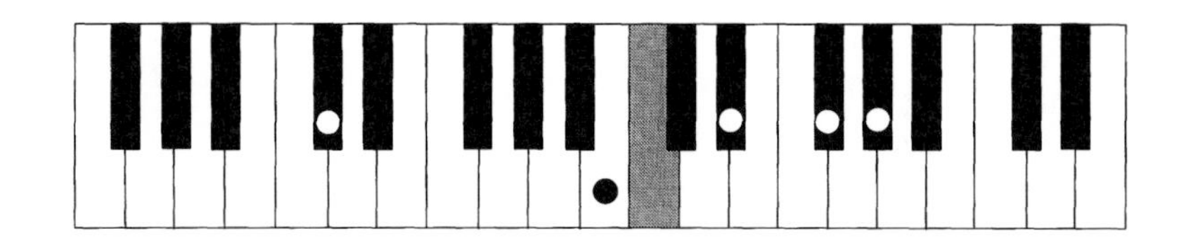

D♭ dominant 9th with augmented 5th - D♭9+ or D♭9aug

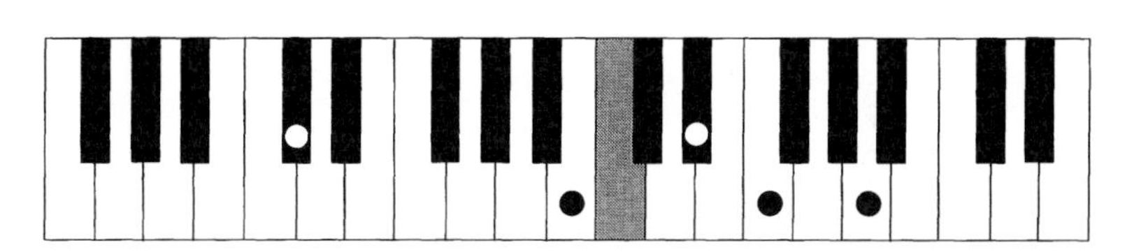

D♭ dominant 9th with sharpened 11th - D♭9(♯11)
with flattened 5th - D♭9(♭5)

D♭ dominant 11th - D♭11

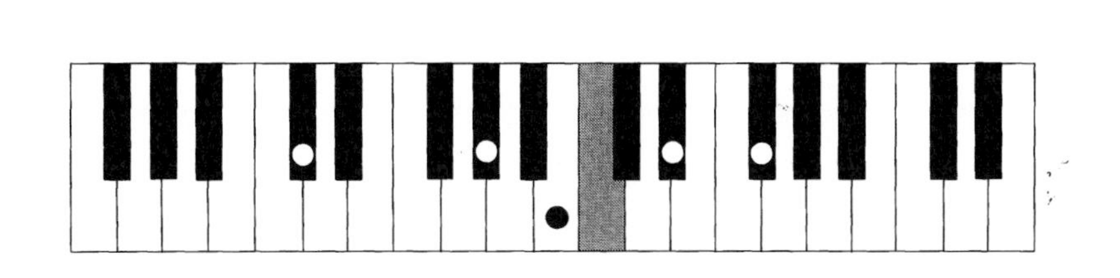

The C♯ Collection

C♯ dominant 11th with flattened 9th - C♯11(♭9)

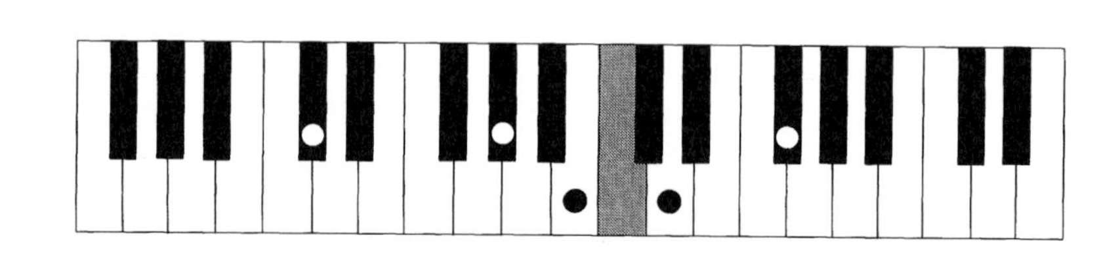

C♯ dominant 13th - C♯13

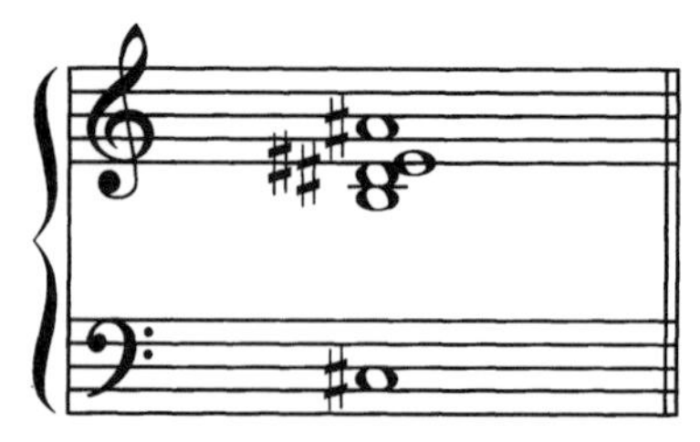

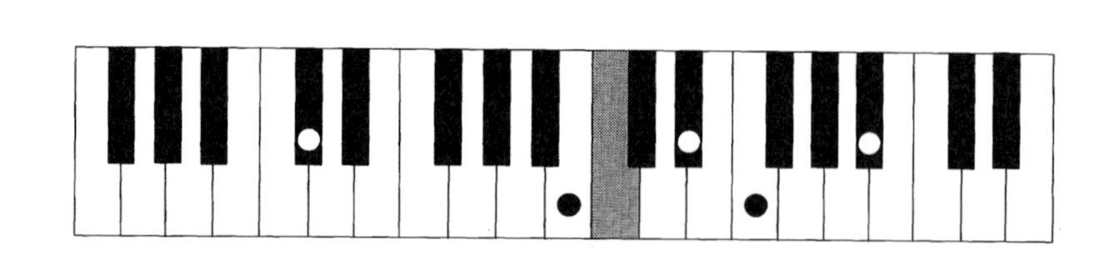

C♯ dominant 13th with flattened 9th - C♯13(♭9)

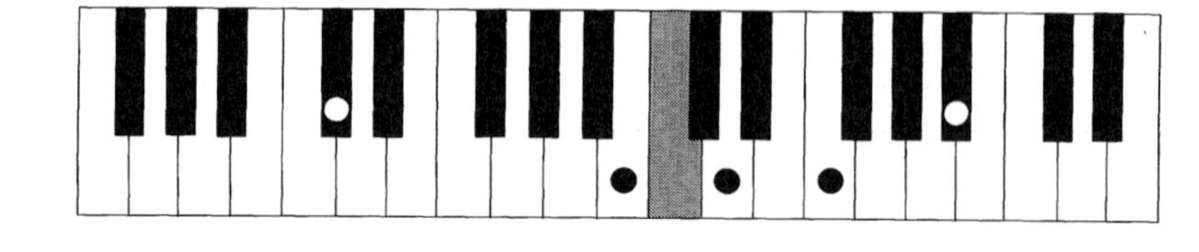

C♯ minor - C♯m

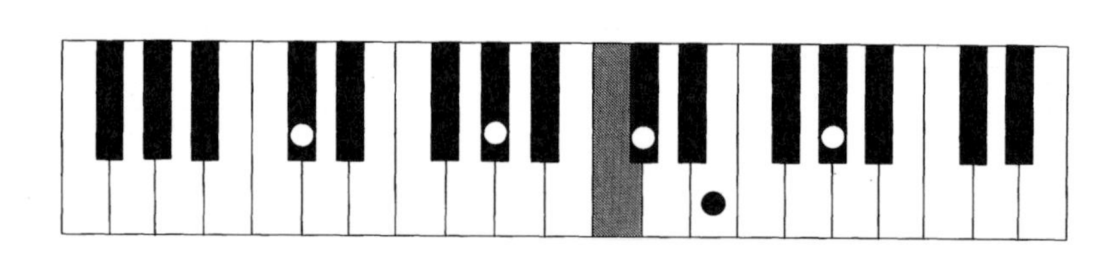

C♯ diminished - C♯° or C♯dim

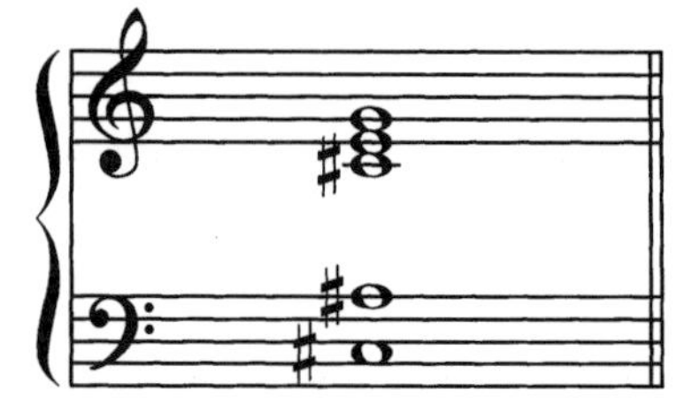

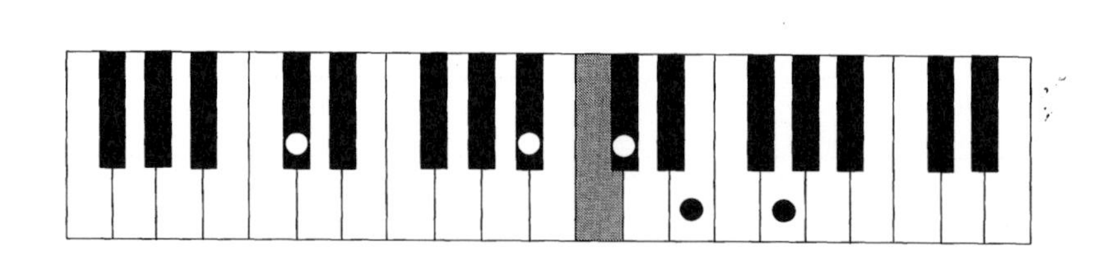

The D♭ Collection

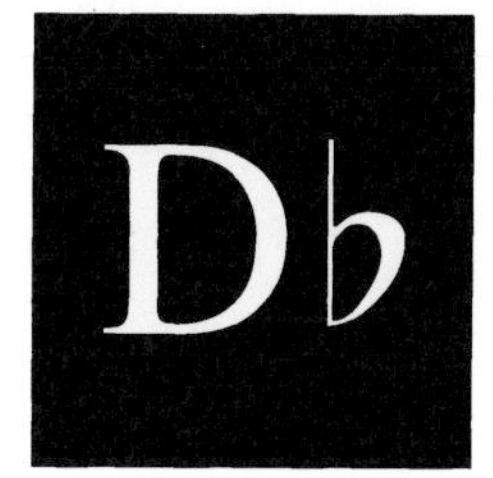

D♭ dominant 11th with flattened 9th - D♭11(♭9)

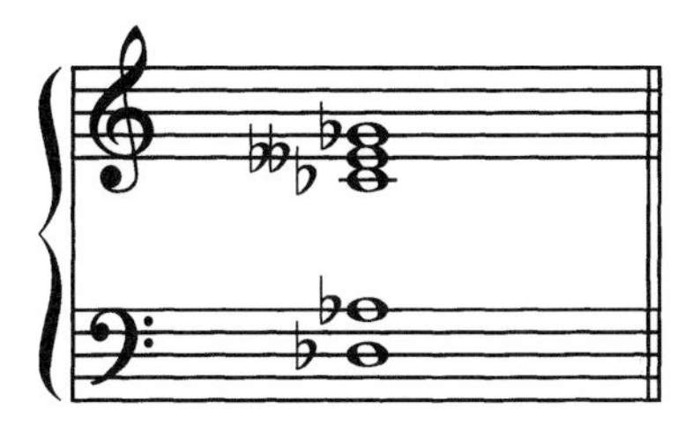

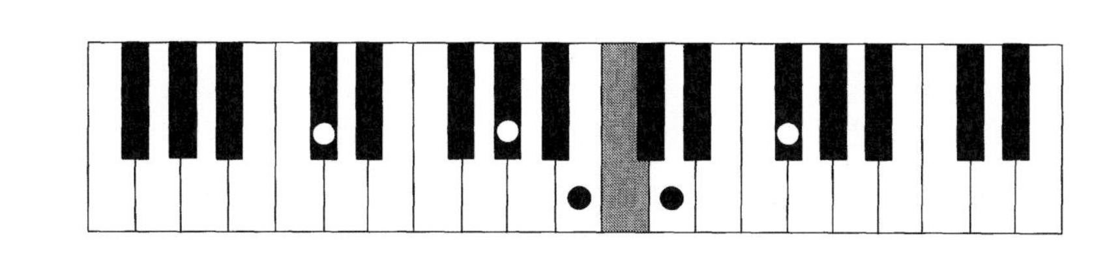

D♭ dominant 13th - D♭13

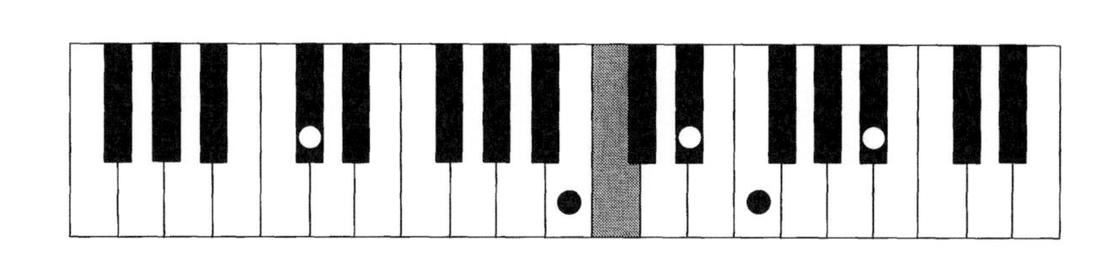

D♭ dominant 13th with flattened 9th - D♭13(♭9)

D♭ minor - D♭m

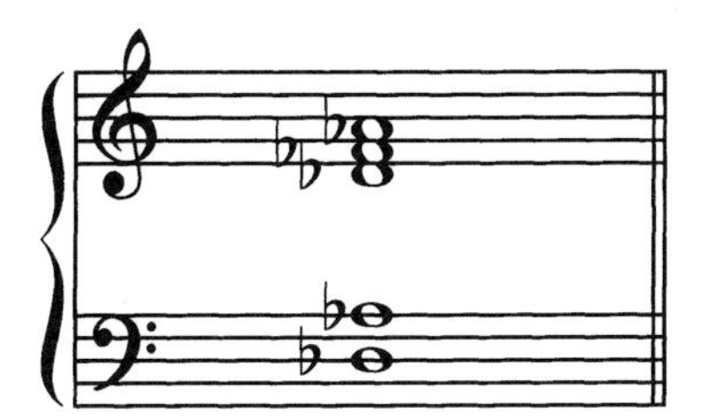

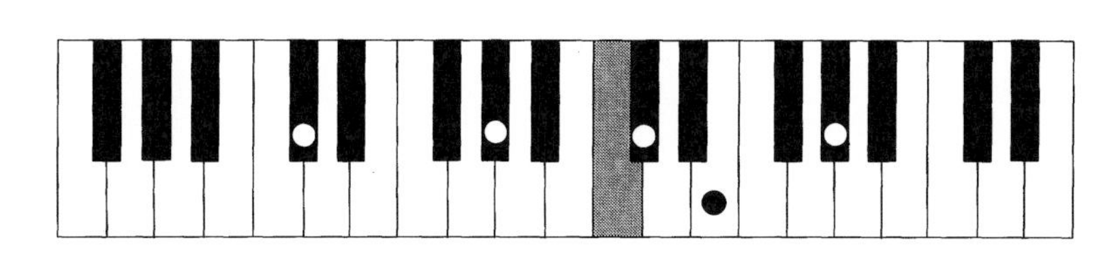

D♭ diminished - D♭° or D♭dim

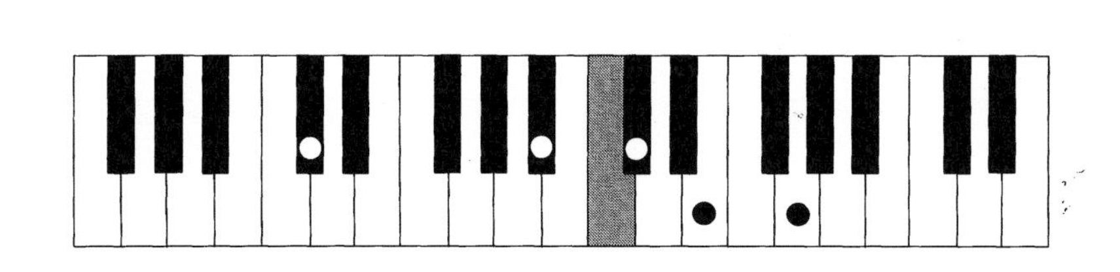

The C♯ Collection

C♯ minor added 6th - C♯m6

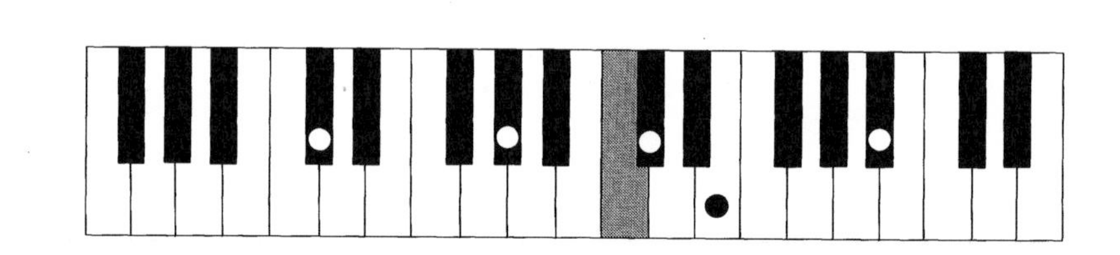

C♯ minor 7th - C♯m7

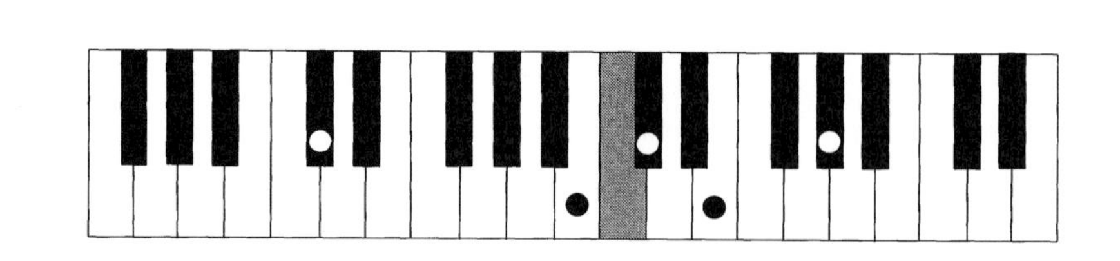

C♯ minor 7th with flattened 5th - C♯m7(♭5)

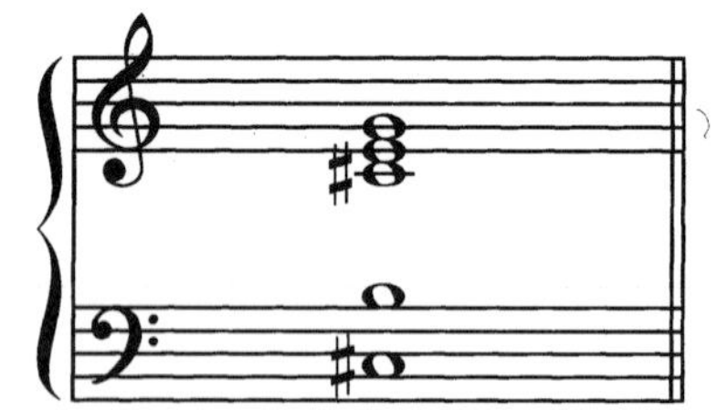

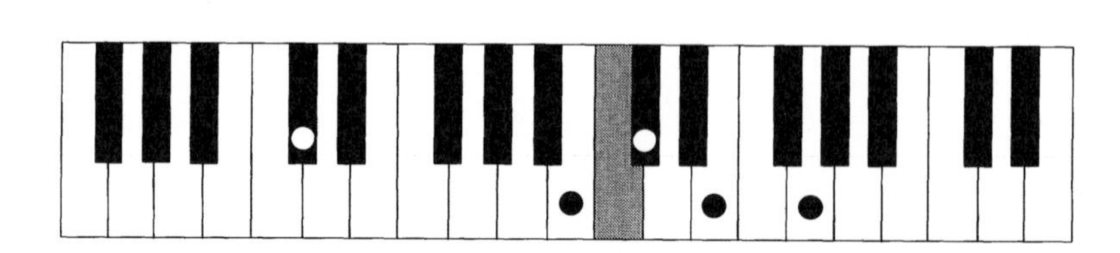

C♯ minor added major 7th - C♯m(maj7)

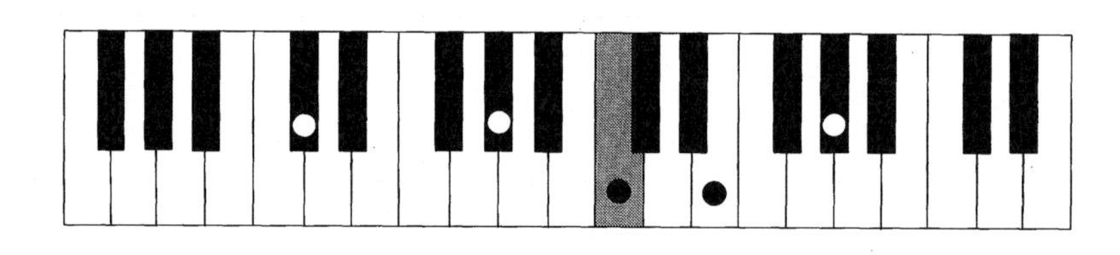

C♯ minor 9th - C♯m9

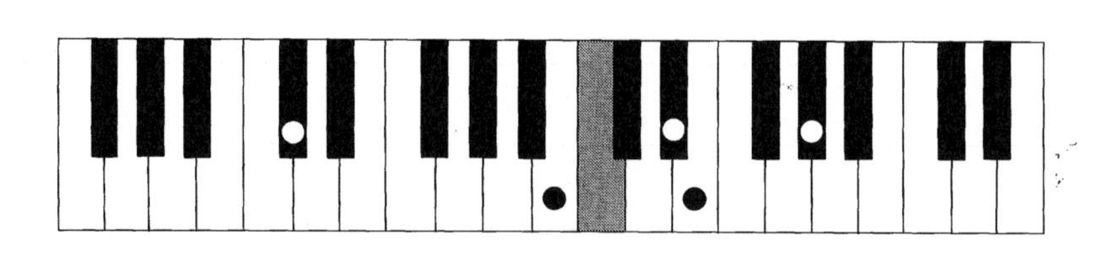

The D♭ Collection

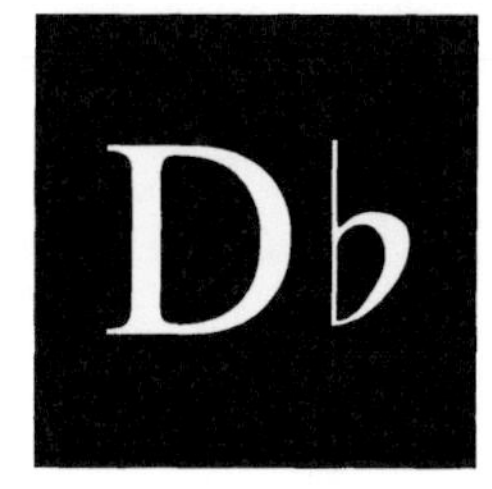

D♭ minor added 6th - D♭m6

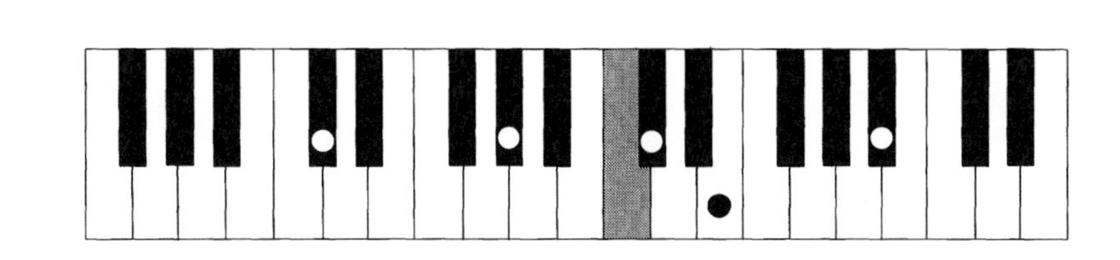

D♭ minor 7th - D♭m7

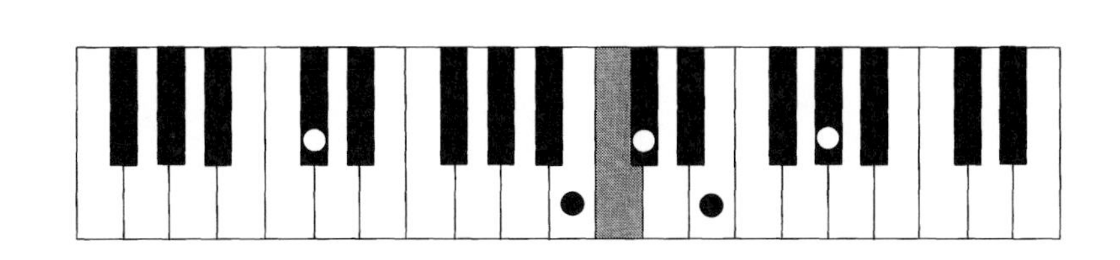

D♭ minor 7th with flattened 5th - D♭m7(♭5)

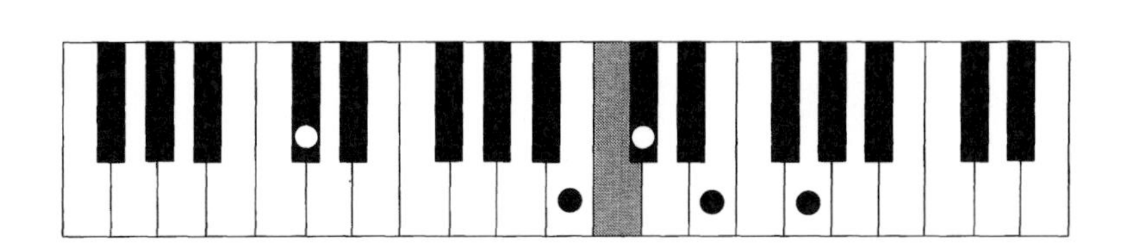

D♭ minor added major 7th - D♭m(maj7)

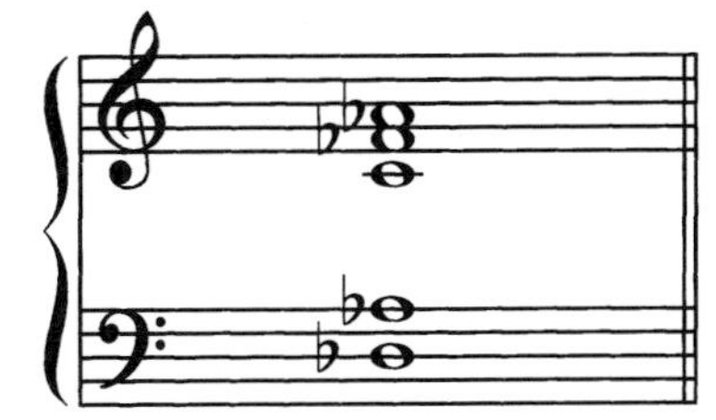

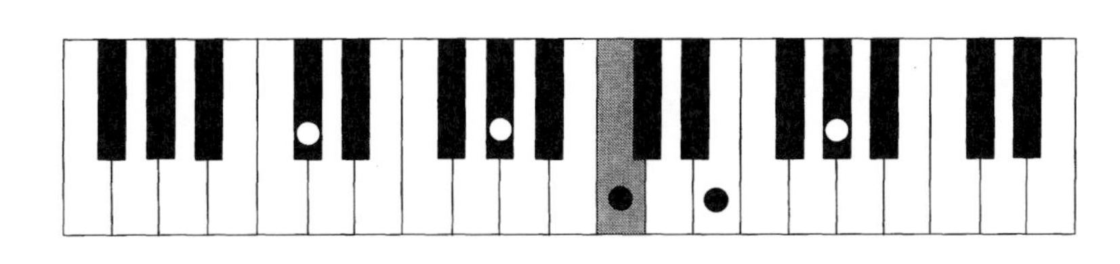

D♭ minor 9th - D♭m9

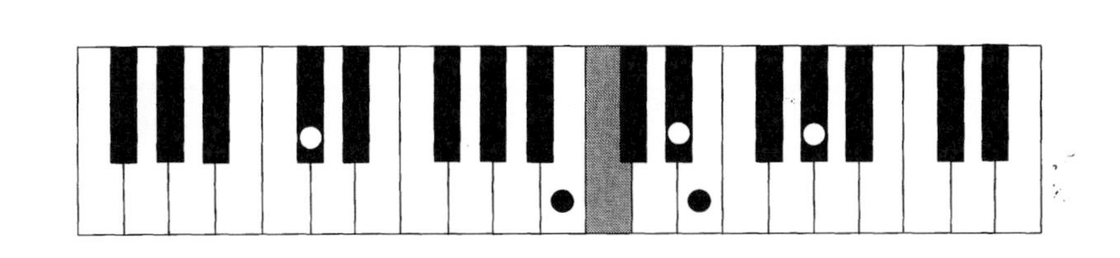

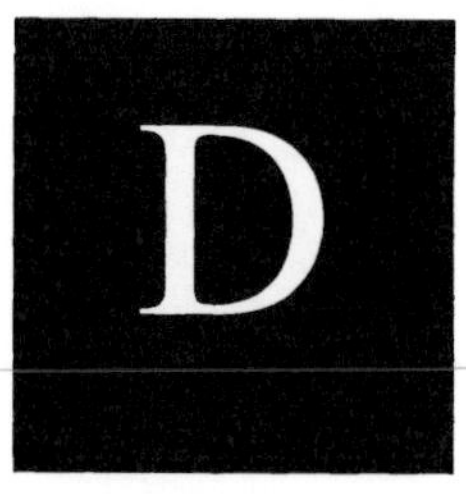

The D Collection

D major - D

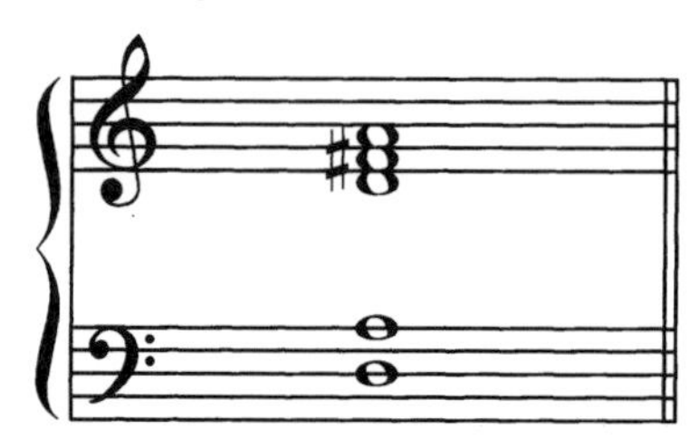

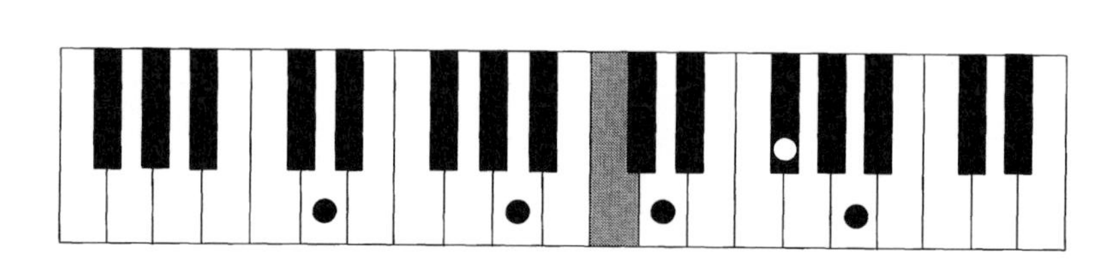

D suspended 4th - Dsus or Dsus4

D augmented 5th - D+ or Daug

D added 6th - D6

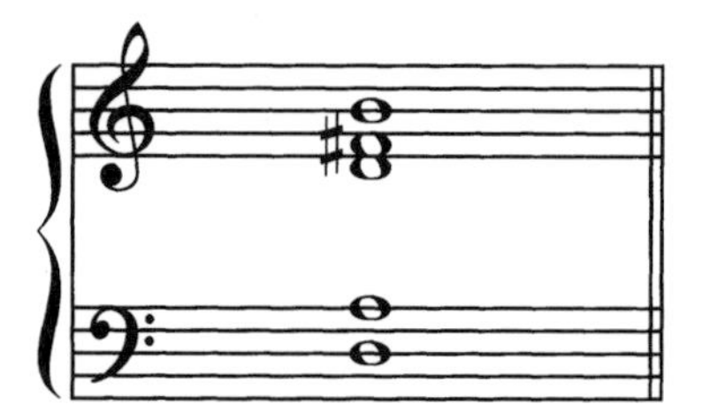

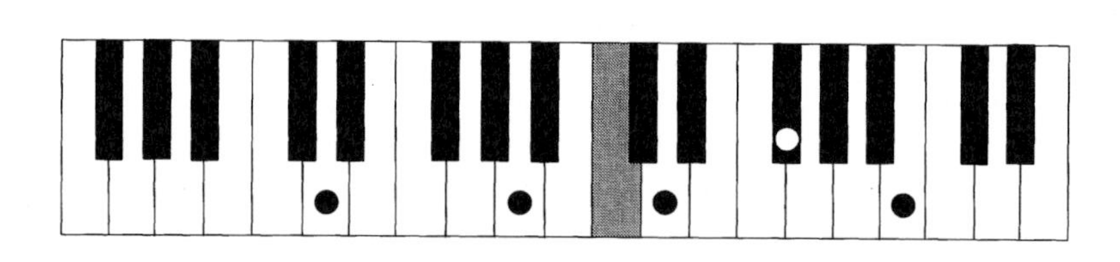

D added 6th and 9th - D6/9

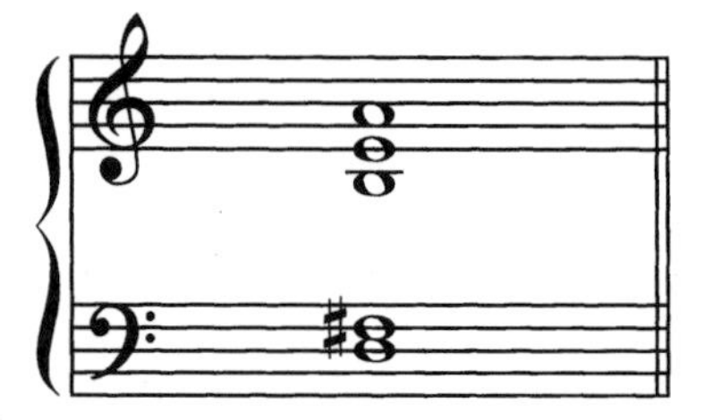

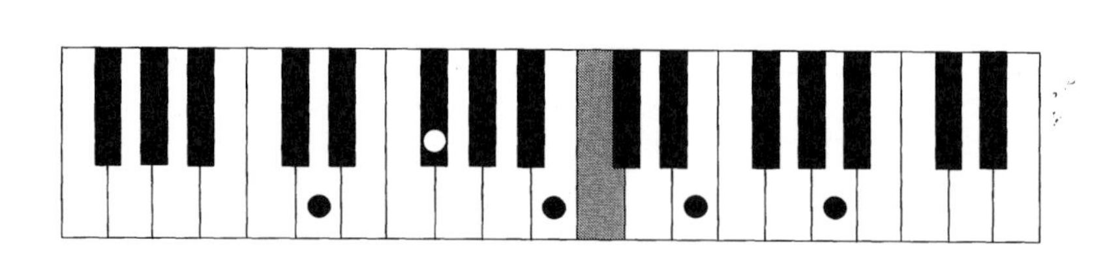

The D Collection

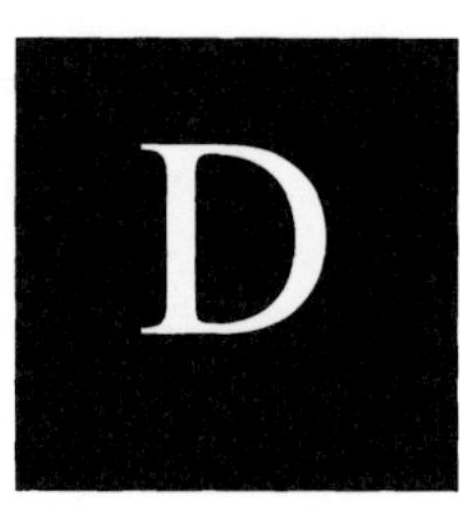

D major 7th - Dmaj7

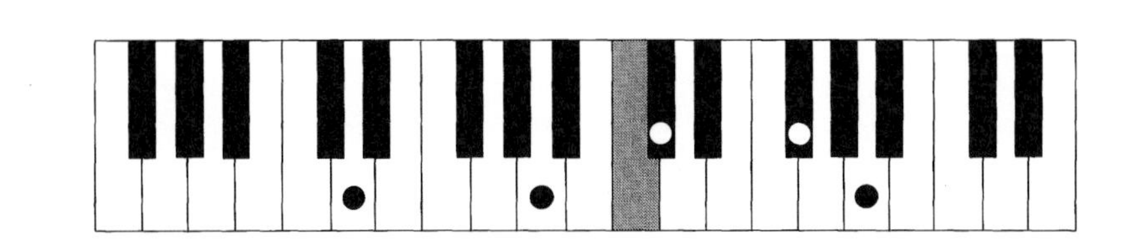

D dominant 7th - D7

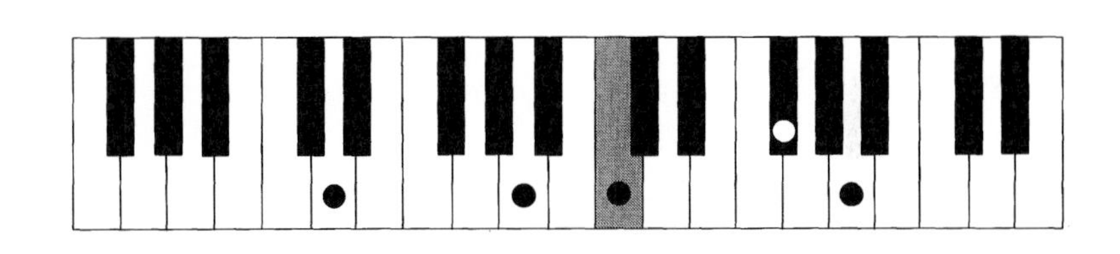

D dominant 7th with suspended 4th - D7sus or D7sus4

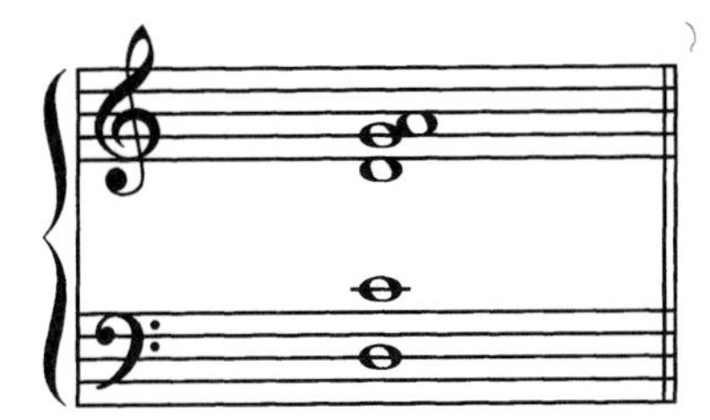

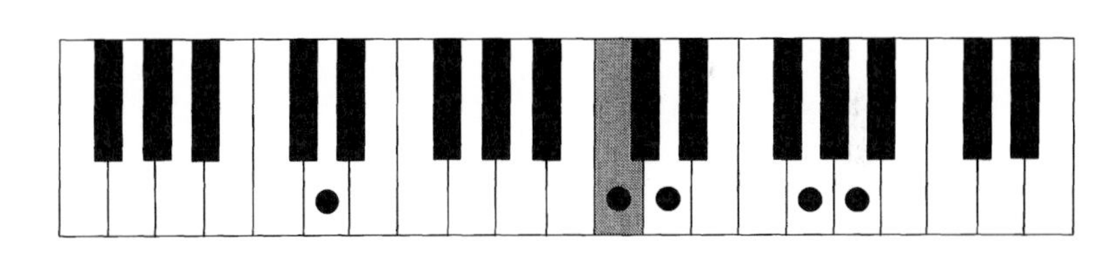

D dominant 7th with flattened 5th - D7(♭5)

D dominant 7th with augmented 5th - D7+ or D7aug

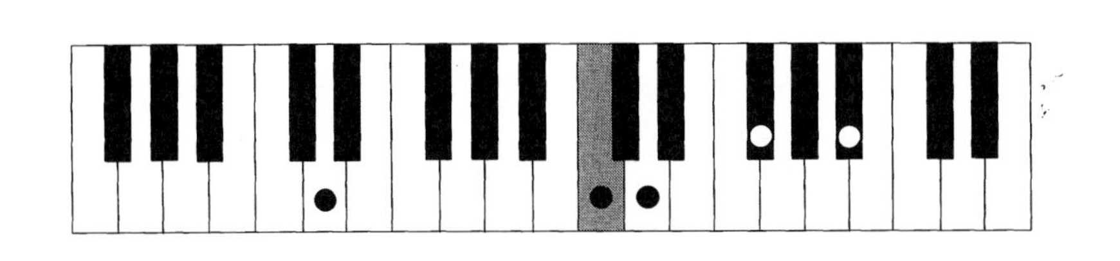

The D Collection

D dominant 7th with flattened 9th - D7(♭9)

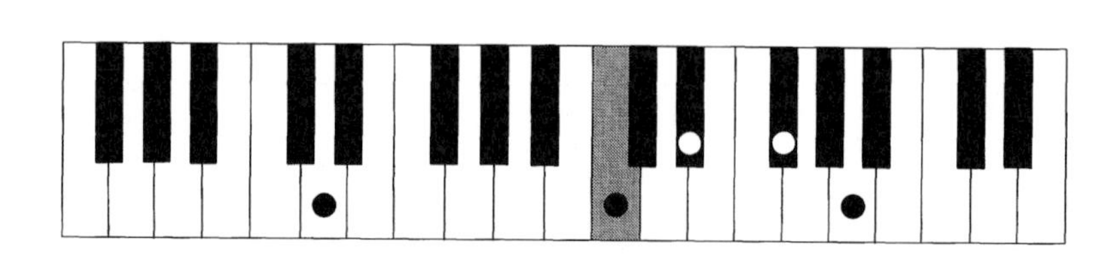

D dominant 7th with flattened 9th and 5th - D7(♭9/♭5)

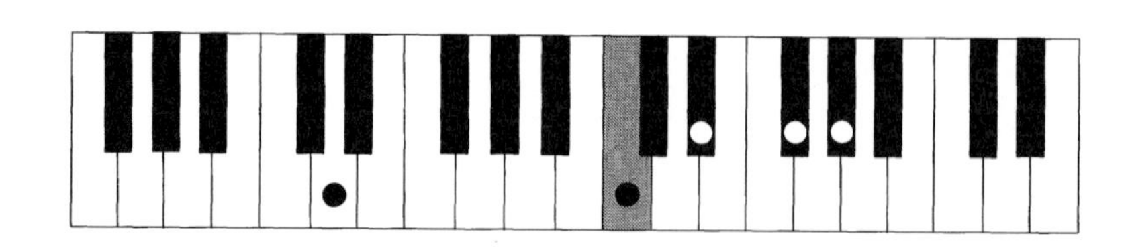

D dominant 7th with sharpened 9th - D7(♯9)

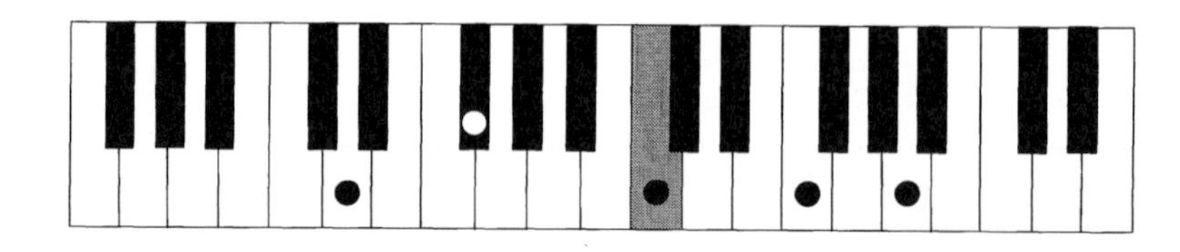

D added 9th - Dadd9

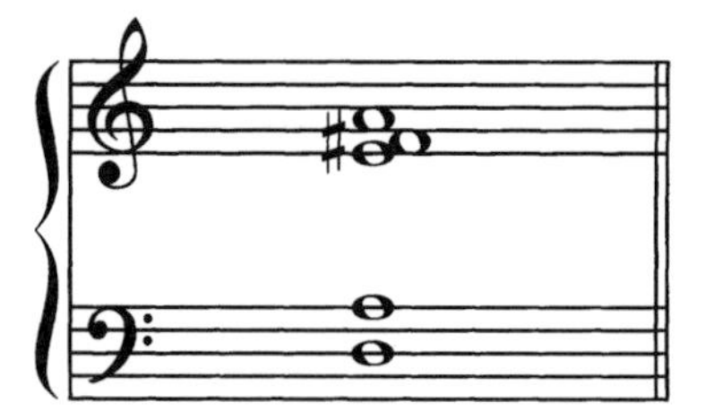

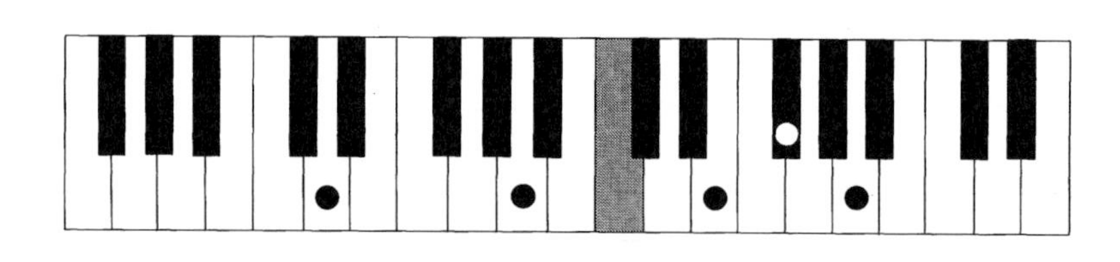

D major 9th - Dmaj9

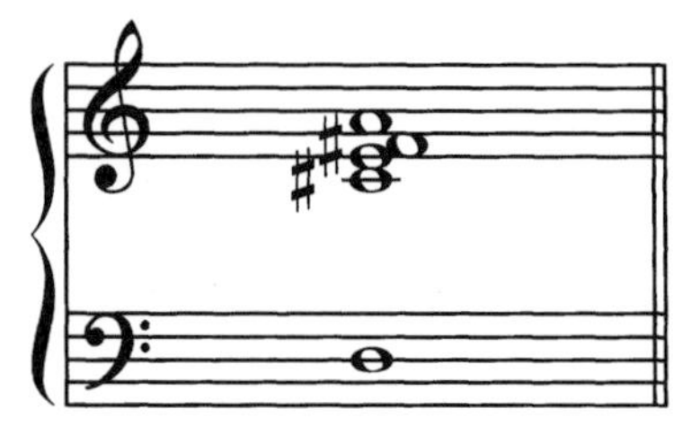

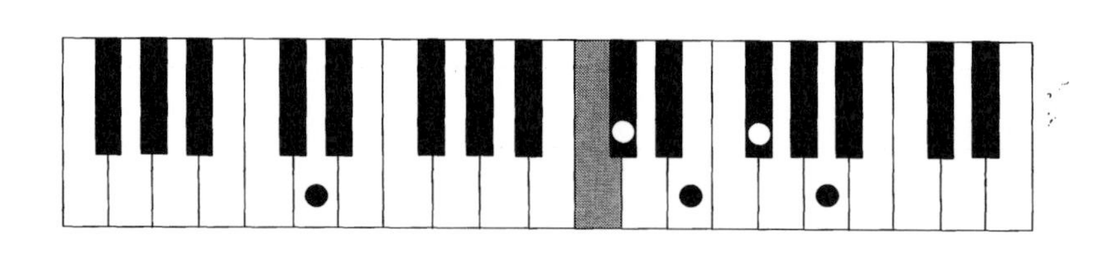

The D Collection

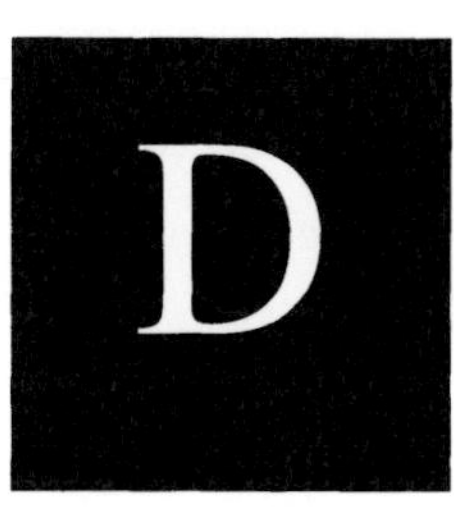

D dominant 9th - D9

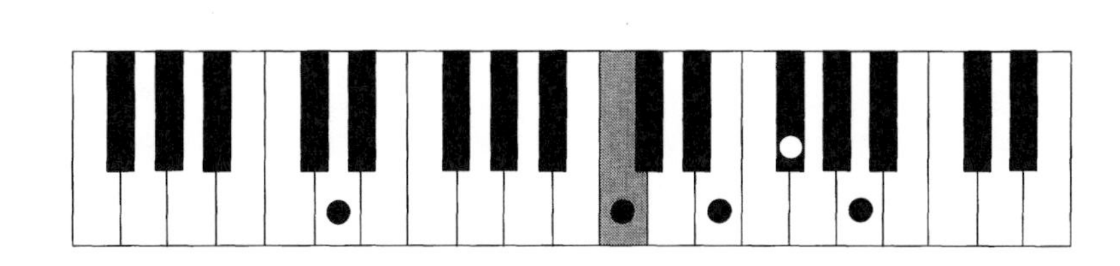

D dominant 9th with suspended 4th - D9sus or D9sus4

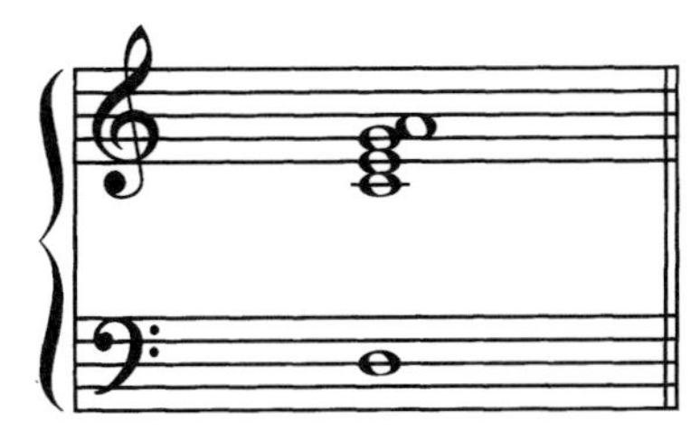

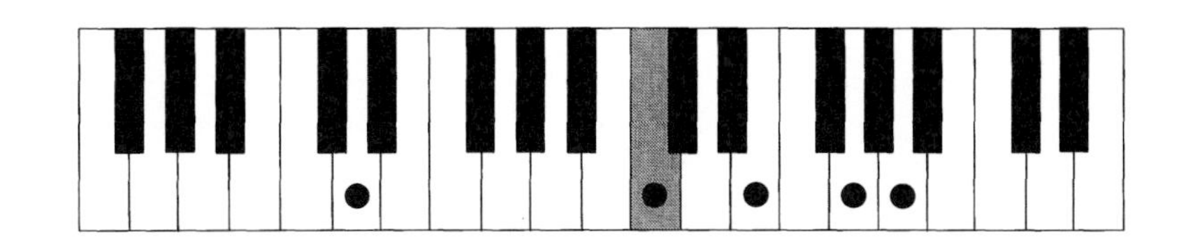

D dominant 9th with augmented 5th - D9+ or D9aug

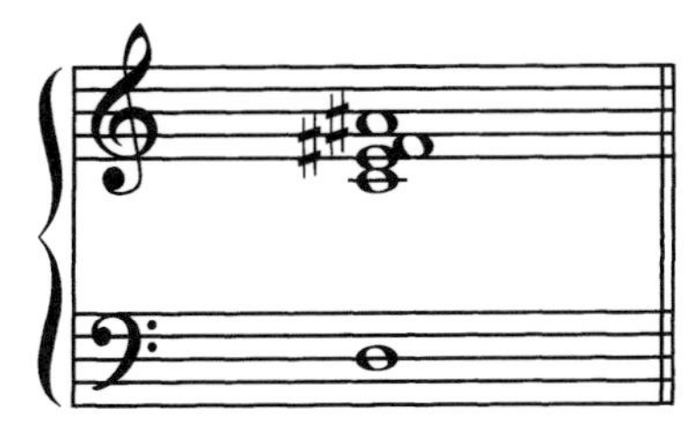

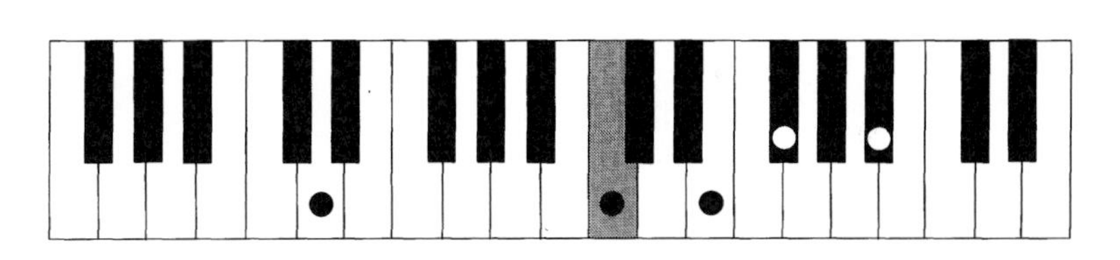

D dominant 9th with sharpened 11th - D9(♯11)
with flattened 5th - D9(♭5)

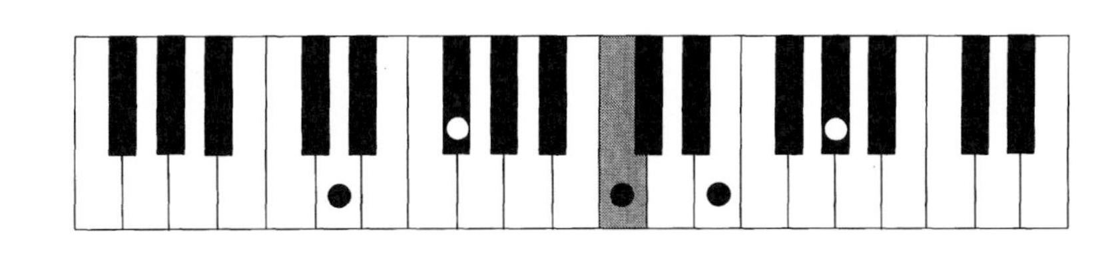

D dominant 11th - D11

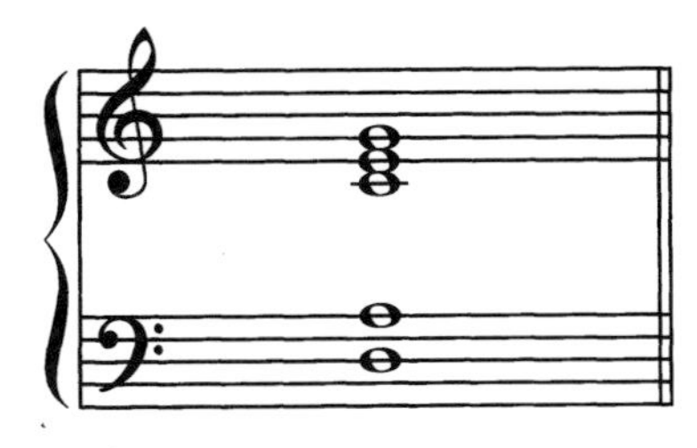

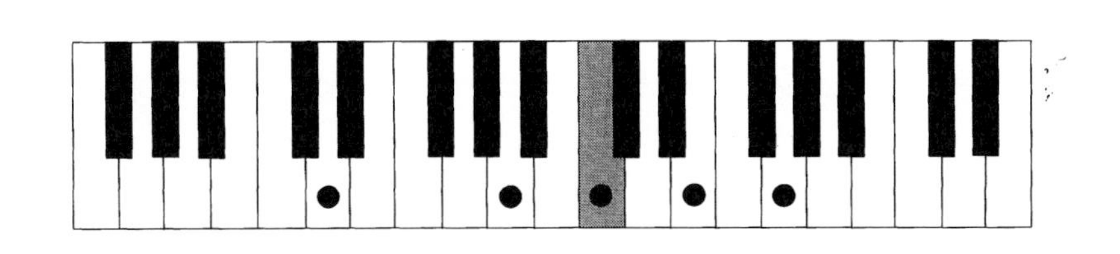

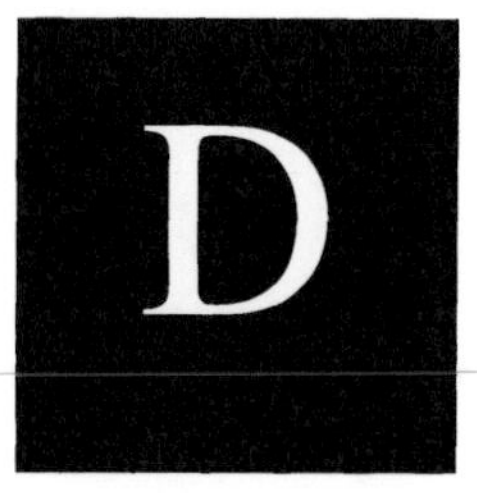

The D Collection

D dominant 11th with flattened 9th - D11(♭9)

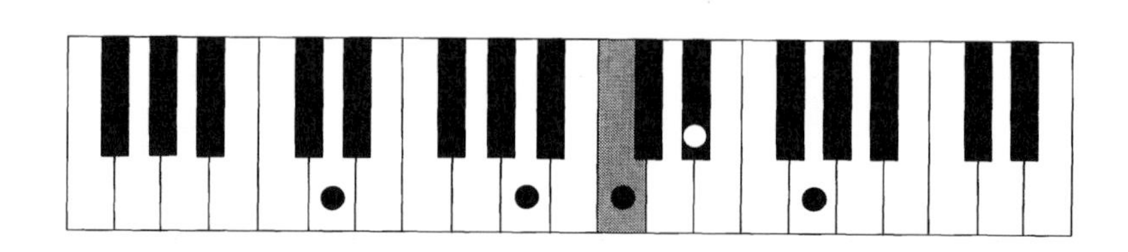

D dominant 13th - D13

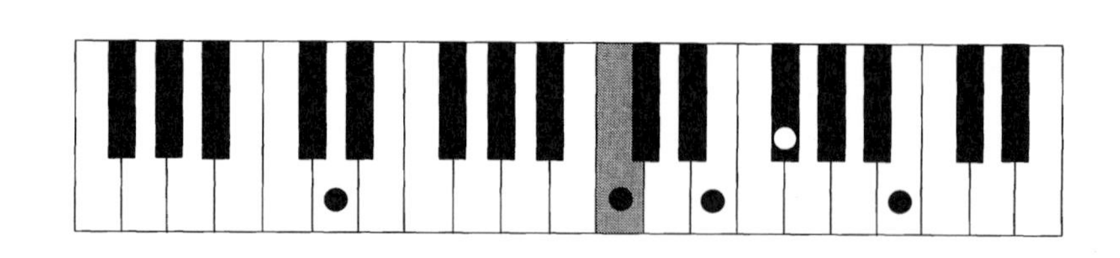

D dominant 13th with flattened 9th - D13(♭9)

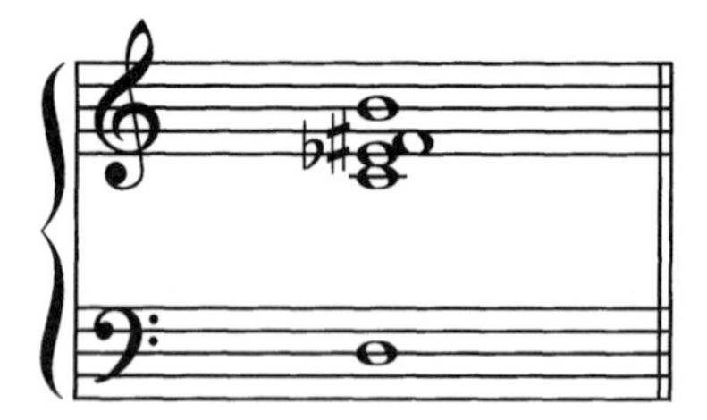

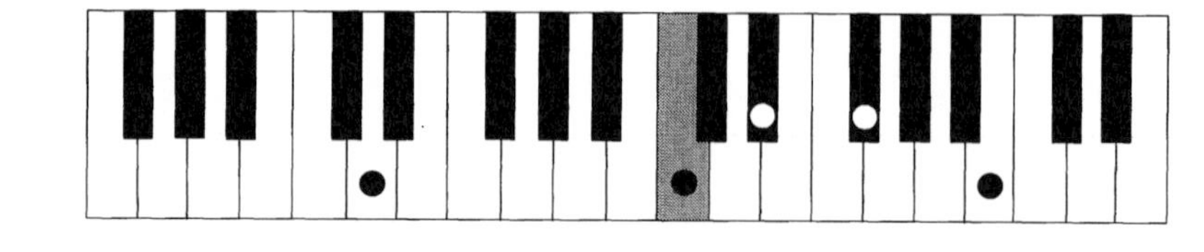

D minor - Dm

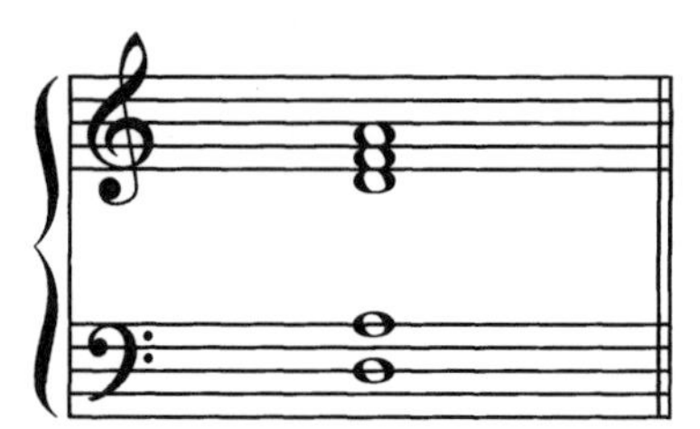

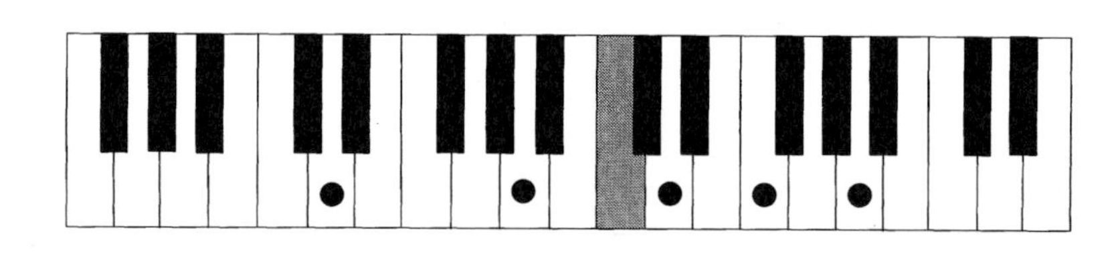

D diminished - D° or Ddim

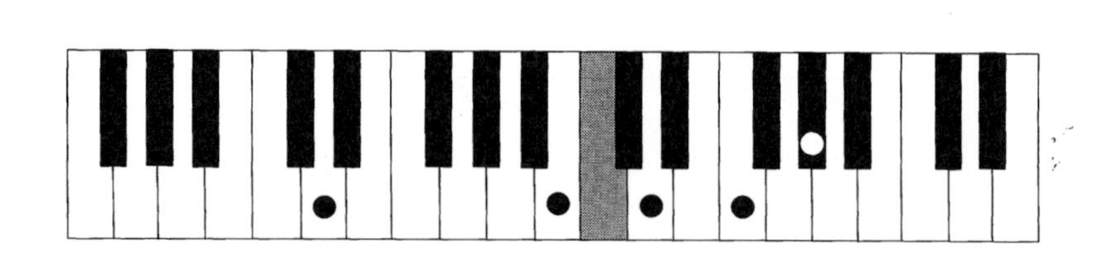

The D Collection

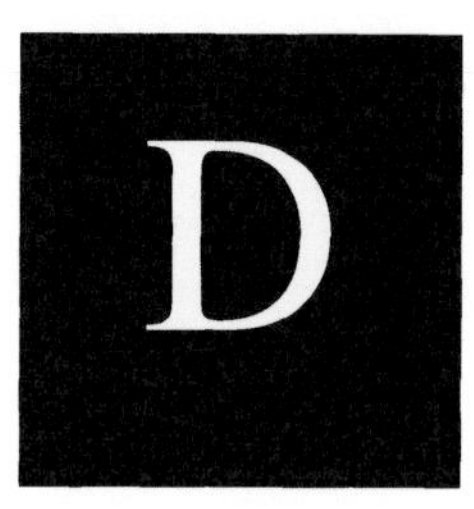

D minor added 6th - Dm6

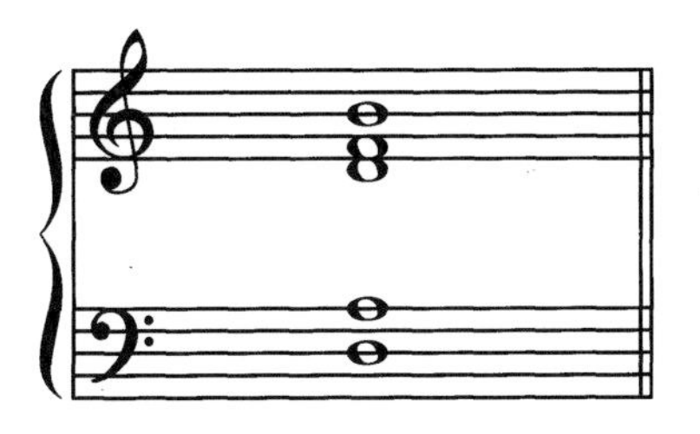

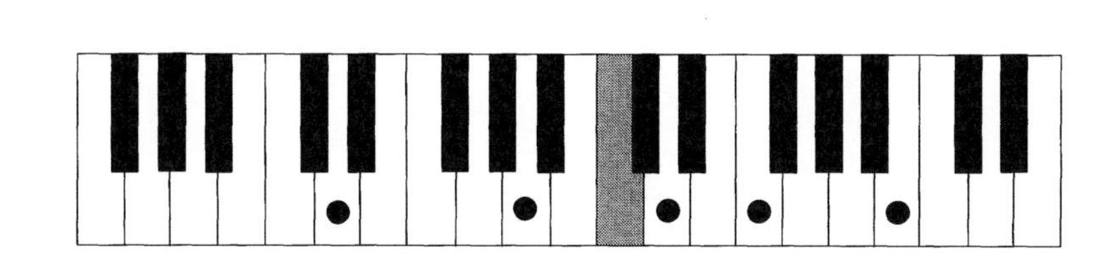

D minor 7th - Dm7

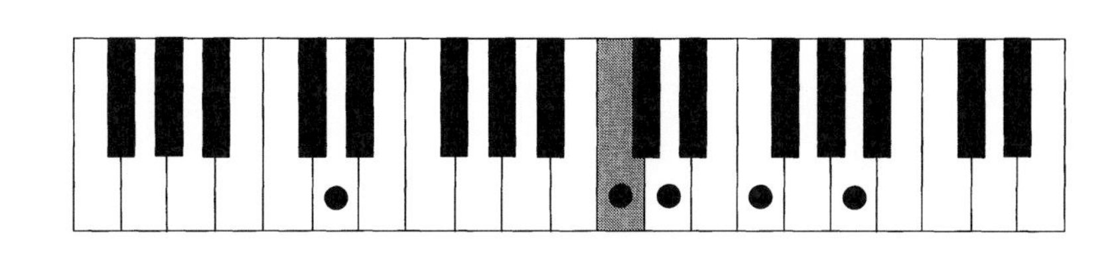

D minor 7th with flattened 5th - Dm7(♭5)

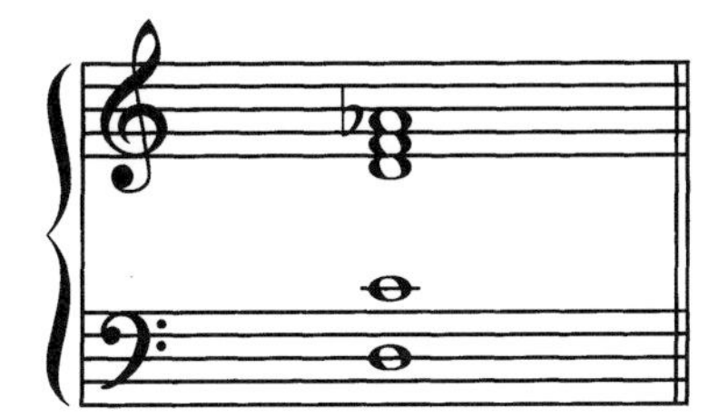

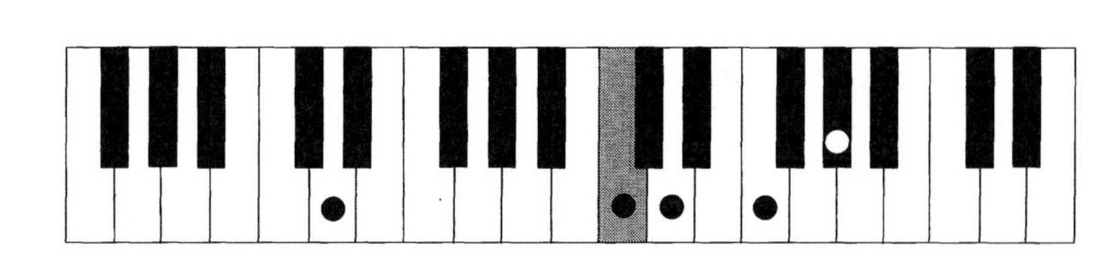

D minor added major 7th - Dm(maj7)

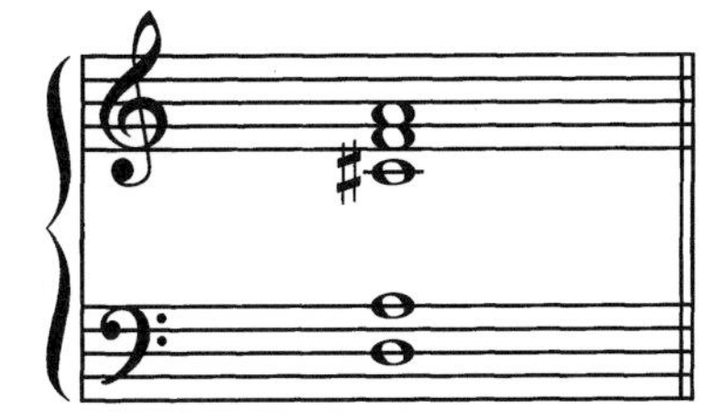

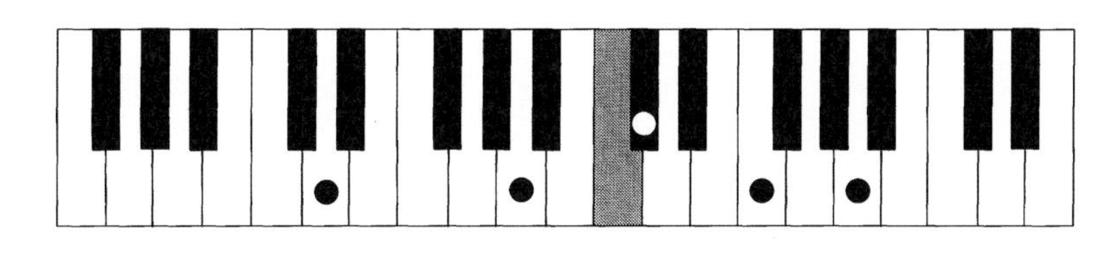

D minor 9th - Dm9

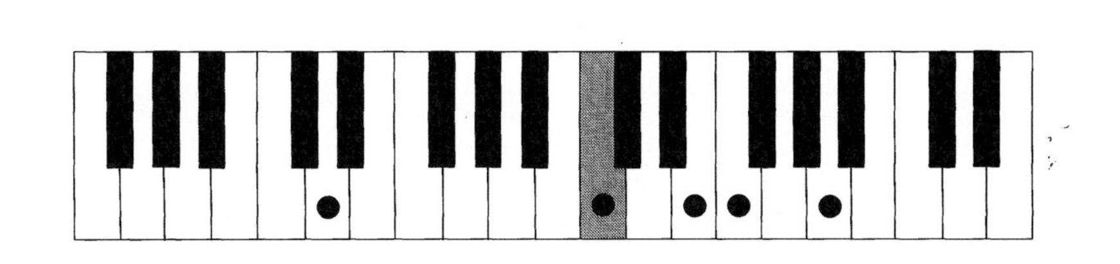

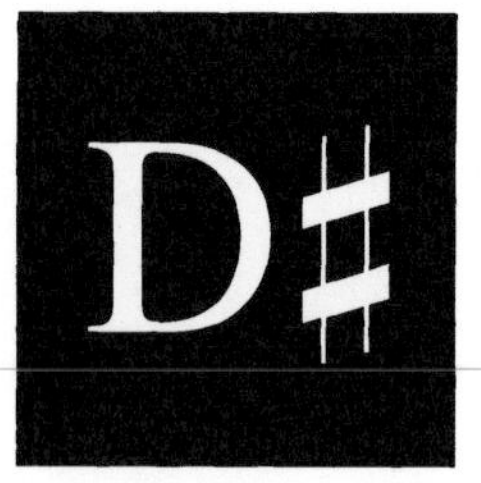

The D♯ Collection

D♯ major - D♯

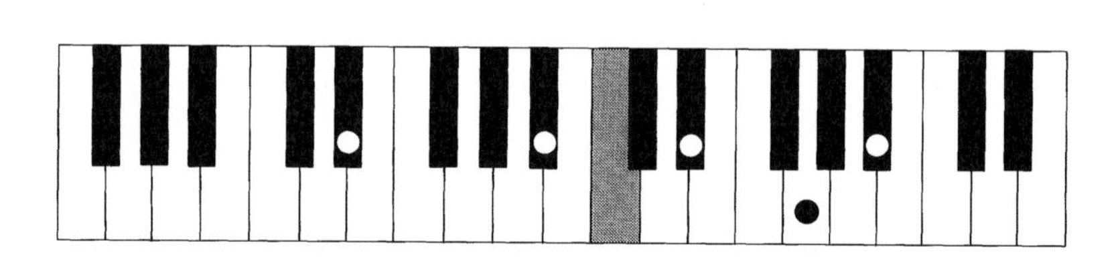

D♯ suspended 4th - D♯sus or D♯sus4

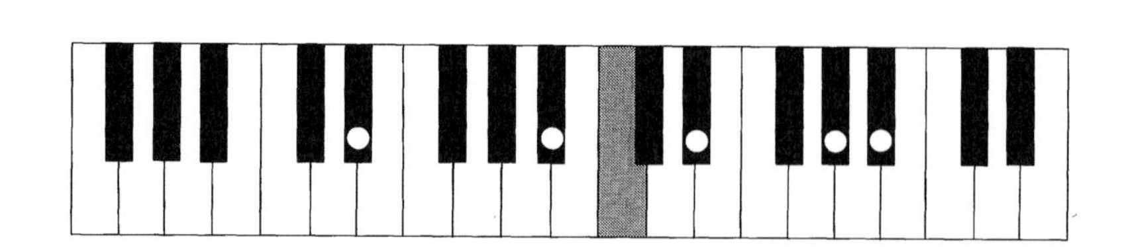

D♯ augmented 5th - D♯+ or D♯aug

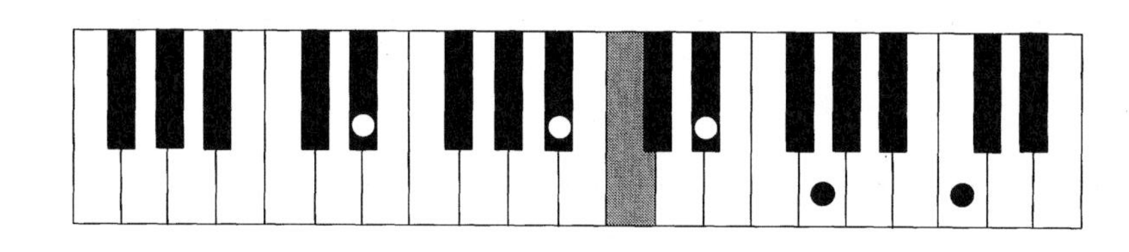

D♯ added 6th - D♯6

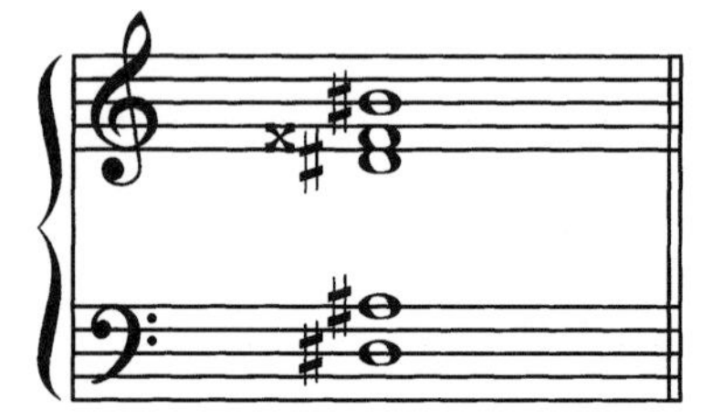

D♯ added 6th and 9th - D♯6/9

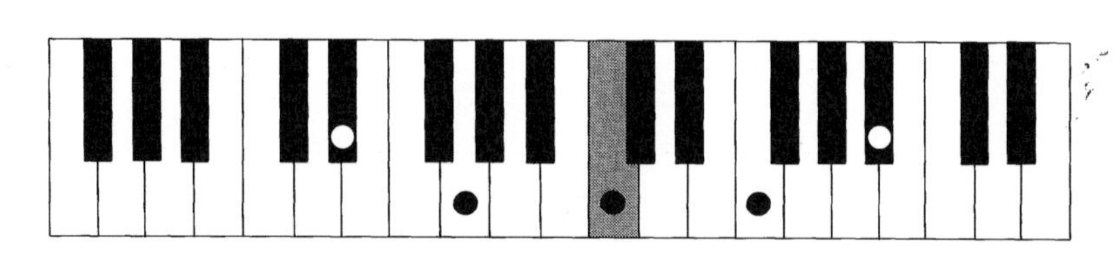

D♯ and E♭ are the same note spelled in different ways, depending on the key you are in.
For this reason, D♯ and E♭ chords are grouped together on facing pages.

The E♭ Collection

E♭ major - E♭

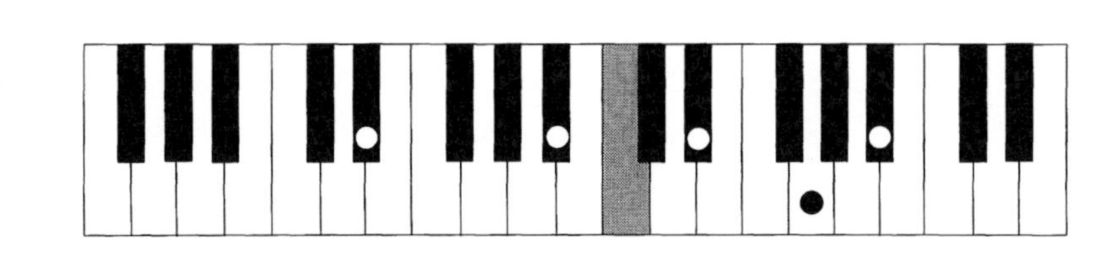

E♭ suspended 4th - E♭sus or E♭sus4

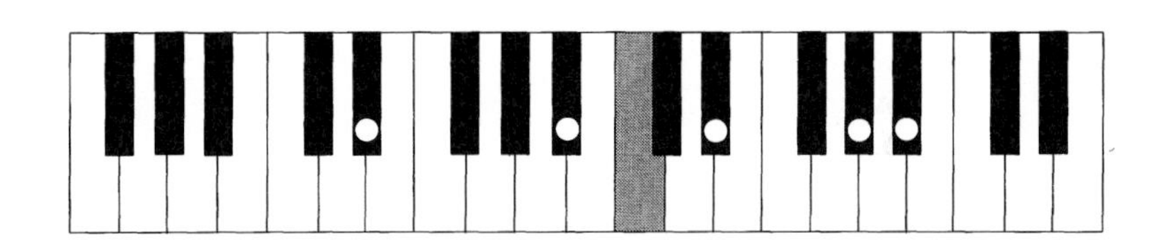

E♭ augmented 5th - E♭+ or E♭aug

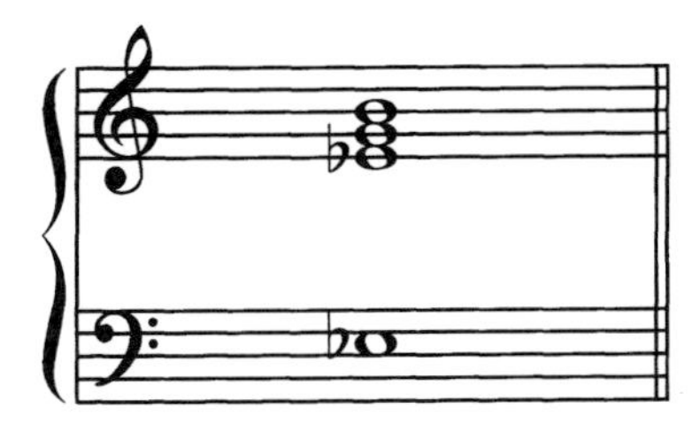

E♭ added 6th - E♭6

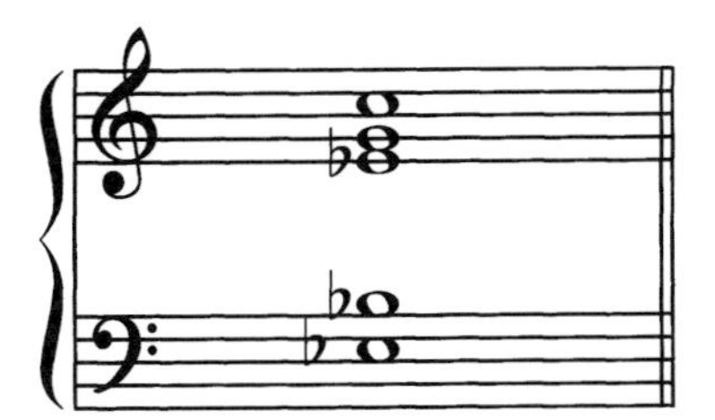

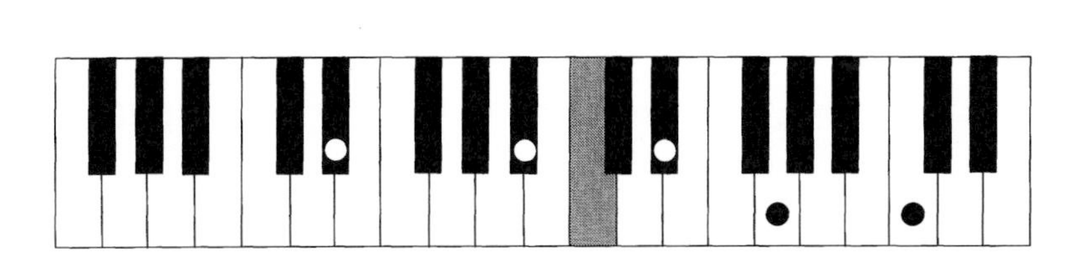

E♭ added 6th and 9th - E♭6/9

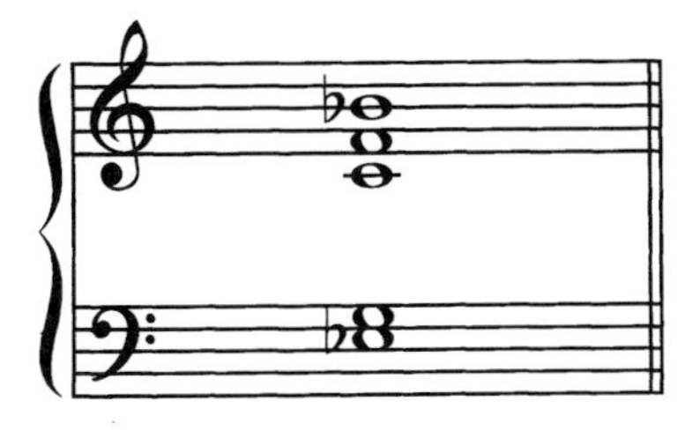

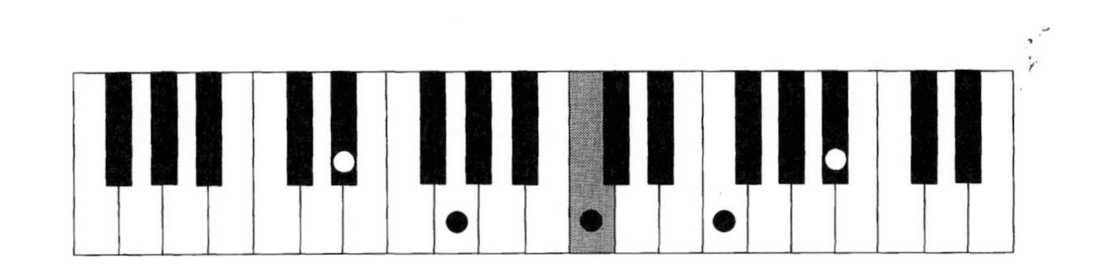

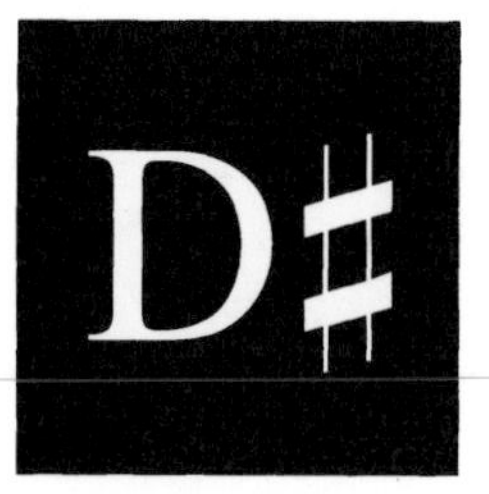

The D♯ Collection

D♯ major 7th - D♯maj7

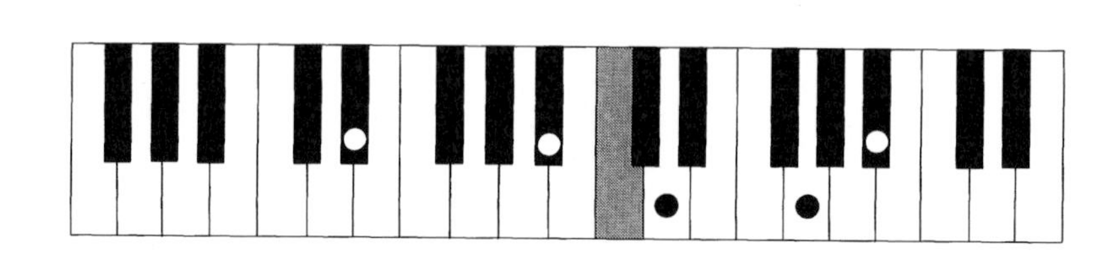

D♯ dominant 7th - D♯7

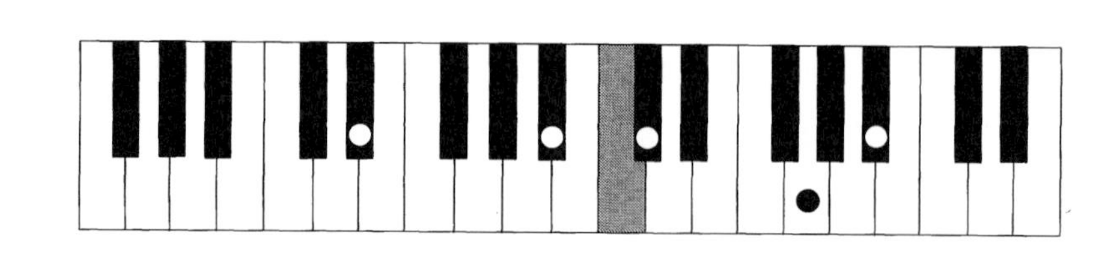

D♯ dominant 7th with suspended 4th - D♯7sus or D♯7sus4

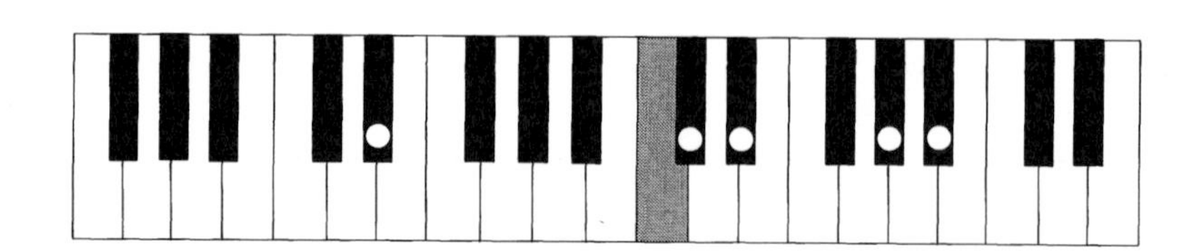

D♯ dominant 7th with flattened 5th - D♯7(♭5)

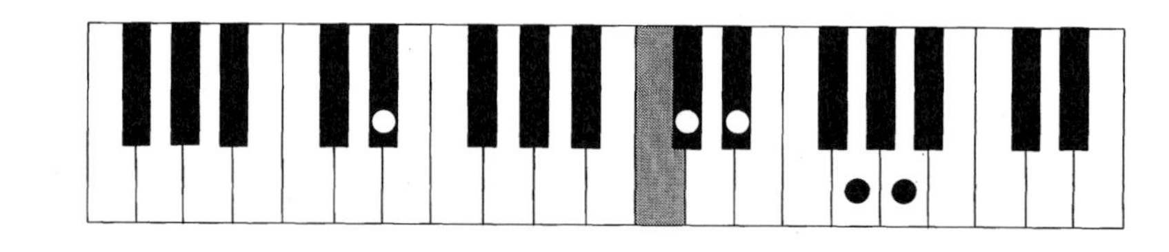

D♯ dominant 7th with augmented 5th - D♯7+ or D♯7aug

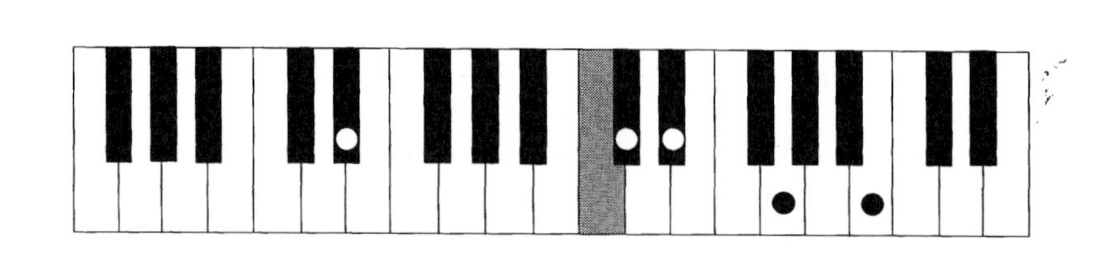

The E♭ Collection

E♭ major 7th - E♭maj7

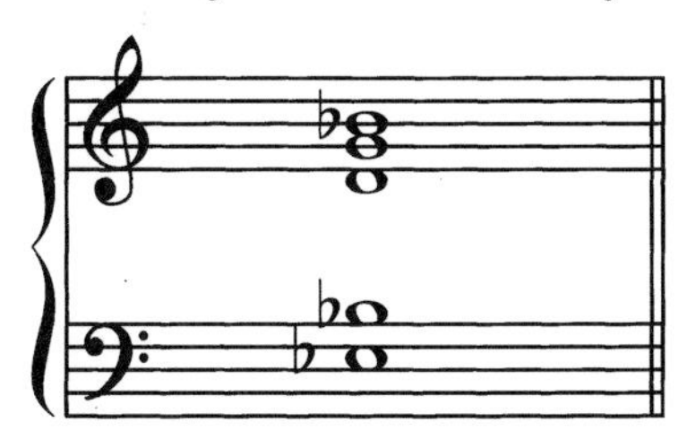

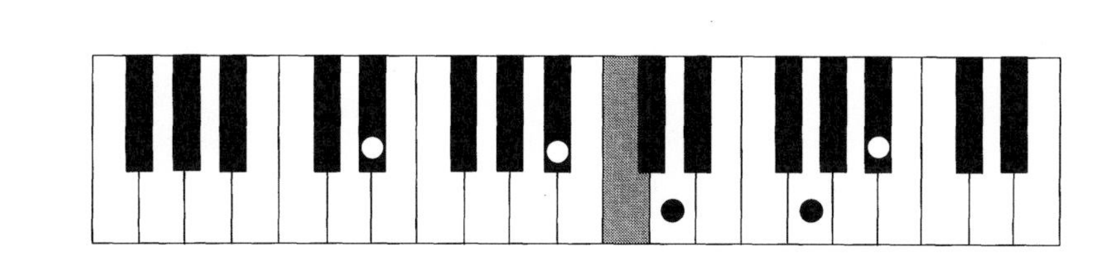

E♭ dominant 7th - E♭7

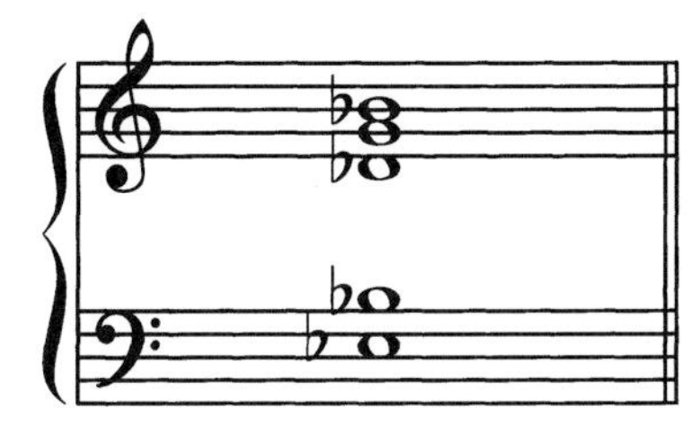

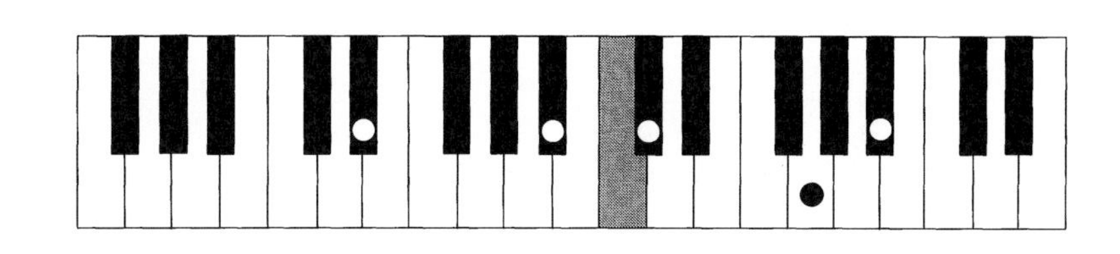

E♭ dominant 7th with suspended 4th - E♭7sus or E♭7sus4

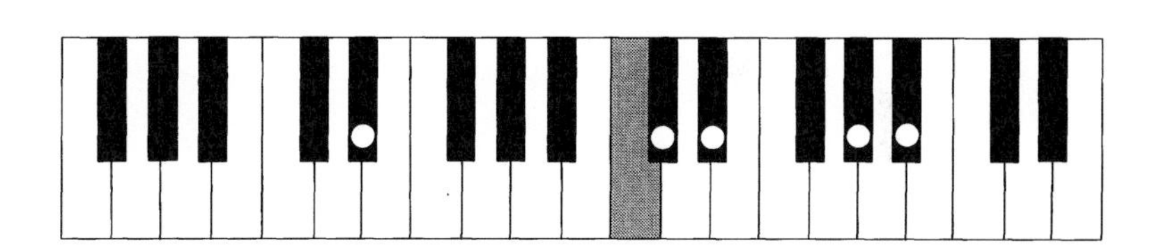

E♭ dominant 7th with flattened 5th - E♭7(♭5)

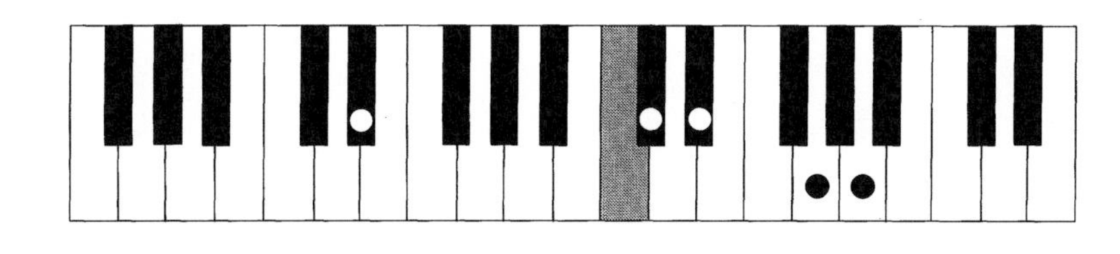

E♭ dominant 7th with augmented 5th - E♭7+ or E♭7aug

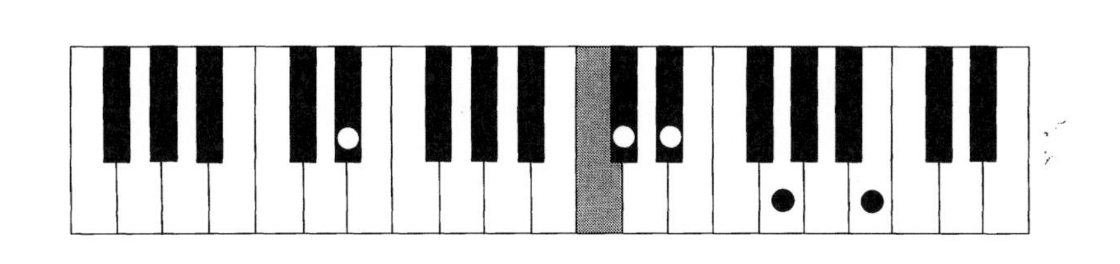

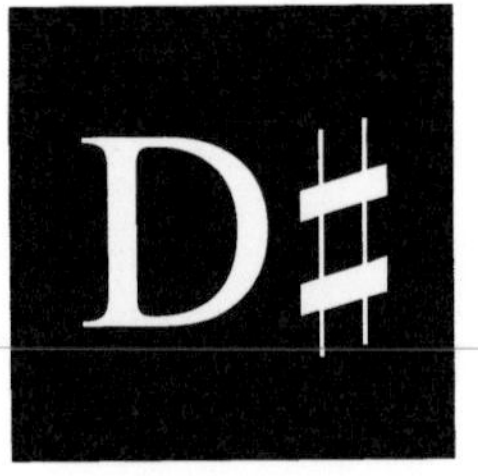

The D♯ Collection

D♯ dominant 7th with flattened 9th - D♯7(♭9)

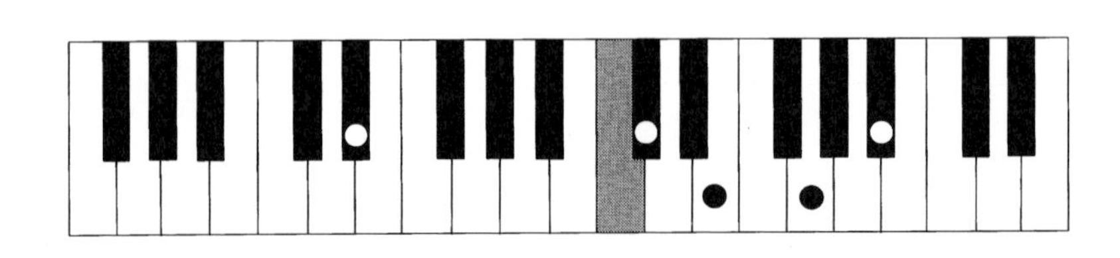

D♯ dominant 7th with flattened 9th and 5th - D♯7(♭9/♭5)

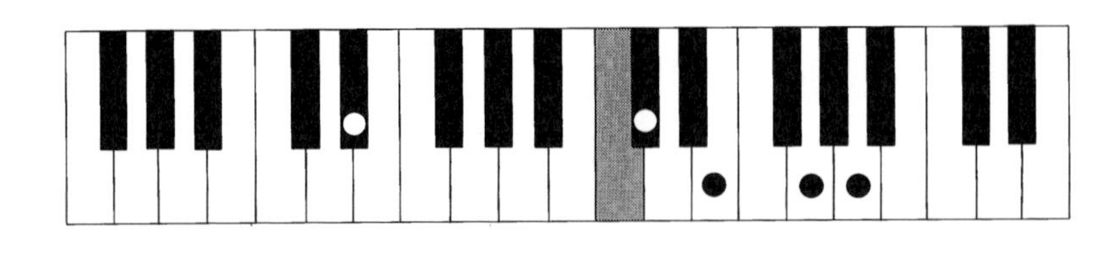

D♯ dominant 7th with sharpened 9th - D♯7(♯9)

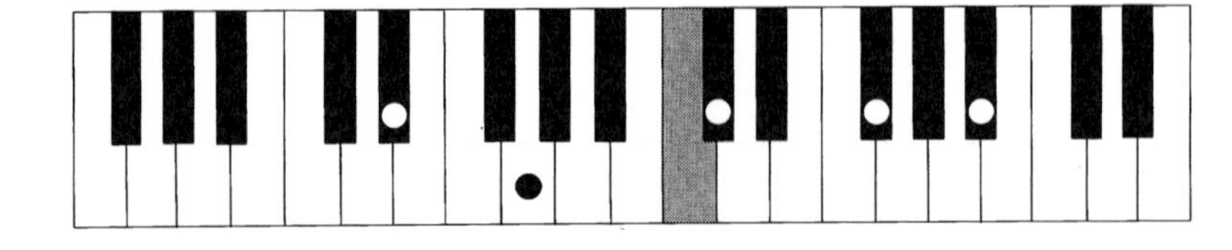

D♯ added 9th - D♯add9

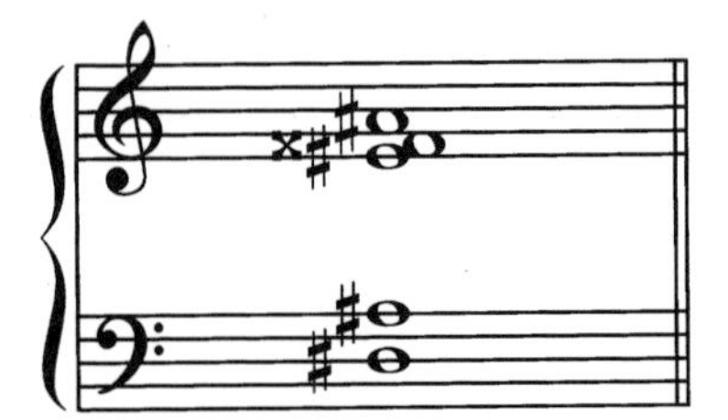
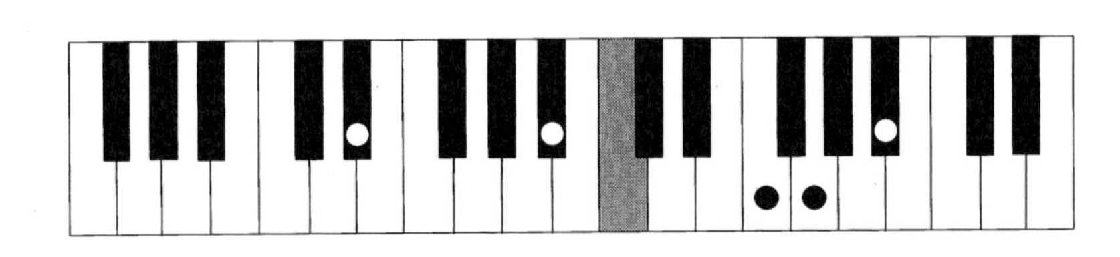

D♯ major 9th - D♯maj9

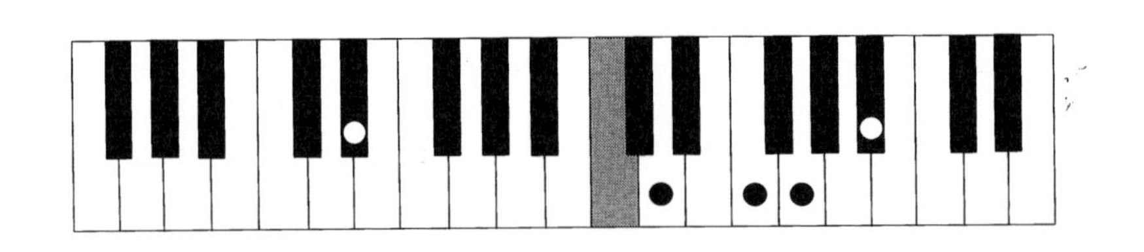

The E♭ Collection

E♭ dominant 7th with flattened 9th - E♭7(♭9)

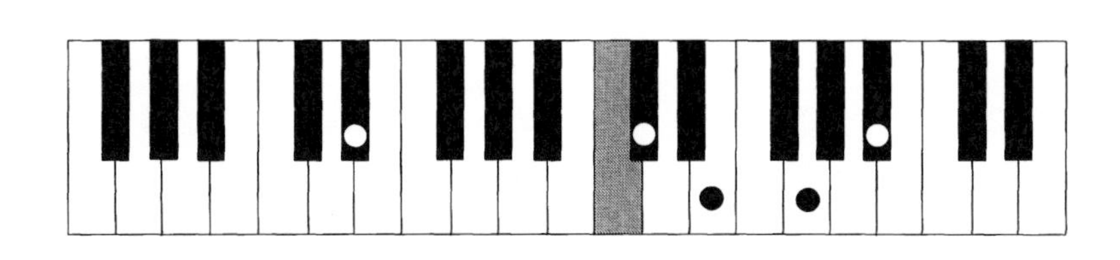

E♭ dominant 7th with flattened 9th and 5th - E♭7(♭9/♭5)

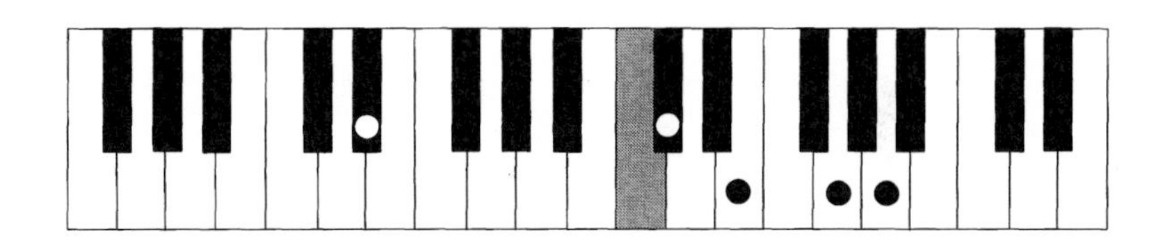

E♭ dominant 7th with sharpened 9th - E♭7(♯9)

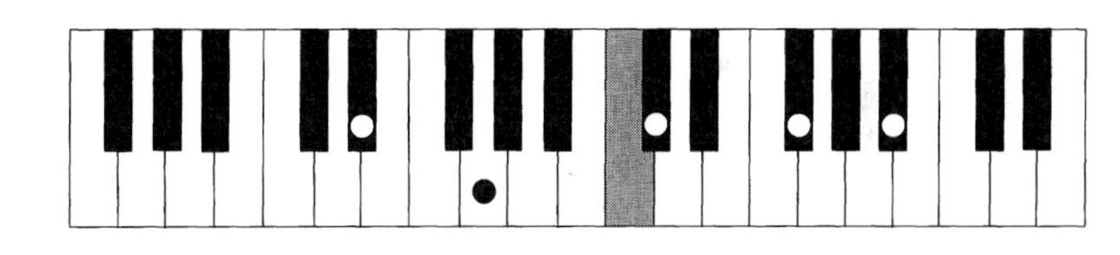

E♭ added 9th - E♭add9

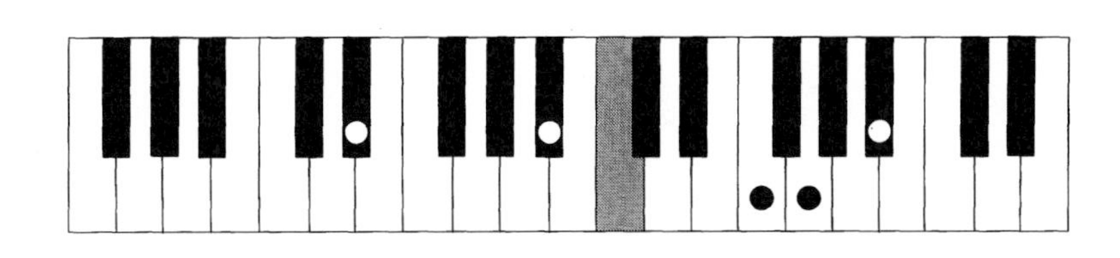

E♭ major 9th - E♭maj9

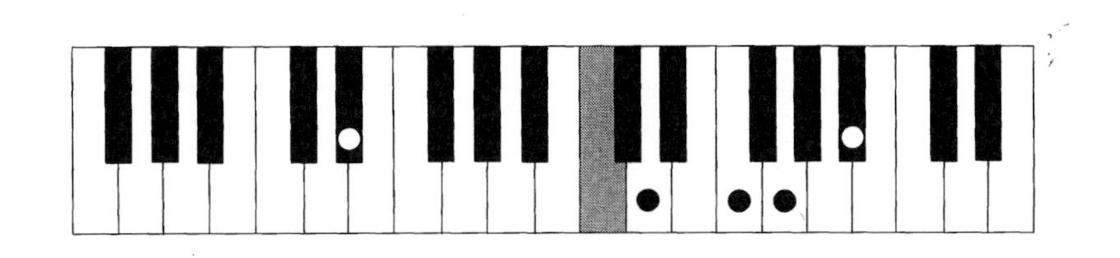

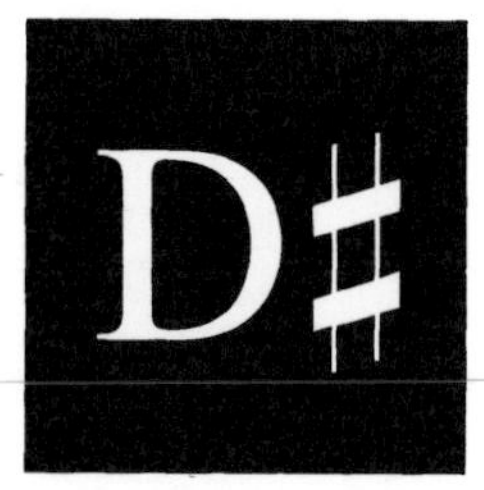

The D♯ Collection

D♯ dominant 9th - D♯9

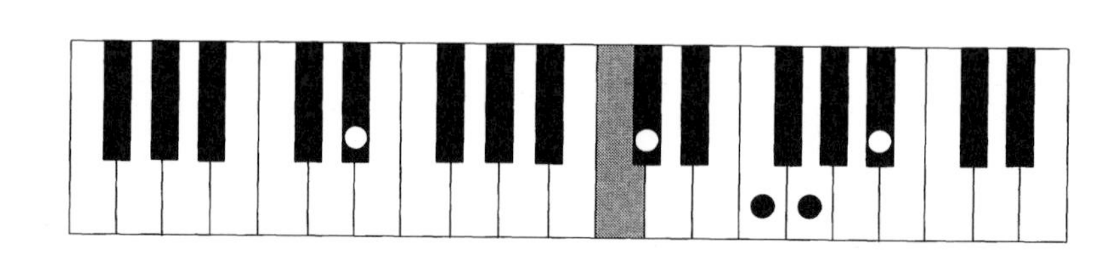

D♯ dominant 9th with suspended 4th - D♯9sus or D♯9sus4

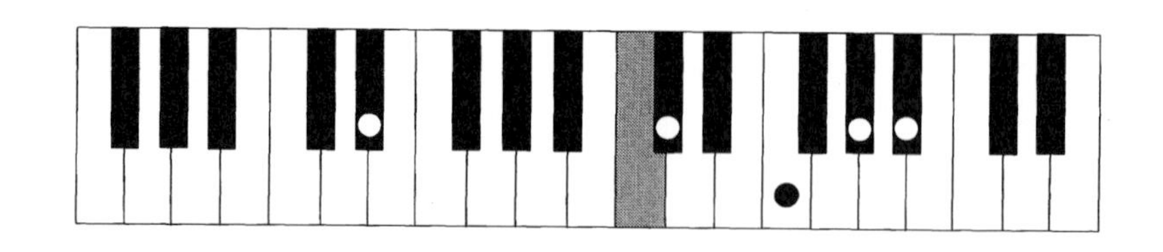

D♯ dominant 9th with augmented 5th - D♯9+ or D♯9aug

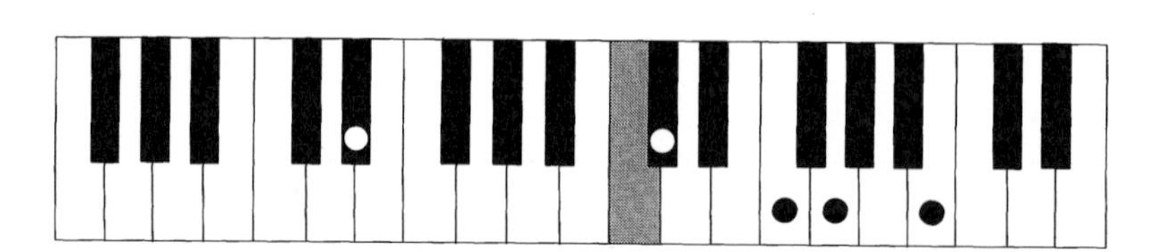

D♯ dominant 9th with sharpened 11th - D♯9(♯11)
with flattened 5th - D♯9(♭5)

D♯ dominant 11th - D♯11

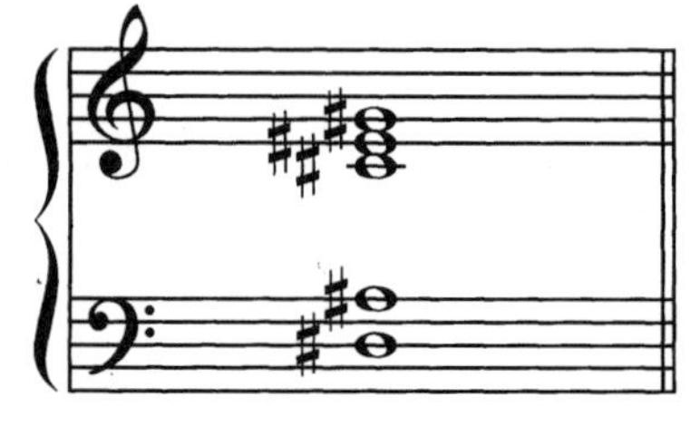

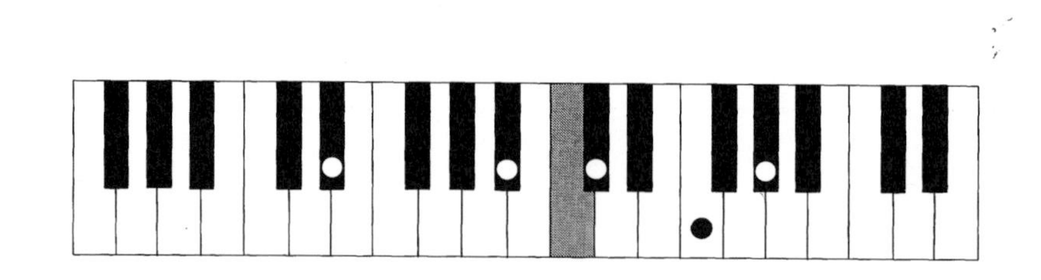

The E♭ Collection

E♭ dominant 9th - E♭9

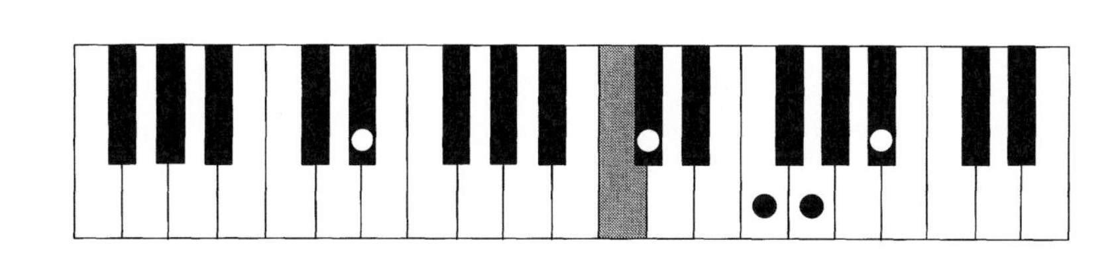

E♭ dominant 9th with suspended 4th - E♭9sus or E♭9sus4

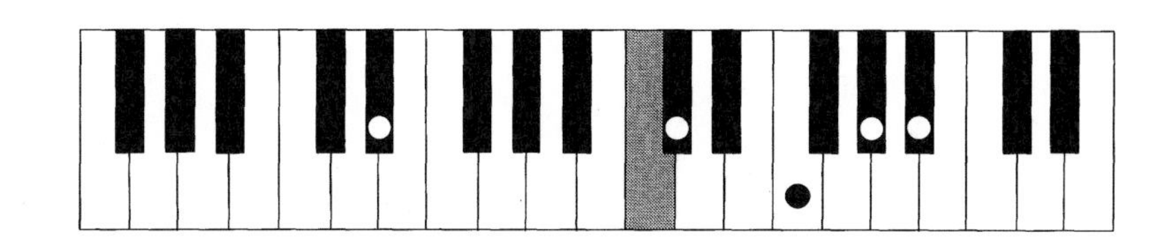

E♭ dominant 9th with augmented 5th - E♭9+ or E♭9aug

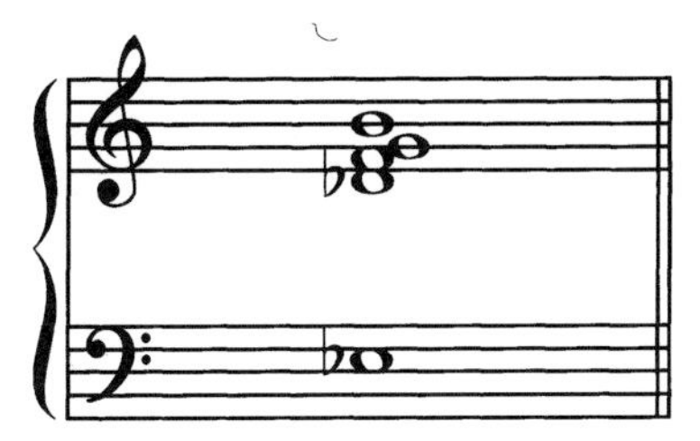

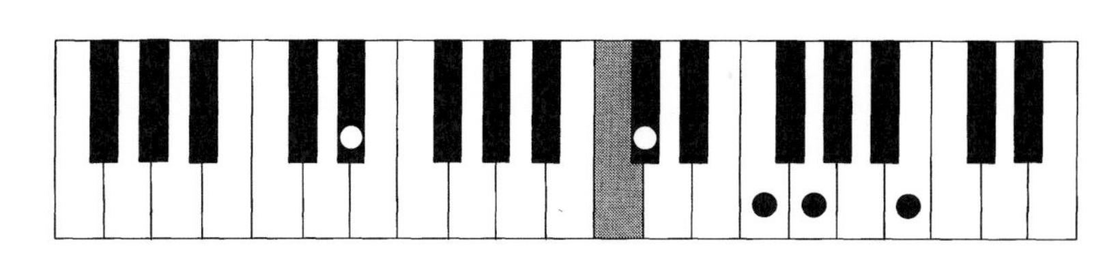

E♭ dominant 9th with sharpened 11th - E♭9(♯11)
with flattened 5th - E♭9(♭5)

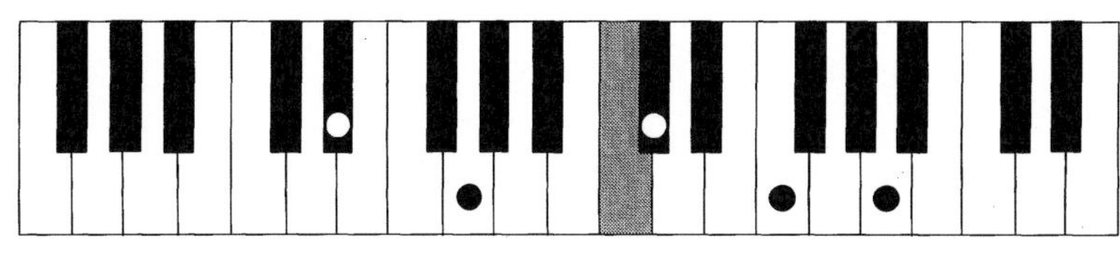

E♭ dominant 11th - E♭11

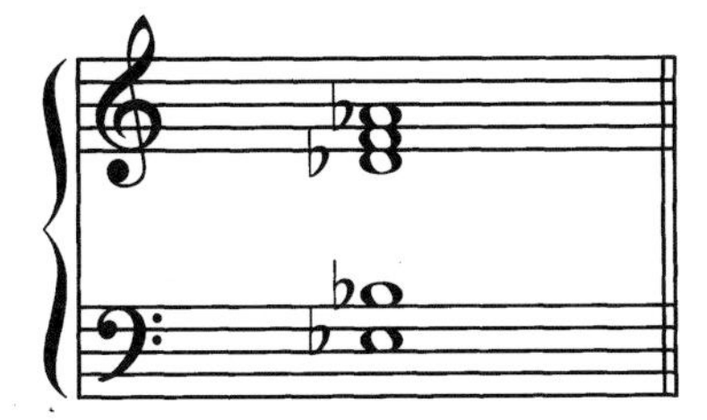

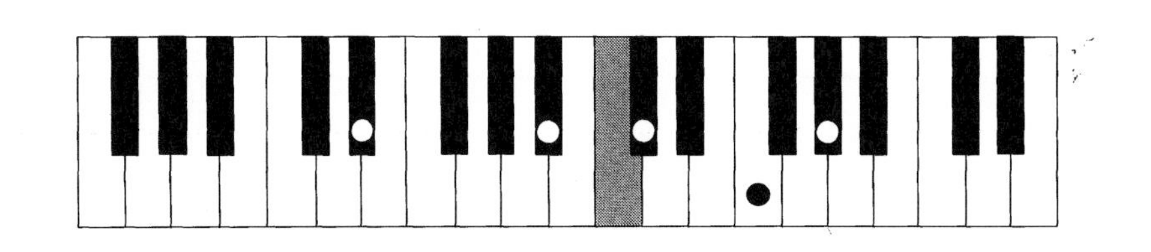

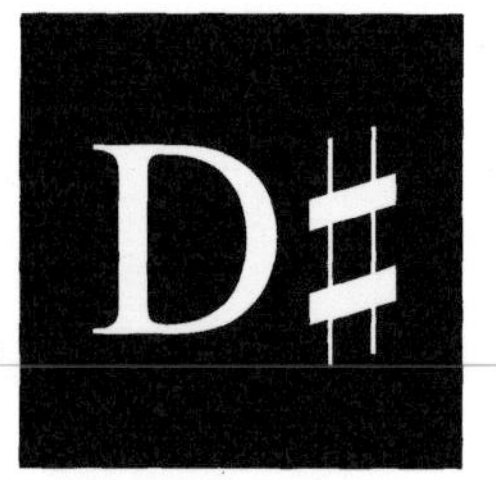

The D♯ Collection

D♯ dominant 11th with flattened 9th - D♯11(♭9)

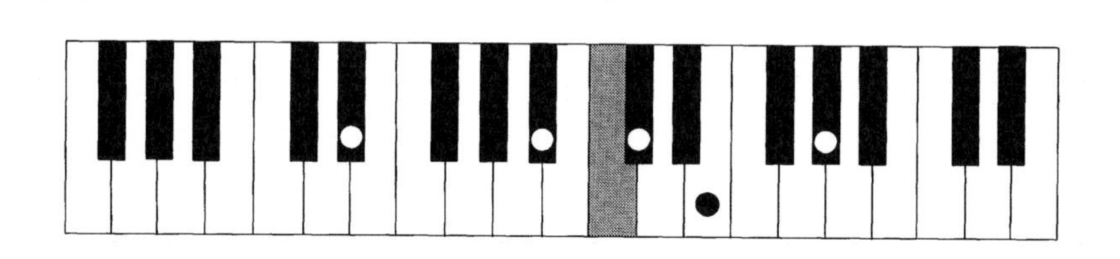

D♯ dominant 13th - D♯13

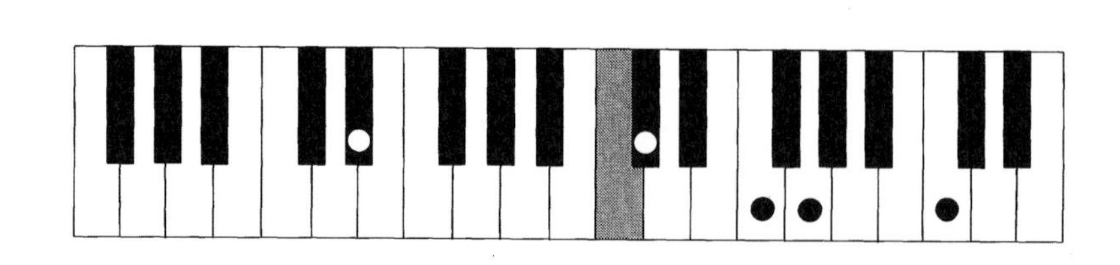

D♯ dominant 13th with flattened 9th - D♯13(♭9)

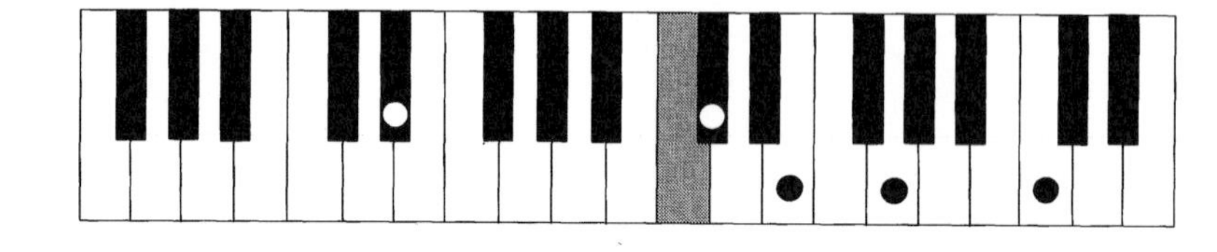

D♯ minor - D♯m

D♯ diminished - D♯° or D♯dim

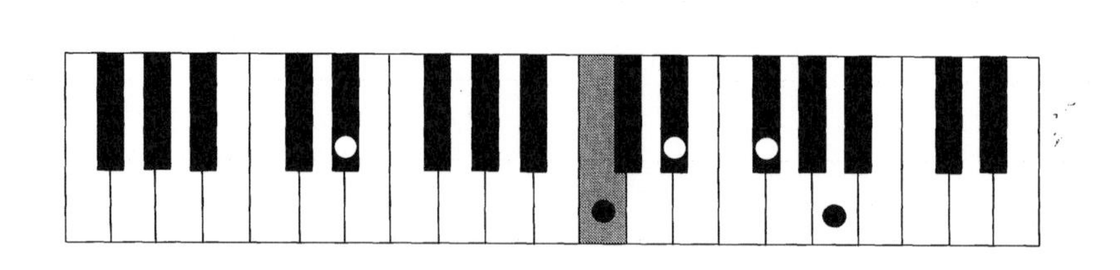

The E♭ Collection

E♭ dominant 11th with flattened 9th - E♭11(♭9)

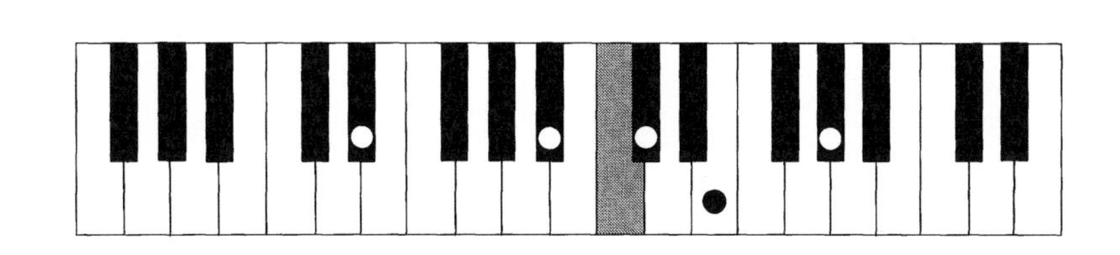

E♭ dominant 13th - E♭13

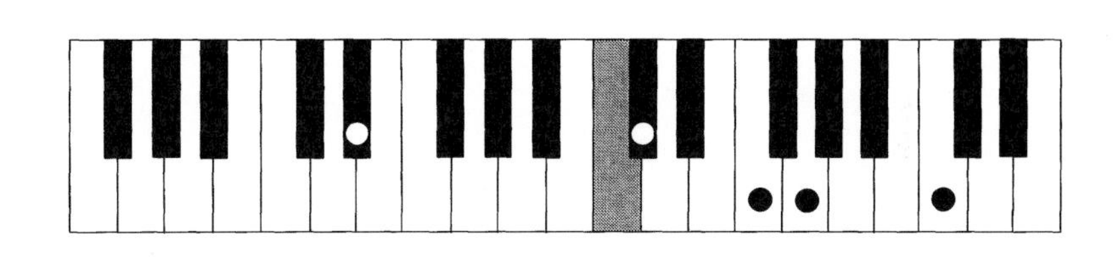

E♭ dominant 13th with flattened 9th - E♭13(♭9)

E♭ minor - E♭m

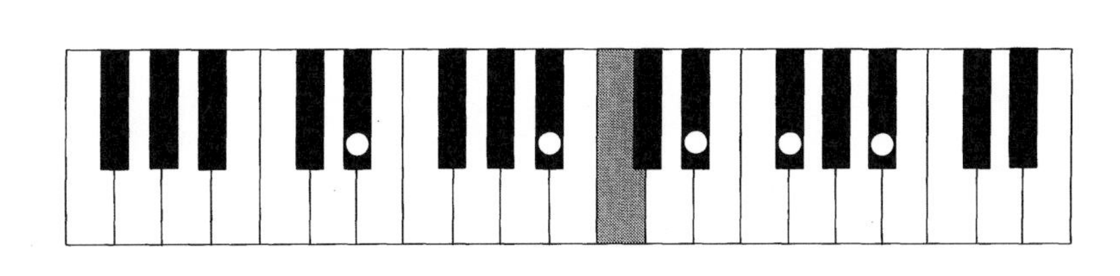

E♭ diminished - E♭° or E♭dim

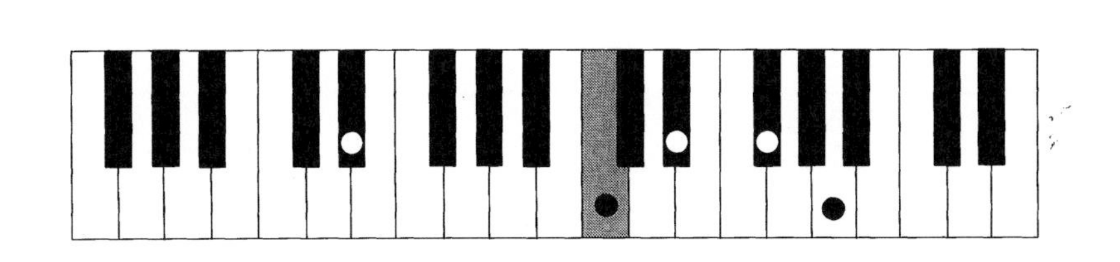

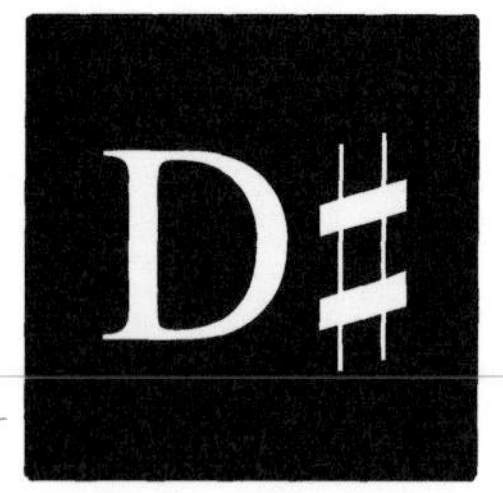

The D♯ Collection

D♯ minor added 6th - D♯m6

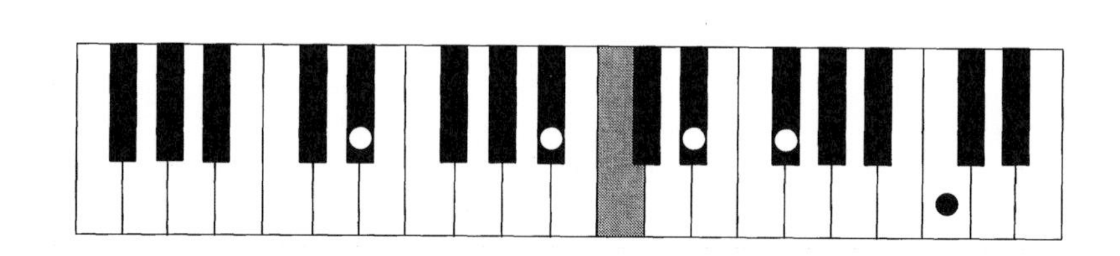

D♯ minor 7th - D♯m7

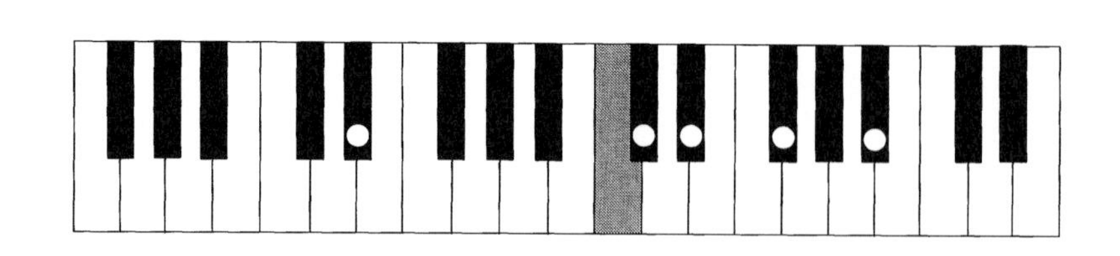

D♯ minor 7th with flattened 5th - D♯m7(♭5)

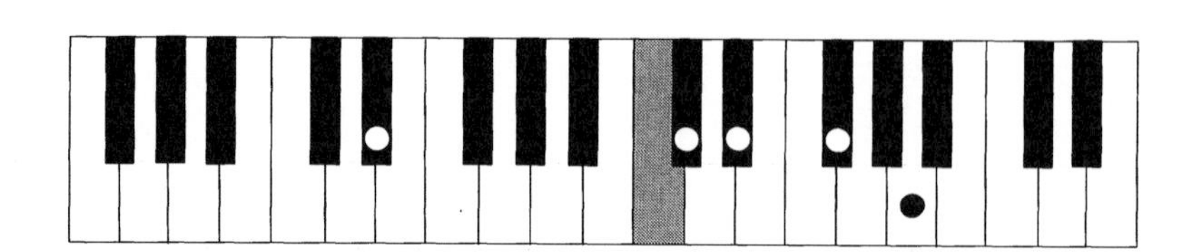

D♯ minor added major 7th - D♯m(maj7)

D♯ minor 9th - D♯m9

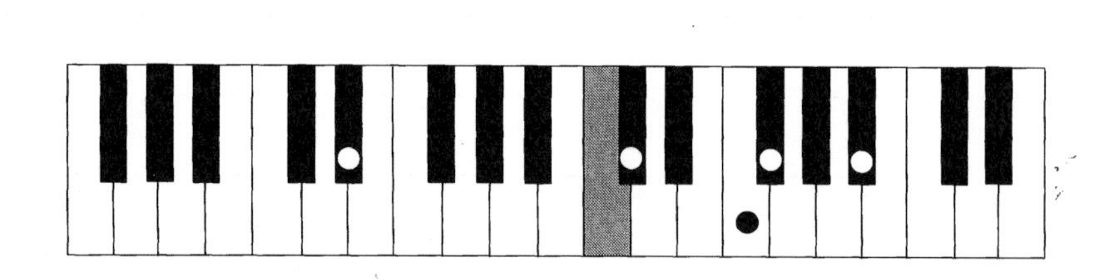

The E♭ Collection

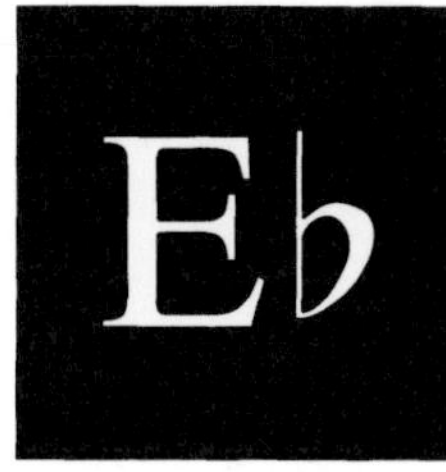

E♭ minor added 6th - E♭m6

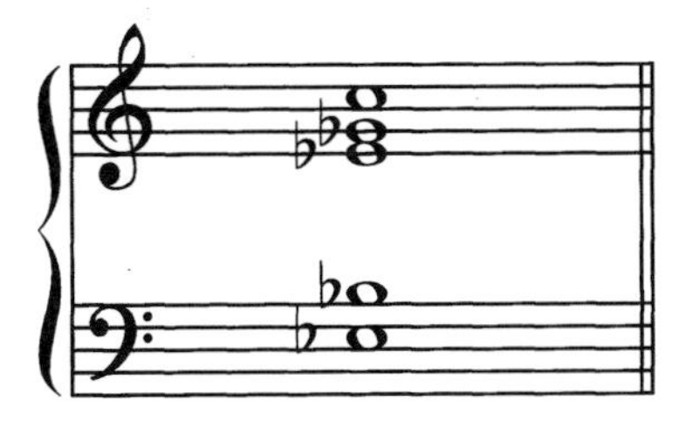

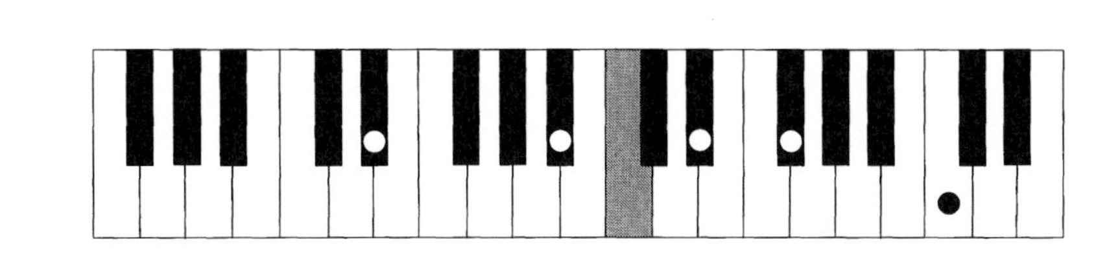

E♭ minor 7th -E♭m7

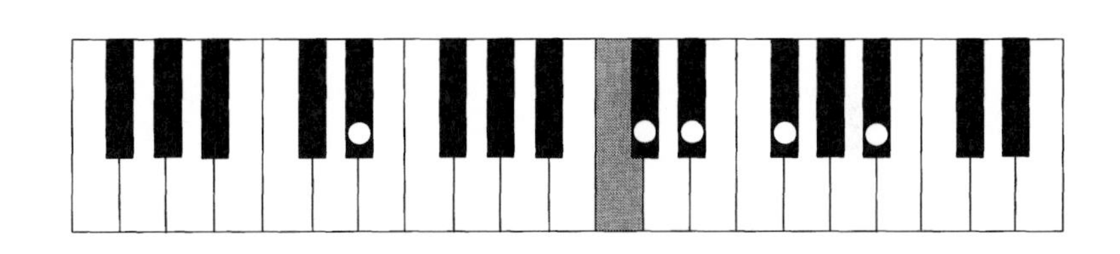

E♭ minor 7th with flattened 5th - E♭m7(♭5)

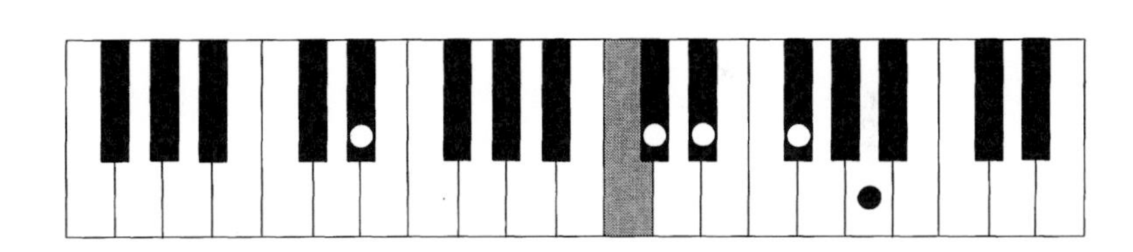

E♭ minor added major 7th - E♭m(maj7)

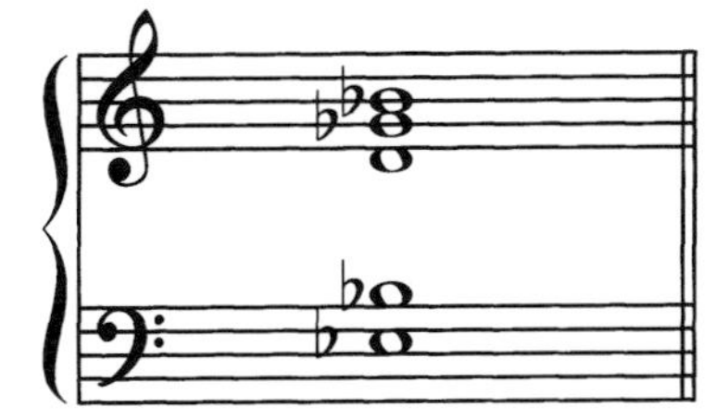

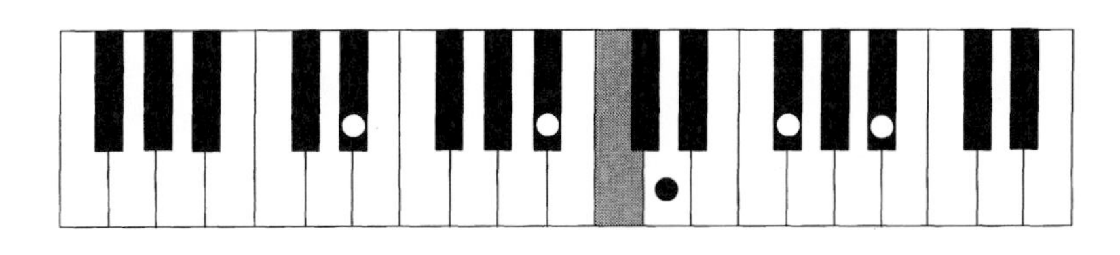

E♭ minor 9th - E♭m9

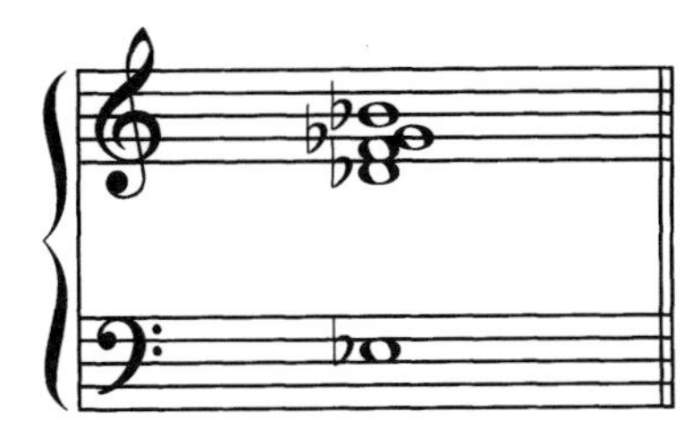

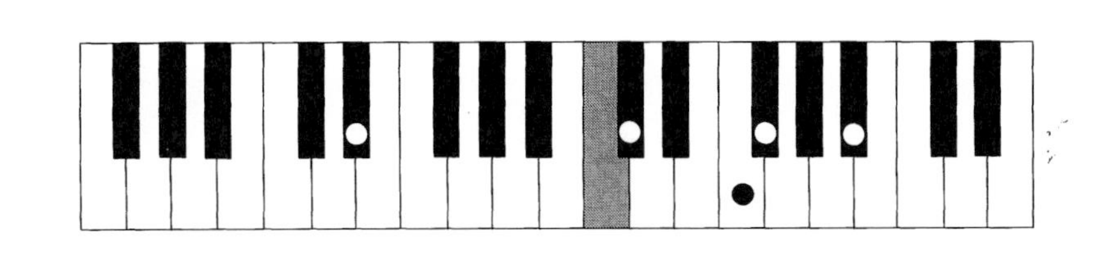

The E Collection

E major - E

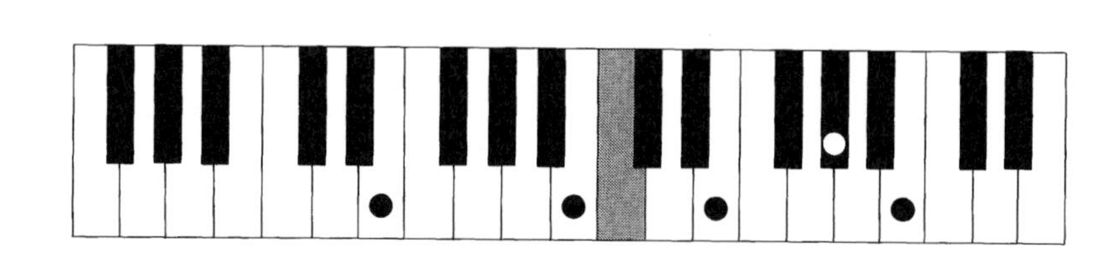

E suspended 4th - Esus or Esus4

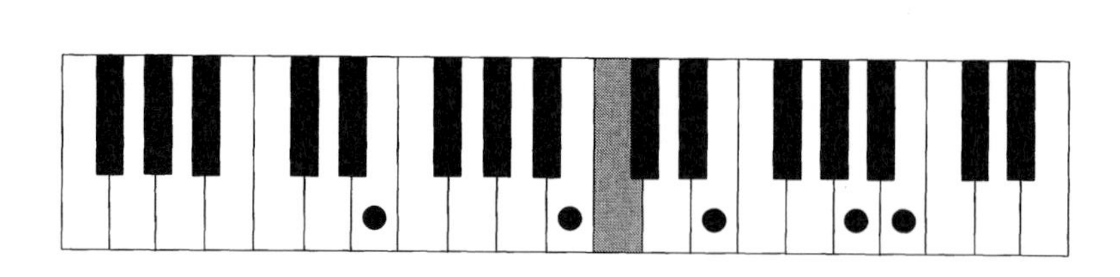

E augmented 5th - E+ or Eaug

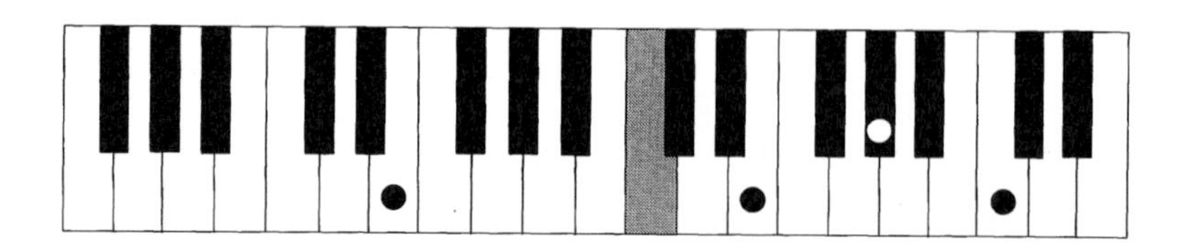

E added 6th - E6

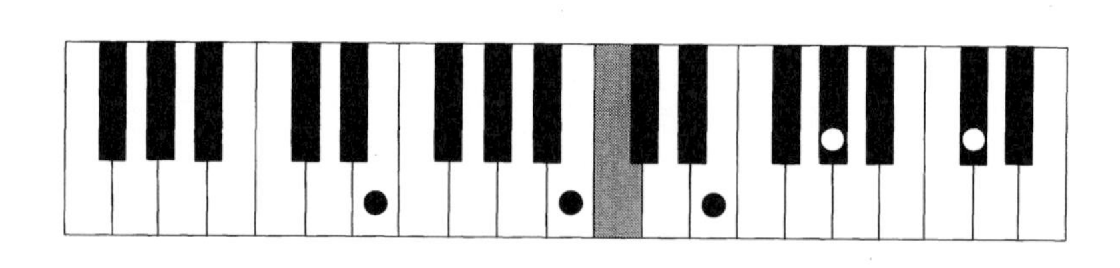

E added 6th and 9th - E6/9

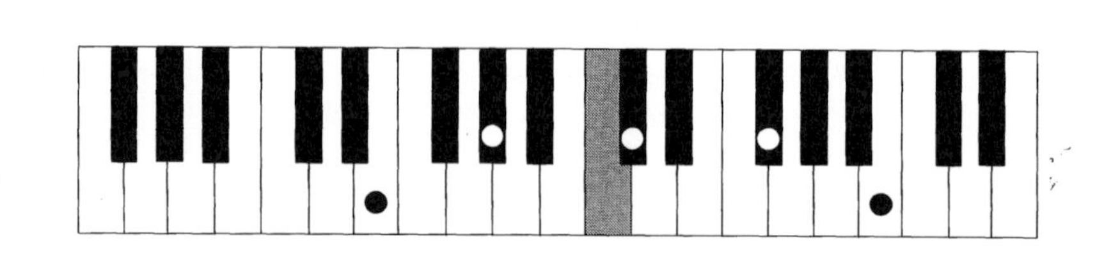

The E Collection

E major 7th - Emaj7

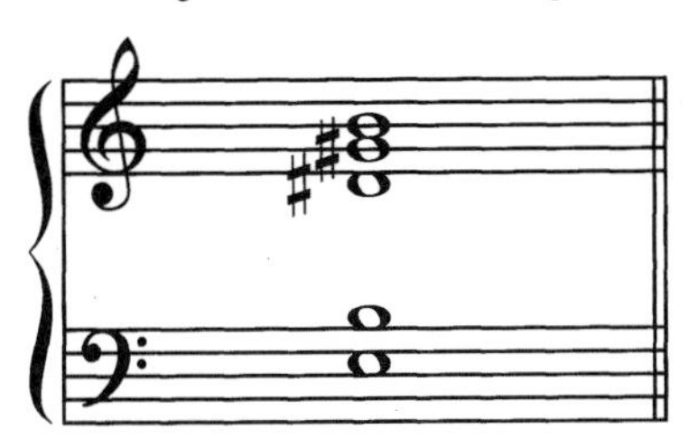

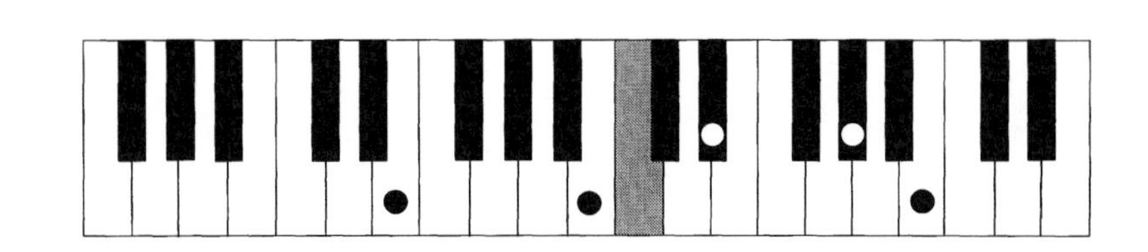

E dominant 7th - E7

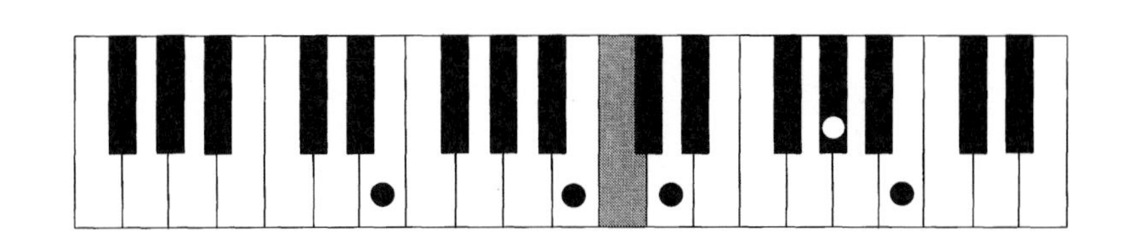

E dominant 7th with suspended 4th - E7sus or E7sus4

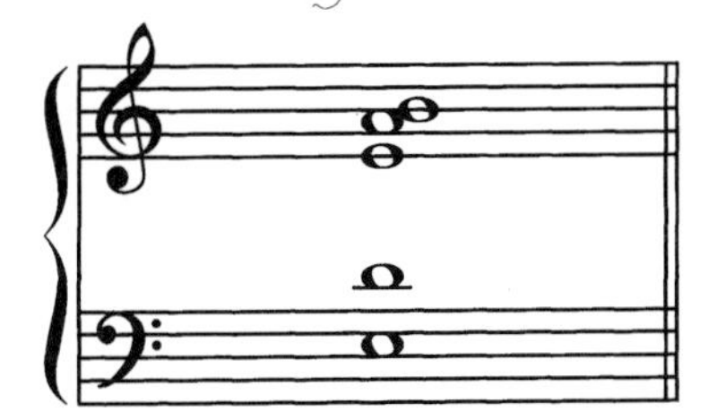

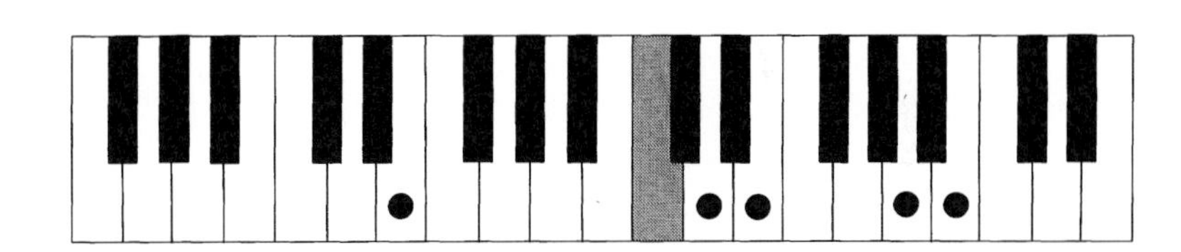

E dominant 7th with flattened 5th - E7(♭5)

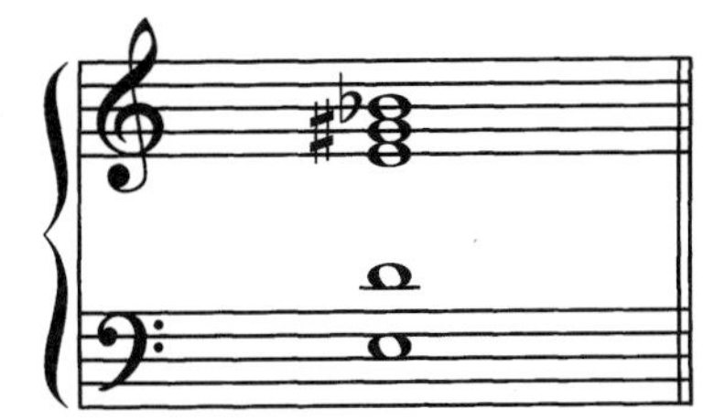

E dominant 7th with augmented 5th - E7+ or E7aug

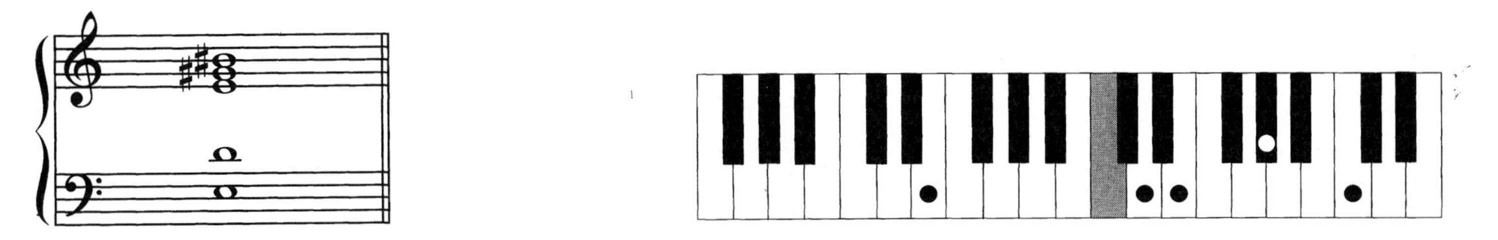

The E Collection

E dominant 7th with flattened 9th - E7(♭9)

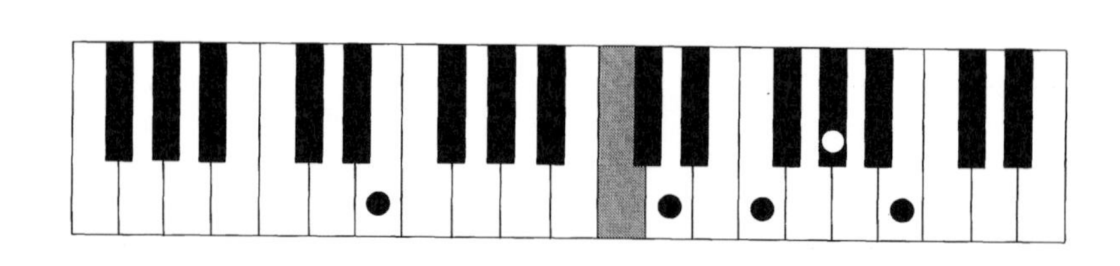

E dominant 7th with flattened 9th and 5th - E7(♭9/♭5)

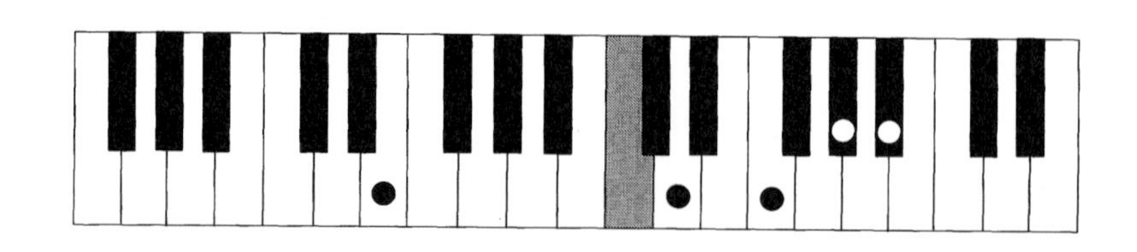

E dominant 7th with sharpened 9th - E7(♯9)

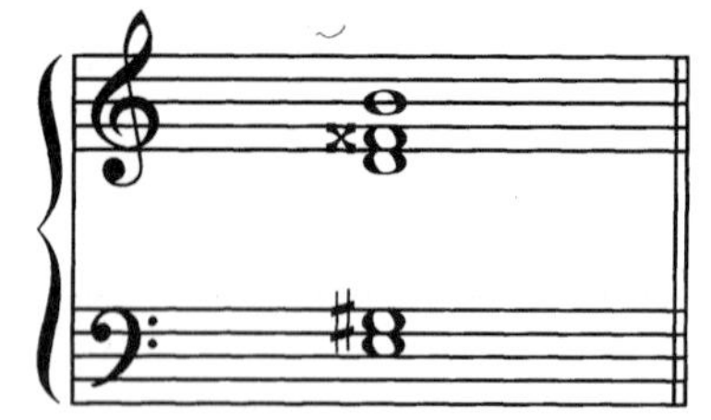

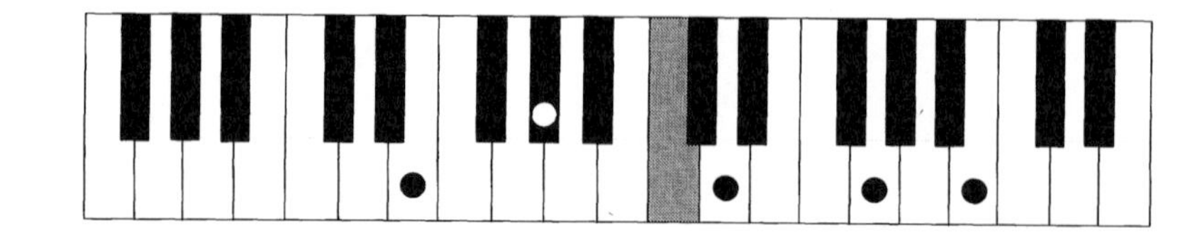

E added 9th - Eadd9

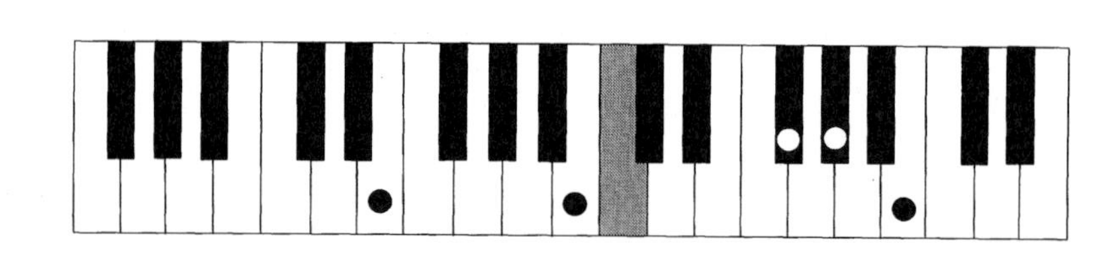

E major 9th - Emaj9

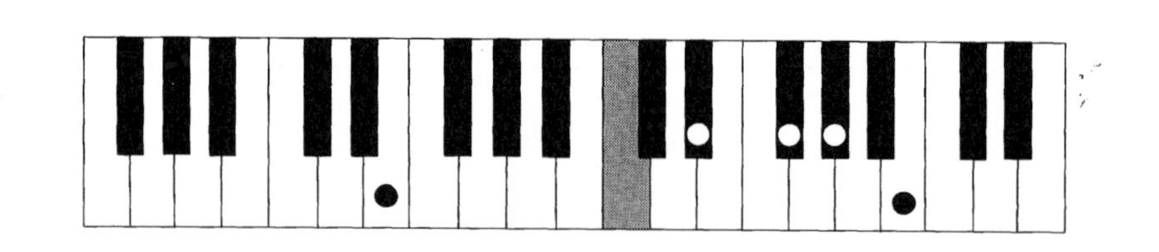

The E Collection

E dominant 9th - E9

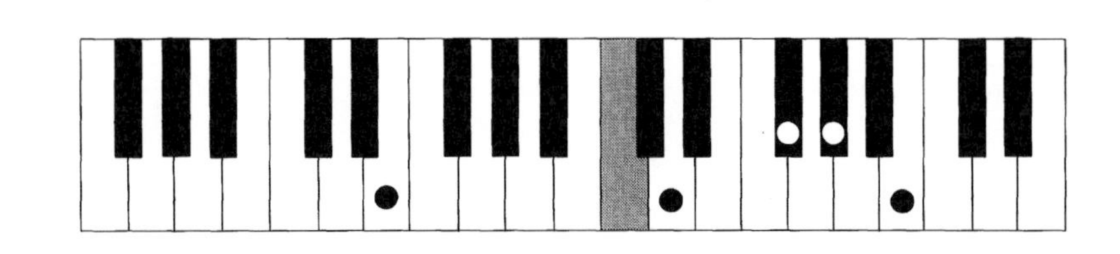

E dominant 9th with suspended 4th - E9sus or E9sus4

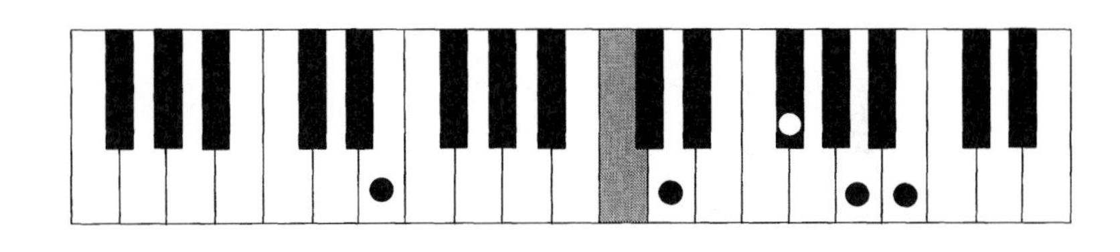

E dominant 9th with augmented 5th - E9+ or E9aug

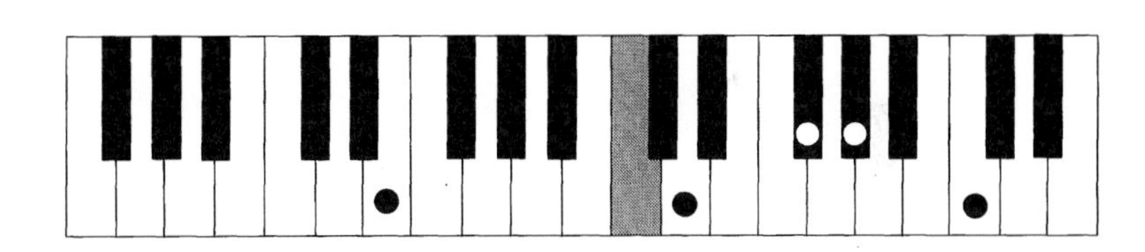

E dominant 9th with sharpened 11th - E9(♯11)
with flattened 5th - E9(♭5)

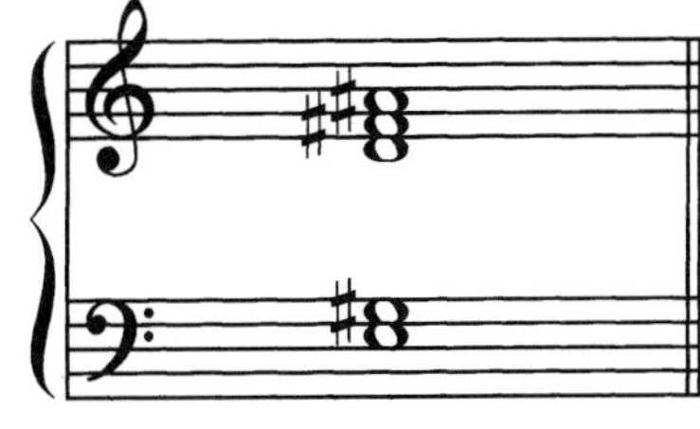

E dominant 11th - E11

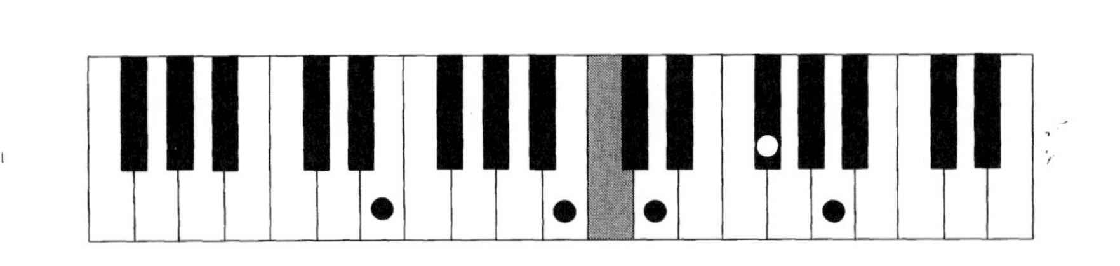

The E Collection

E dominant 11th with flattened 9th - E11(♭9)

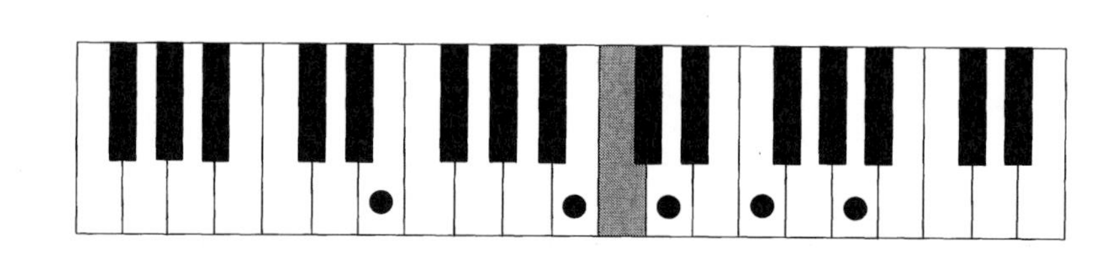

E dominant 13th - E13

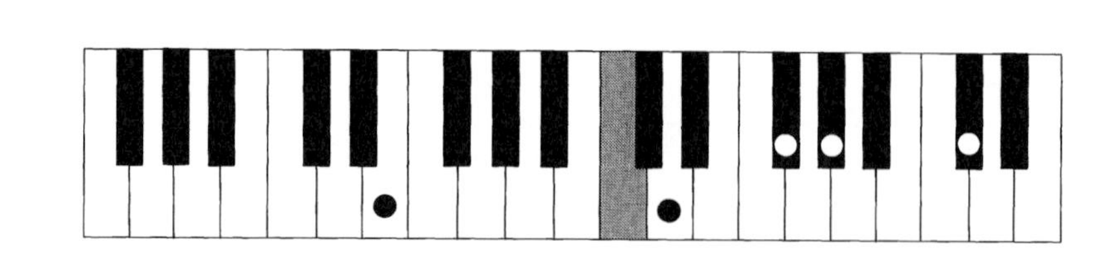

E dominant 13th with flattened 9th - E13(♭9)

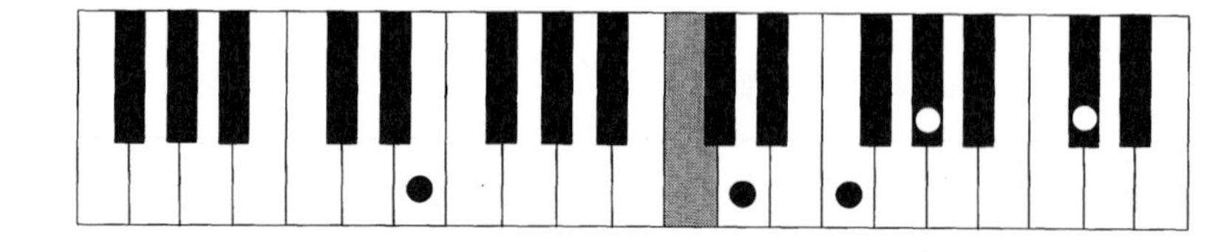

E minor - Em

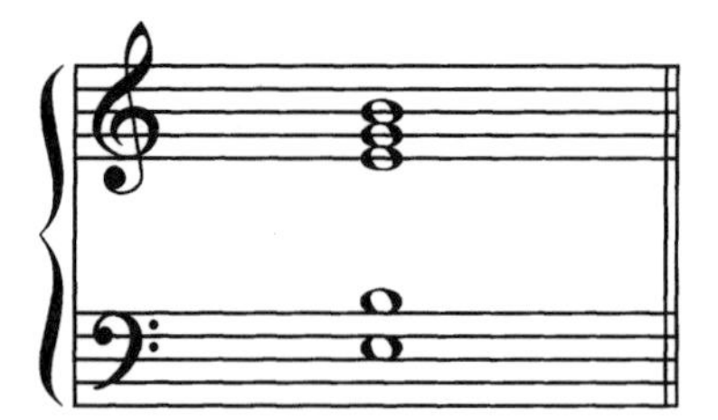

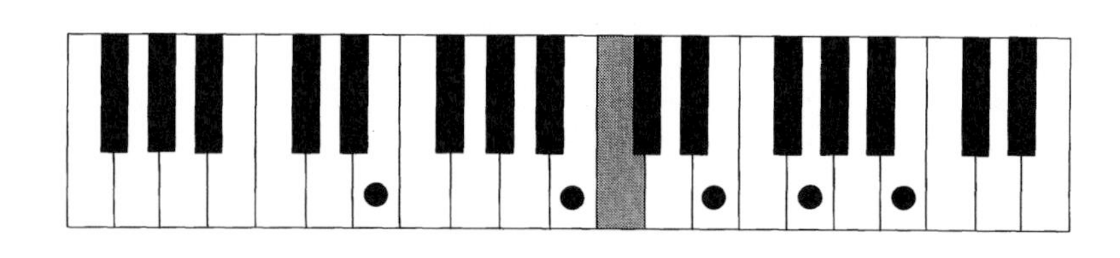

E diminished - E° or Edim

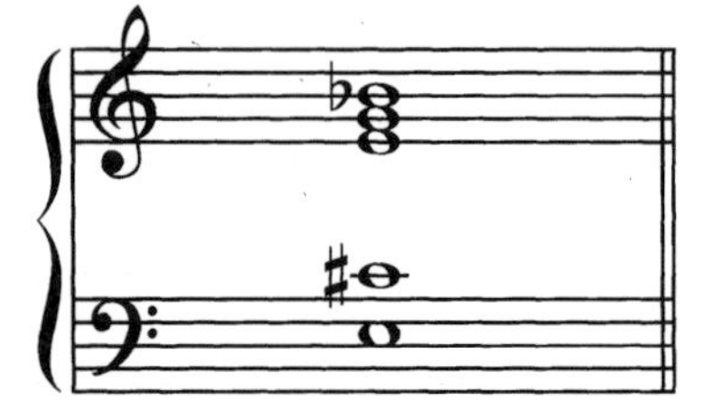

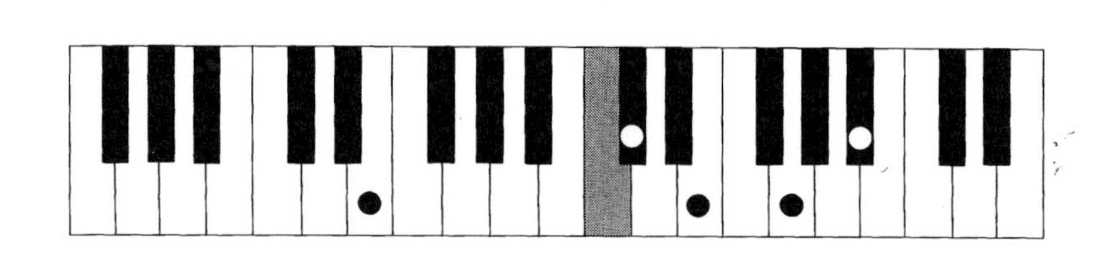

The E Collection

E minor added 6th - Em6

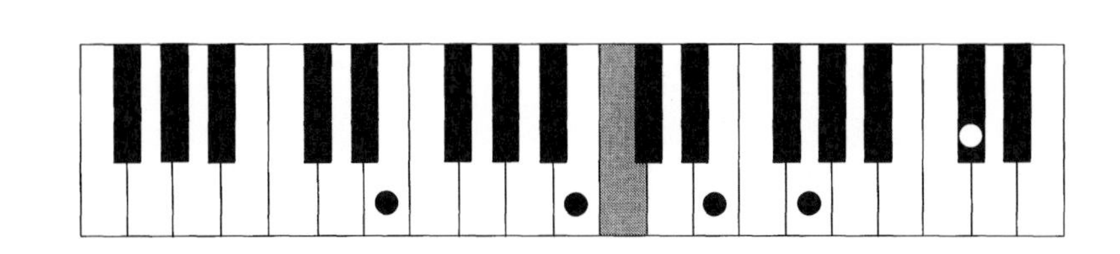

E minor 7th - Em7

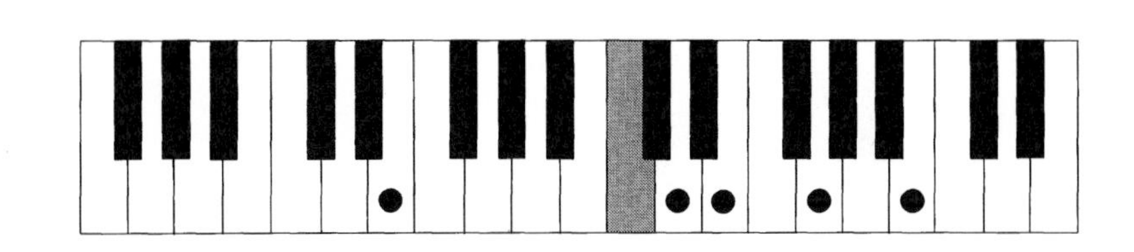

E minor 7th with flattened 5th - Em7(♭5)

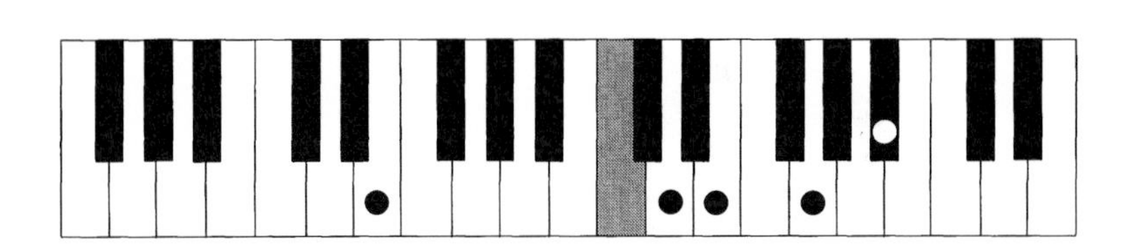

E minor added major 7th - Em(maj7)

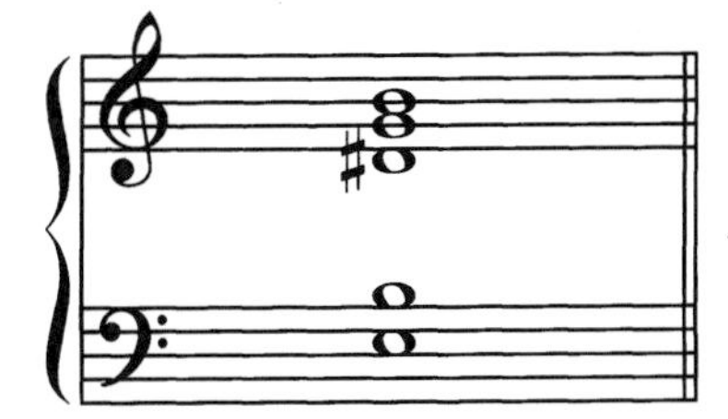

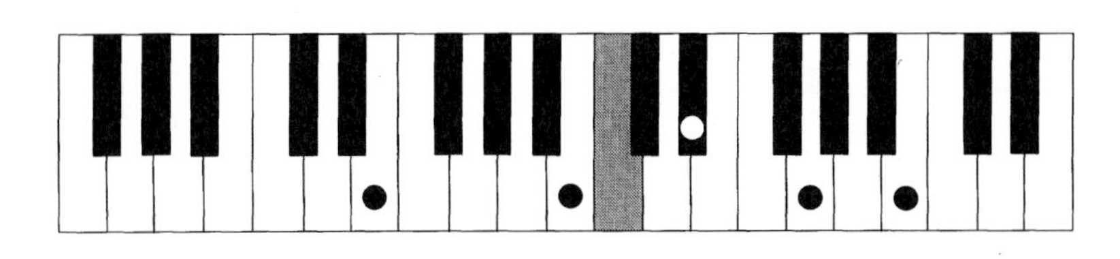

E minor 9th - Em9

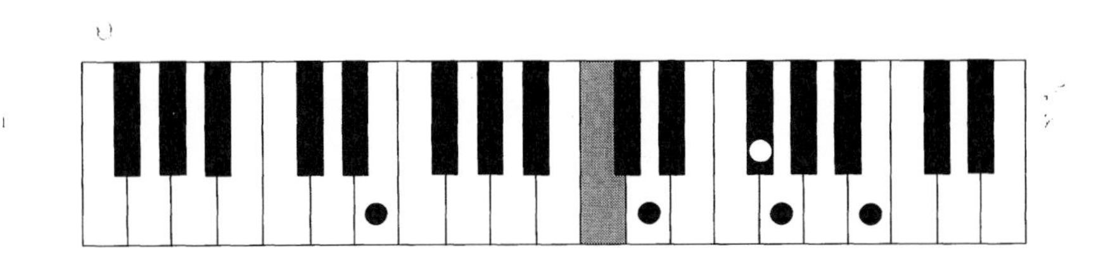

The F Collection

F major - F

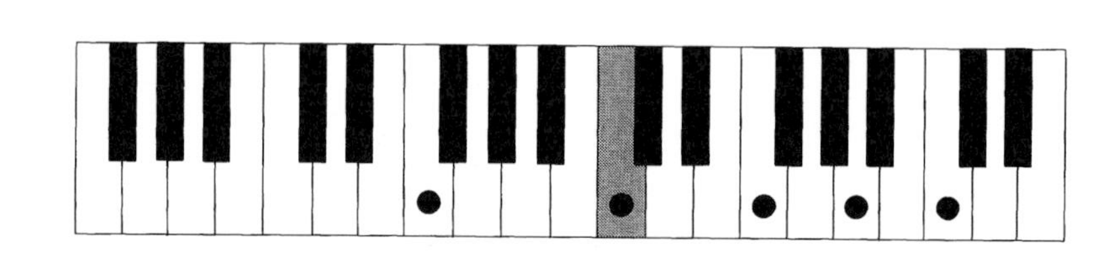

F suspended 4th - Fsus or Fsus4

F augmented 5th - F+ or Faug

F added 6th - F6

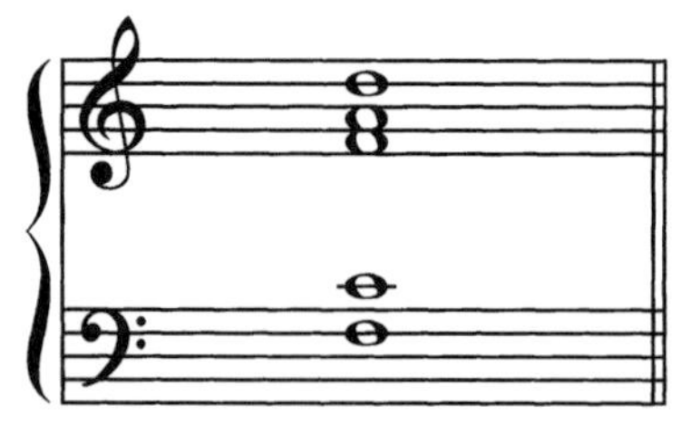

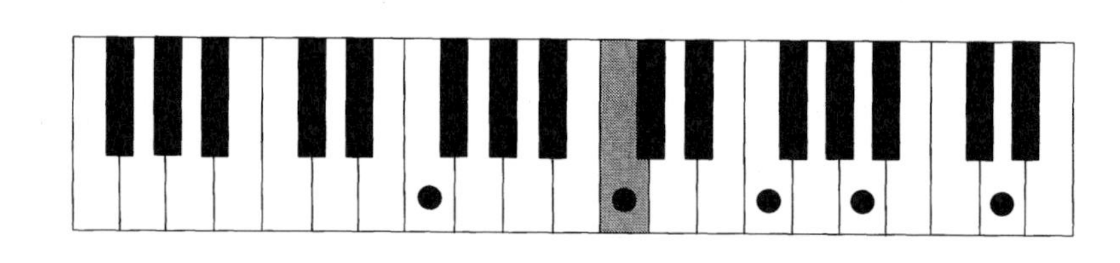

F added 6th and 9th - F6/9

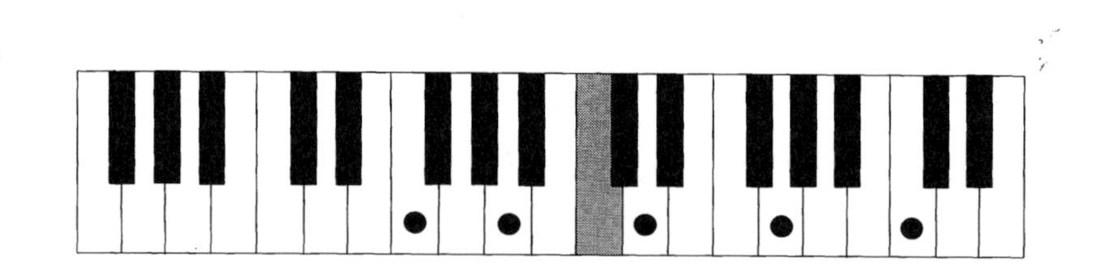

The F Collection

F major 7th - Fmaj7

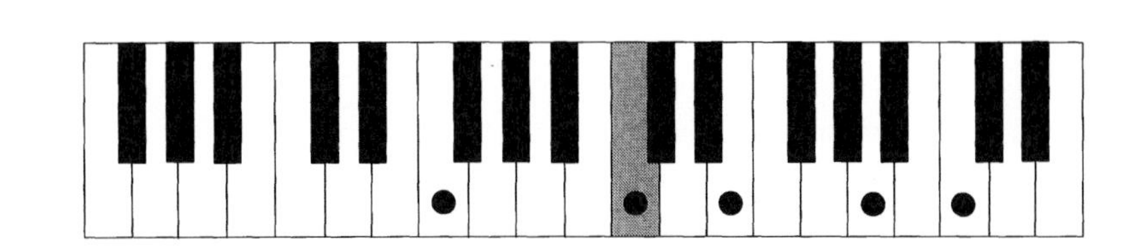

F dominant 7th - F7

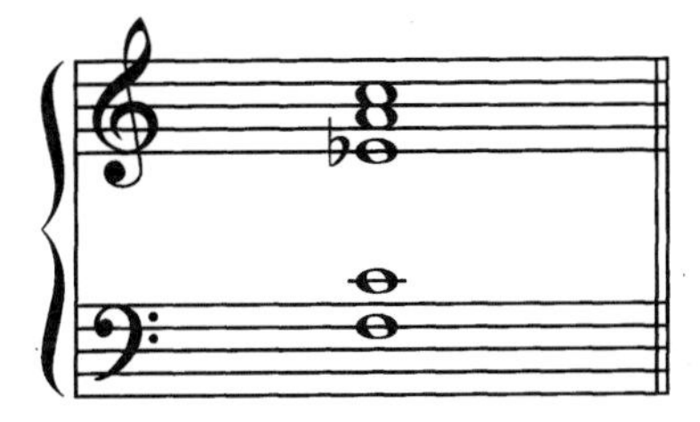

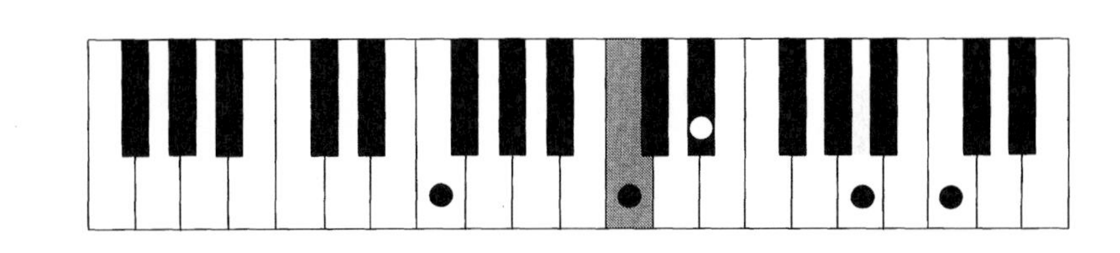

F dominant 7th with suspended 4th - F7sus or F7sus4

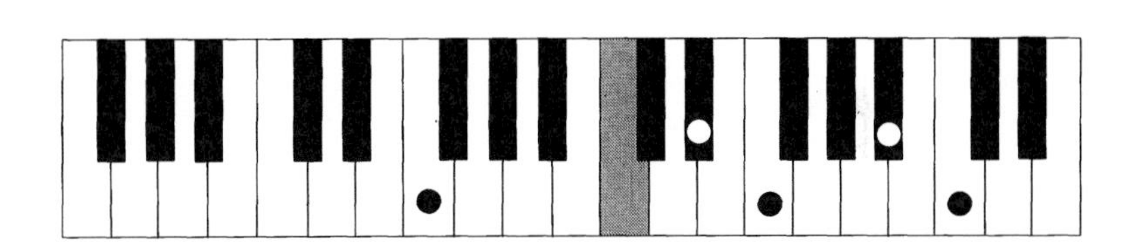

F dominant 7th with flattened 5th - F7(♭5)

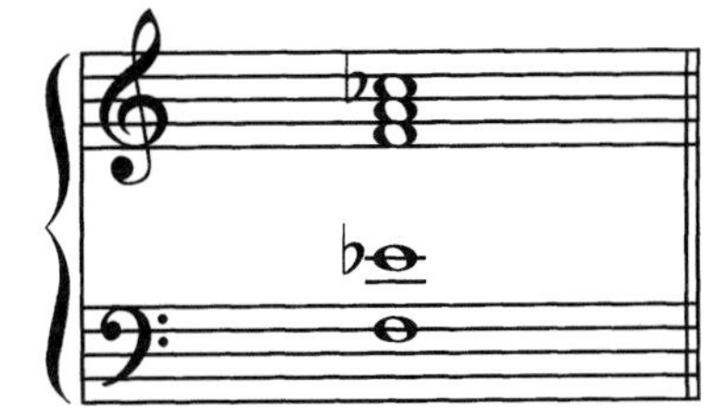

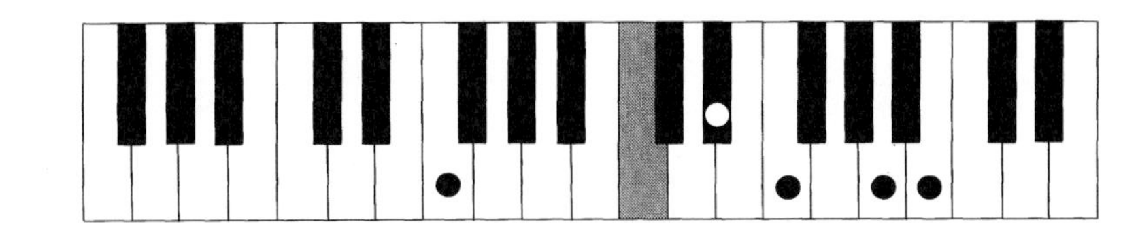

F dominant 7th with augmented 5th - F7+ or F7aug

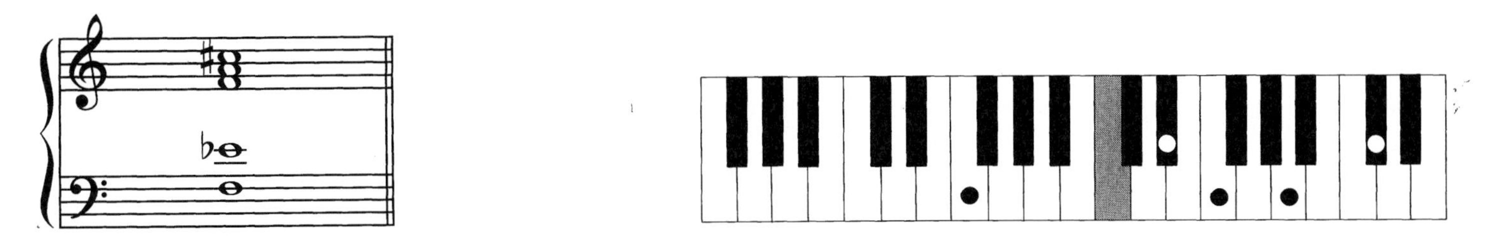

The F Collection

F dominant 7th with flattened 9th - F7(♭9)

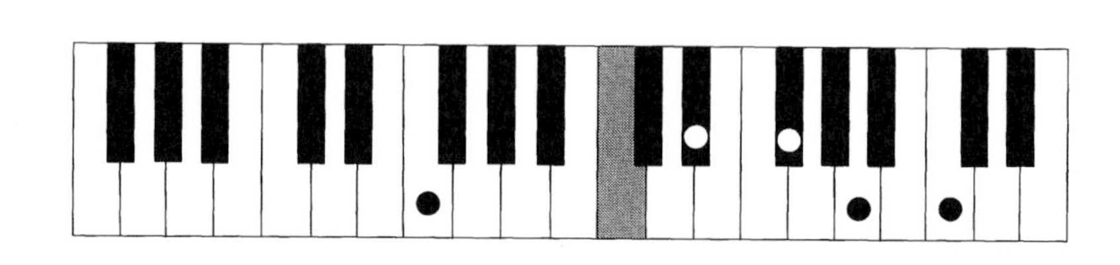

F dominant 7th with flattened 9th and 5th - F7(♭9/♭5)

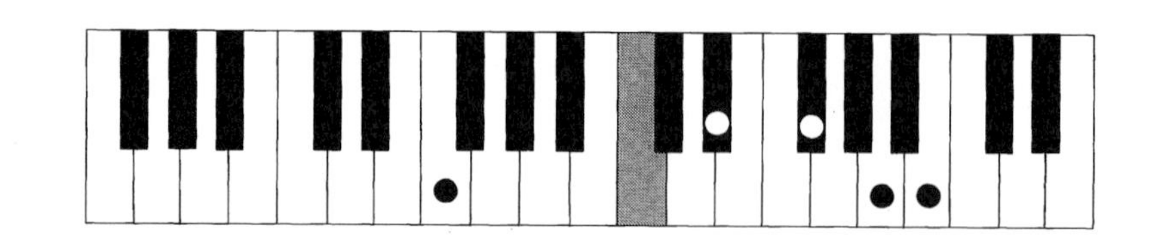

F dominant 7th with sharpened 9th - F7(♯9)

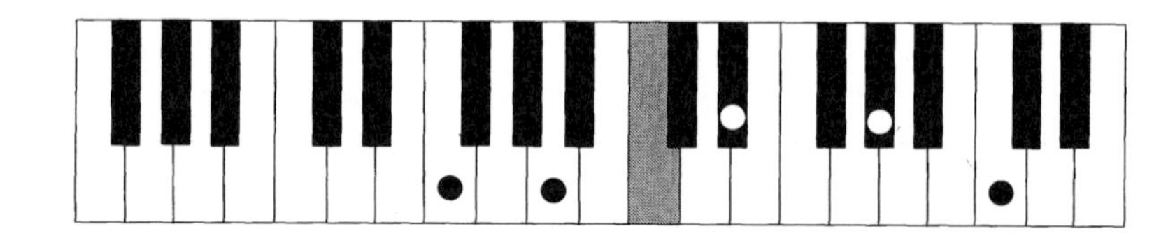

F added 9th - Fadd9

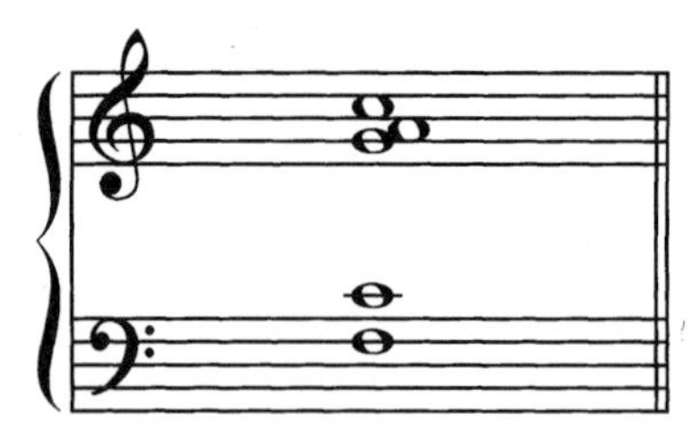

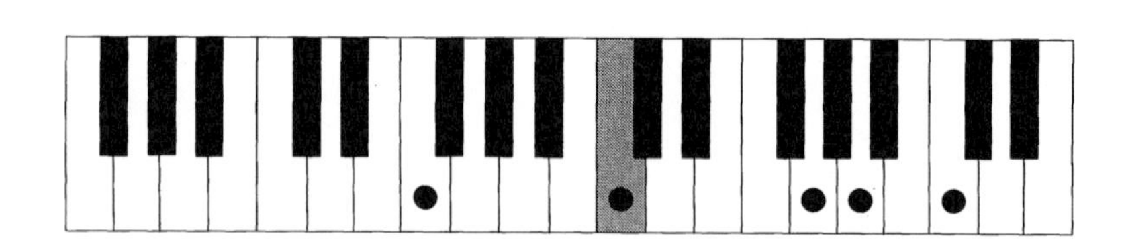

F major 9th - Fmaj9

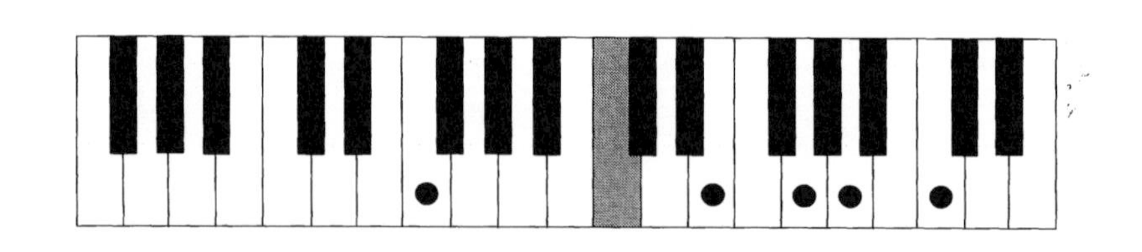

The F Collection

F dominant 9th - F9

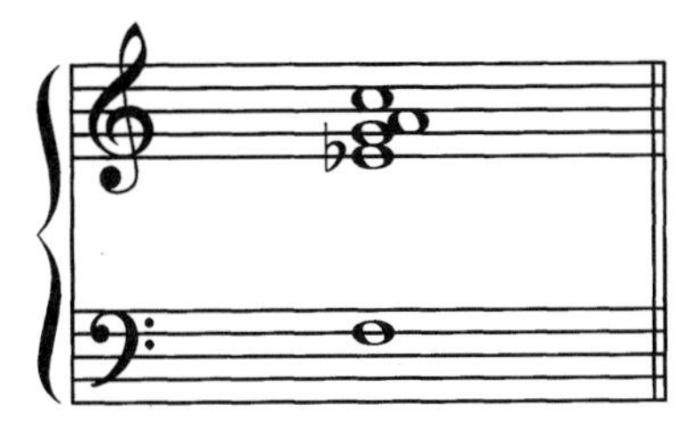
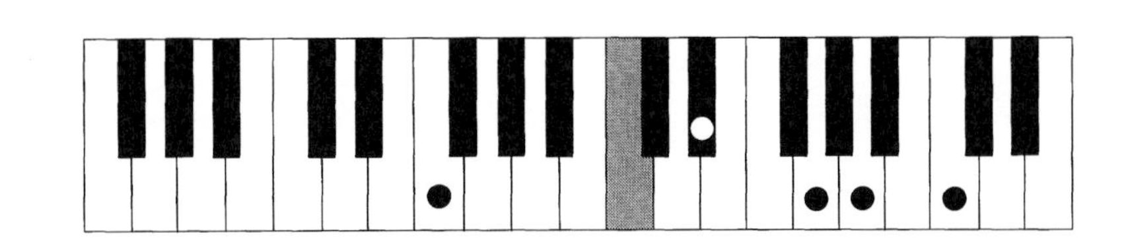

F dominant 9th with suspended 4th - F9sus or F9sus4

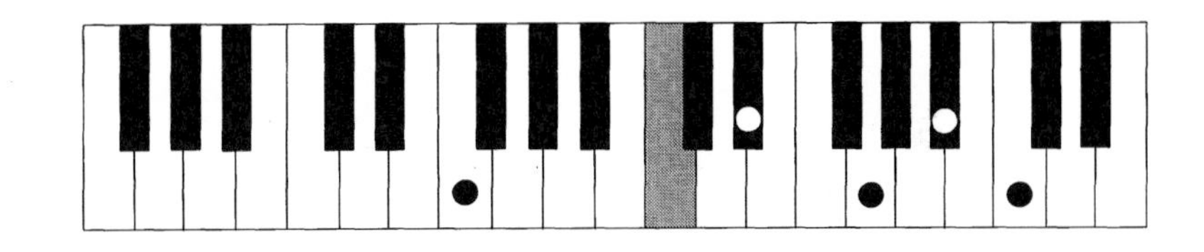

F dominant 9th with augmented 5th - F9+ or F9aug

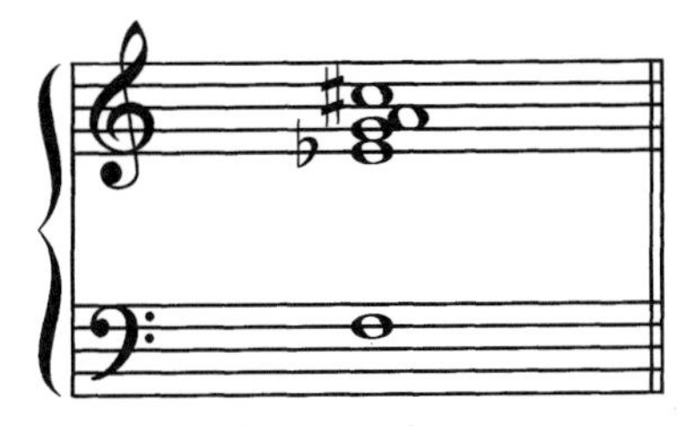
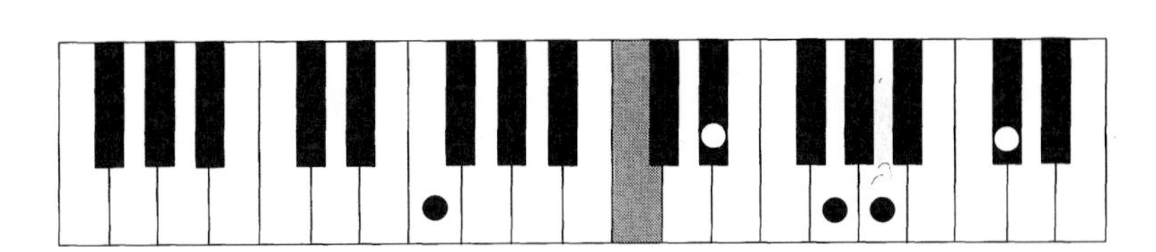

F dominant 9th with sharpened 11th - F9(♯11)
with flattened 5th - F9(♭5)

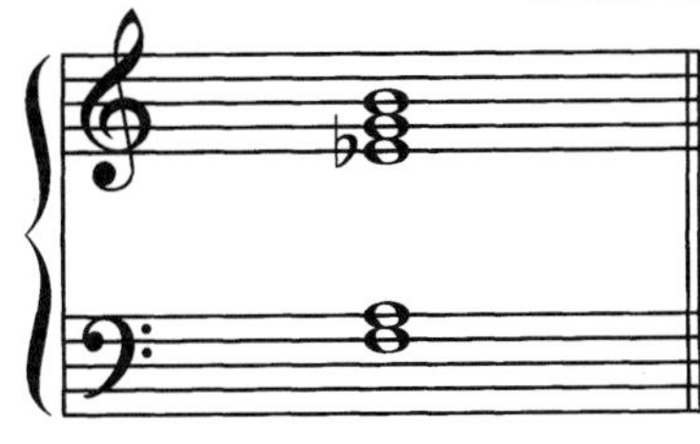

F dominant 11th - F11

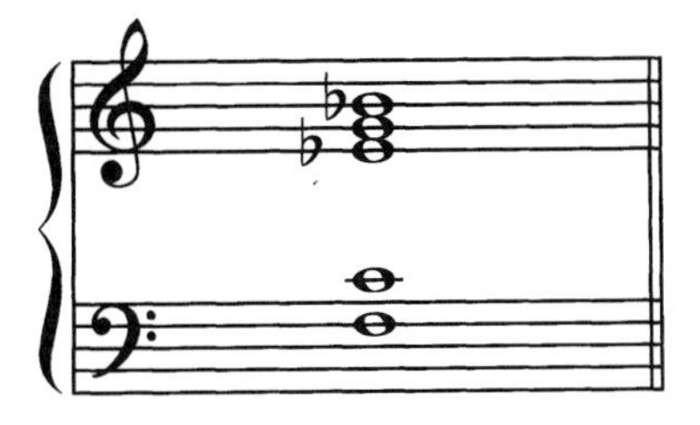
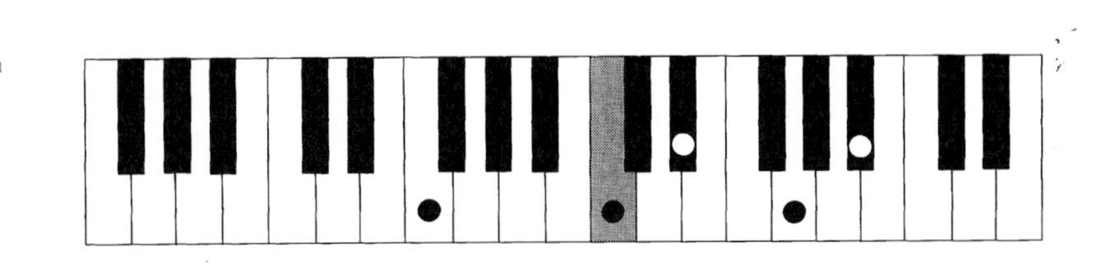

The F Collection

F dominant 11th with flattened 9th - F11(♭9)

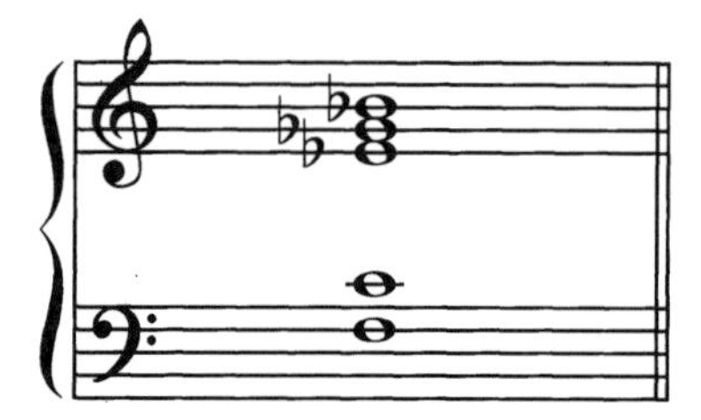

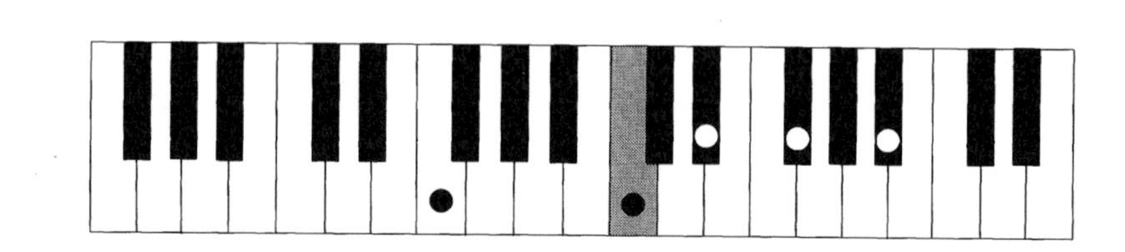

F dominant 13th - F13

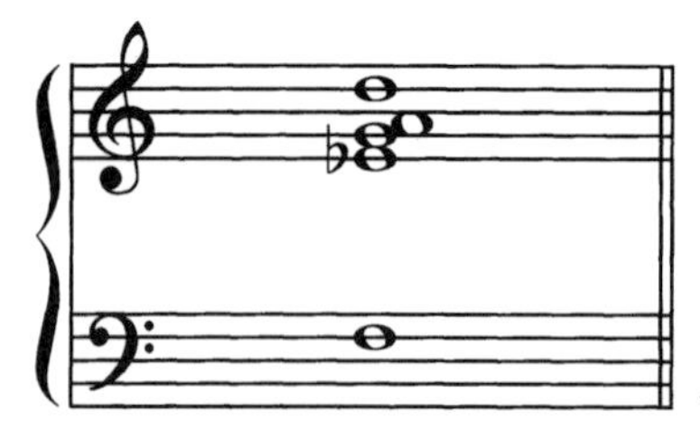

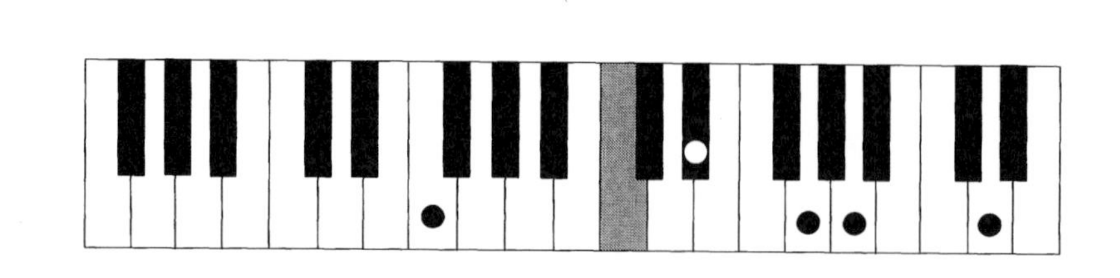

F dominant 13th with flattened 9th - F13(♭9)

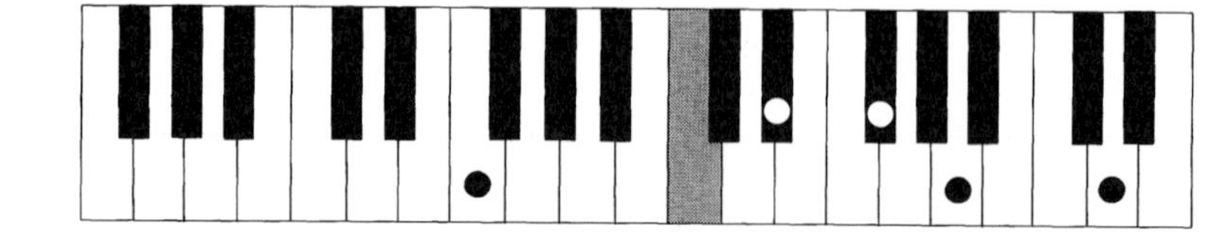

F minor - Fm

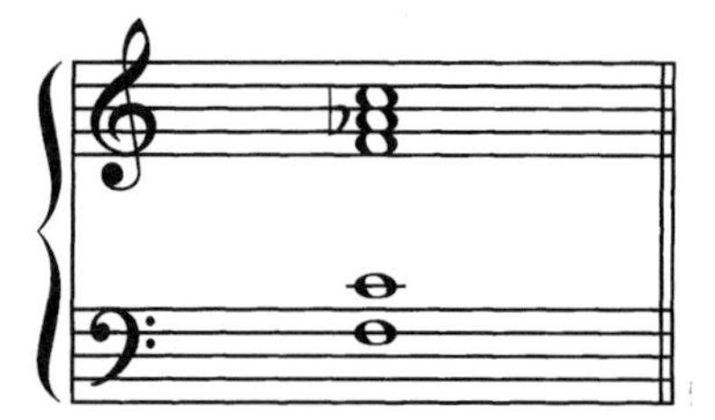

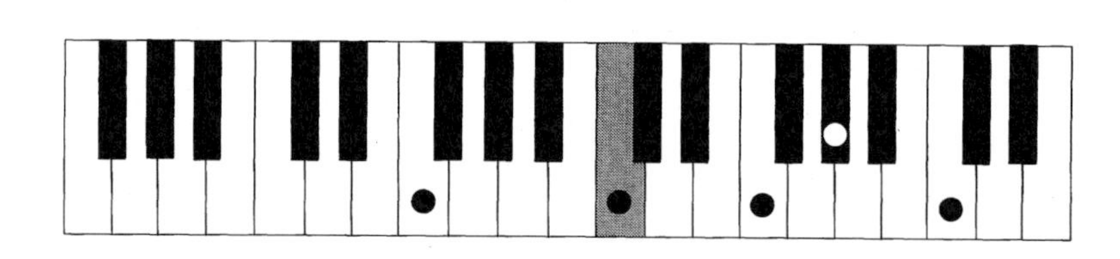

F diminished - F° or Fdim

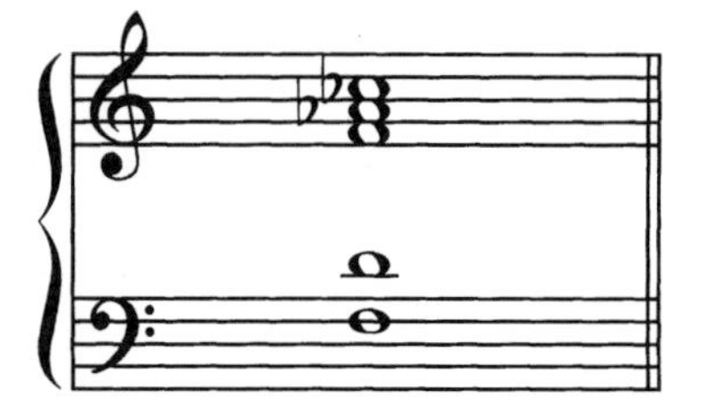

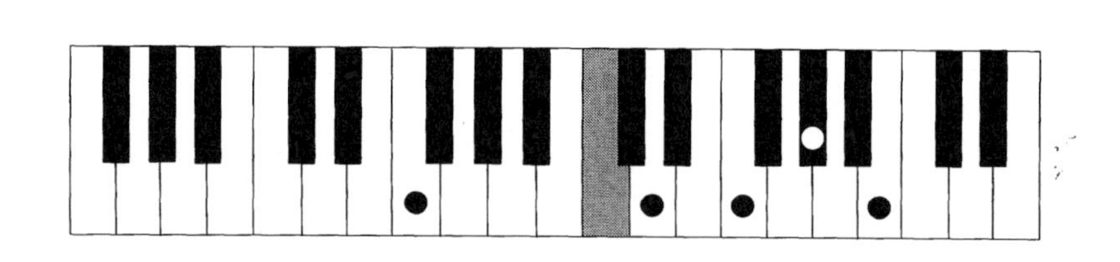

The F Collection

F minor added 6th - Fm6

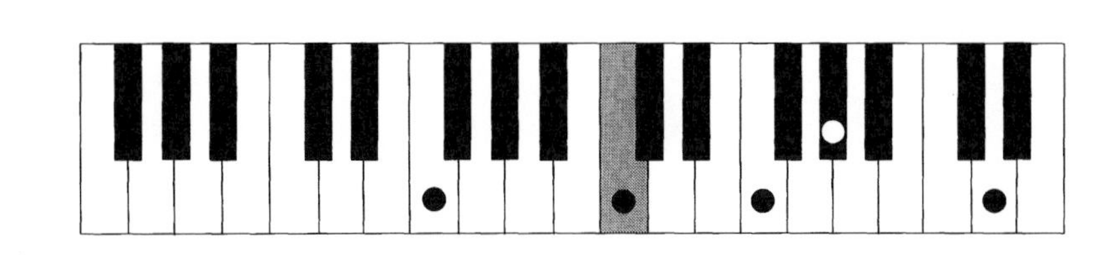

F minor 7th - Fm7

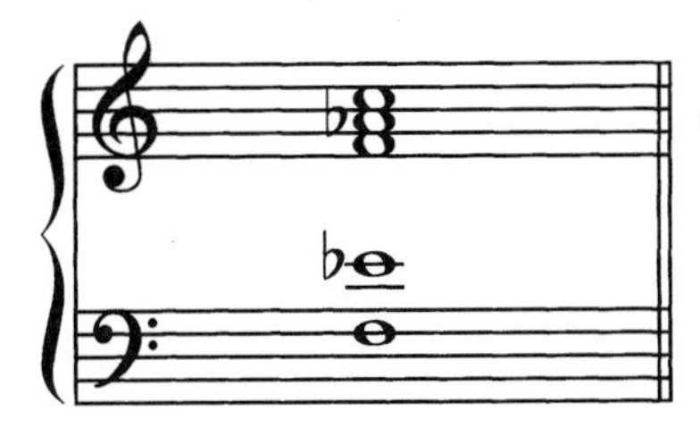

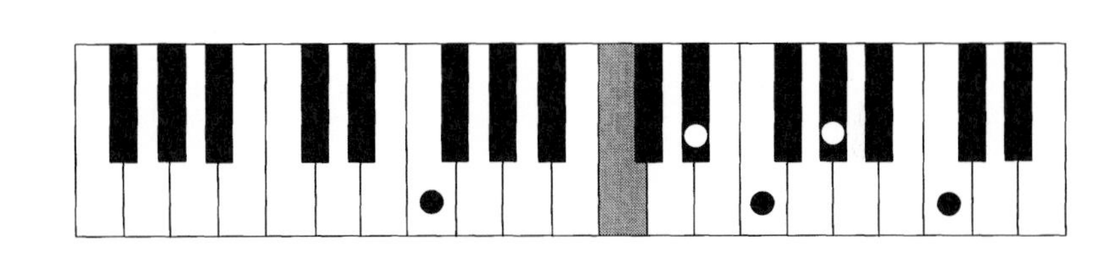

F minor 7th with flattened 5th - Fm7(♭5)

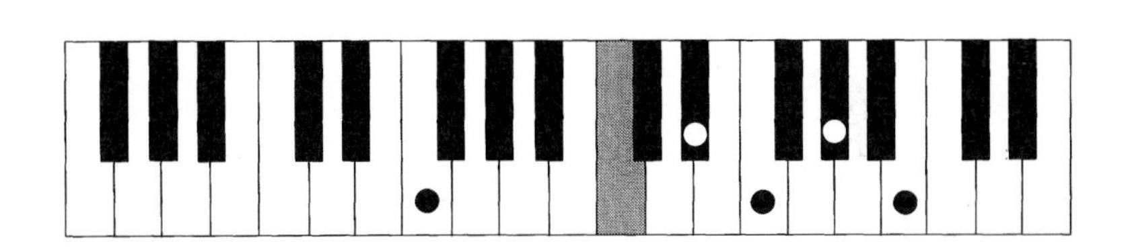

F minor added major 7th - Fm(maj7)

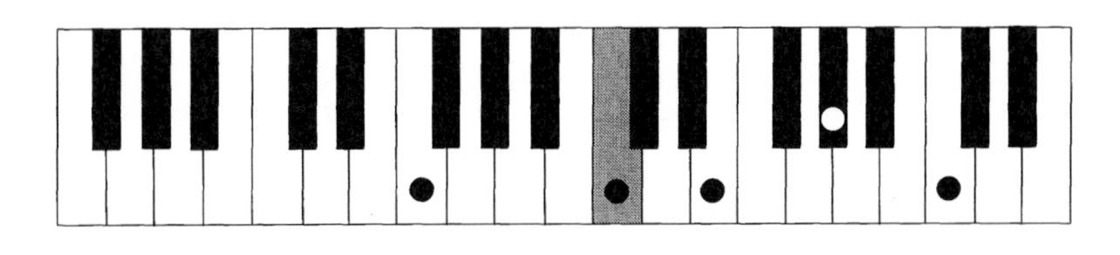

F minor 9th - Fm9

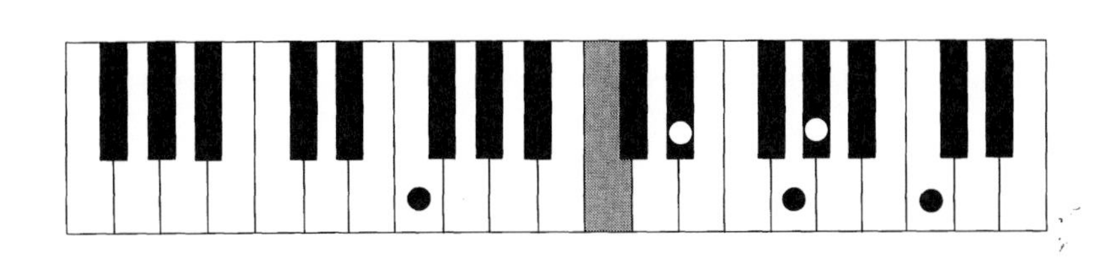

The F♯ Collection

F♯ major - F♯

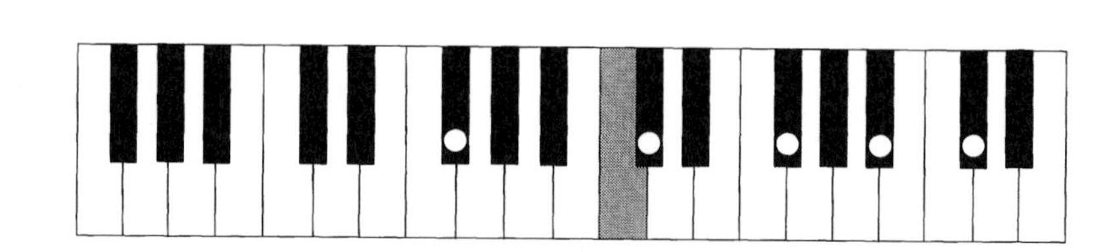

F♯ suspended 4th - F♯sus or F♯sus4

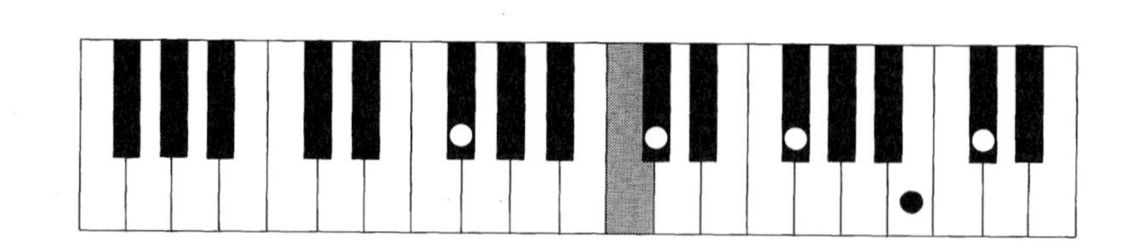

F♯ augmented 5th - F♯+ or F♯aug

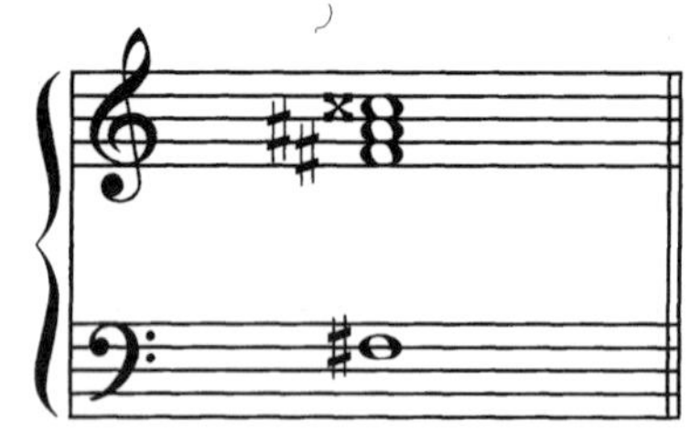

F♯ added 6th - F♯6

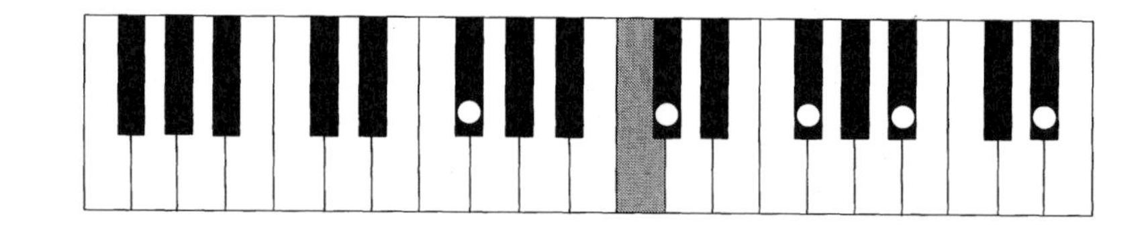

F♯ added 6th and 9th - F♯6/9

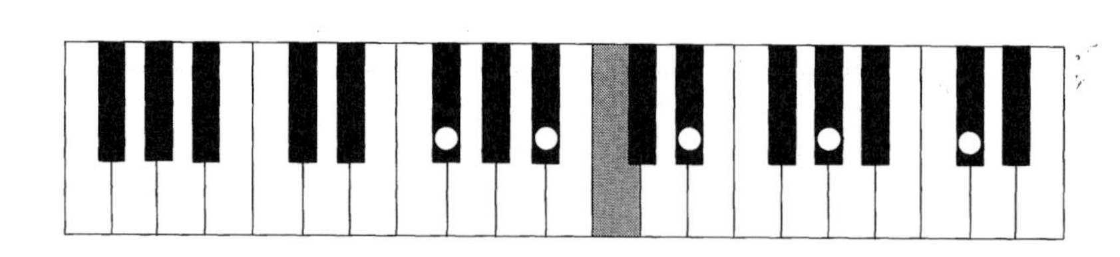

F♯ and G♭ are the same note spelled in different ways, depending on the key you are in.
For this reason, F♯ and G♭ chords are grouped together on facing pages.

The G♭ Collection

G♭ major - G♭

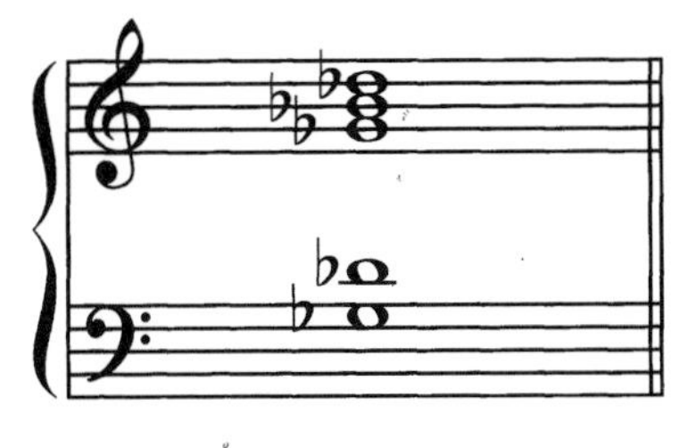

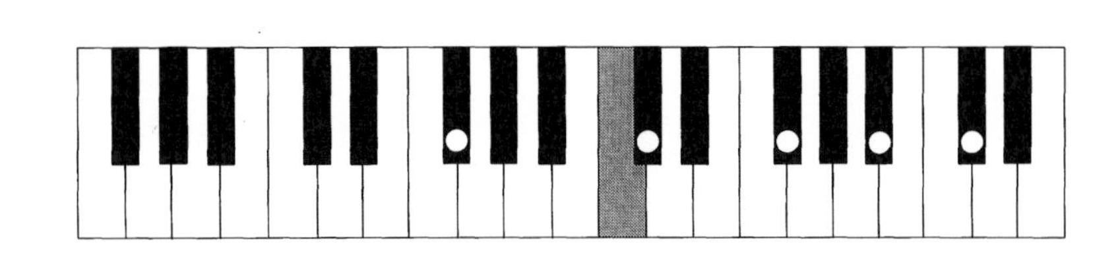

G♭ suspended 4th - G♭sus or G♭sus4

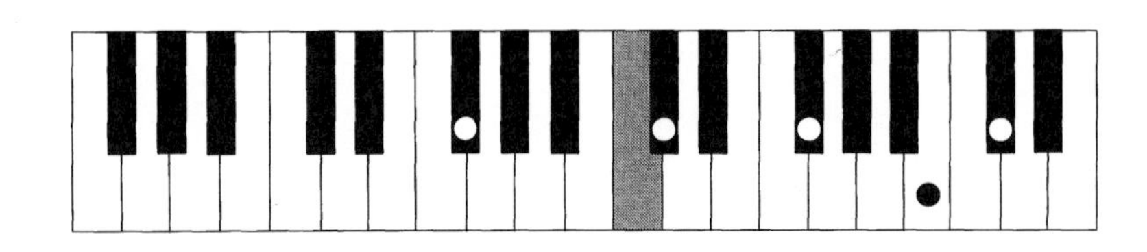

G♭ augmented 5th - G♭+ or G♭aug

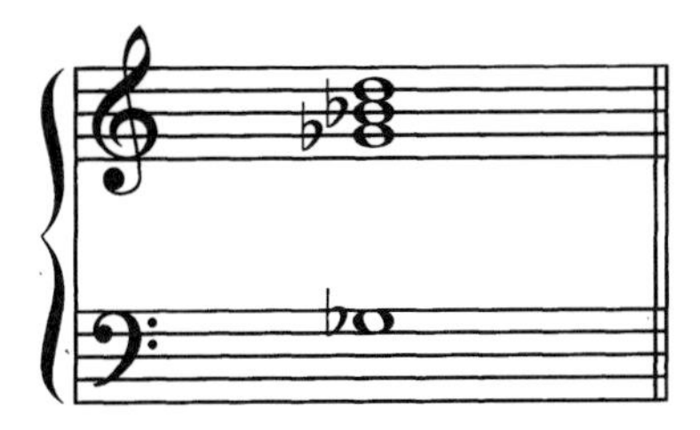

G♭ added 6th - G♭6

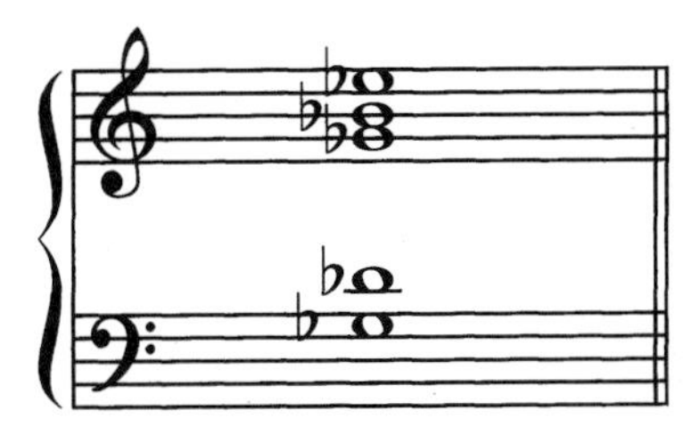

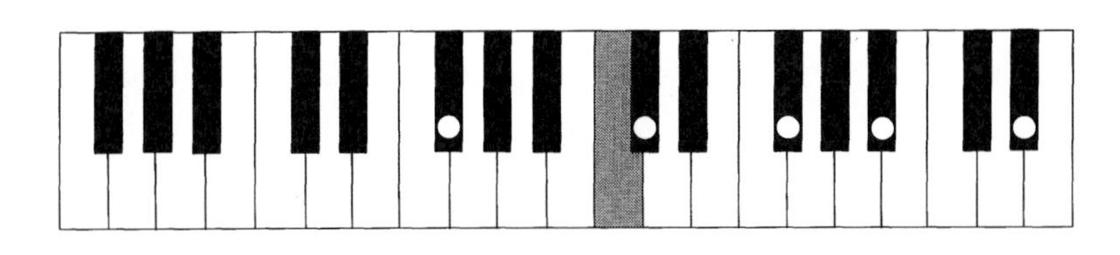

G♭ added 6th and 9th - G♭6/9

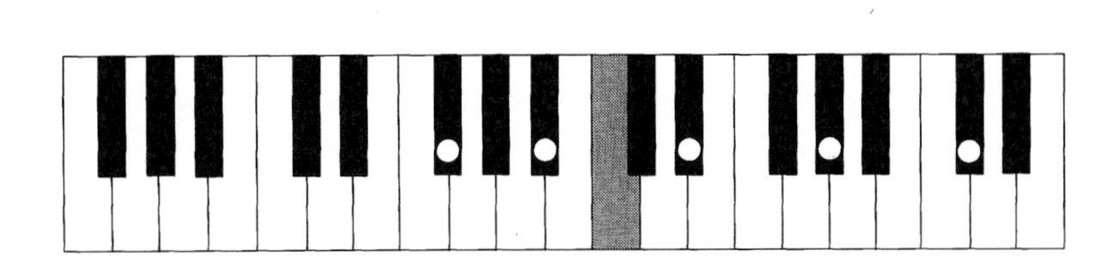

The F♯ Collection

F♯ major 7th - F♯maj7

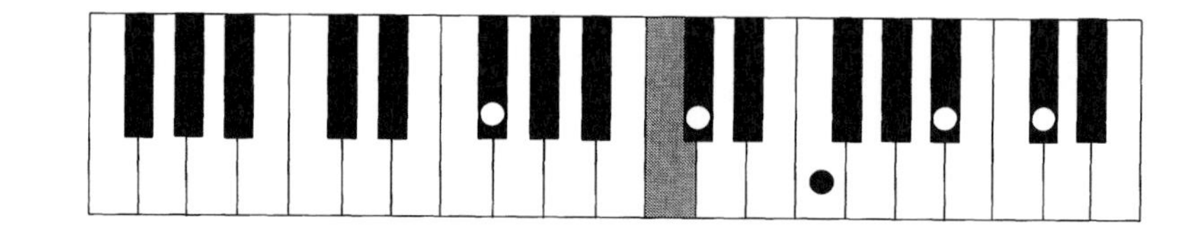

F♯ dominant 7th - F♯7

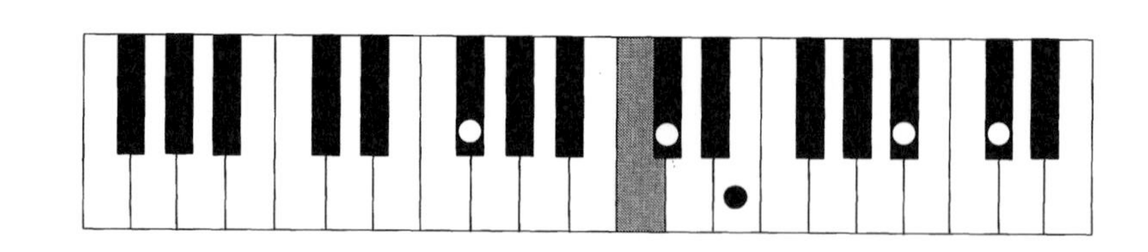

F♯ dominant 7th with suspended 4th - F♯7sus or F♯7sus4

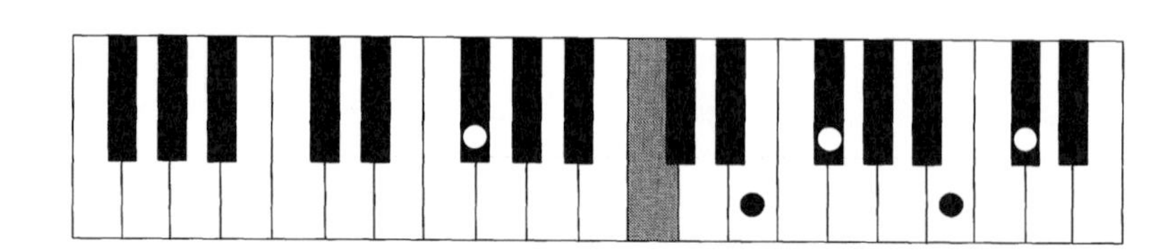

F♯ dominant 7th with flattened 5th - F♯7(♭5)

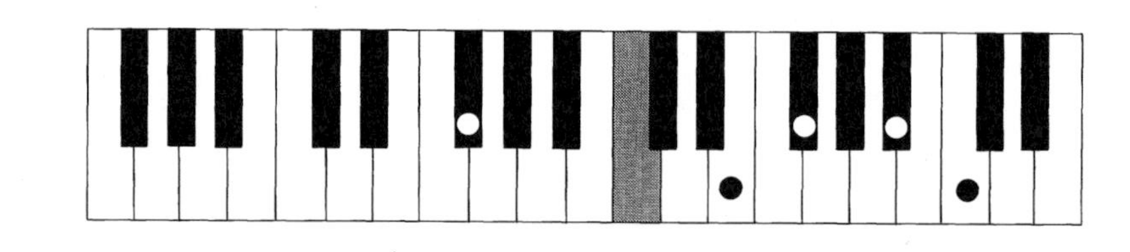

F♯ dominant 7th with augmented 5th - F♯7+ or F♯7aug

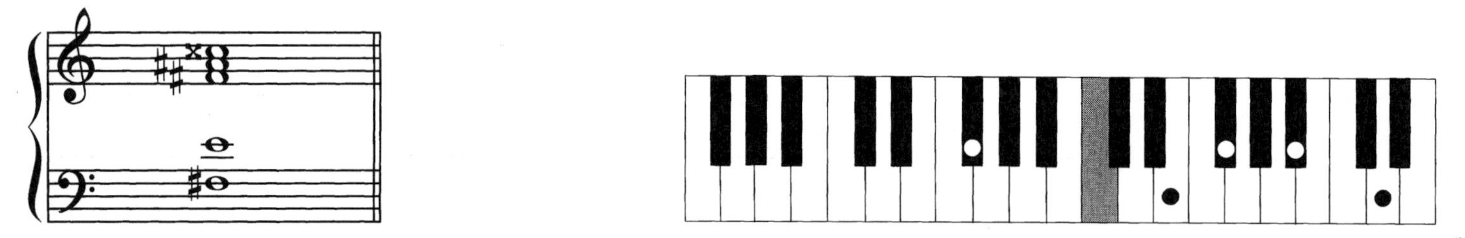

The G♭ Collection

G♭ major 7th - G♭maj7

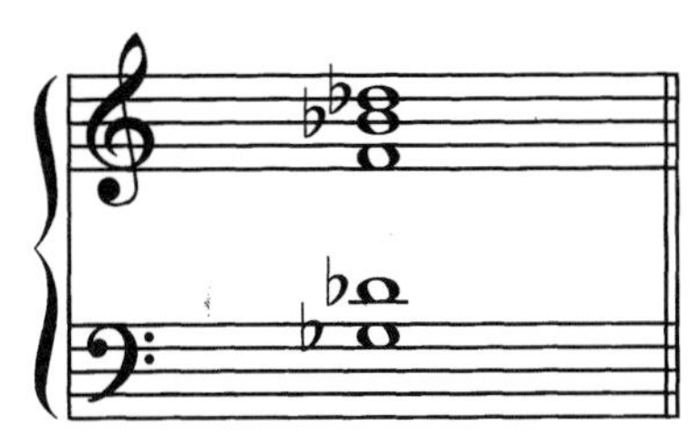

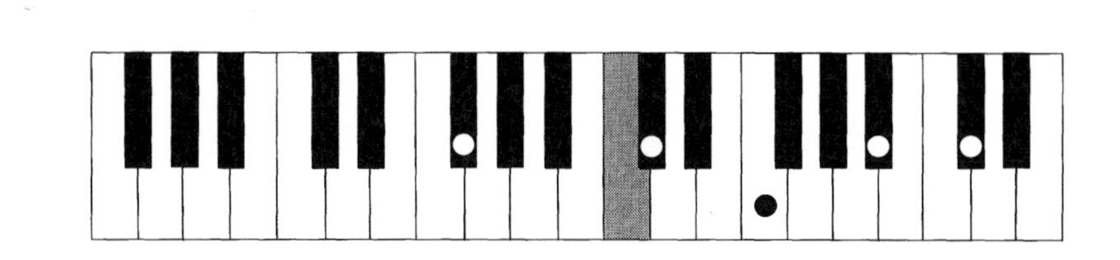

G♭ dominant 7th - G♭7

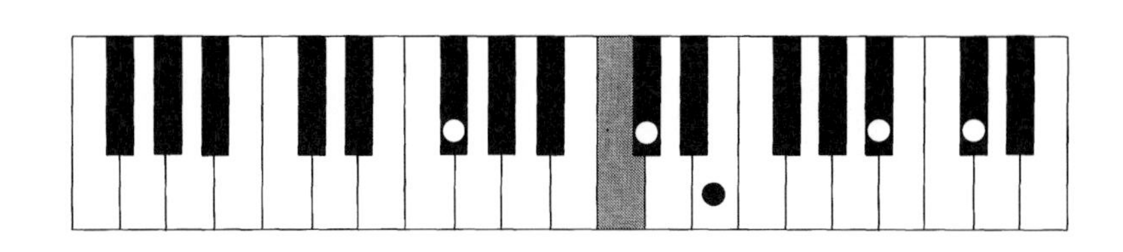

G♭ dominant 7th with suspended 4th - G♭7sus or G♭7sus4

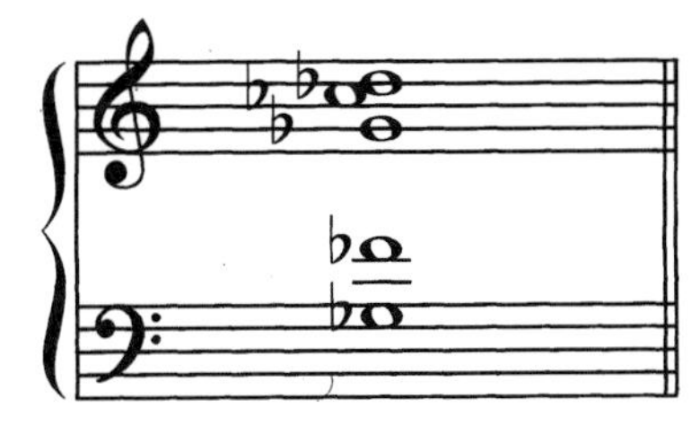

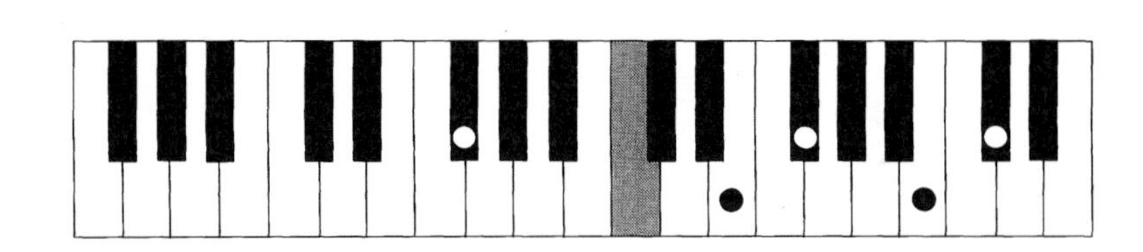

G♭ dominant 7th with flattened 5th - G♭7(♭5)

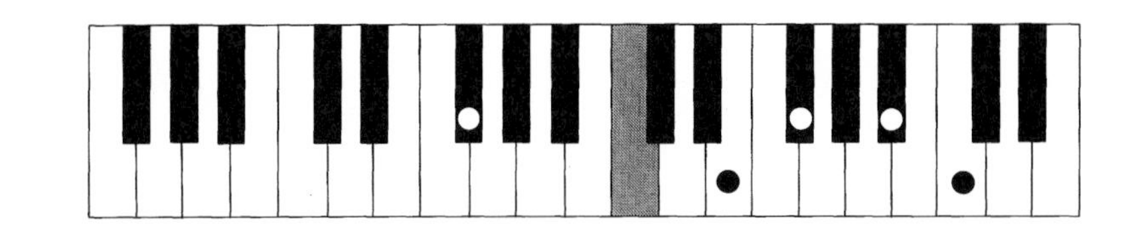

G♭ dominant 7th with augmented 5th - G♭7+ or G♭7aug

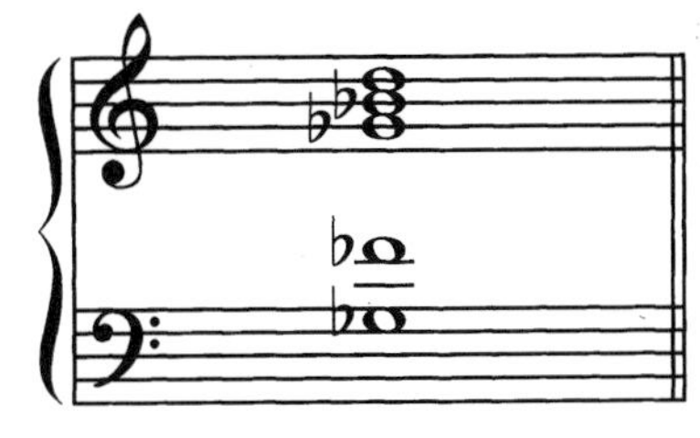

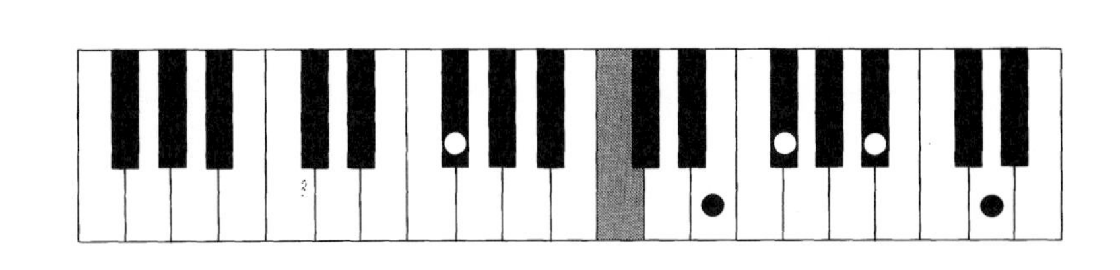

The F♯ Collection

F♯ dominant 7th with flattened 9th - F♯7(♭9)

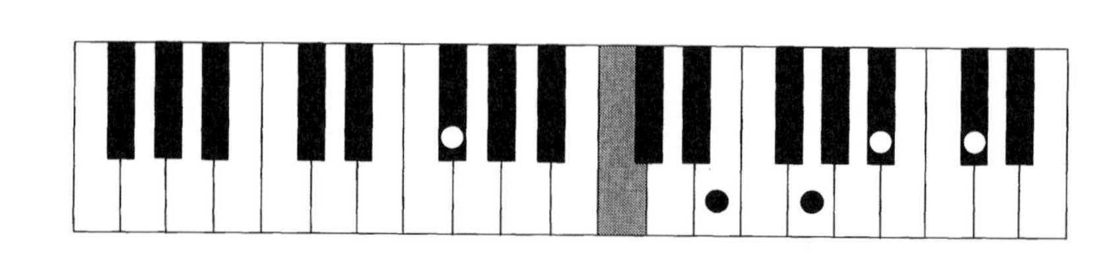

F♯ dominant 7th with flattened 9th and 5th - F♯7(♭9/♭5)

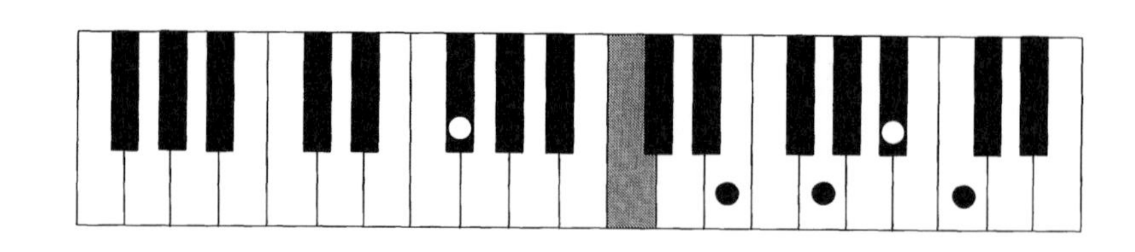

F♯ dominant 7th with sharpened 9th - F♯7(♯9)

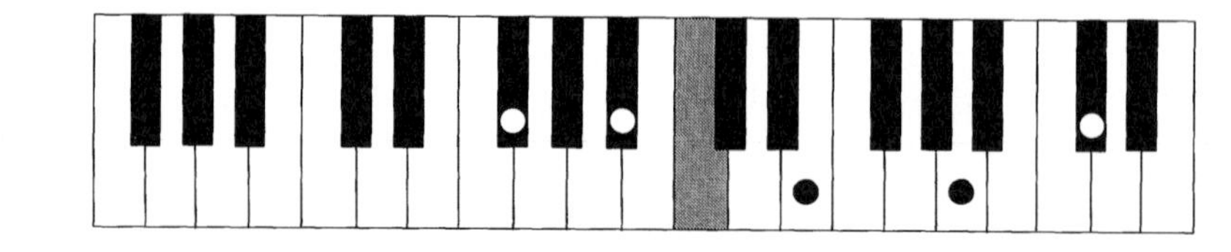

F♯ added 9th - F♯add9

F♯ major 9th - F♯maj9

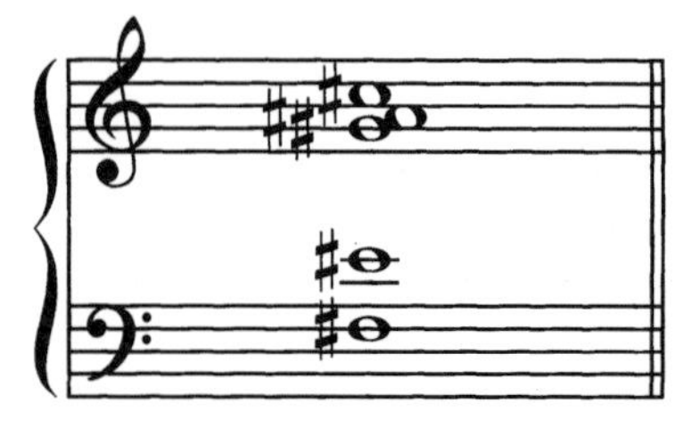

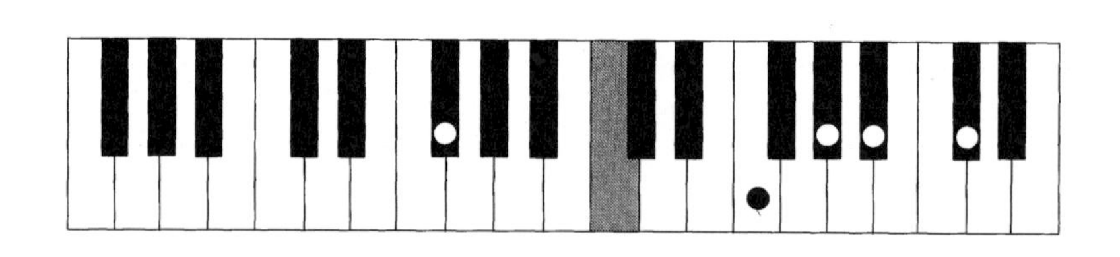

The G♭ Collection

G♭ dominant 7th with flattened 9th - G♭7(♭9)

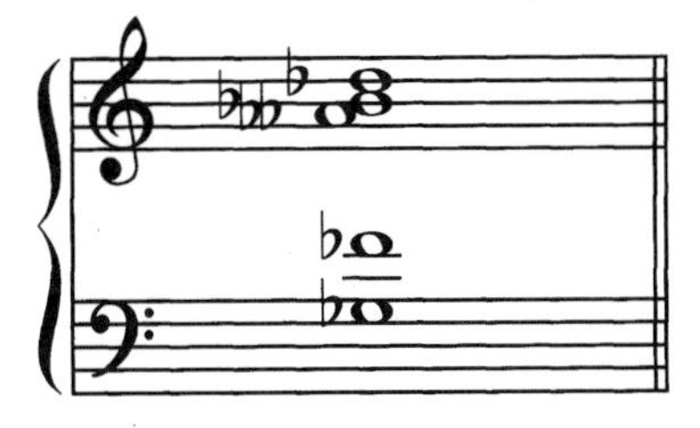

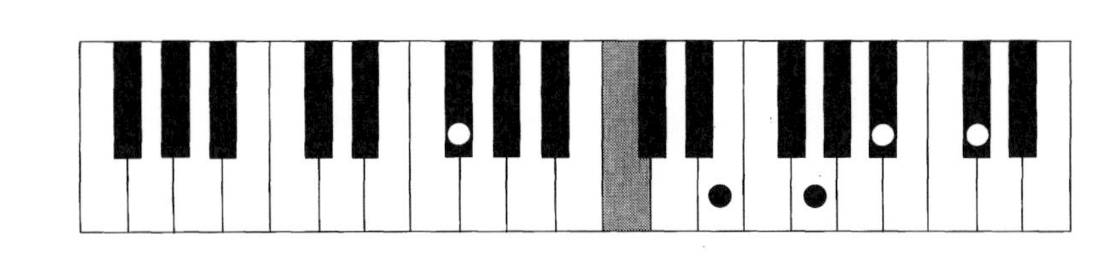

G♭ dominant 7th with flattened 9th and 5th - G♭7(♭9/♭5)

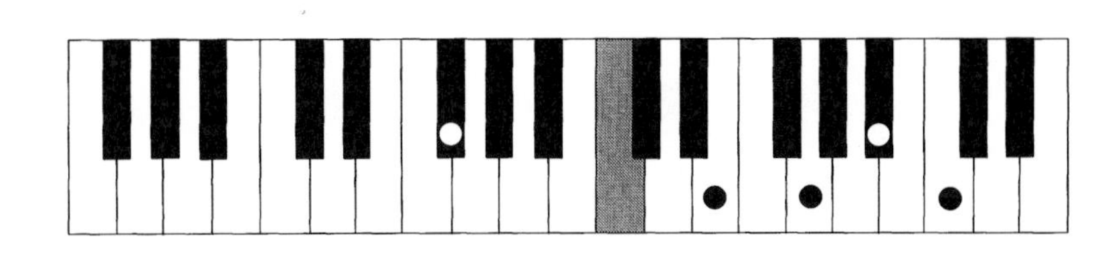

G♭ dominant 7th with sharpened 9th - G♭7(♯9)

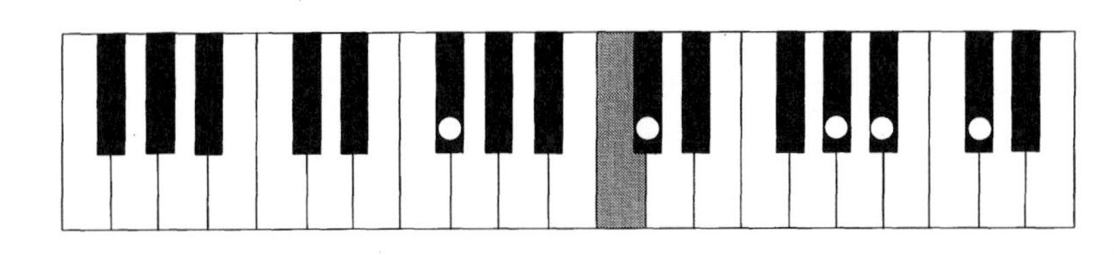

G♭ added 9th - G♭add9

G♭ major 9th - G♭maj9

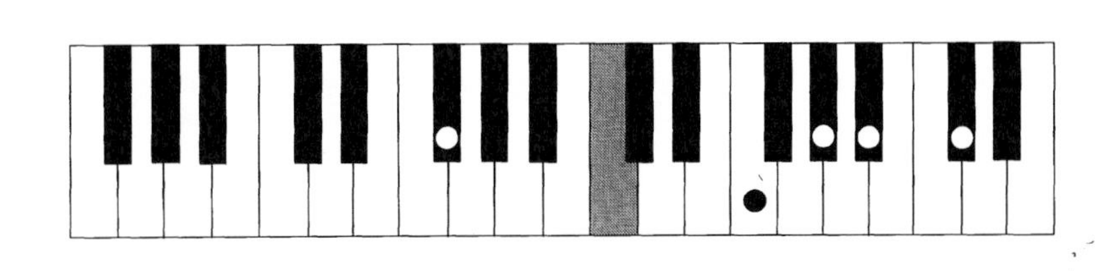

The F♯ Collection

F♯ dominant 9th - F♯9

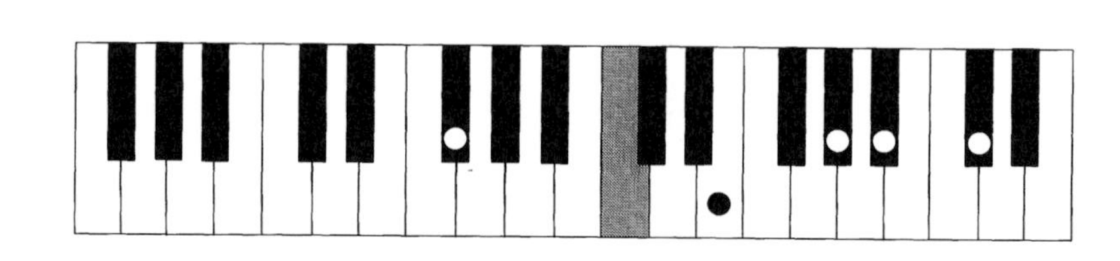

F♯ dominant 9th with suspended 4th - F♯9sus or F♯9sus4

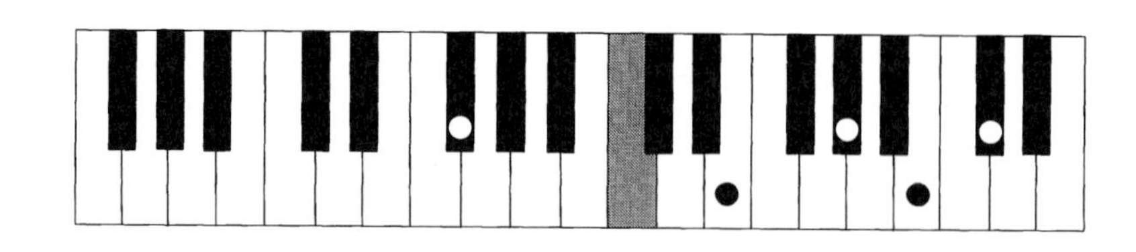

F♯ dominant 9th with augmented 5th - F♯9+ or F♯9aug

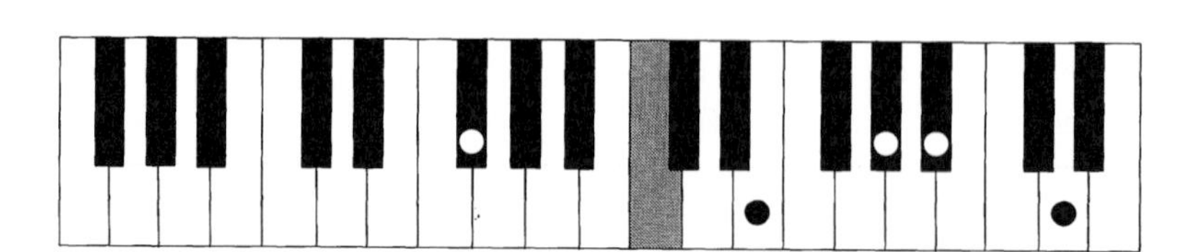

F♯ dominant 9th with sharpened 11th - F♯9(♯11)
with flattened 5th - F♯9(♭5)

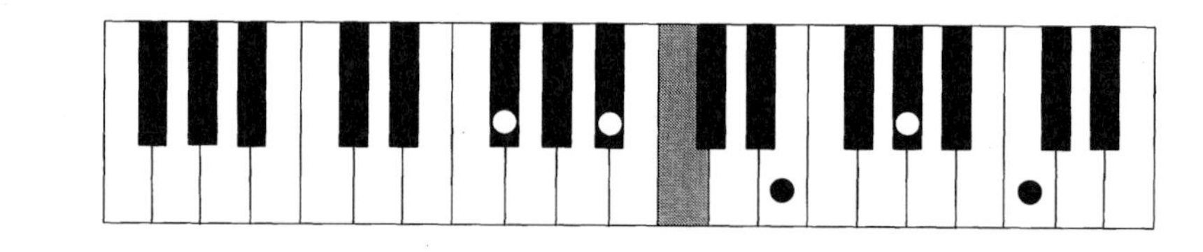

F♯ dominant 11th - F♯11

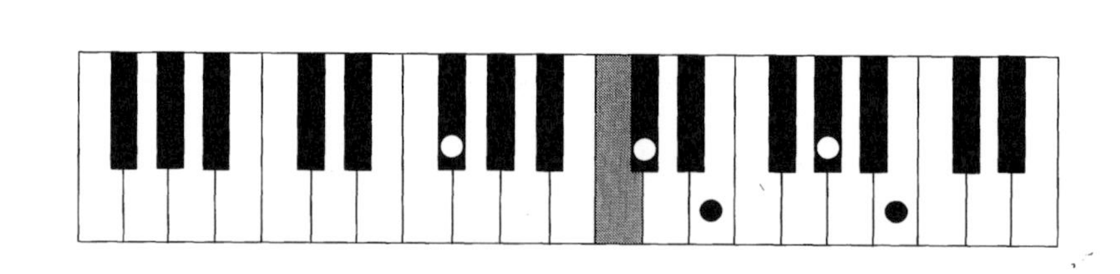

The G♭ Collection

G♭ dominant 9th - G♭9

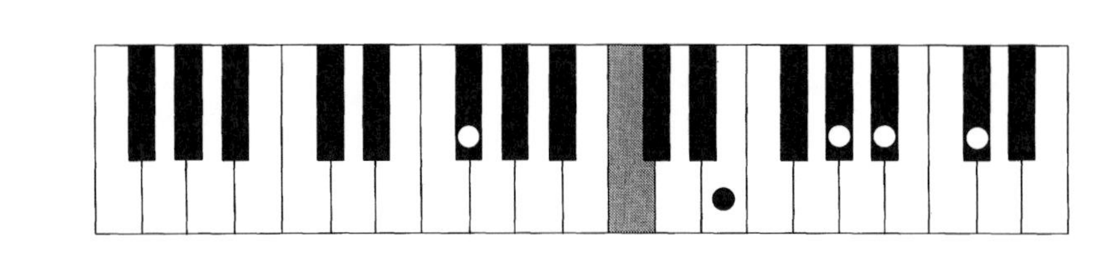

G♭ dominant 9th with suspended 4th - G♭9sus or G♭9sus4

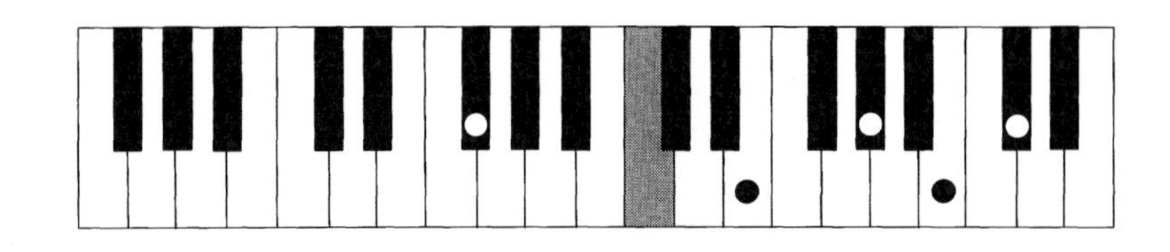

G♭ dominant 9th with augmented 5th - G♭9+ or G♭9aug

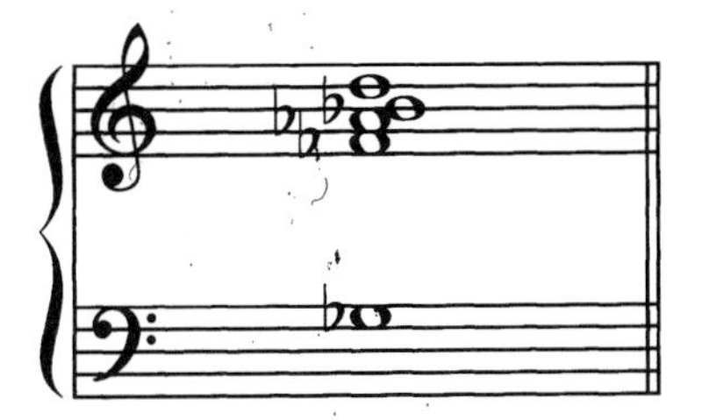

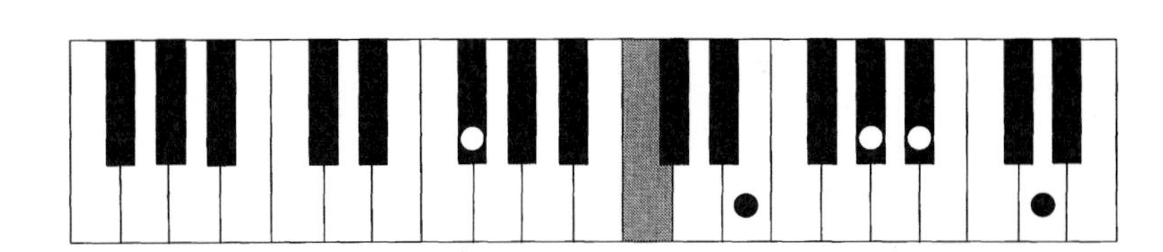

G♭ dominant 9th with sharpened 11th - G♭9(♯11)
with flattened 5th - G♭9(♭5)

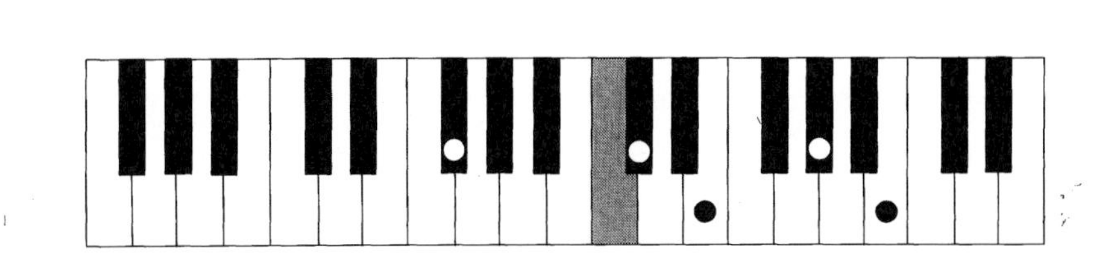

G♭ dominant 11th - G♭11

The F♯ Collection

F♯ dominant 11th with flattened 9th - F♯11(♭9)

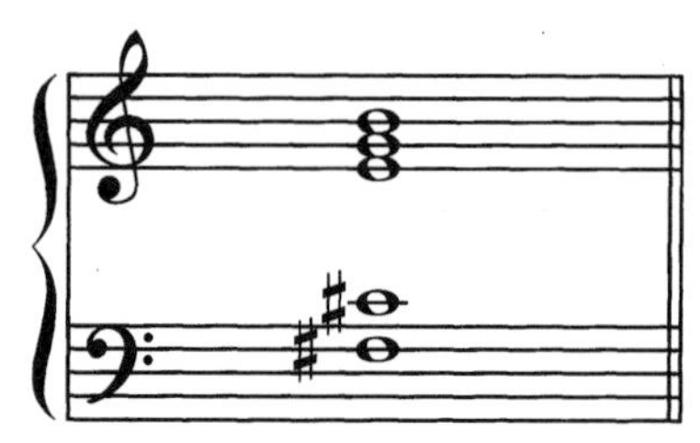

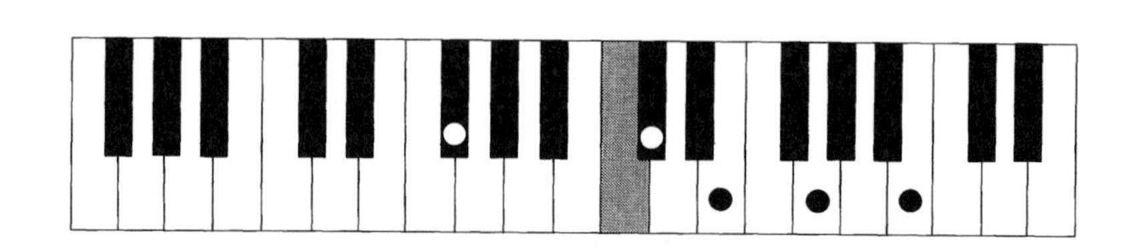

F♯ dominant 13th - F♯13

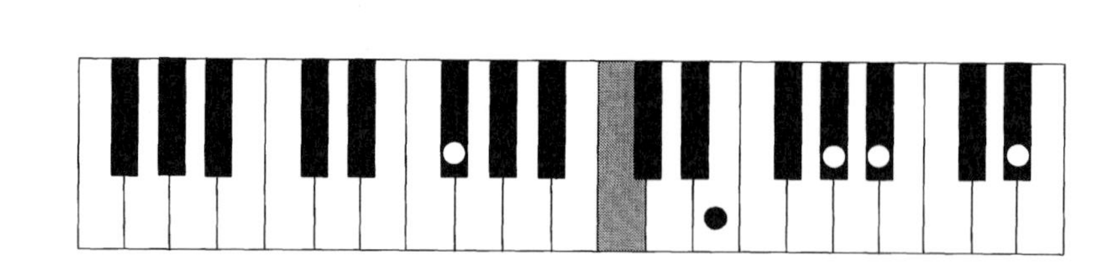

F♯ dominant 13th with flattened 9th - F♯13(♭9)

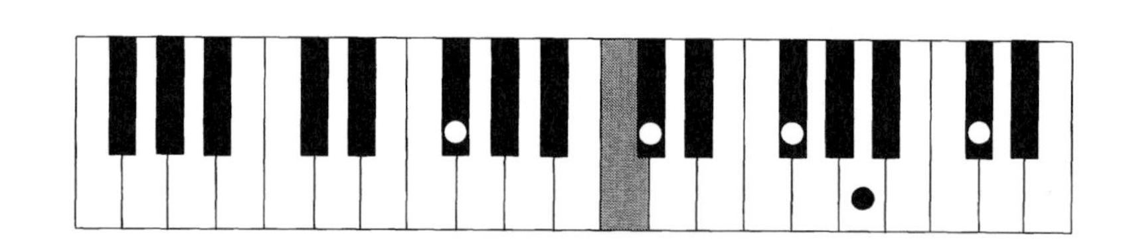

F♯ minor - F♯m

F♯ diminished - F♯° or F♯dim

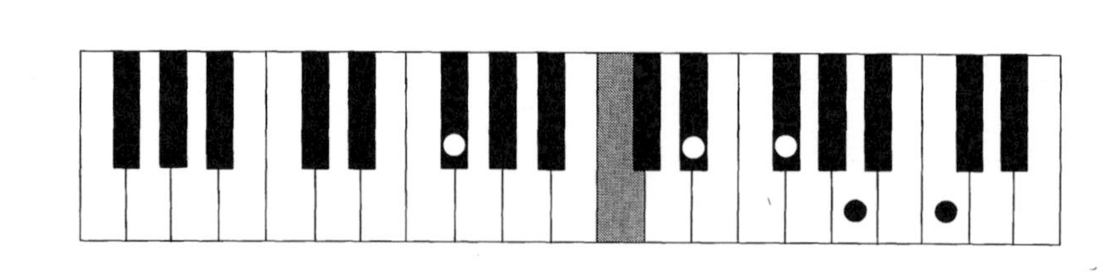

The G♭ Collection

G♭ dominant 11th with flattened 9th - G♭11(♭9)

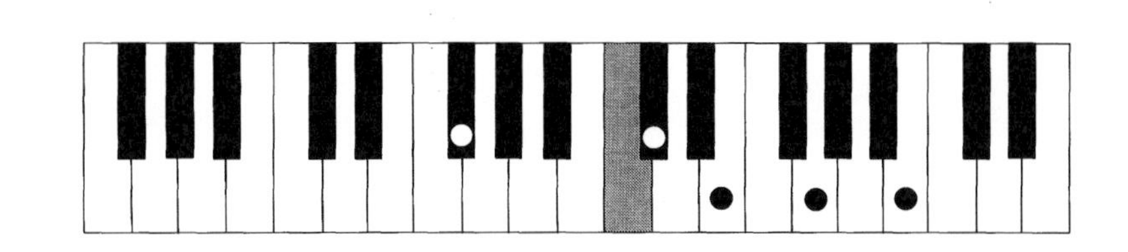

G♭ dominant 13th - G♭13

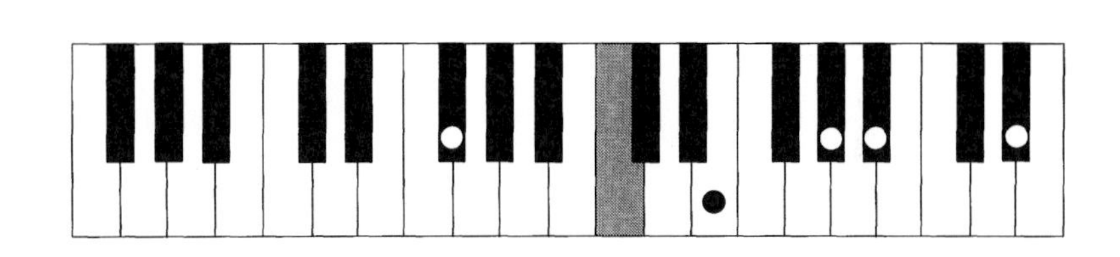

G♭ dominant 13th with flattened 9th - G♭13(♭9)

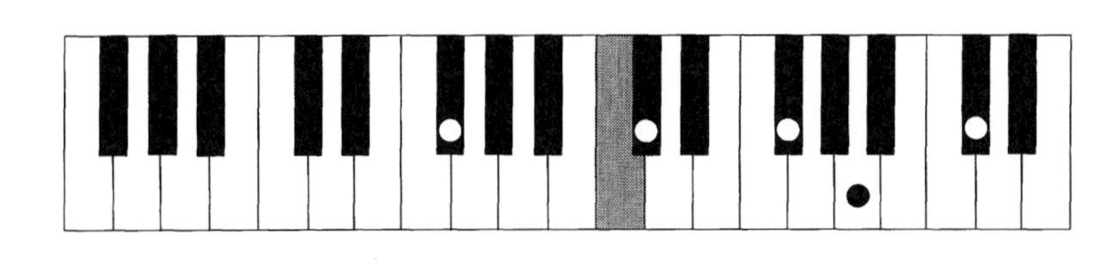

G♭ minor - G♭m

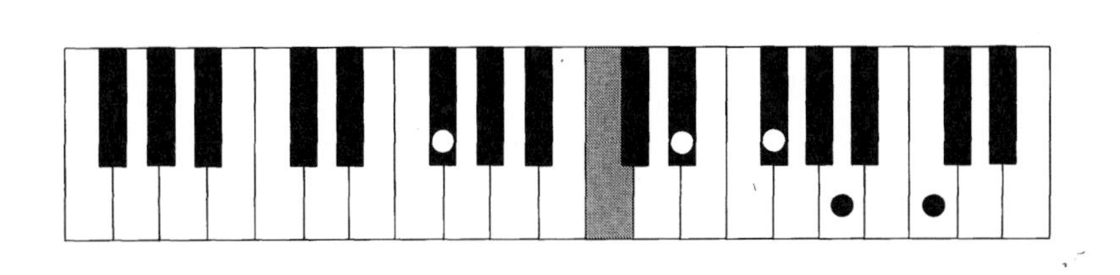

G♭ diminished - G♭° or G♭dim

The F♯ Collection

F♯ minor added 6th - F♯m6

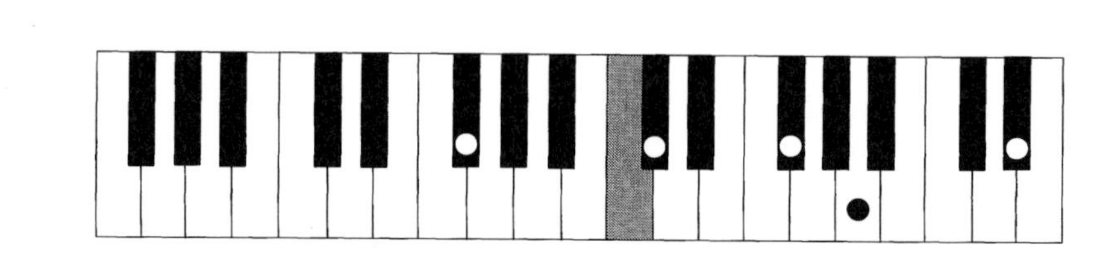

F♯ minor 7th - F♯m7

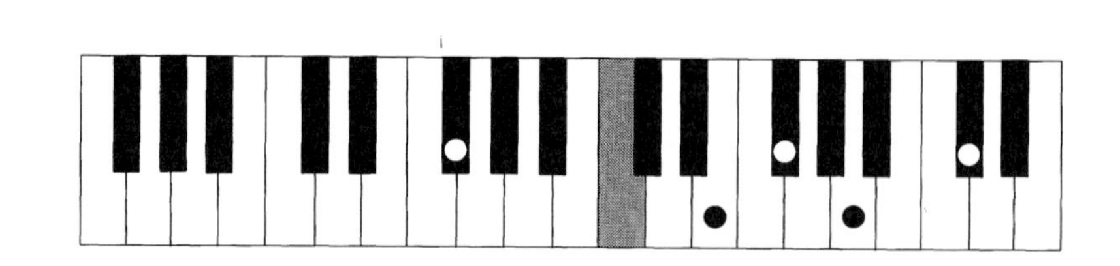

F♯ minor 7th with flattened 5th - F♯m7(♭5)

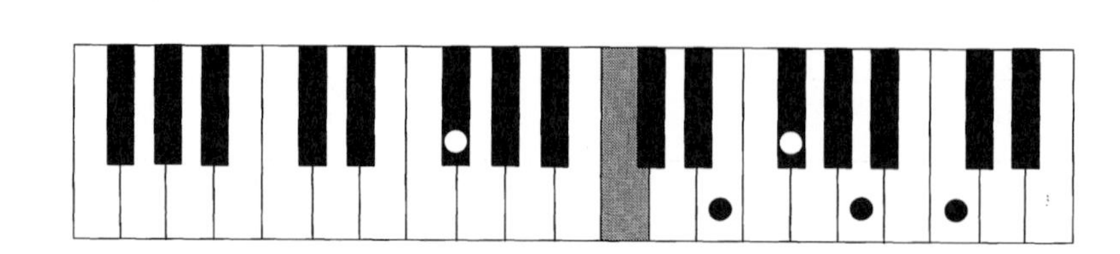

F♯ minor added major 7th - F♯m(maj7)

F♯ minor 9th - F♯m9

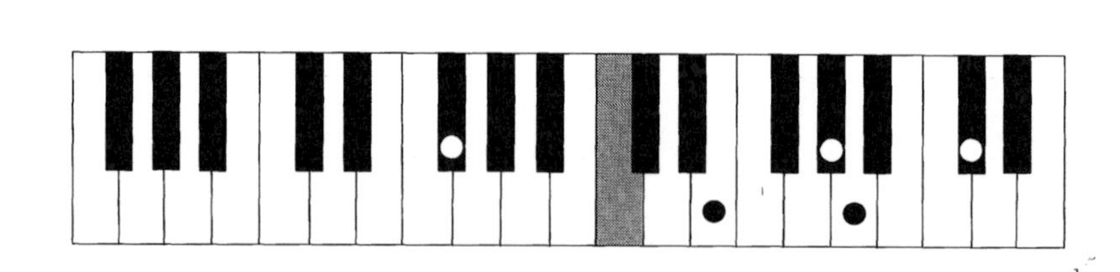

The G♭ Collection

G♭ minor added 6th - G♭m6

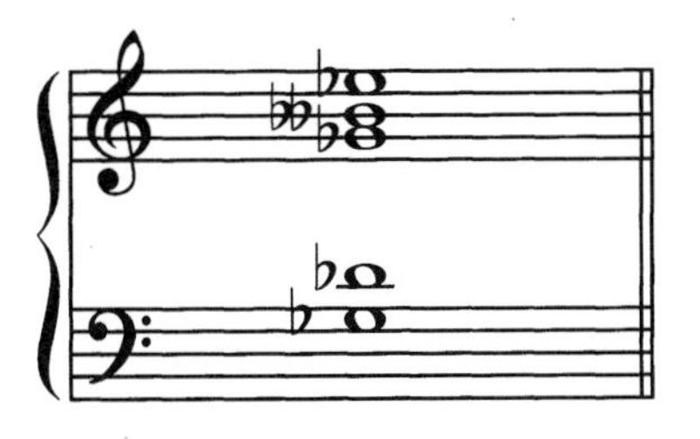

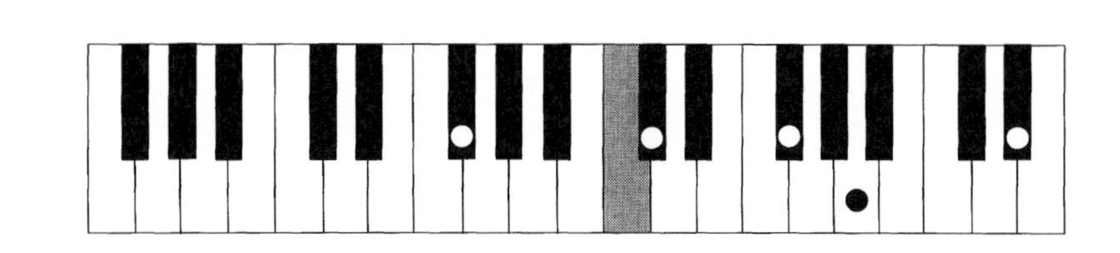

G♭ minor 7th - G♭m7

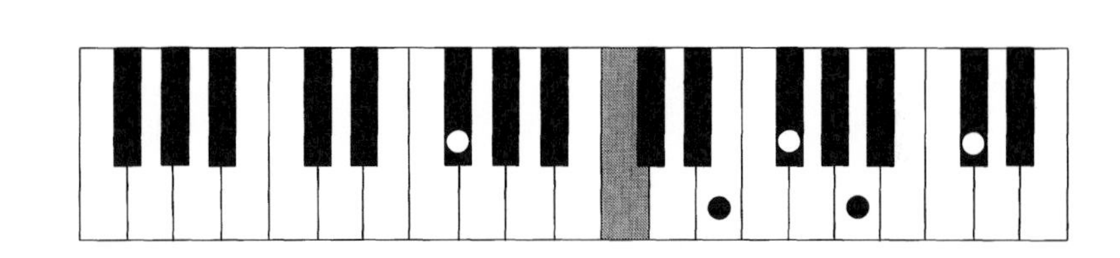

G♭ minor 7th with flattened 5th - G♭m7(♭5)

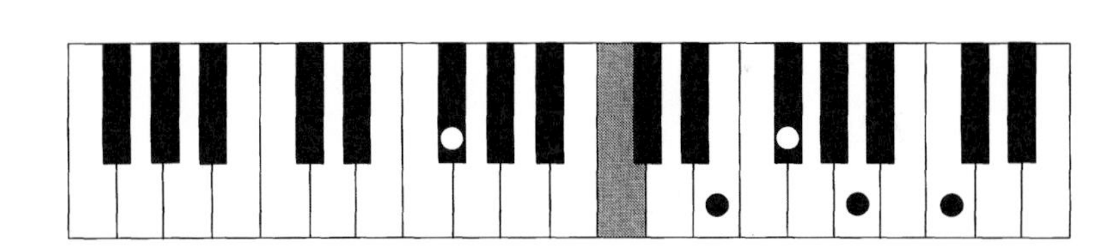

G♭ minor added major 7th - G♭m(maj7)

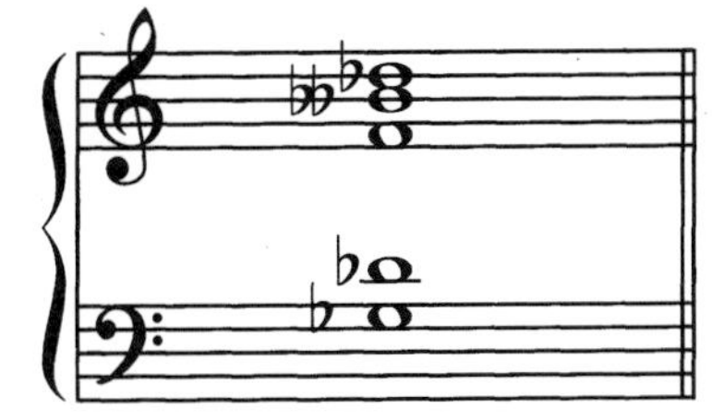

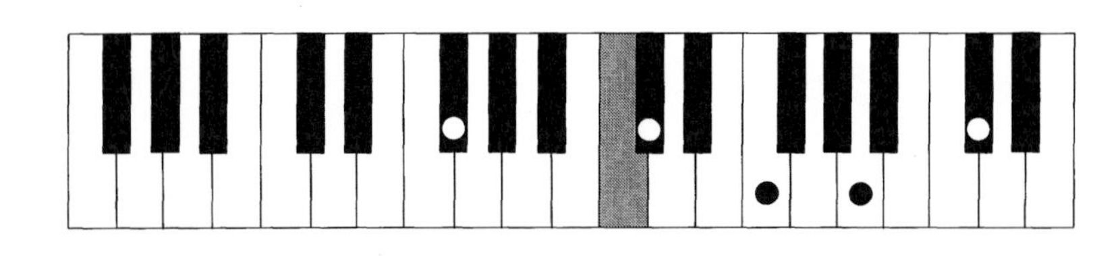

G♭ minor 9th - G♭m9

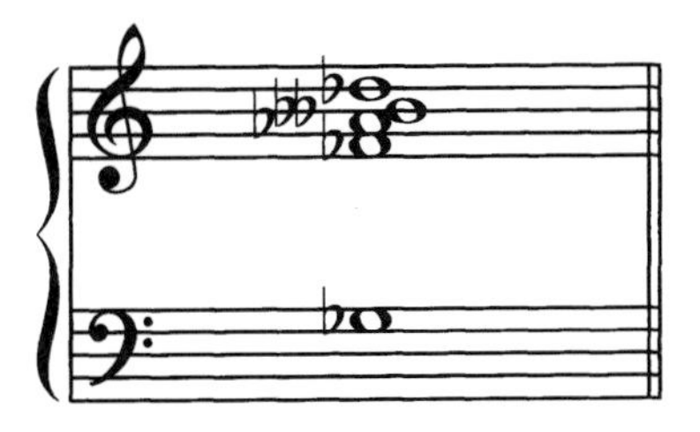

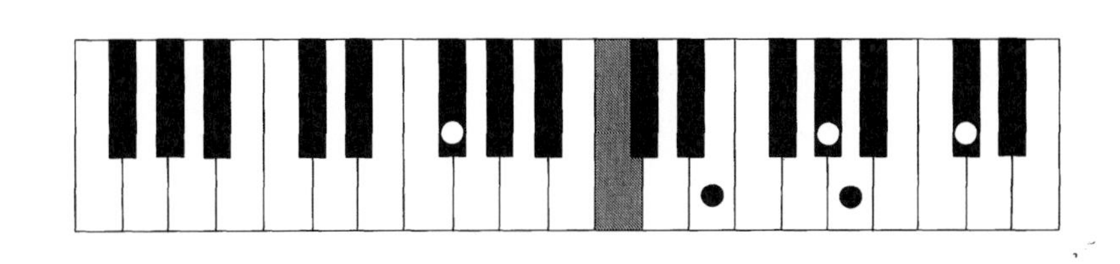

The G Collection

G major - G

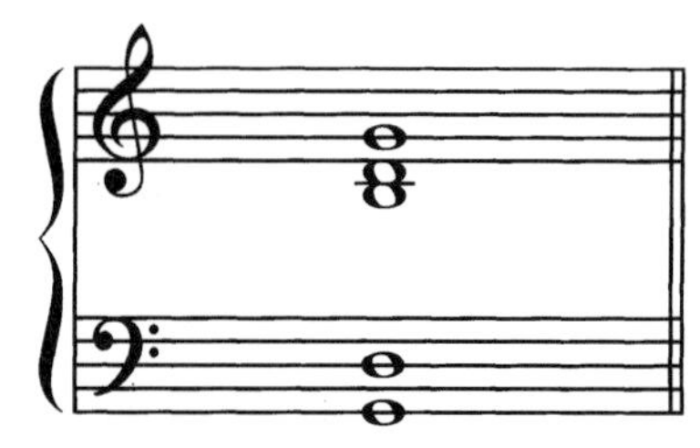

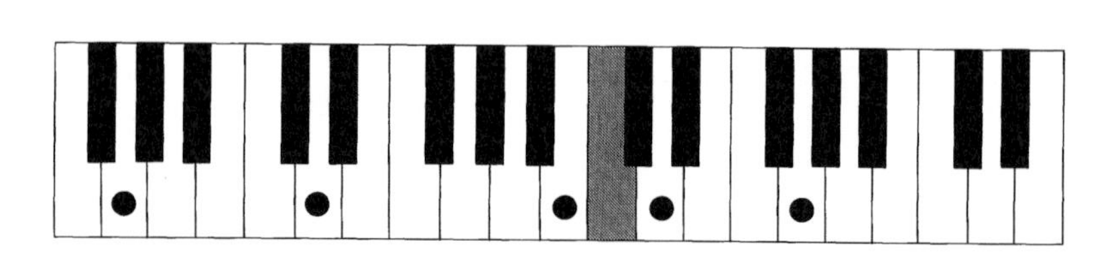

G suspended 4th - Gsus or Gsus4

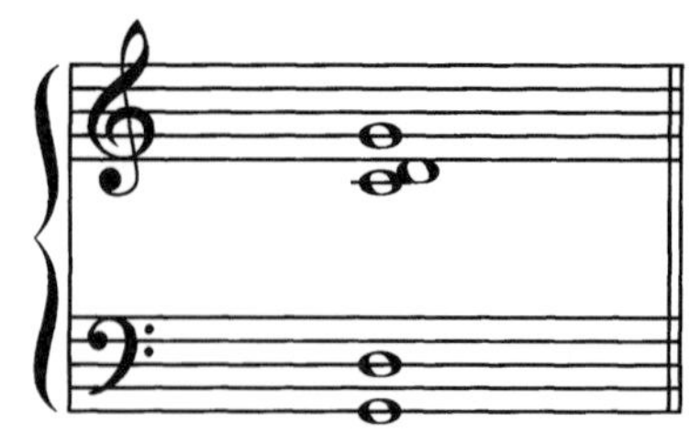

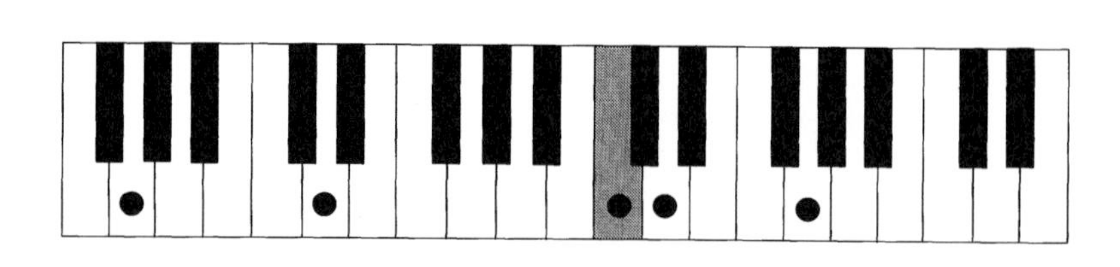

G augmented 5th - G+ or Gaug

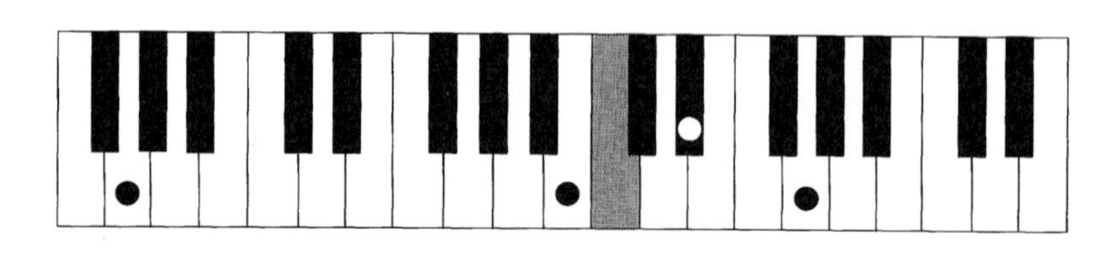

G added 6th - G6

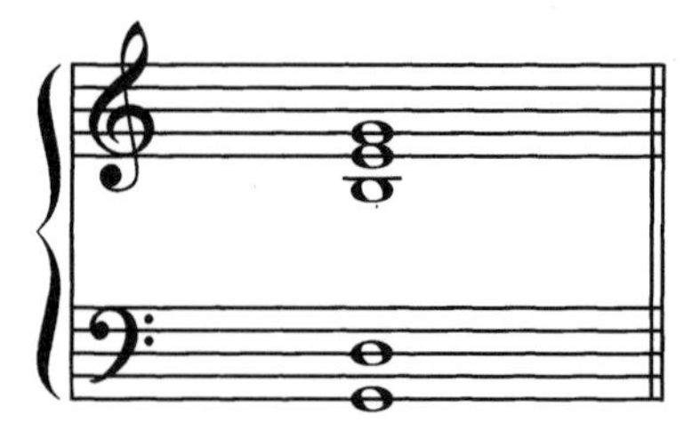

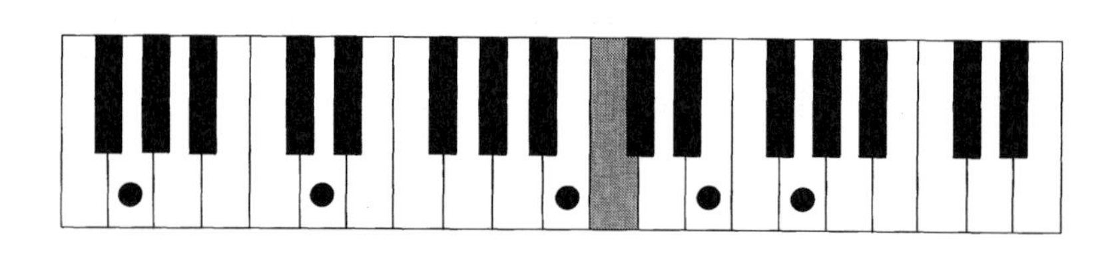

G added 6th and 9th - G6/9

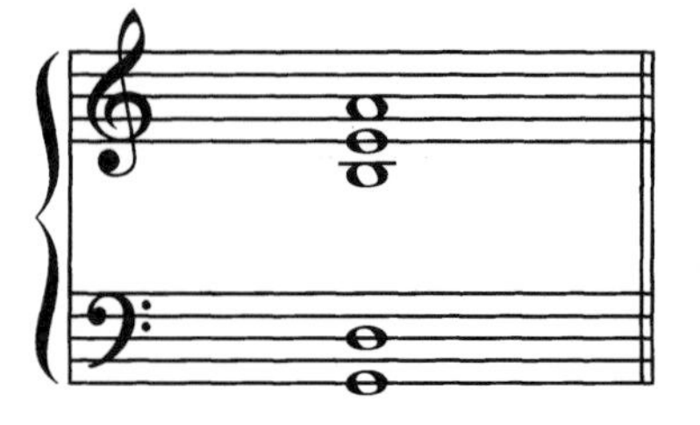

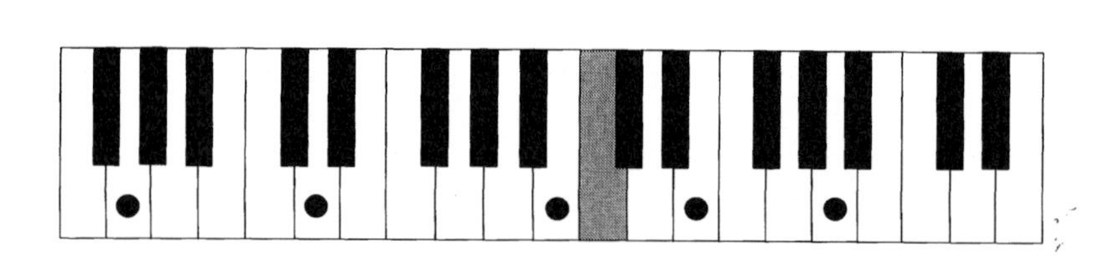

The G Collection

G major 7th - Gmaj7

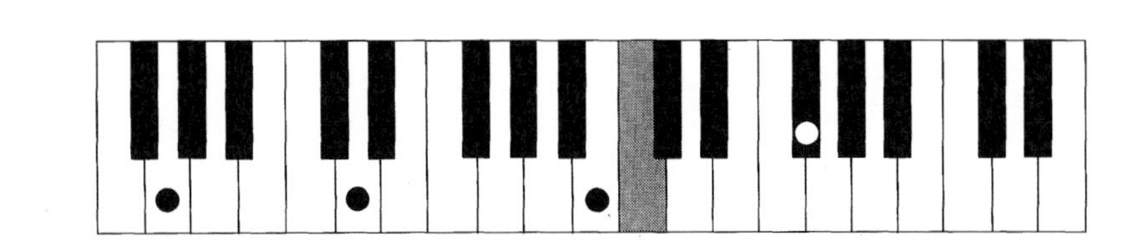

G dominant 7th - G7

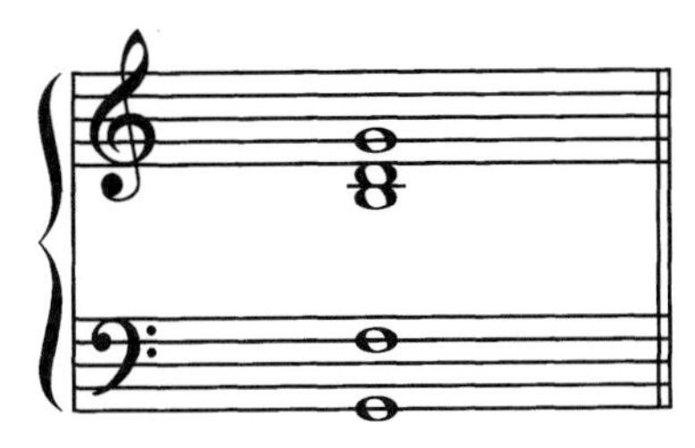

G dominant 7th with suspended 4th - G7sus or G7sus4

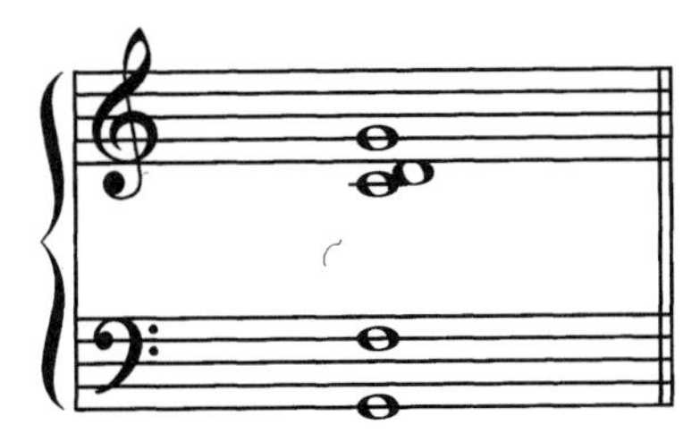

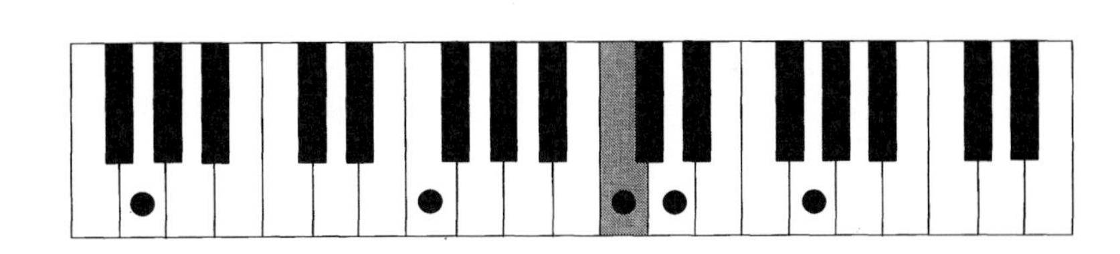

G dominant 7th with flattened 5th - G7(♭5)

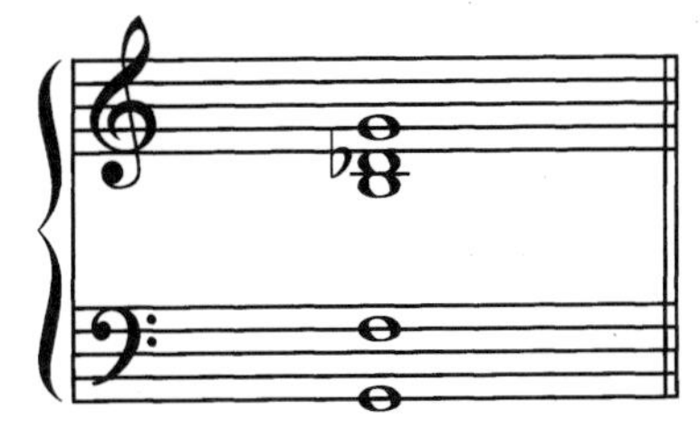

G dominant 7th with augmented 5th - G7+ or G7aug

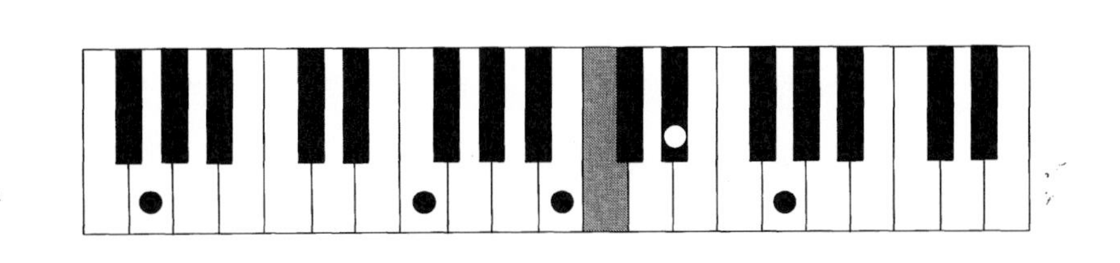

The G Collection

G dominant 7th with flattened 9th - G7(♭9)

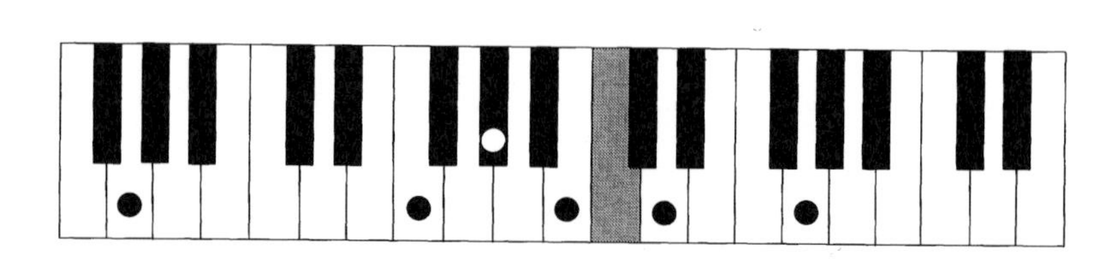

G dominant 7th with flattened 9th and 5th - G7(♭9/♭5)

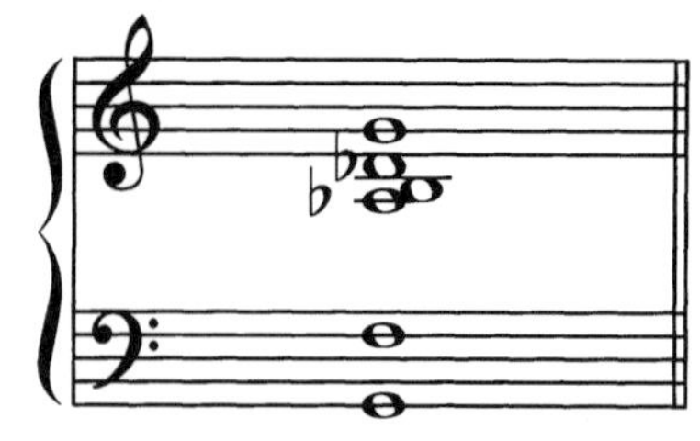

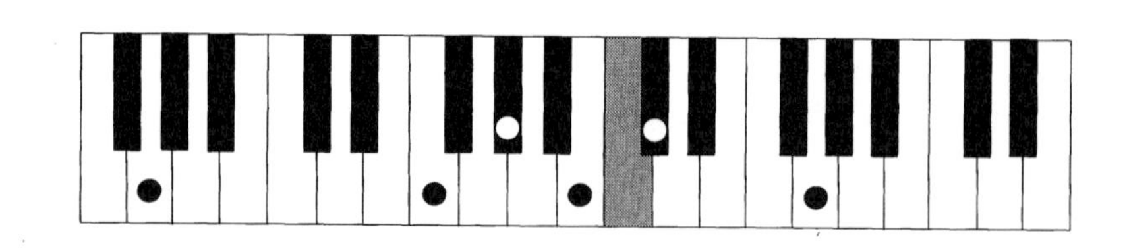

G dominant 7th with sharpened 9th - G7(♯9)

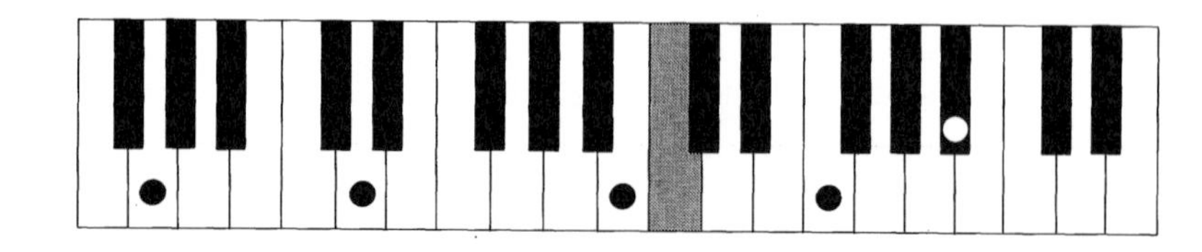

G added 9th - Gadd9

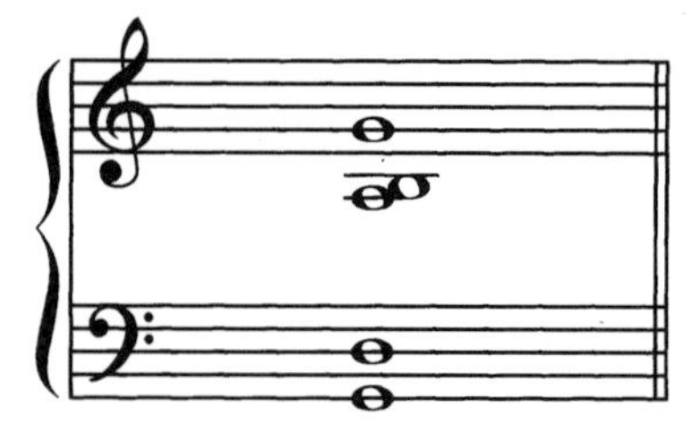

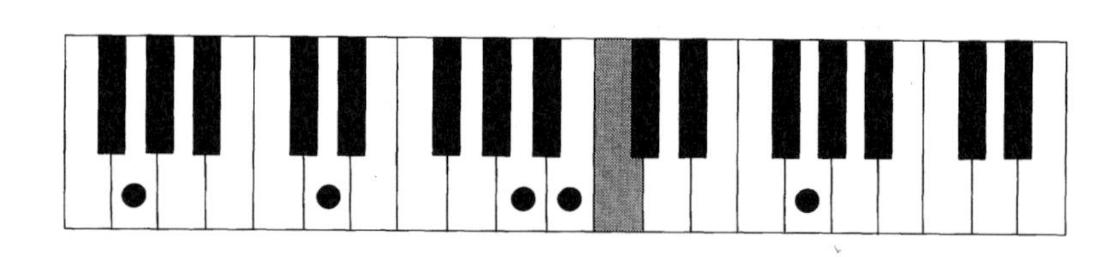

G major 9th - Gmaj9

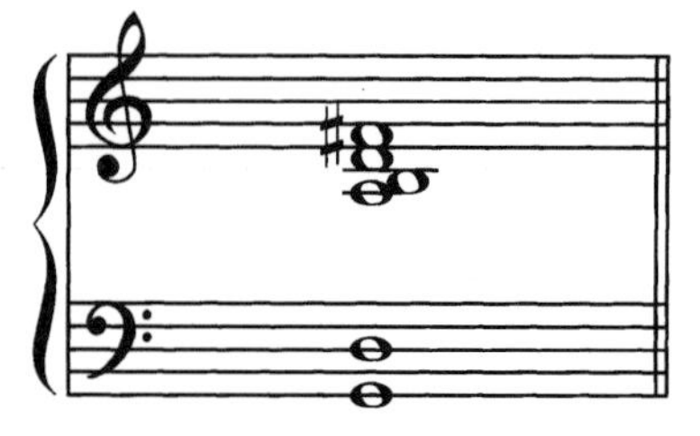

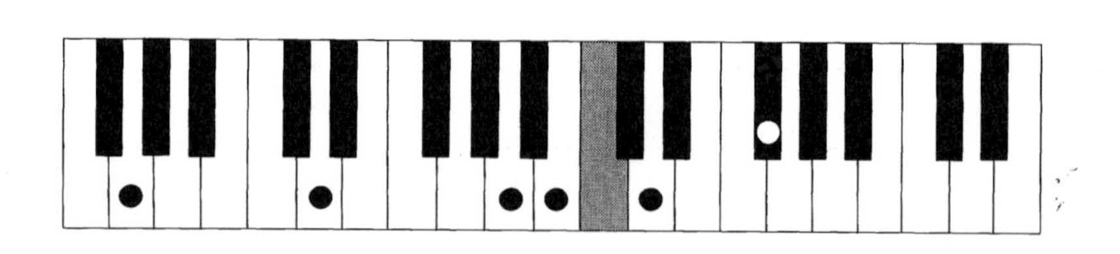

The G Collection

G dominant 9th - G9

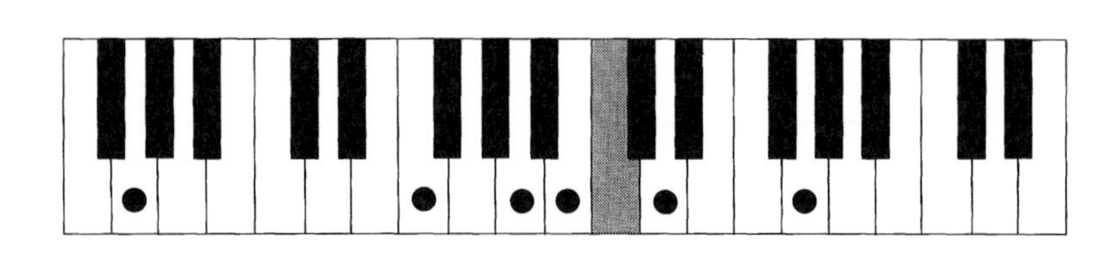

G dominant 9th with suspended 4th - G9sus or G9sus4

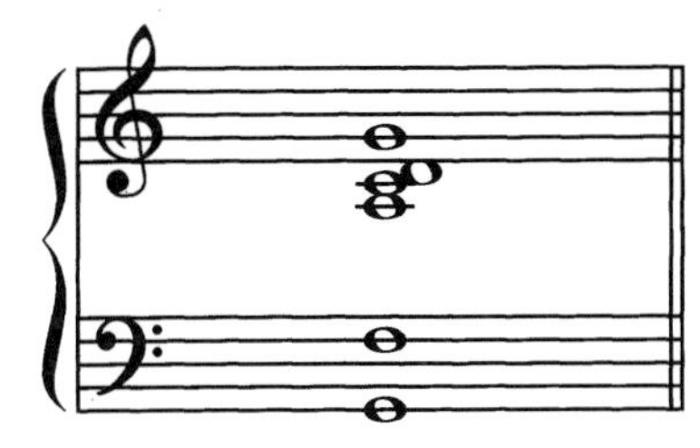

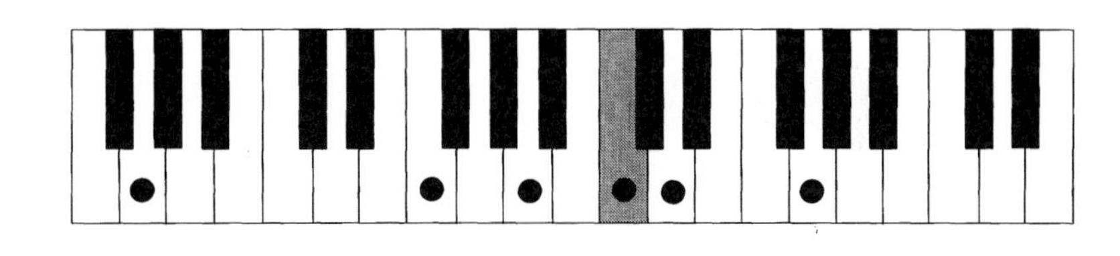

G dominant 9th with augmented 5th - G9+ or G9aug

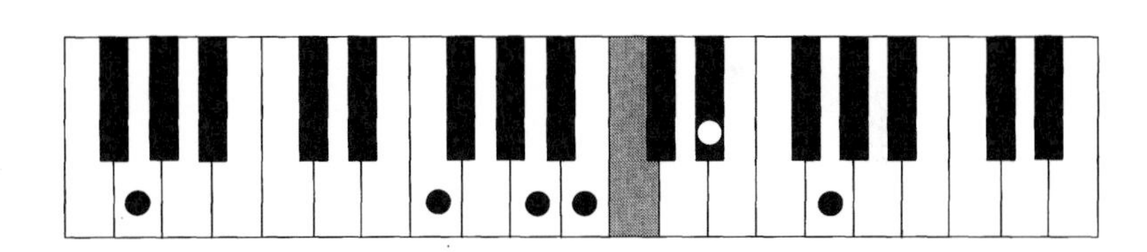

G dominant 9th with sharpened 11th - G9(♯11)
with flattened 5th - G9(♭5)

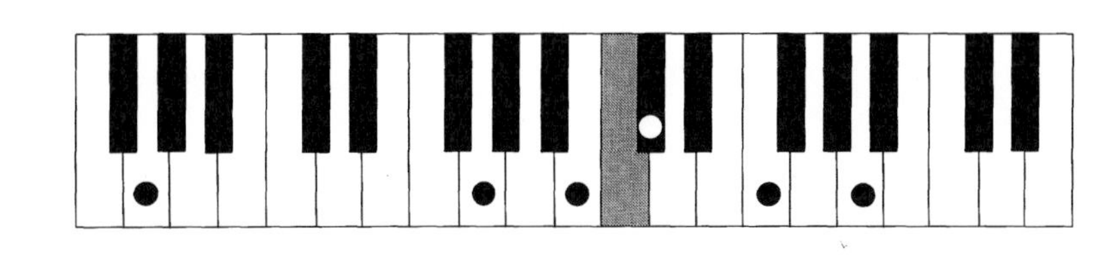

G dominant 11th - G11

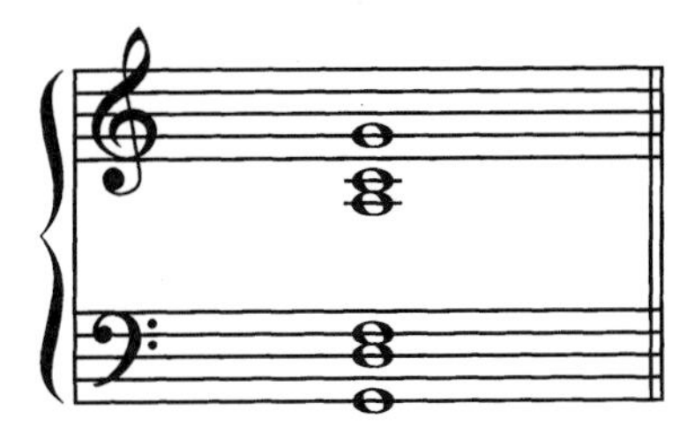

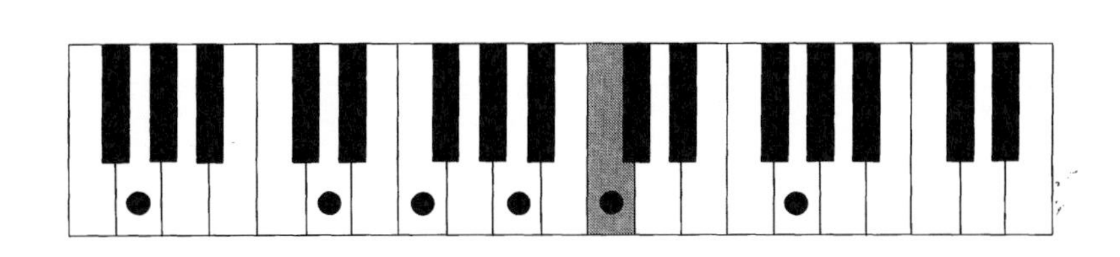

The G Collection

G dominant 11th with flattened 9th - G11(♭9)

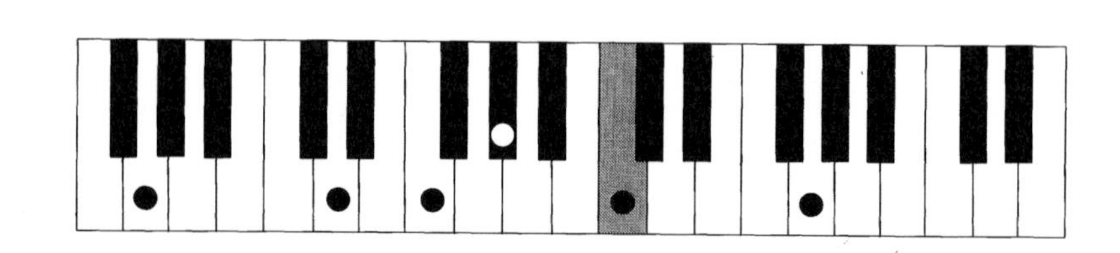

G dominant 13th - G13

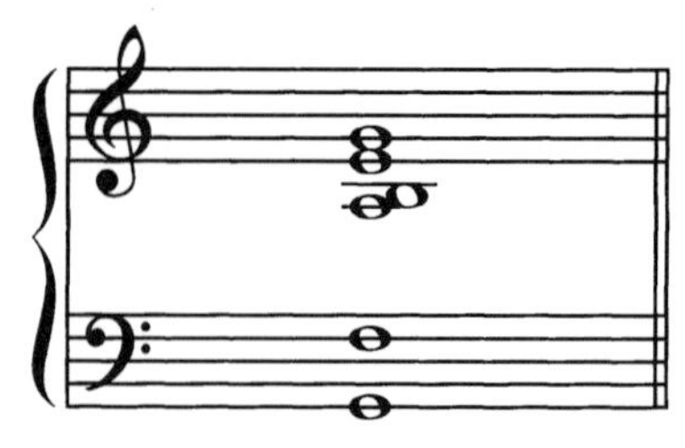

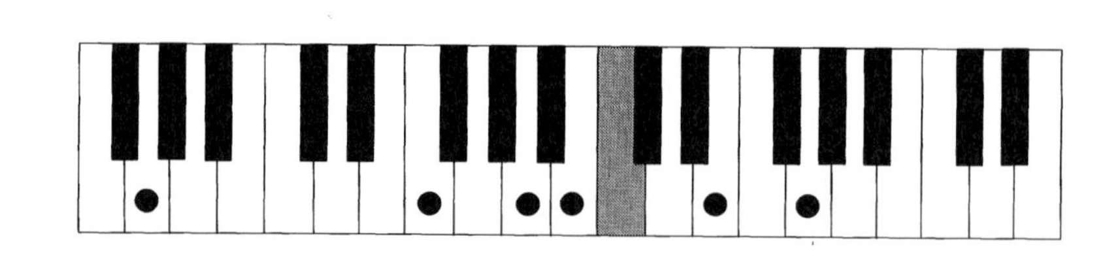

G dominant 13th with flattened 9th - G13(♭9)

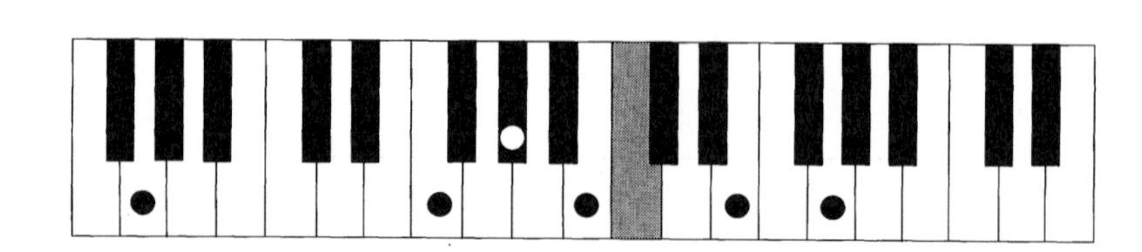

G minor - Gm

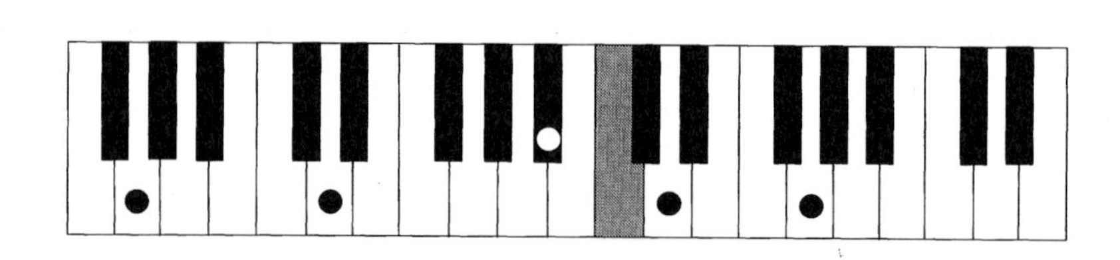

G diminished - G° or Gdim

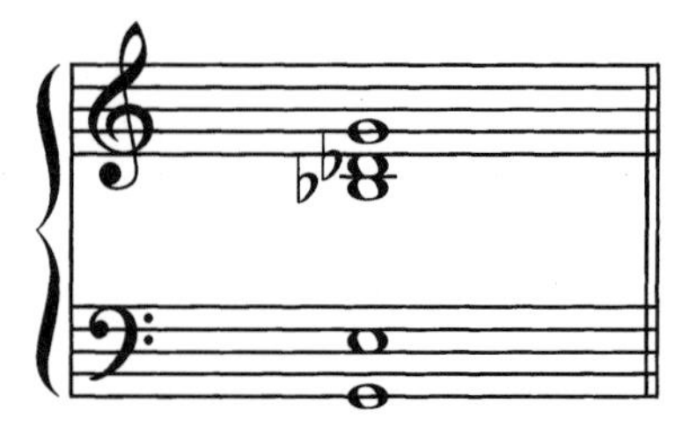

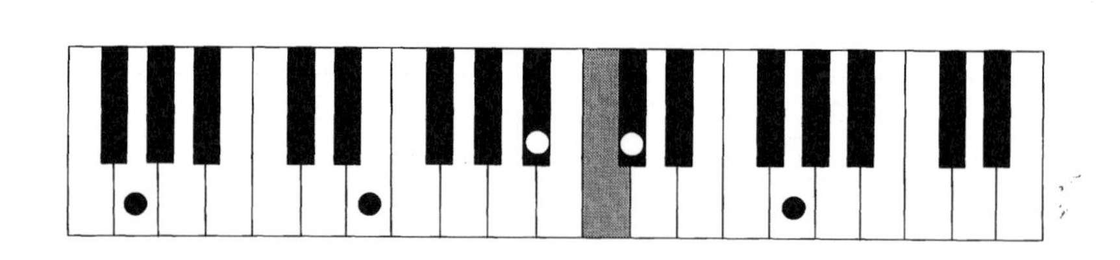

The G Collection

G minor added 6th - Gm6

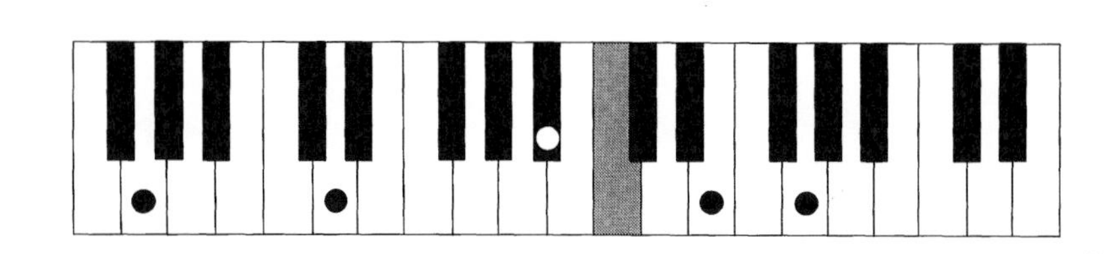

G minor 7th - Gm7

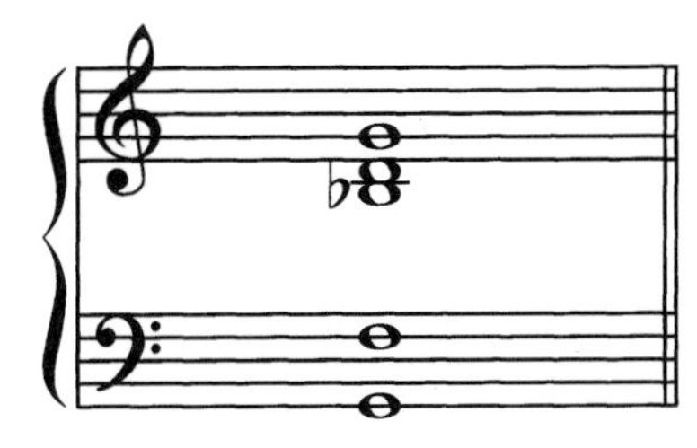

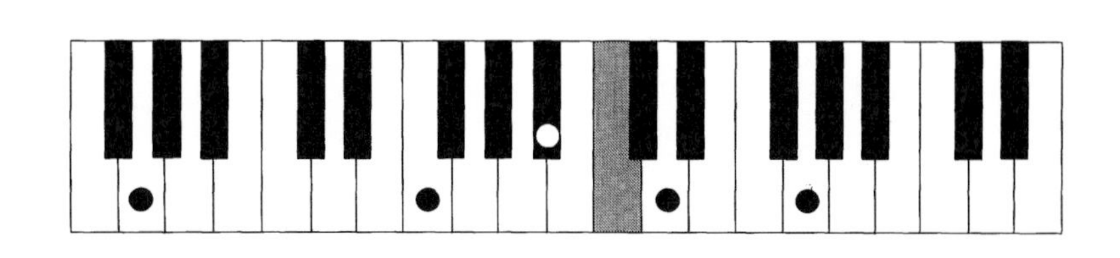

G minor 7th with flattened 5th - Gm7(♭5)

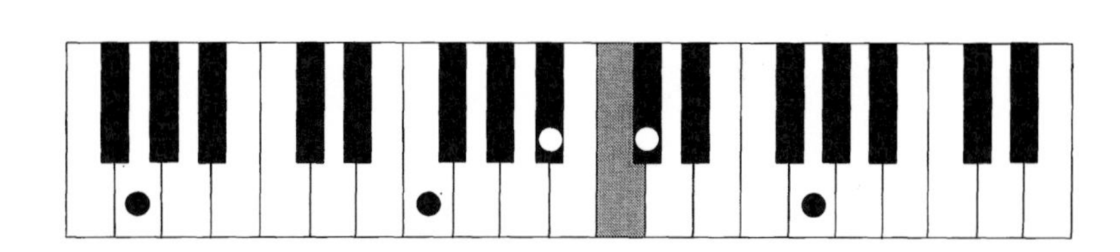

G minor added major 7th - Gm(maj7)

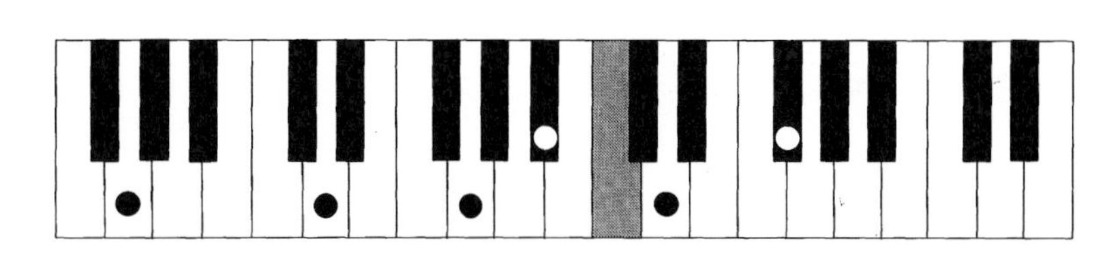

G minor 9th - Gm9

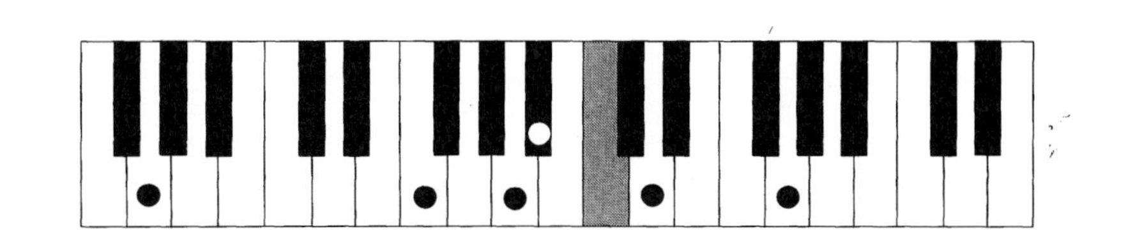

The G♯ Collection

G♯ major - G♯

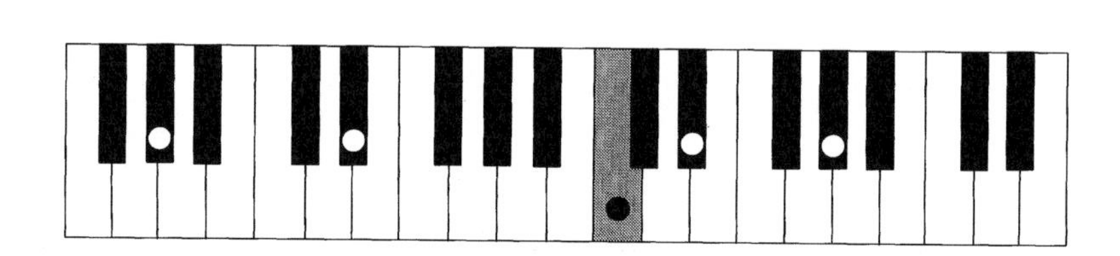

G♯ suspended 4th - G♯sus or G♯sus4

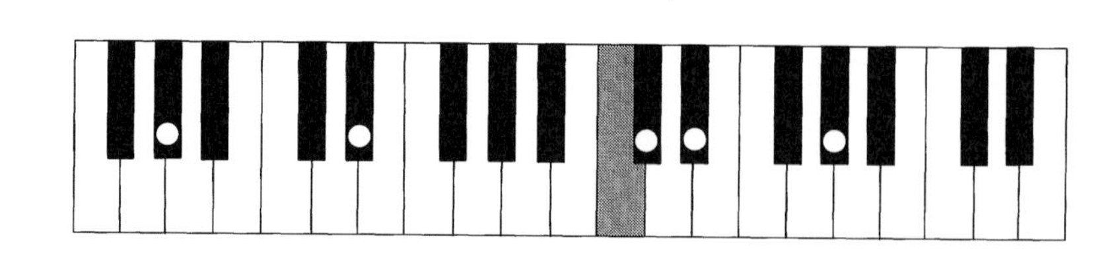

G♯ augmented 5th - G♯+ or G♯aug

G♯ added 6th - G♯6

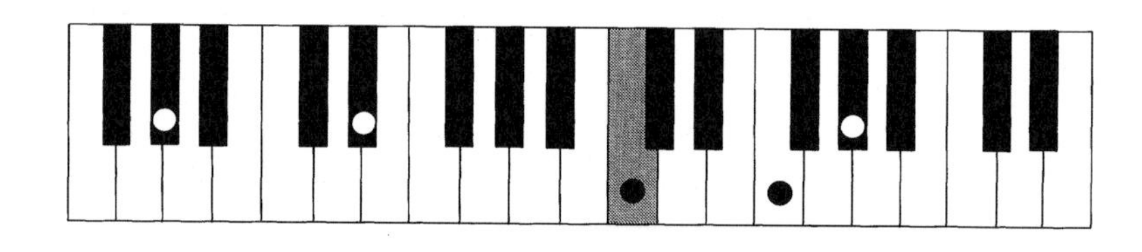

G♯ added 6th and 9th - G♯6/9

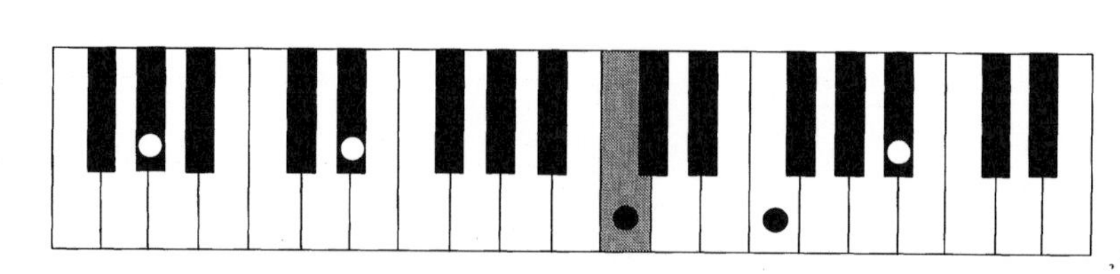

G♯ and A♭ are the same note spelled in different ways, depending on the key you are in.
For this reason, G♯ and A♭ chords are grouped together on facing pages.

The A♭ Collection

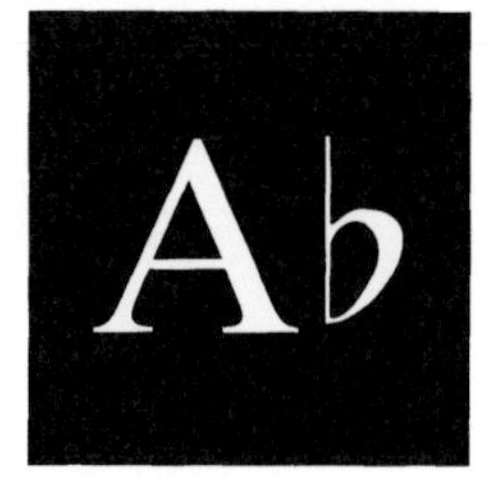

A♭ major - A♭

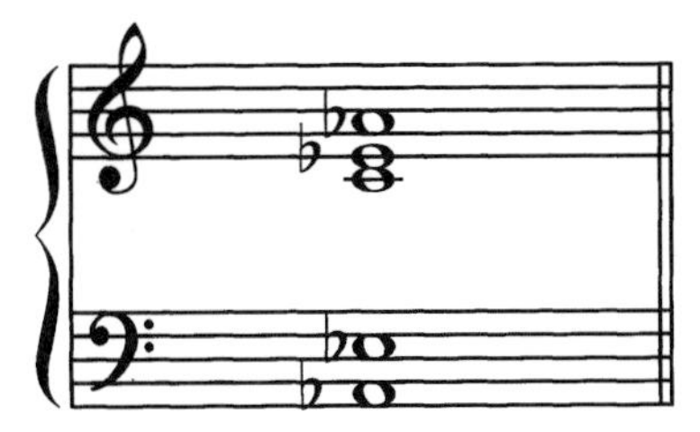

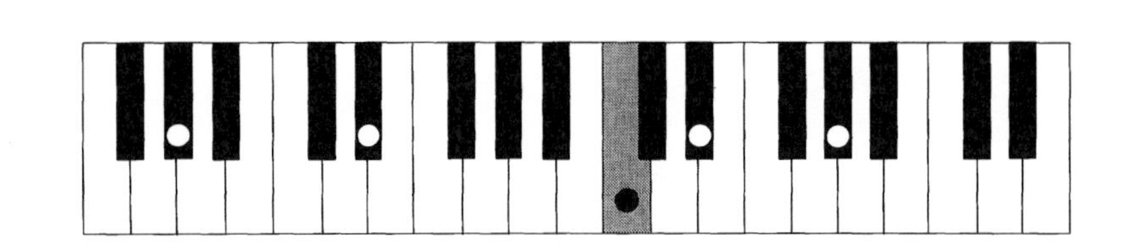

A♭ suspended 4th - A♭sus or A♭sus4

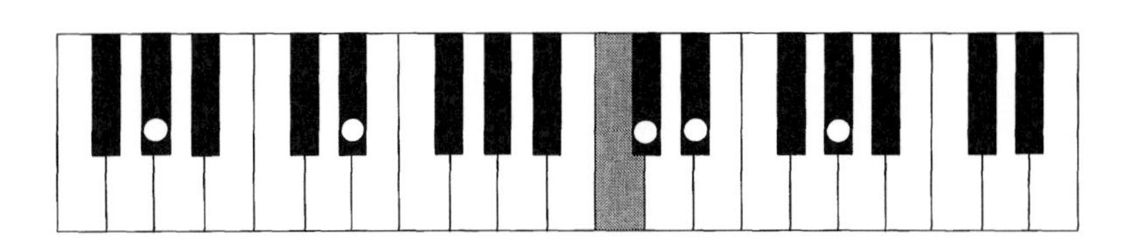

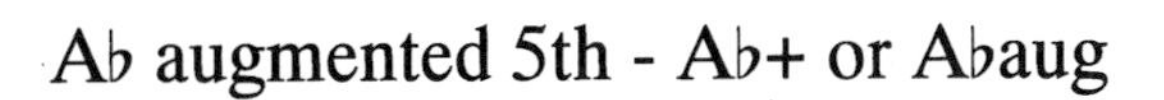
A♭ augmented 5th - A♭+ or A♭aug

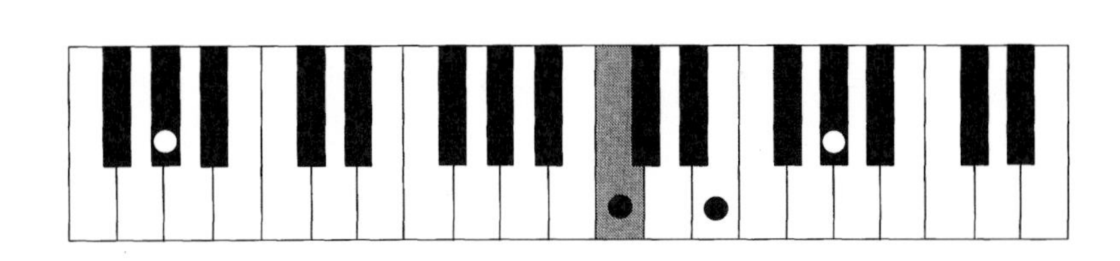

A♭ added 6th - A♭6

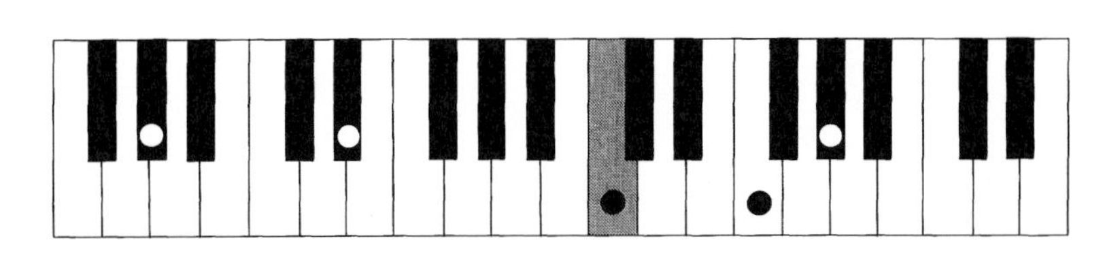

A♭ added 6th and 9th - A♭6/9

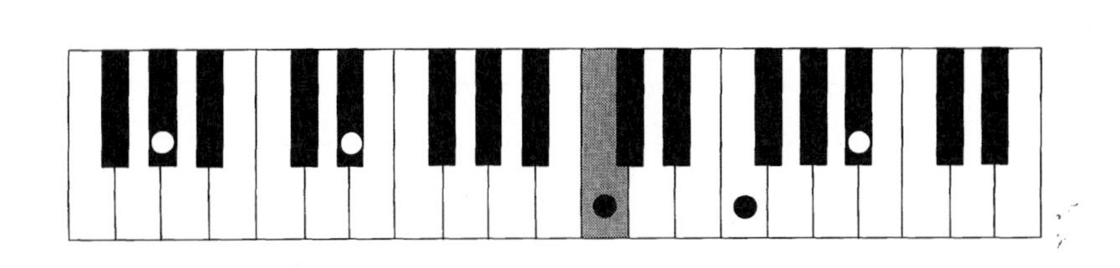

The G♯ Collection

G♯ major 7th - G♯maj7

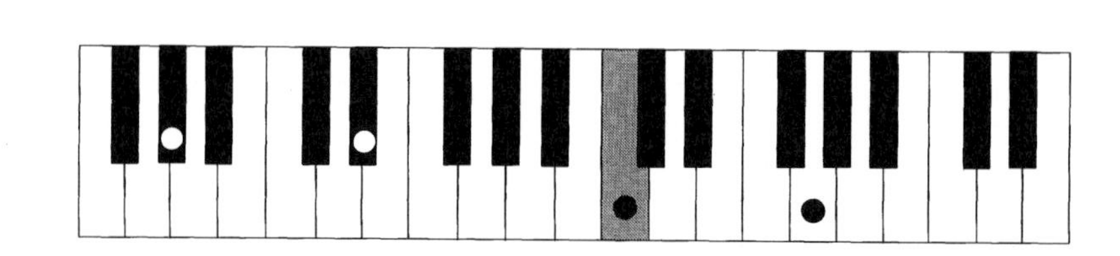

G♯ dominant 7th - G♯7

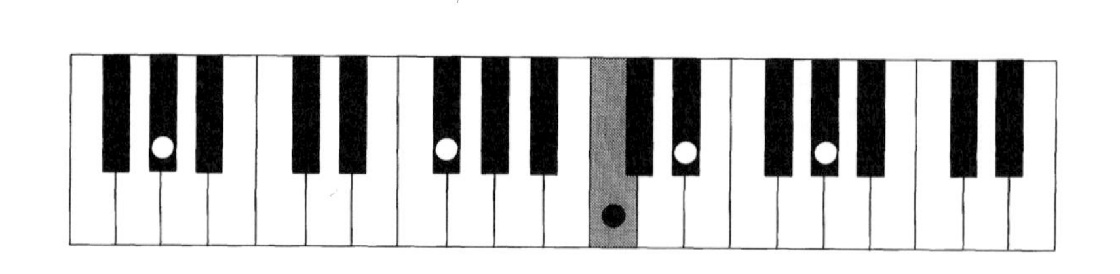

G♯ dominant 7th with suspended 4th - G♯7sus or G♯7sus4

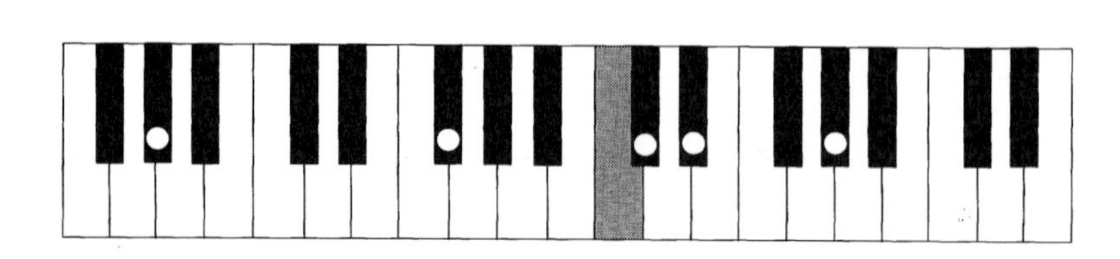

G♯ dominant 7th with flattened 5th - G♯7(♭5)

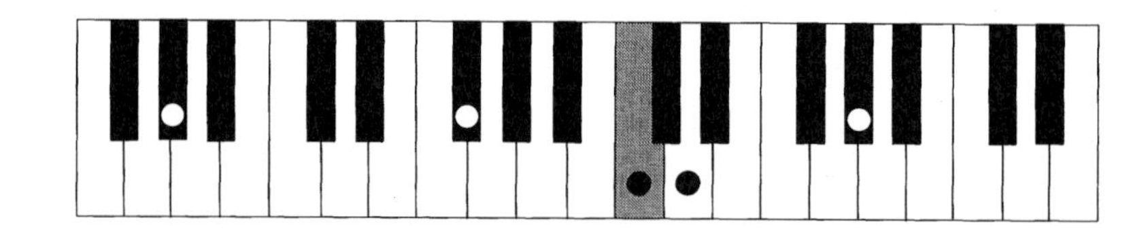

G♯ dominant 7th with augmented 5th - G♯7+ or G♯7aug

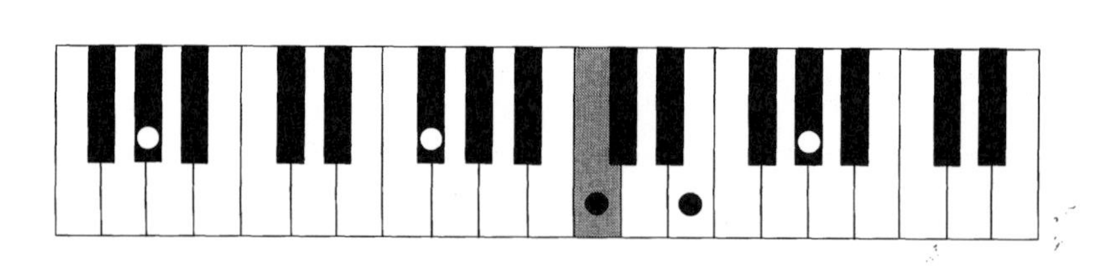

The A♭ Collection

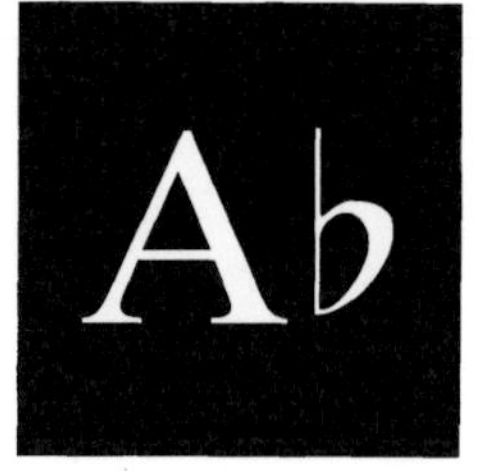

A♭ major 7th - A♭maj7

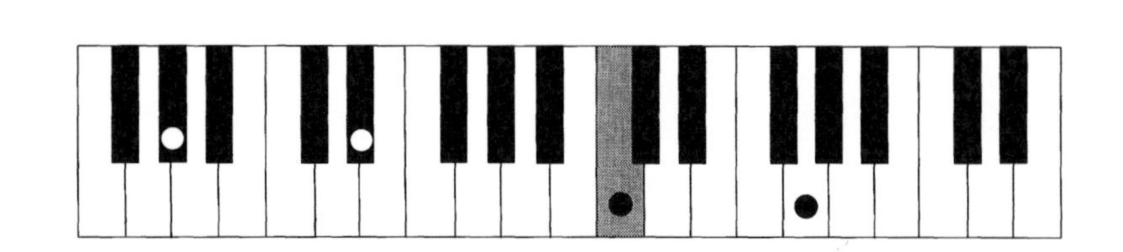

A♭ dominant 7th - A♭7

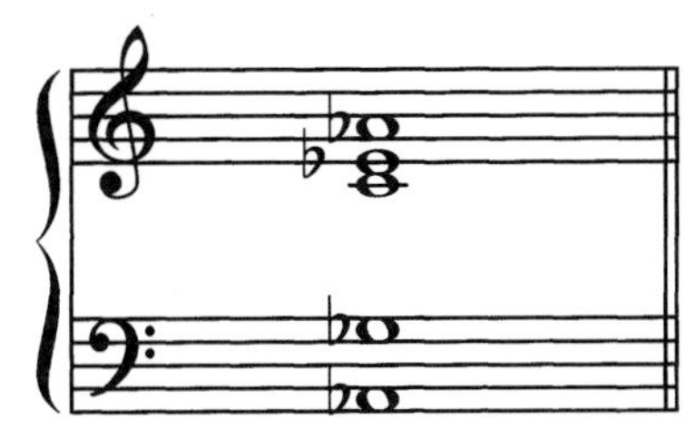

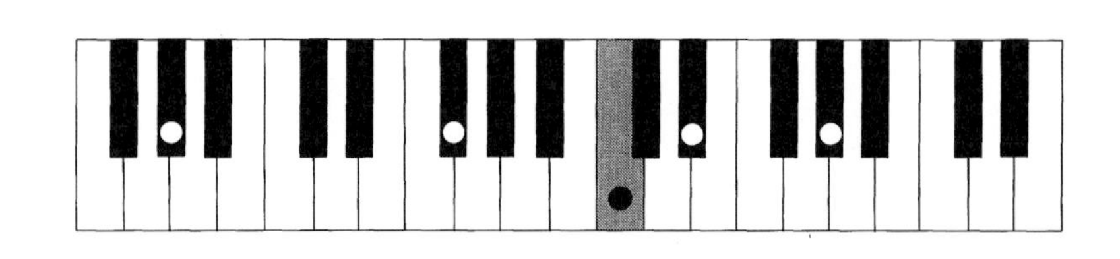

A♭ dominant 7th with suspended 4th - A♭7sus or A♭7sus4

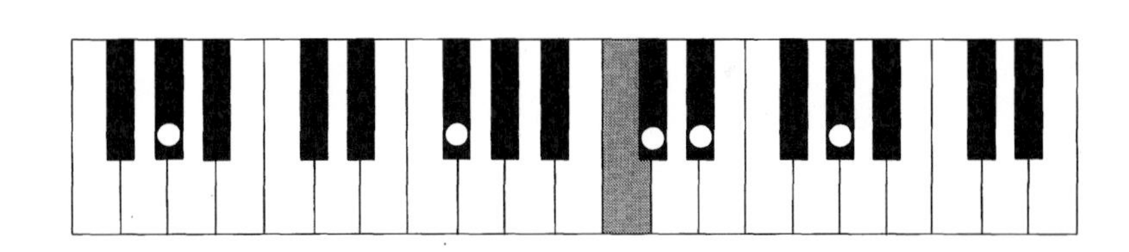

A♭ dominant 7th with flattened 5th - A♭7(♭5)

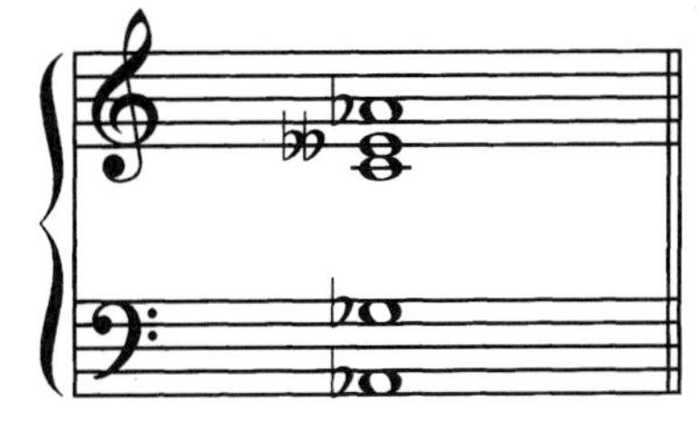

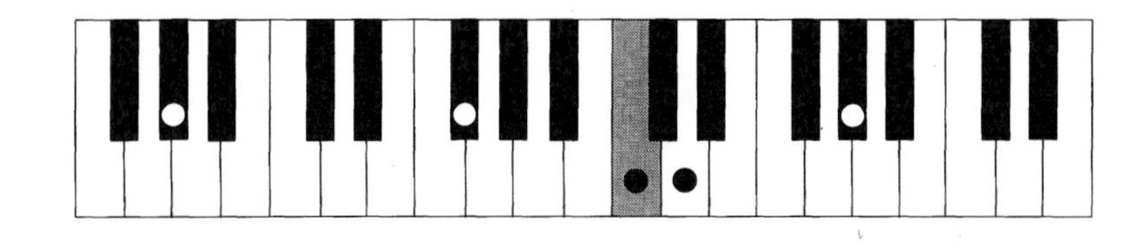

A♭ dominant 7th with augmented 5th - A♭7+ or A♭7aug

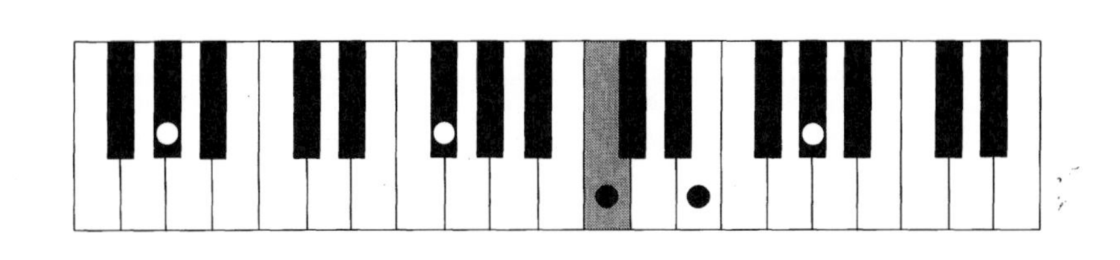

The G♯ Collection

G♯ dominant 7th with flattened 9th - G♯7(♭9)

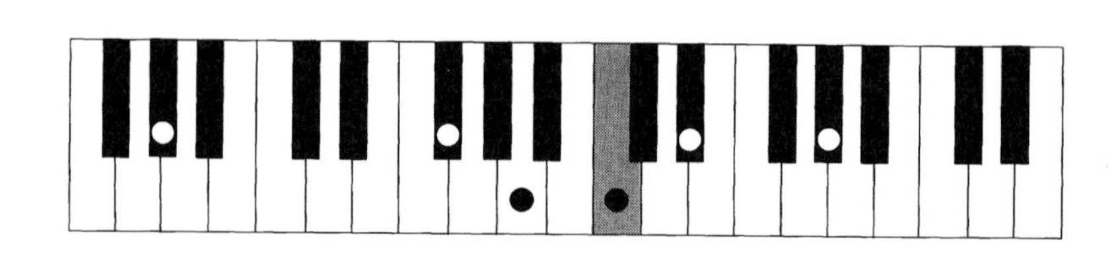

G♯ dominant 7th with flattened 9th and 5th - G♯7(♭9/♭5)

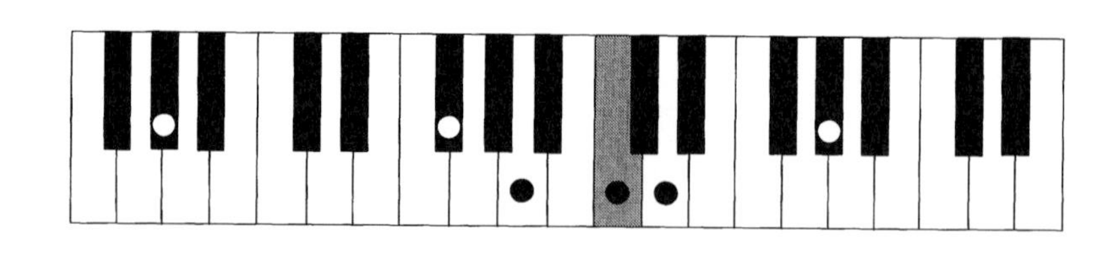

G♯ dominant 7th with sharpened 9th - G♯7(♯9)

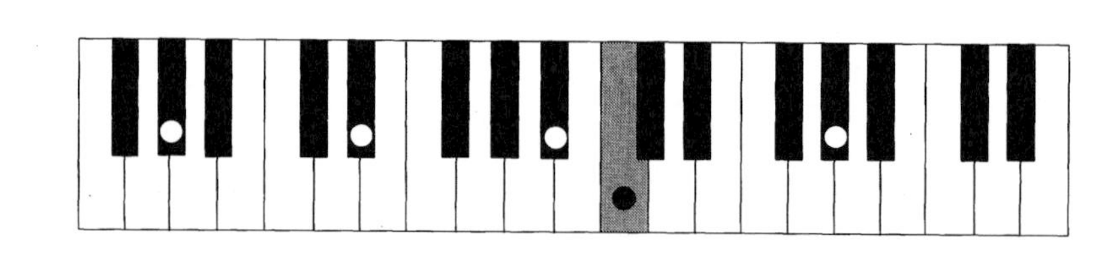

G♯ added 9th - G♯add9

G♯ major 9th - G♯maj9

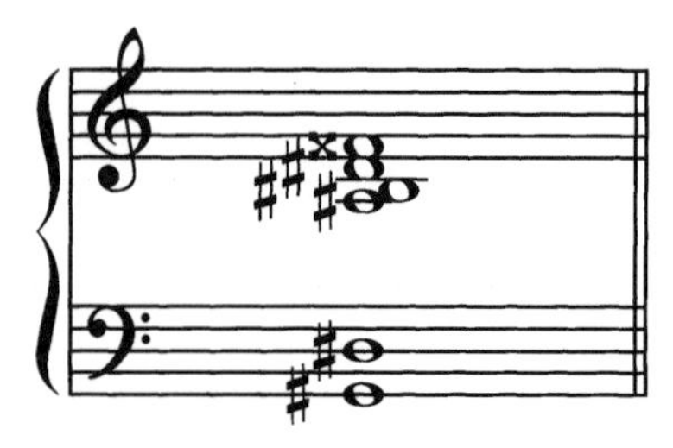

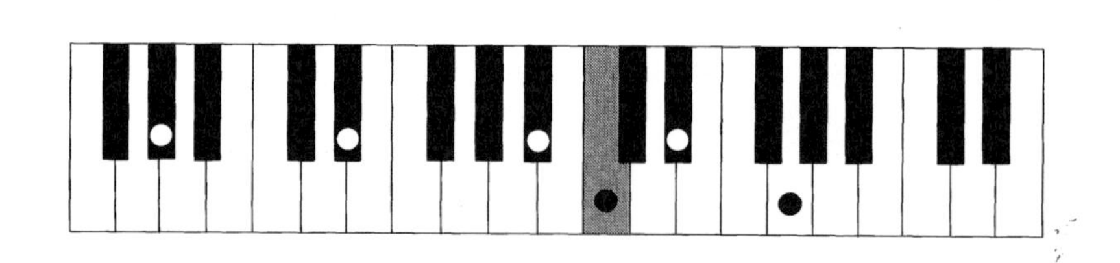

The A♭ Collection

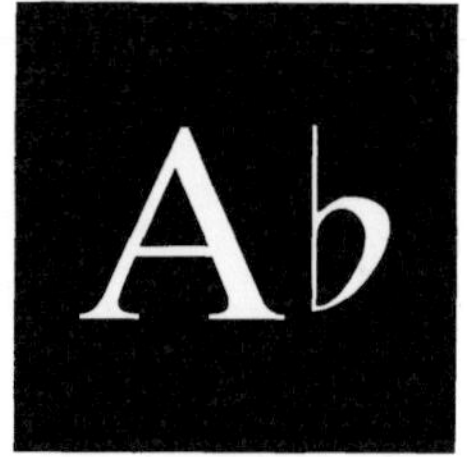

A♭ dominant 7th with flattened 9th - A♭7(♭9)

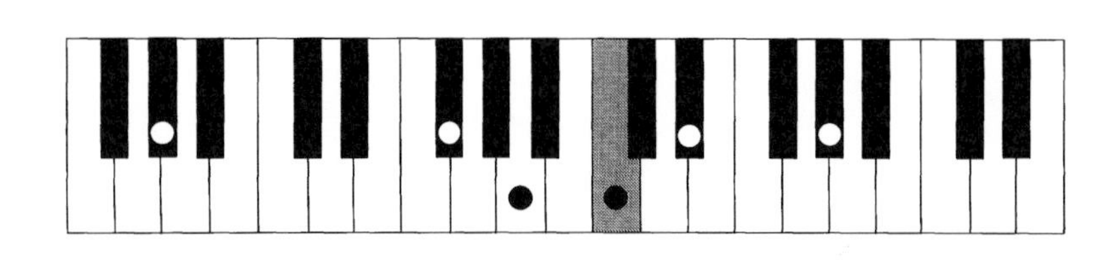

A♭ dominant 7th with flattened 9th and 5th - A♭7(♭9/♭5)

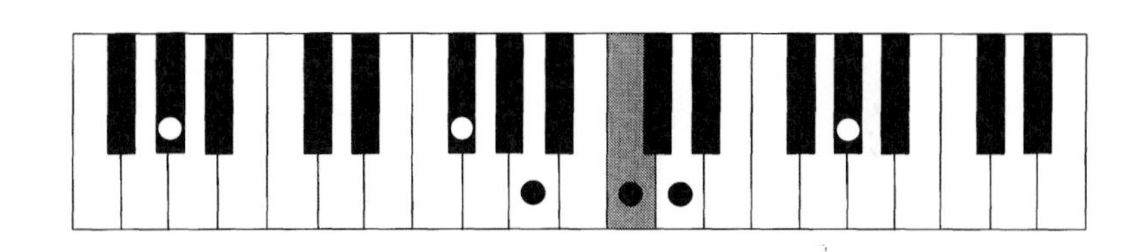

A♭ dominant 7th with sharpened 9th - A♭7(♯9)

A♭ added 9th - A♭add9

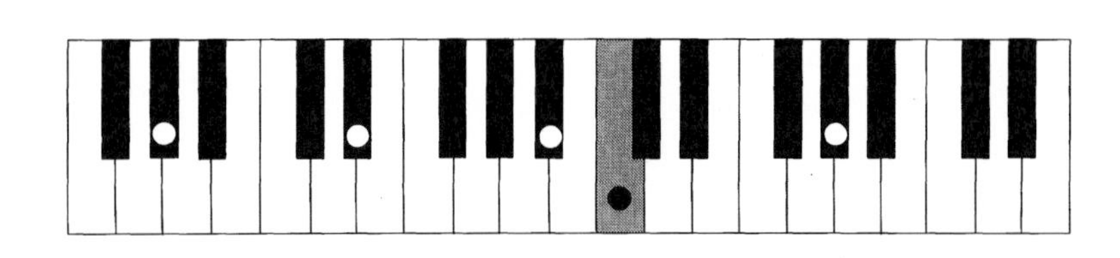

A♭ major 9th - A♭maj9

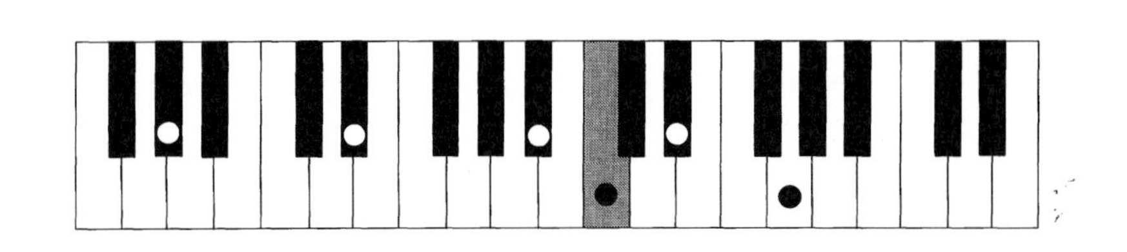

The G♯ Collection

G♯ dominant 9th - G♯9

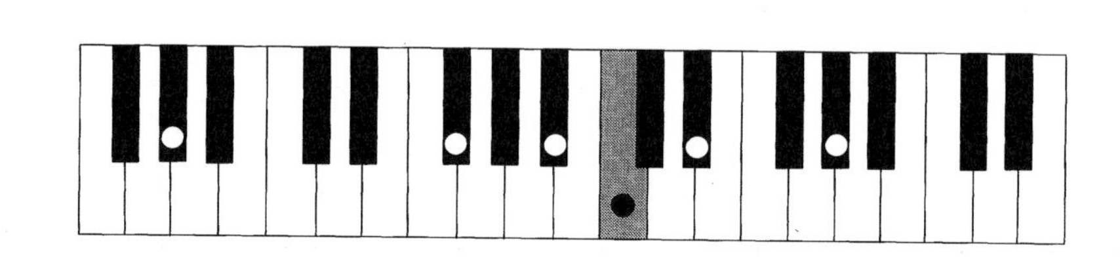

G♯ dominant 9th with suspended 4th - G♯9sus or G♯9sus4

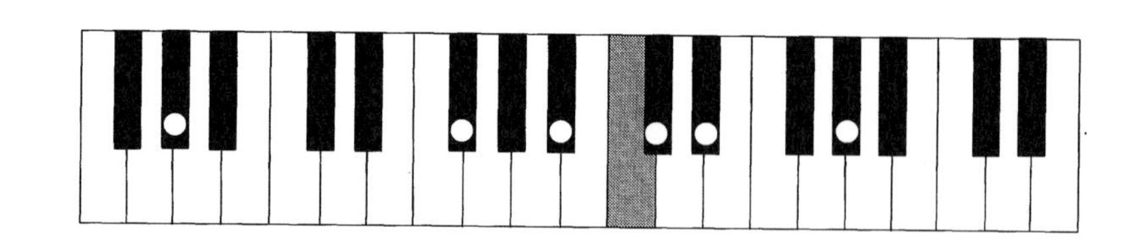

G♯ dominant 9th with augmented 5th - G♯9+ or G♯9aug

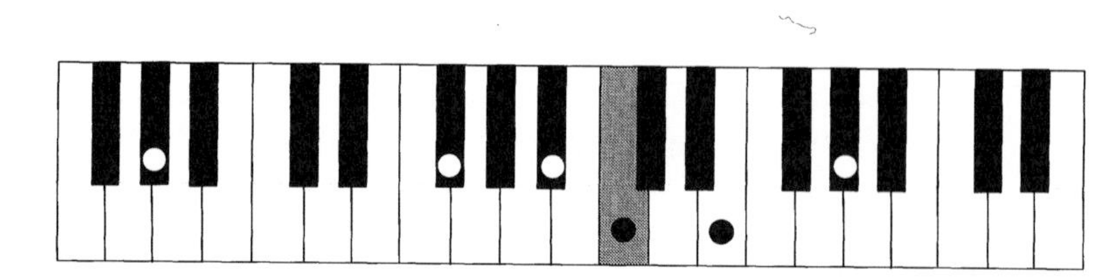

G♯ dominant 9th with sharpened 11th - G♯9(♯11)
with flattened 5th - G♯9(♭5)

G♯ dominant 11th - G♯11

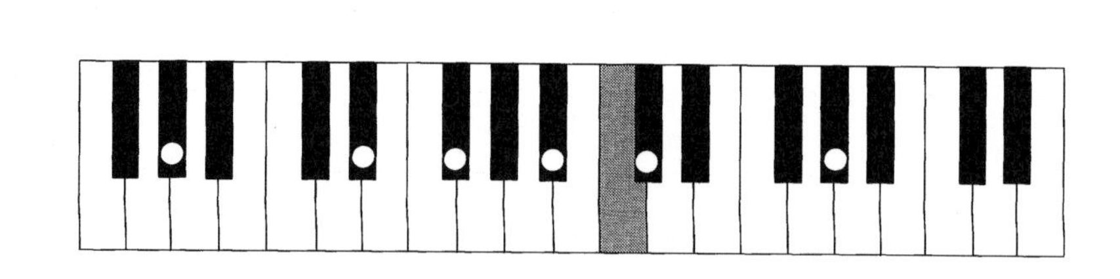

The A♭ Collection

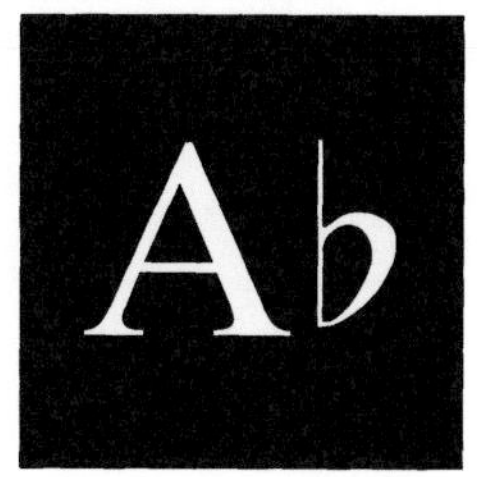

A♭ dominant 9th - A♭9

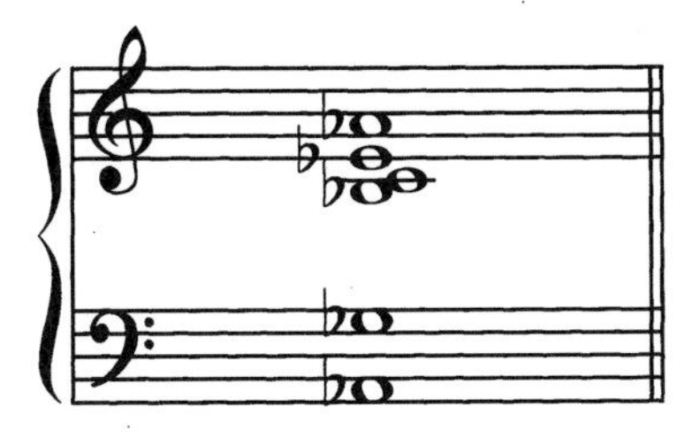

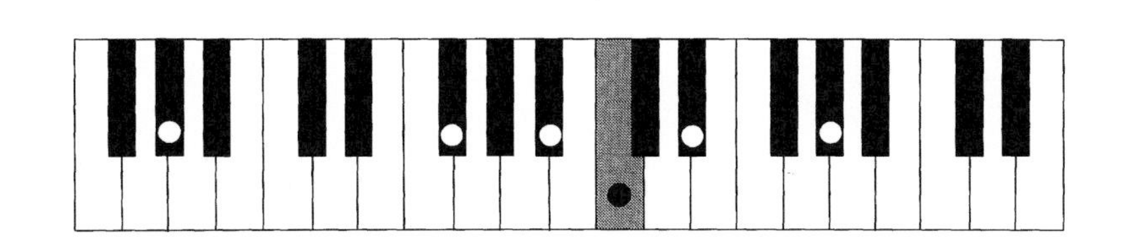

A♭ dominant 9th with suspended 4th - A♭9sus or A♭9sus4

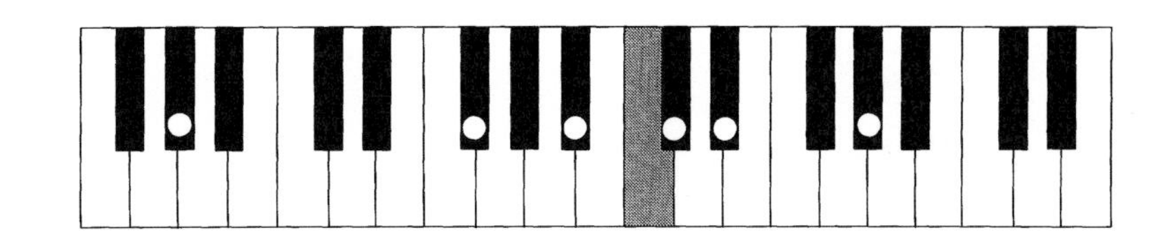

A♭ dominant 9th with augmented 5th - A♭9+ or A♭9aug

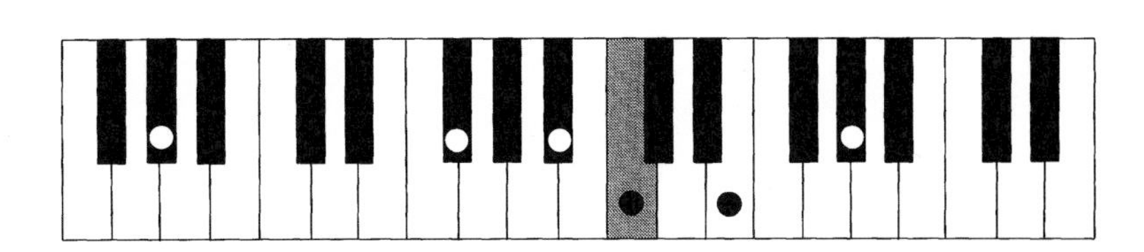

A♭ dominant 9th with sharpened 11th - A♭9(♯11)
with flattened 5th - A♭9(♭5)

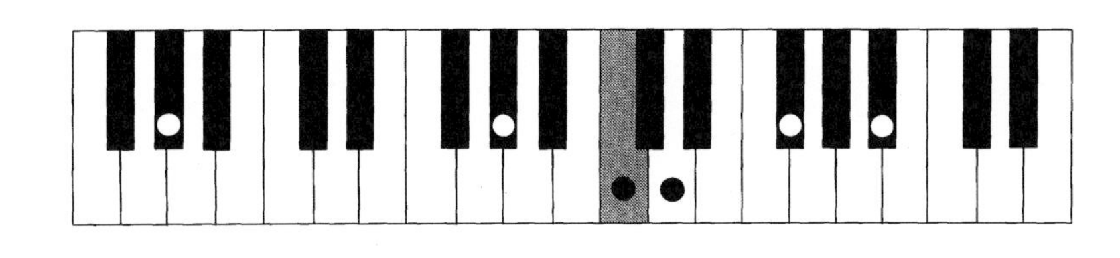

A♭ dominant 11th - A♭11

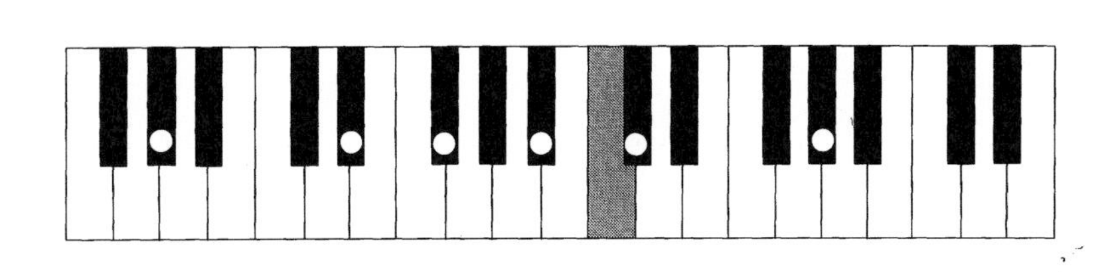

The G♯ Collection

G♯ dominant 11th with flattened 9th - G♯11(♭9)

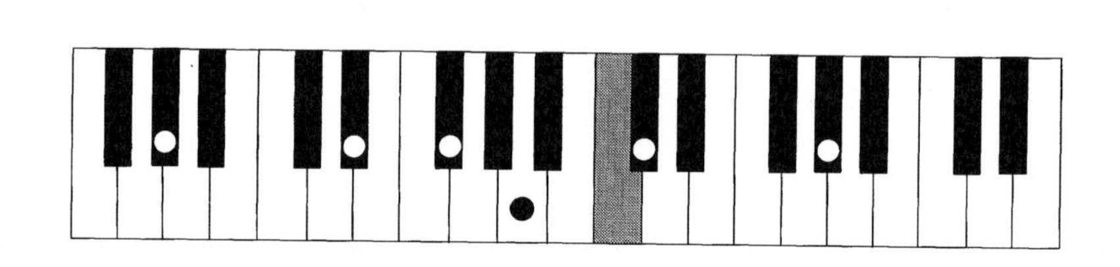

G♯ dominant 13th - G♯13

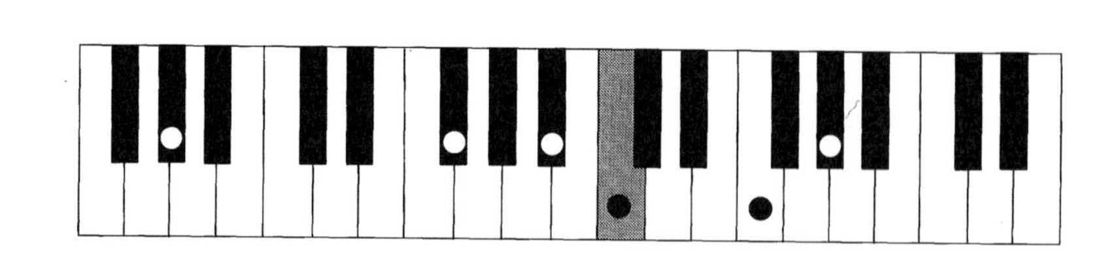

G♯ dominant 13th with flattened 9th - G♯13(♭9)

G♯ minor - G♯m

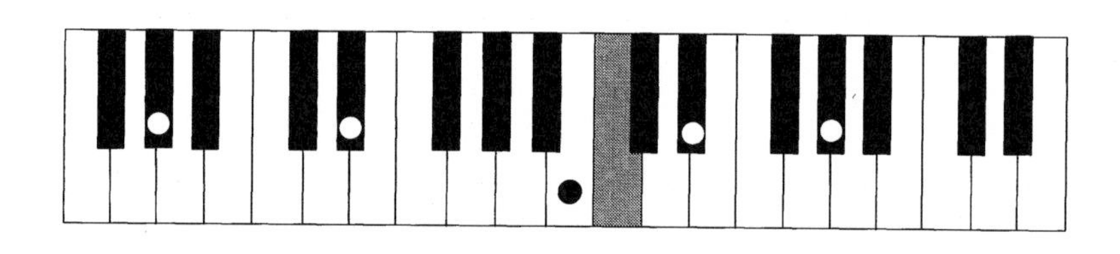

G♯ diminished - G♯° or G♯dim

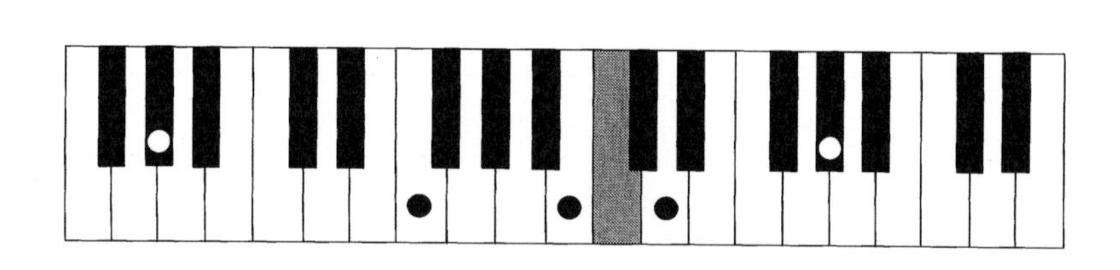

The A♭ Collection

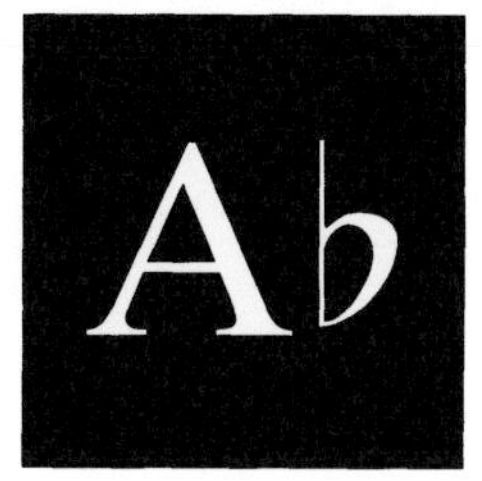

A♭ dominant 11th with flattened 9th - A♭11(♭9)

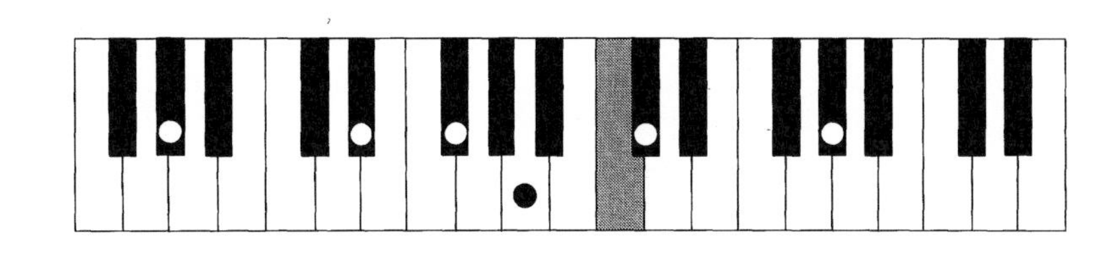

A♭ dominant 13th - A♭13

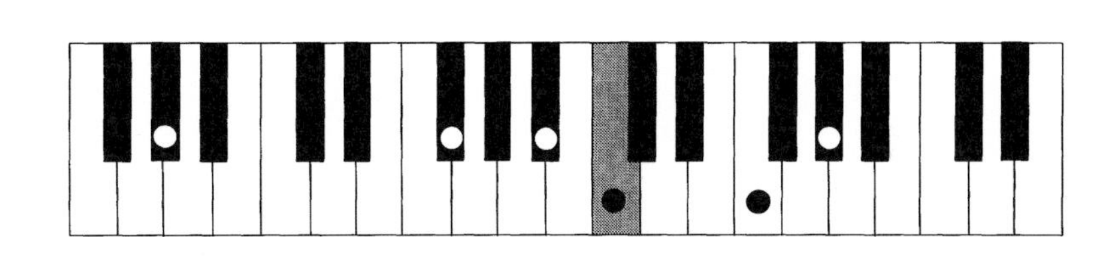

A♭ dominant 13th with flattened 9th - A♭13(♭9)

A♭ minor - A♭m

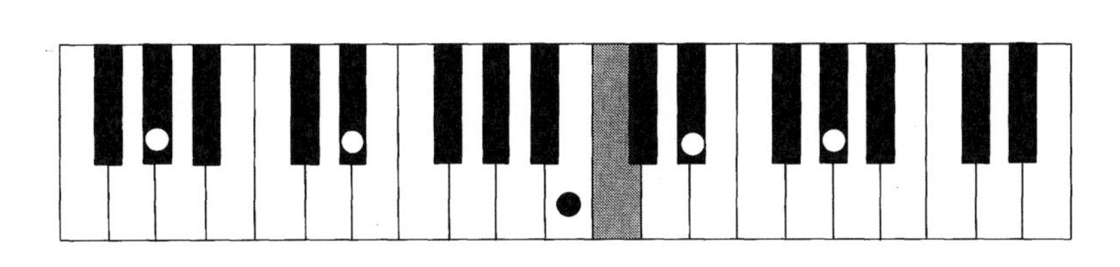

A♭ diminished - A♭° or A♭dim

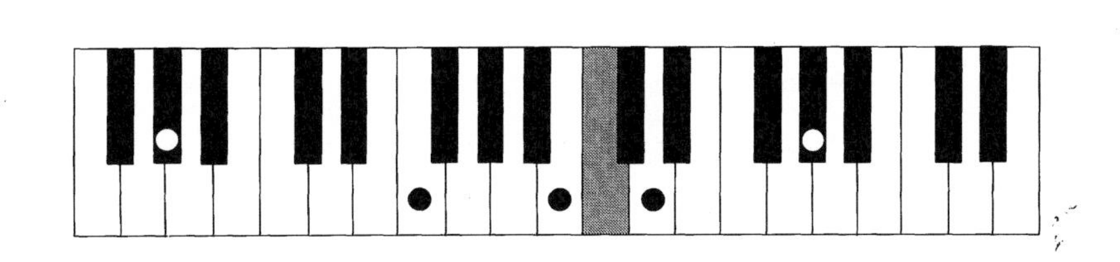

The G♯ Collection

G♯ minor added 6th - G♯m6

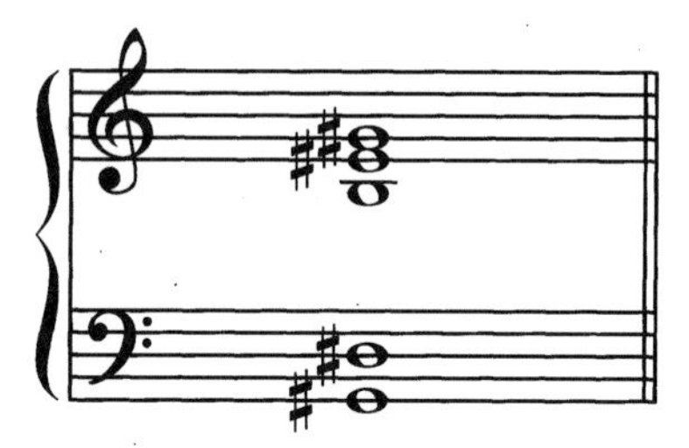

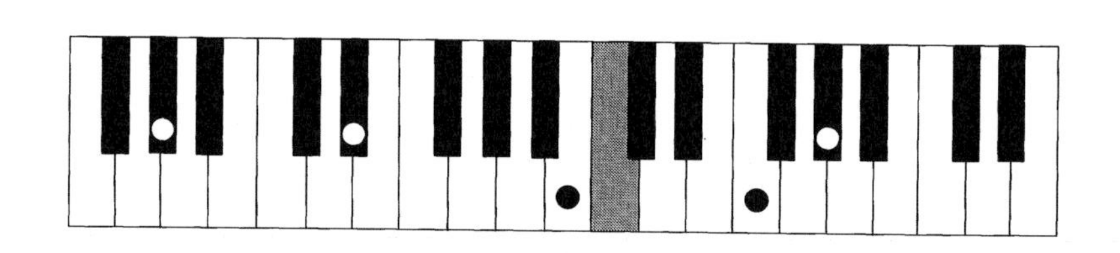

G♯ minor 7th - G♯m7

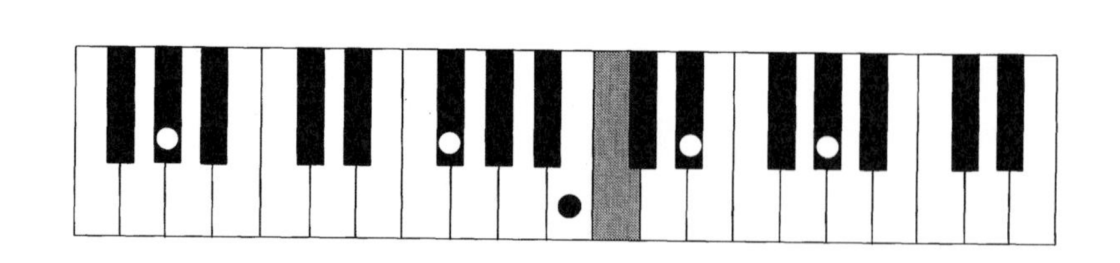

G♯ minor 7th with flattened 5th - G♯m7(♭5)

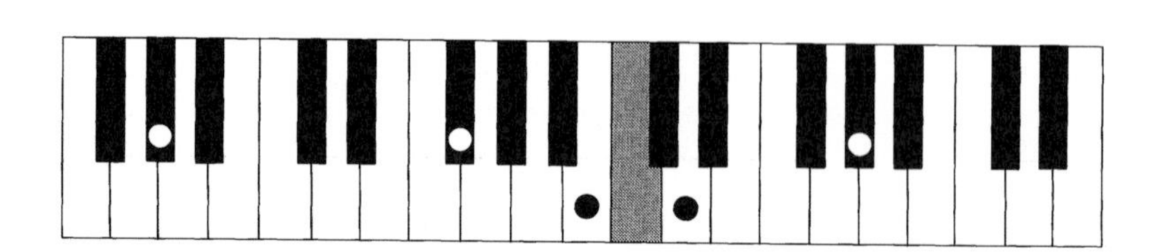

G♯ minor added major 7th - G♯m(maj7)

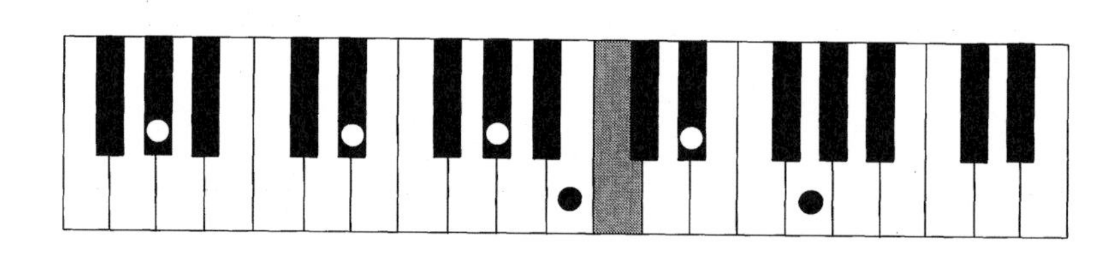

G♯ minor 9th - G♯m9

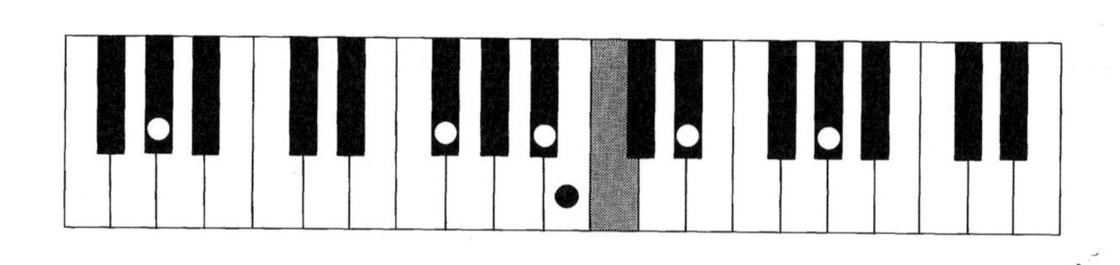

The A♭ Collection

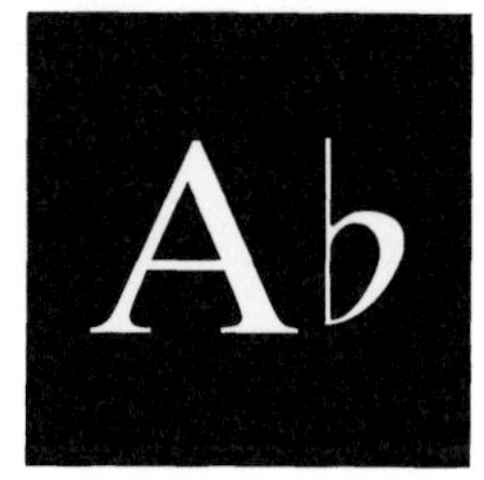

A♭ minor added 6th - A♭m6

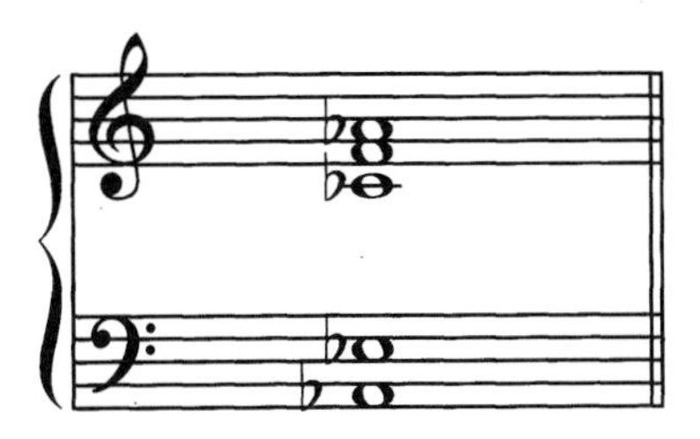

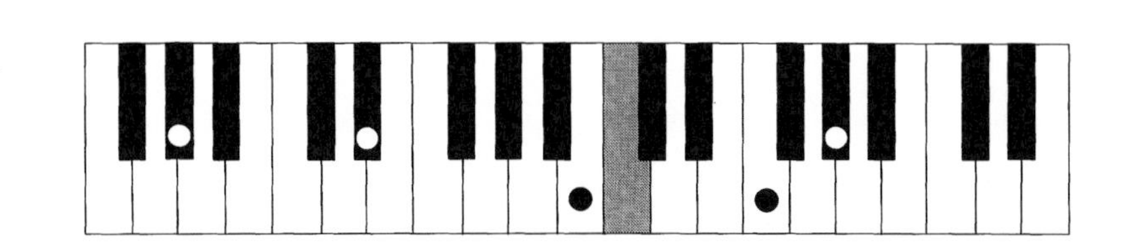

A♭ minor 7th - A♭m7

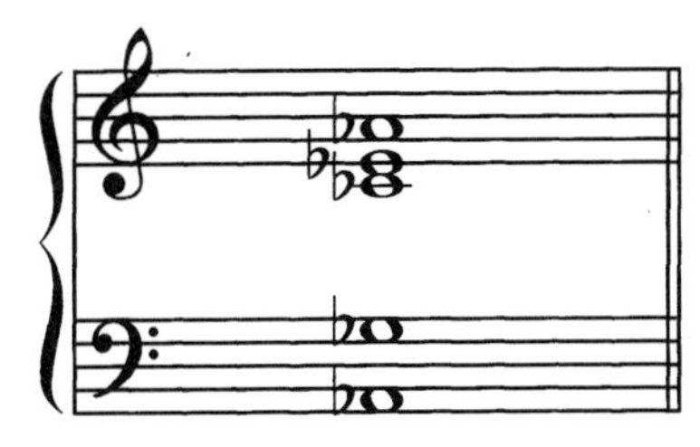

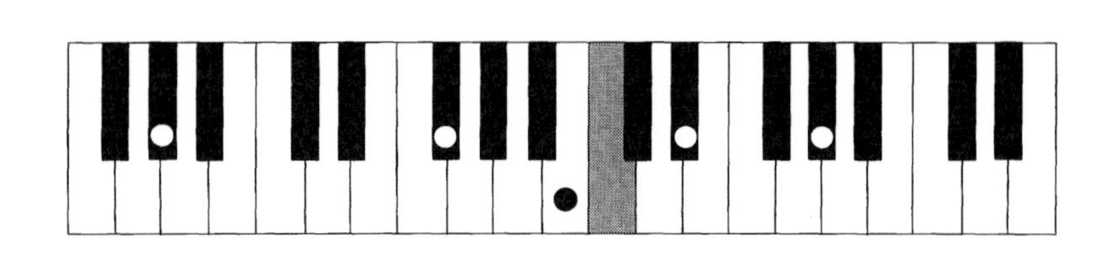

A♭ minor 7th with flattened 5th - A♭m7(♭5)

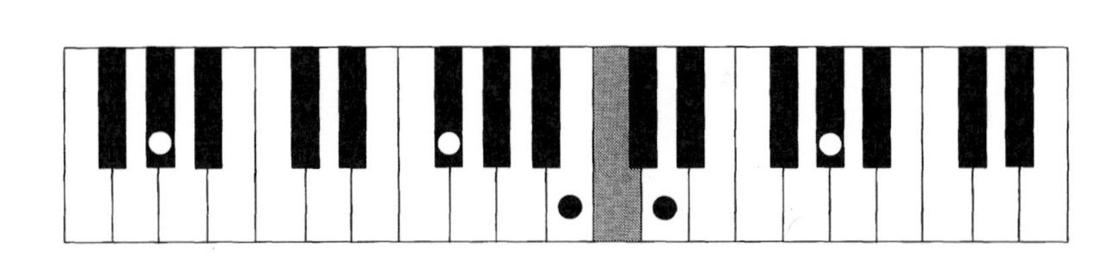

A♭ minor added major 7th - A♭m(maj7)

A♭ minor 9th - A♭m9

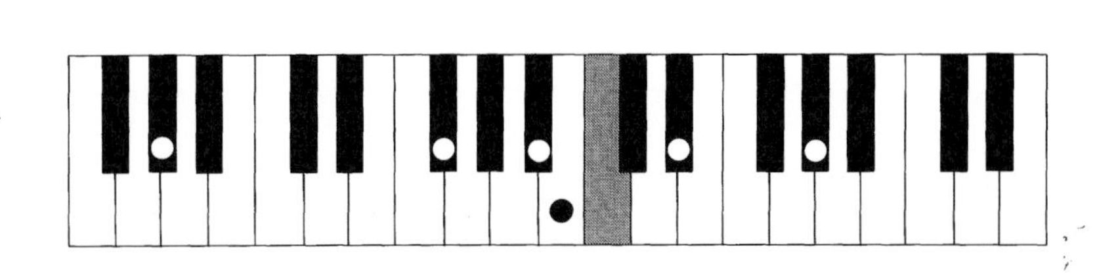

The A Collection

A major - A

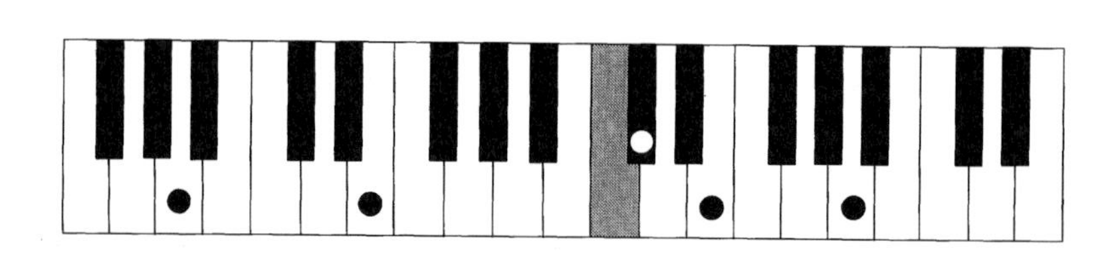

A suspended 4th - Asus or Asus4

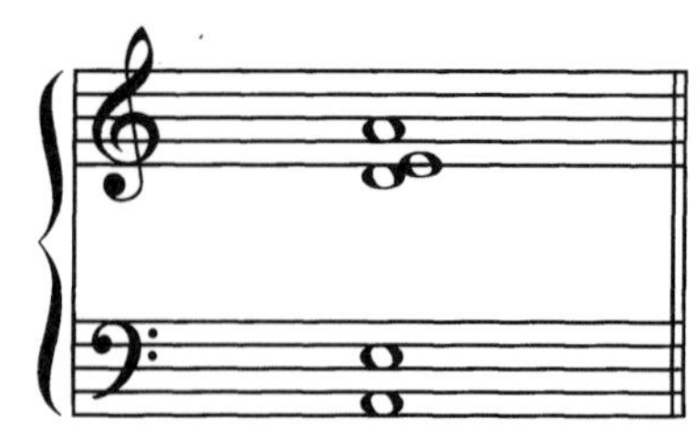

A augmented 5th - A+ or Aaug

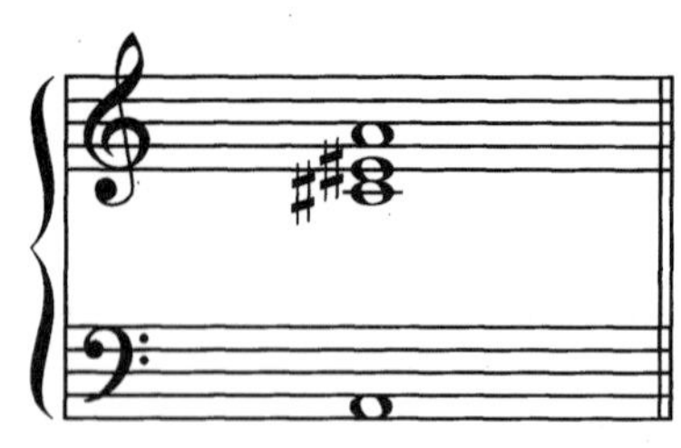

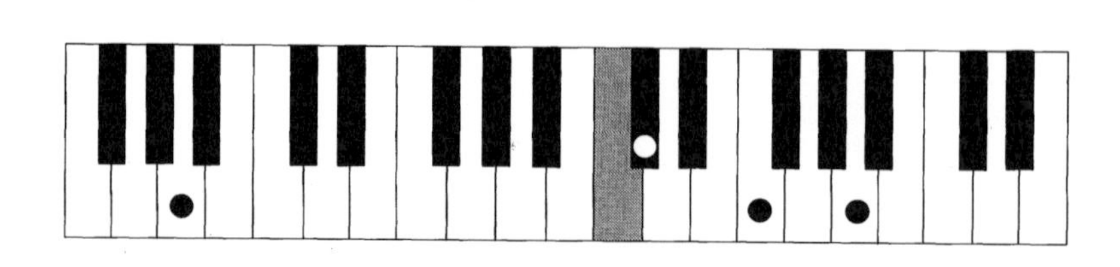

A added 6th - A6

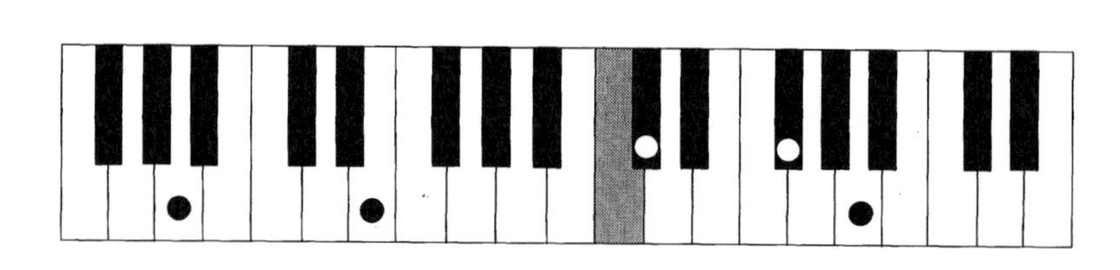

A added 6th and 9th - A6/9

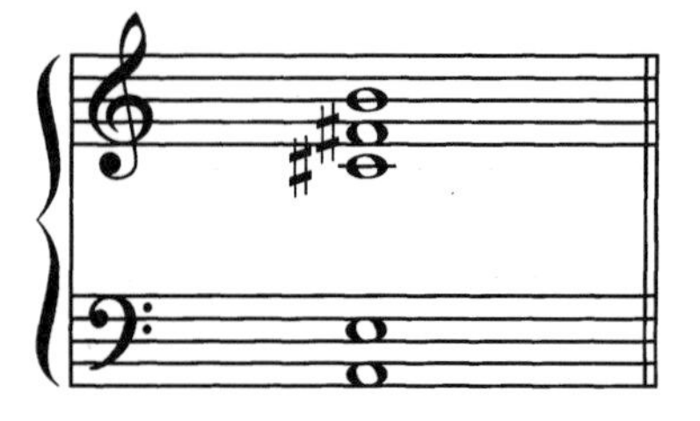

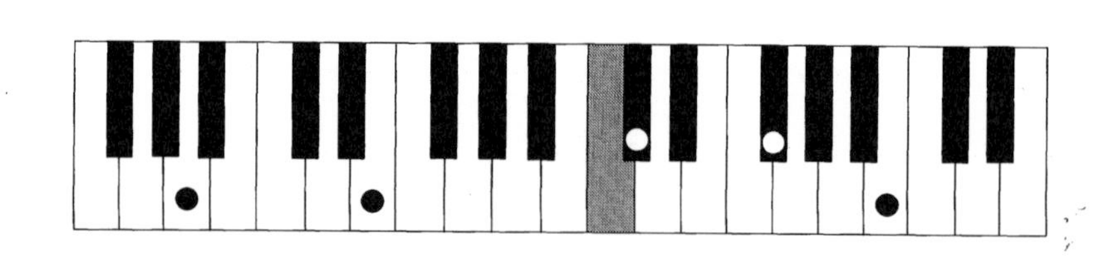

The A Collection

A major 7th - Amaj7

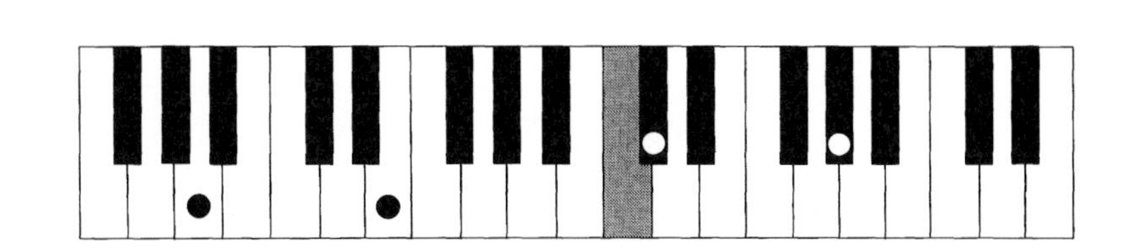

A dominant 7th - A7

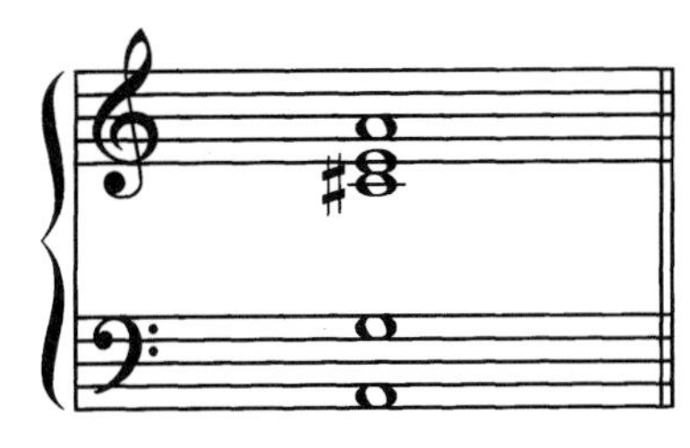

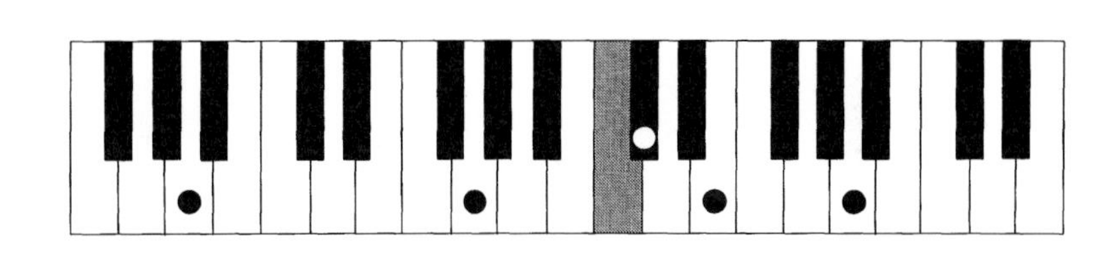

A dominant 7th with suspended 4th - A7sus or A7sus4

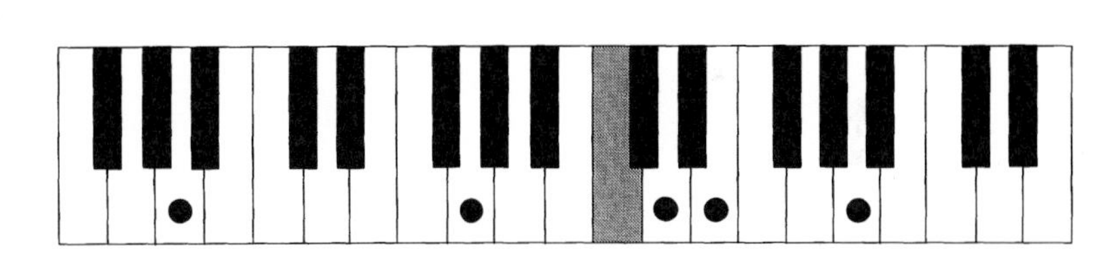

A dominant 7th with flattened 5th - A7(♭5)

A dominant 7th with augmented 5th - A7+ or A7aug

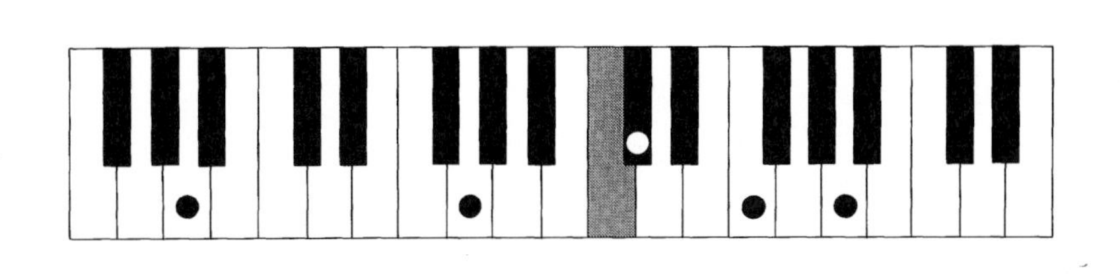

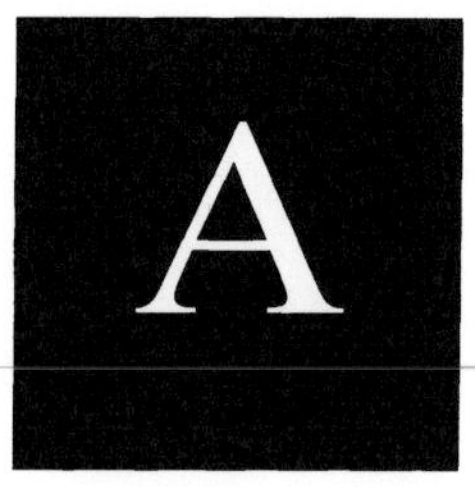

The A Collection

A dominant 7th with flattened 9th - A7(♭9)

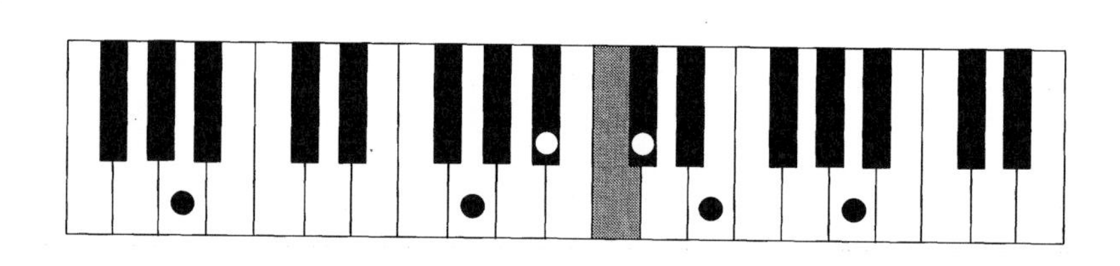

A dominant 7th with flattened 9th and 5th - A7(♭9/♭5)

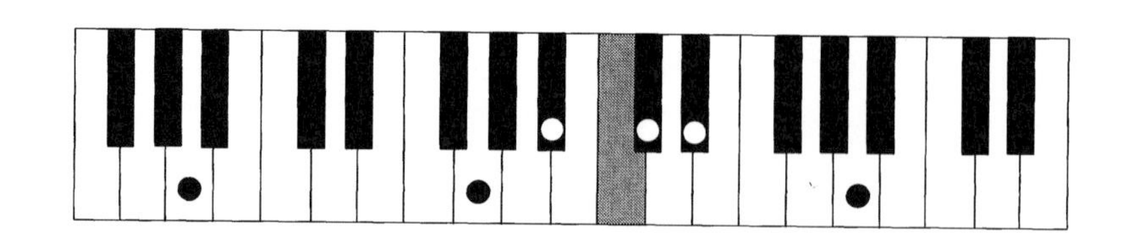

A dominant 7th with sharpened 9th - A7(♯9)

A added 9th - Aadd9

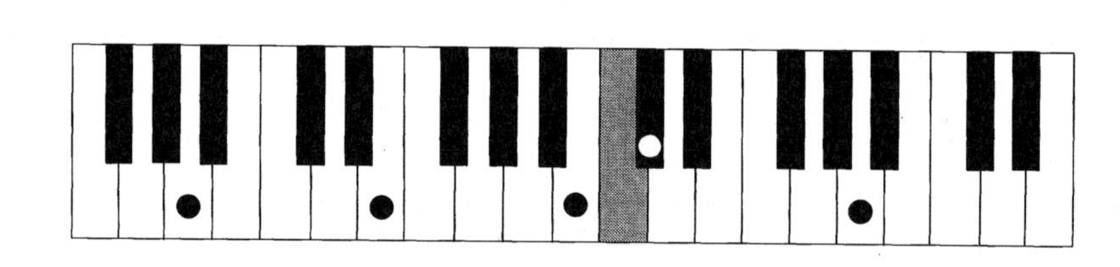

A major 9th - Amaj9

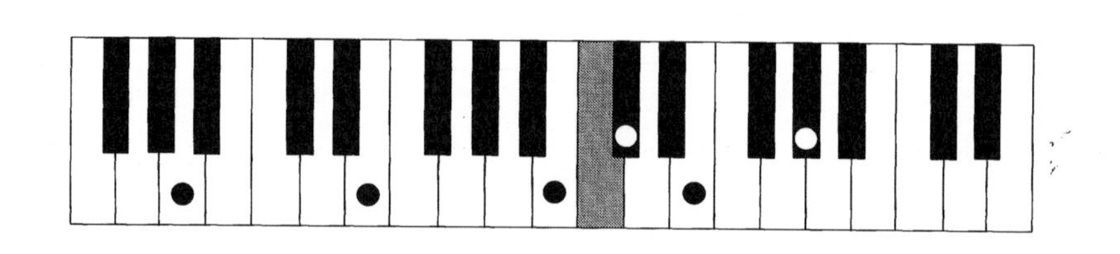

The A Collection

A dominant 9th - A9

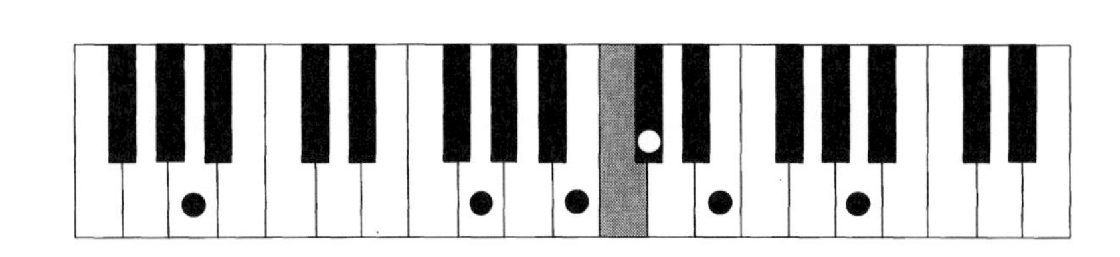

A dominant 9th with suspended 4th - A9sus or A9sus4

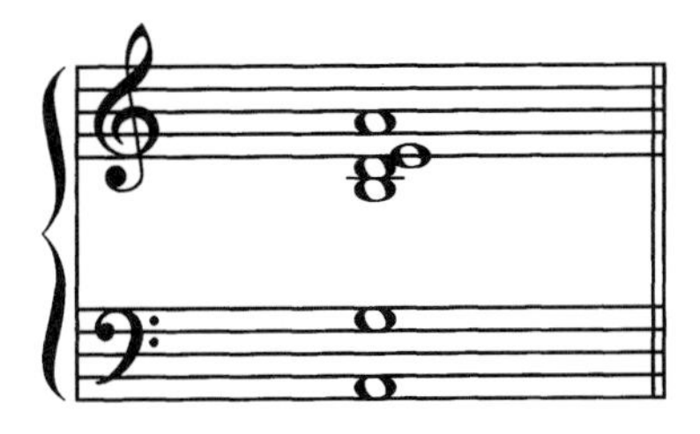

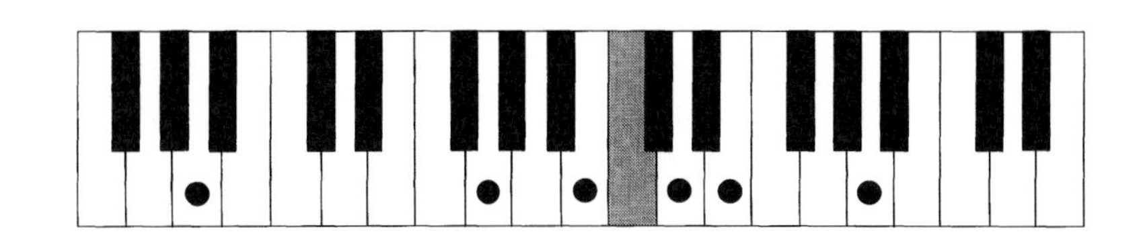

A dominant 9th with augmented 5th - A9+ or A9aug

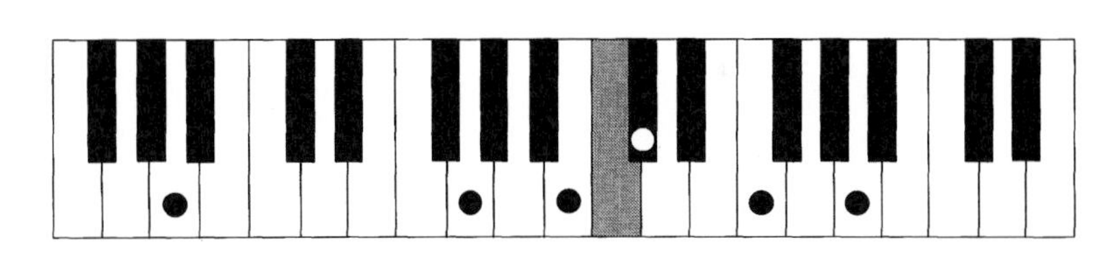

A dominant 9th with sharpened 11th - A9(♯11)
with flattened 5th - A9(♭5)

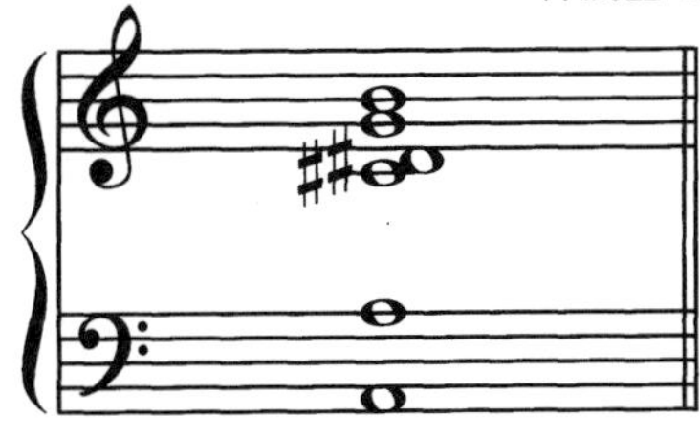

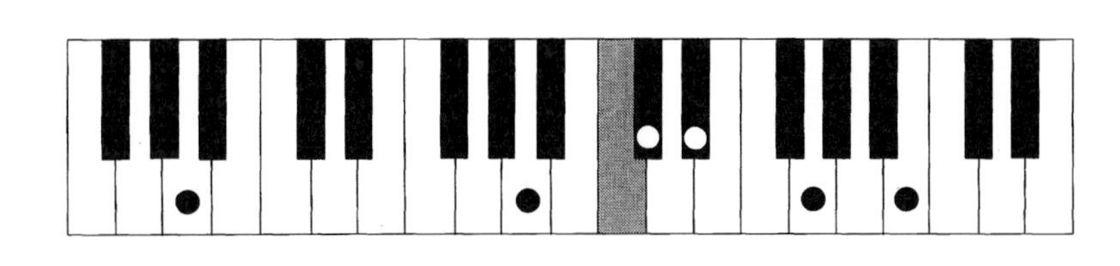

A dominant 11th - A11

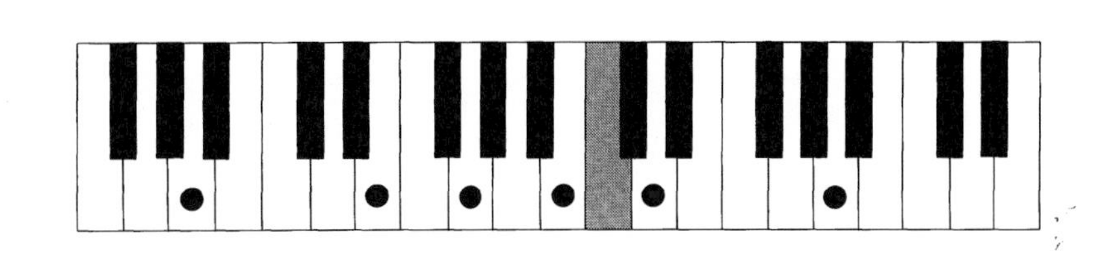

The A Collection

A dominant 11th with flattened 9th - A11(♭9)

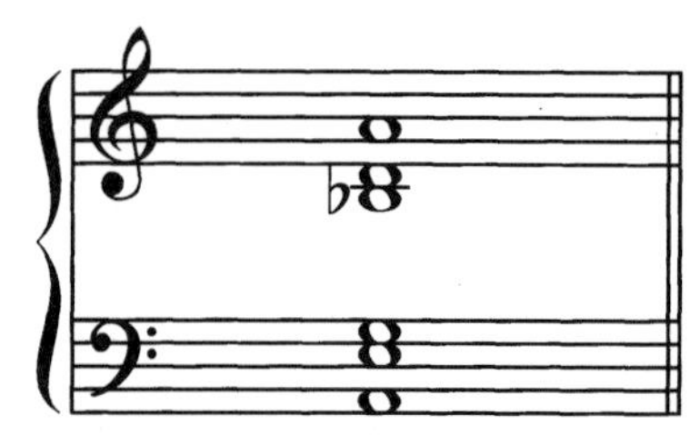

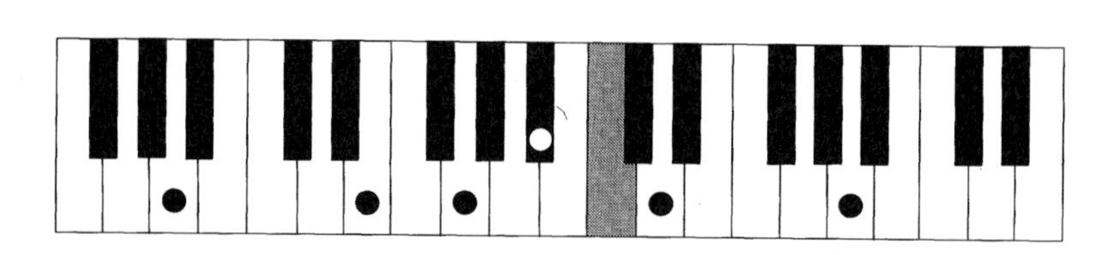

A dominant 13th - A13

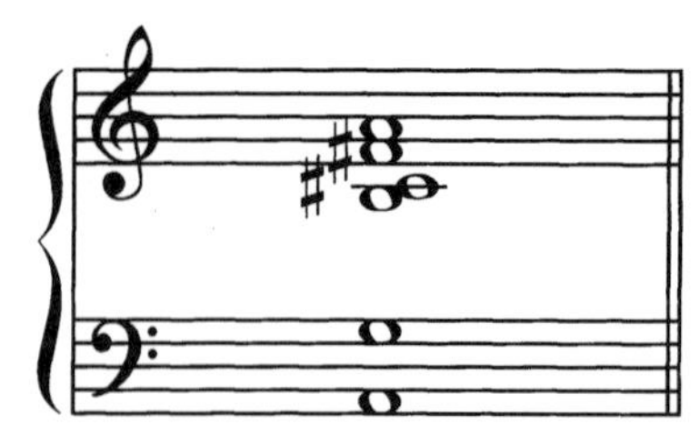

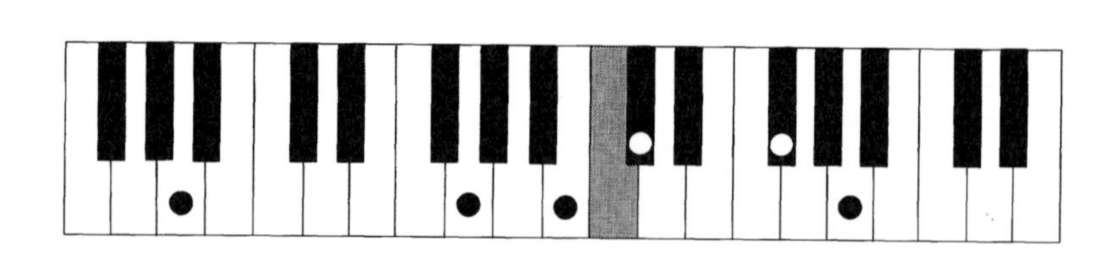

A dominant 13th with flattened 9th - A13(♭9)

A minor - Am

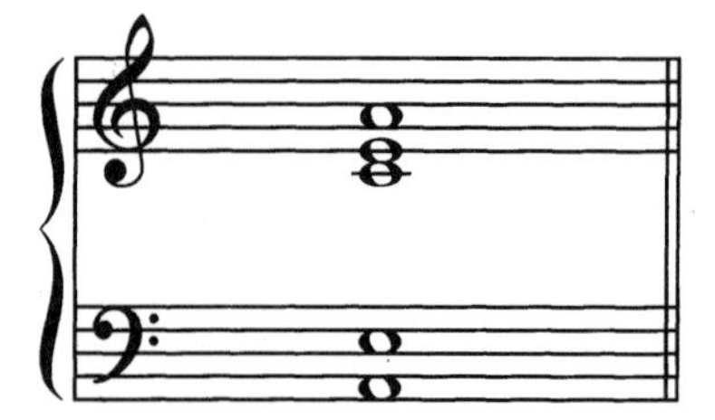

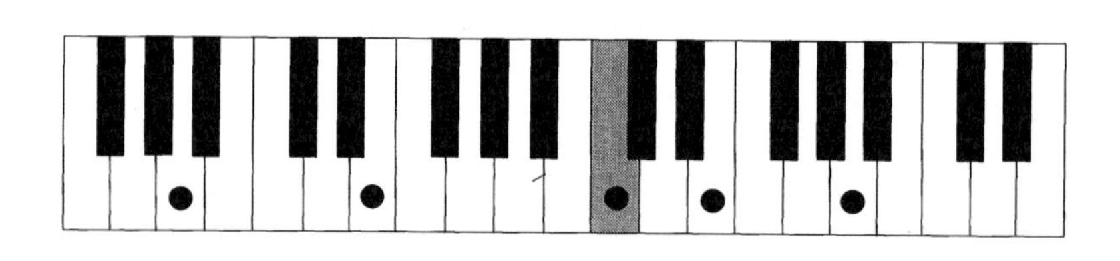

A diminished - A° or Adim

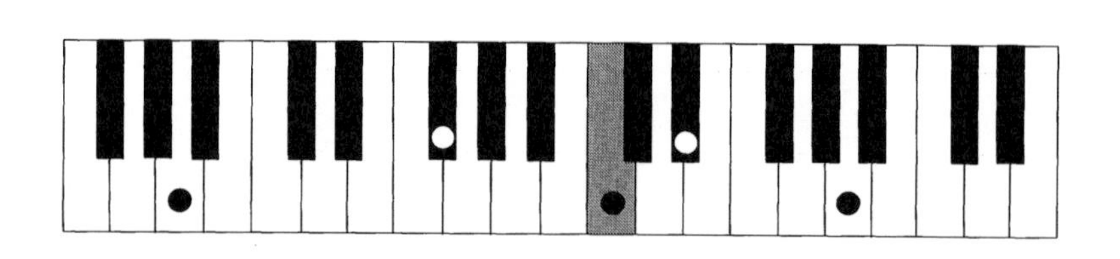

The A Collection

A minor added 6th - Am6

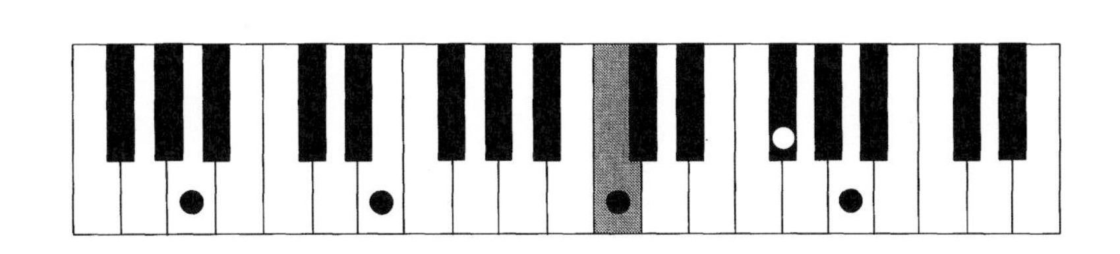

A minor 7th - Am7

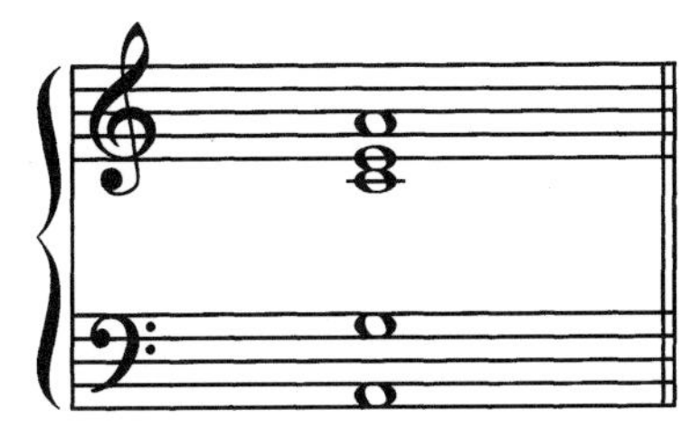

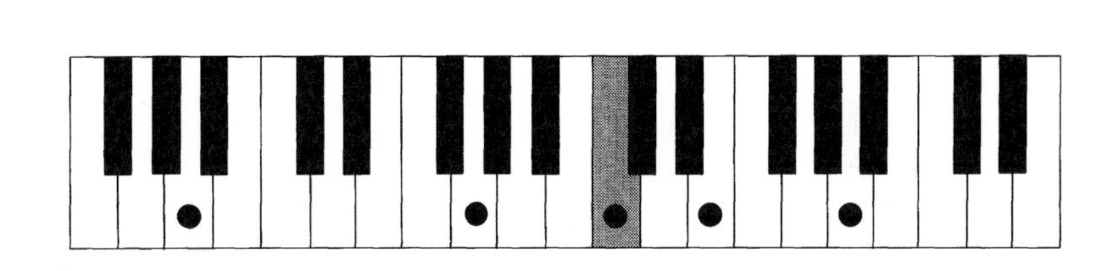

A minor 7th with flattened 5th - Am7(♭5)

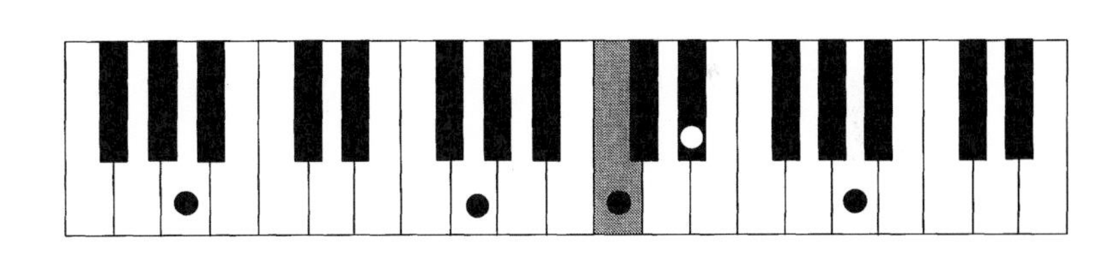

A minor added major 7th - Am(maj7)

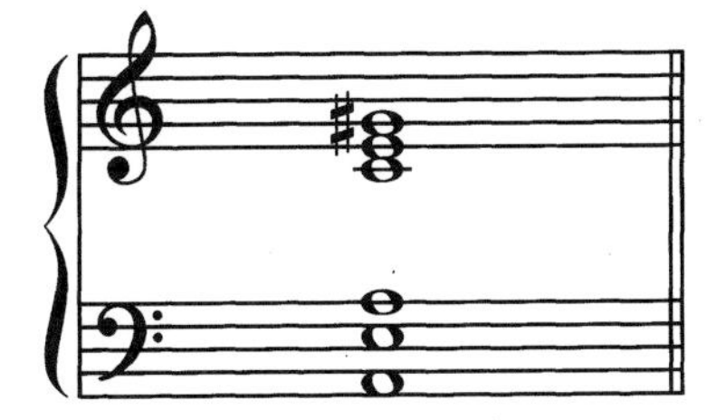

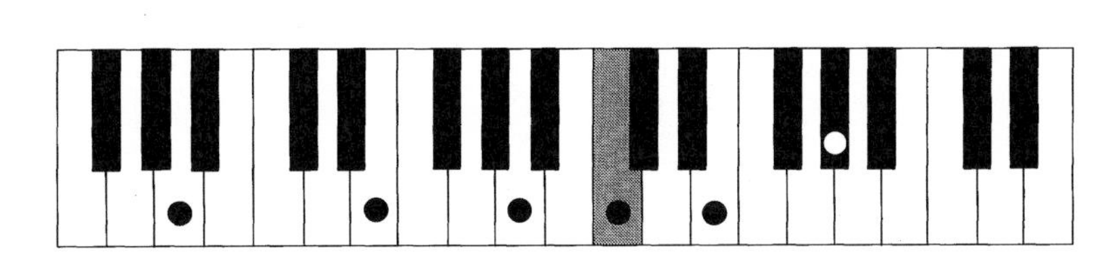

A minor 9th - Am9

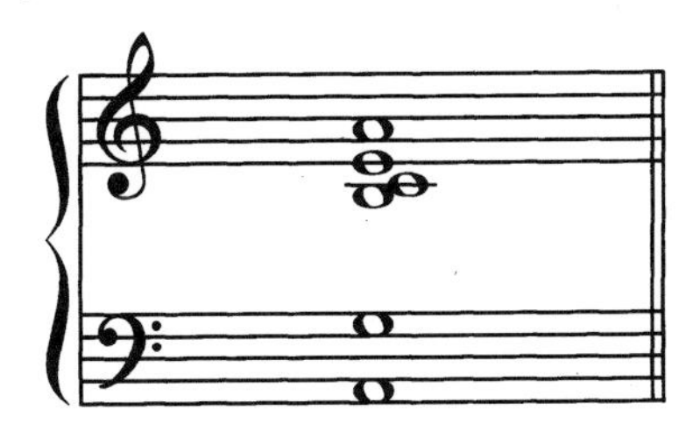

The B♭ Collection

B♭ major - B♭

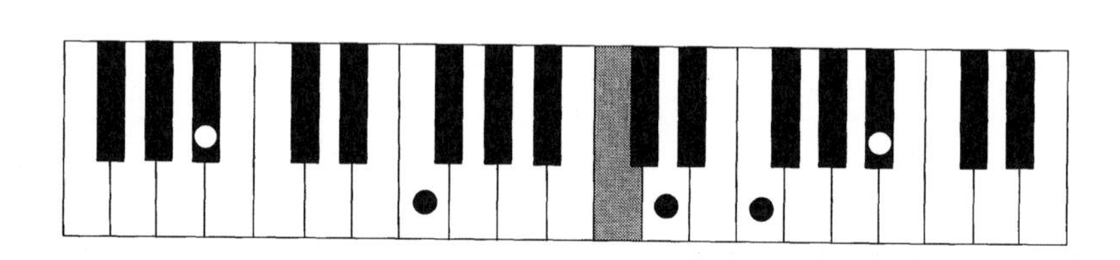

B♭ suspended 4th - B♭sus or B♭sus4

B♭ augmented 5th - B♭+ or B♭aug

B♭ added 6th - B♭6

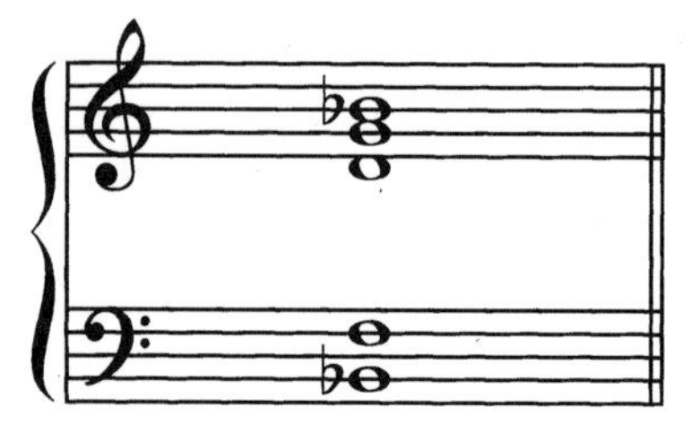

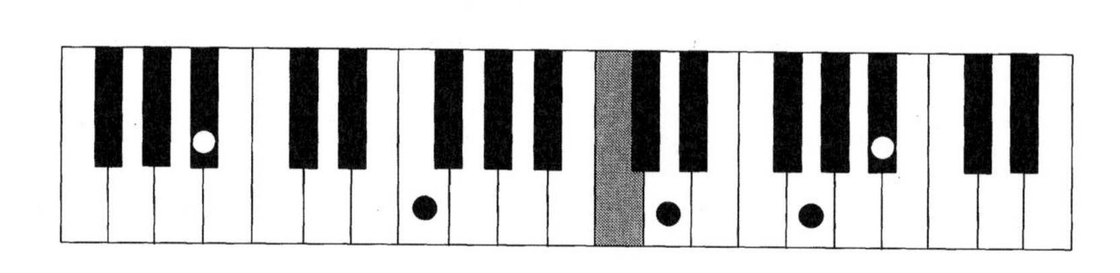

B♭ added 6th and 9th - B♭6/9

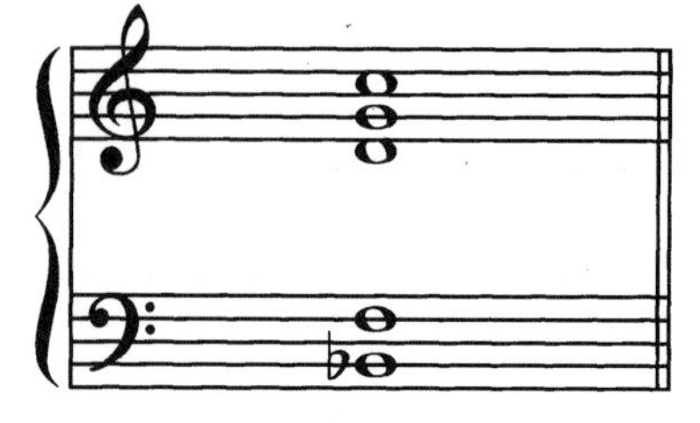

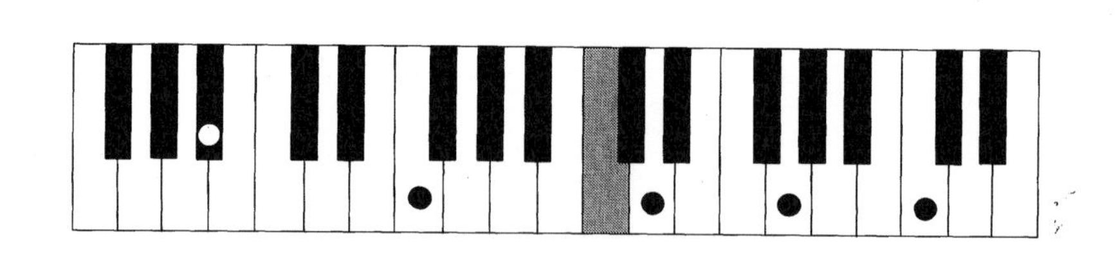

The B♭ Collection

B♭ major 7th - B♭maj7

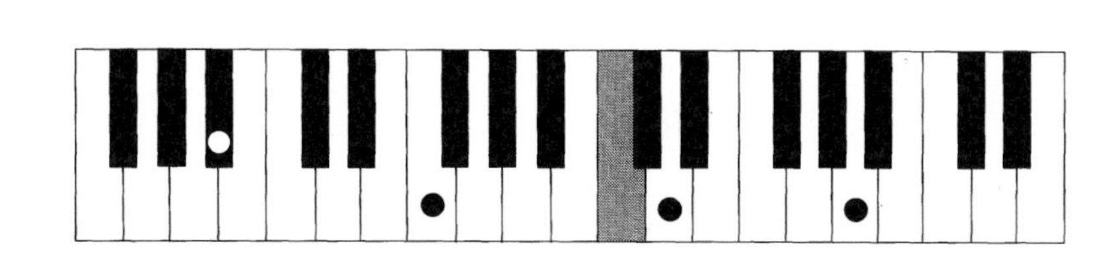

B♭ dominant 7th - B♭7

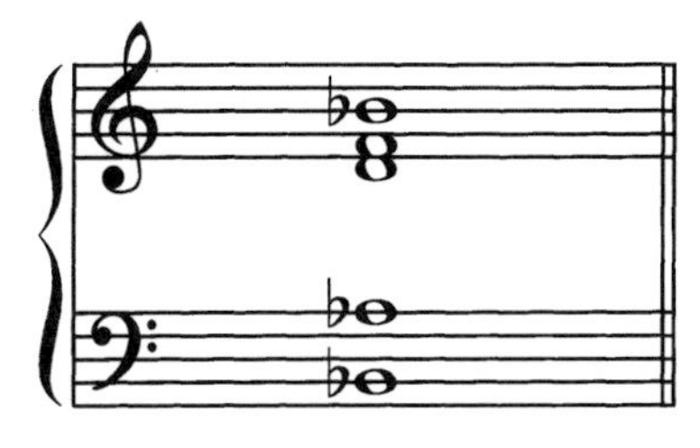

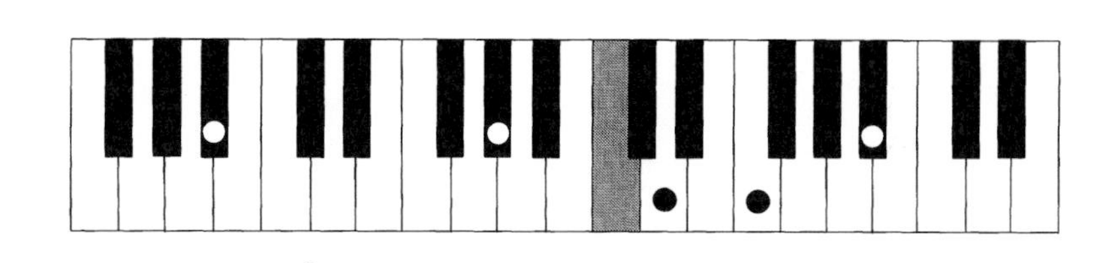

B♭ dominant 7th with suspended 4th - B♭7sus or B♭7sus4

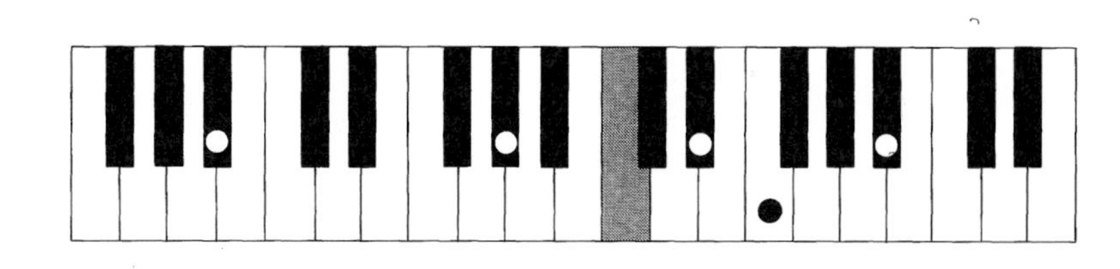

B♭ dominant 7th with flattened 5th - B♭7(♭5)

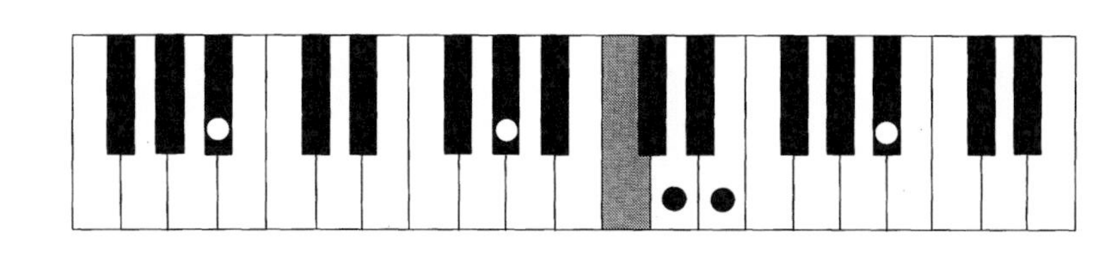

B♭ dominant 7th with augmented 5th - B♭7+ or B♭aug

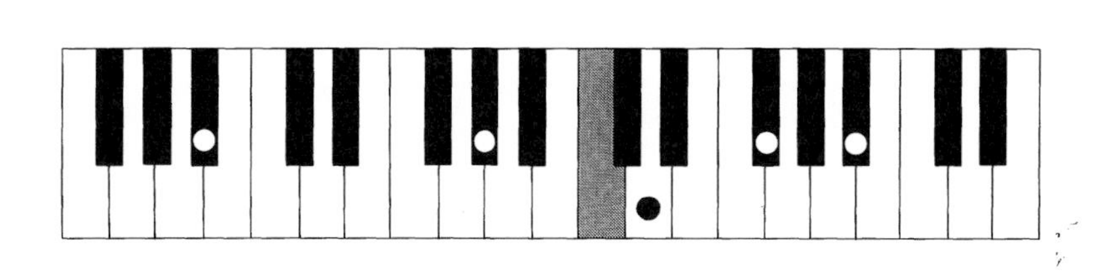

The B♭ Collection

B♭ dominant 7th with flattened 9th - B♭7(♭9)

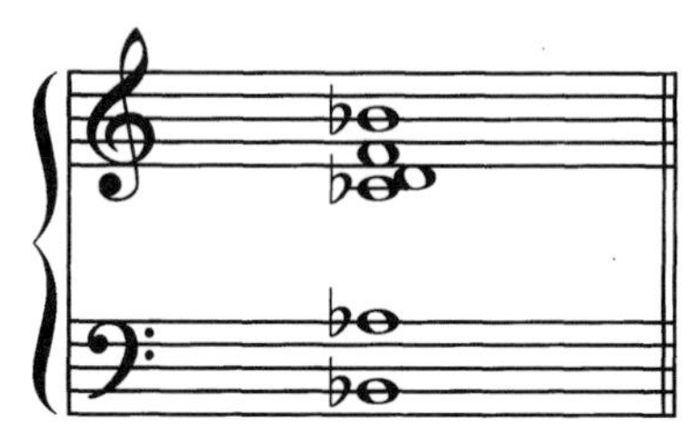

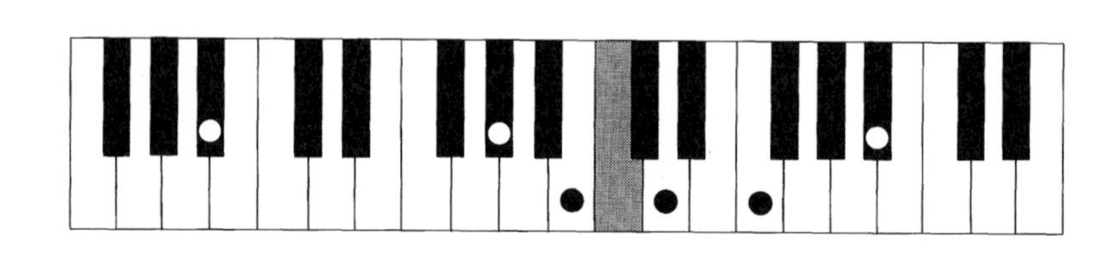

B♭ dominant 7th with flattened 9th and 5th - B♭7(♭9/♭5)

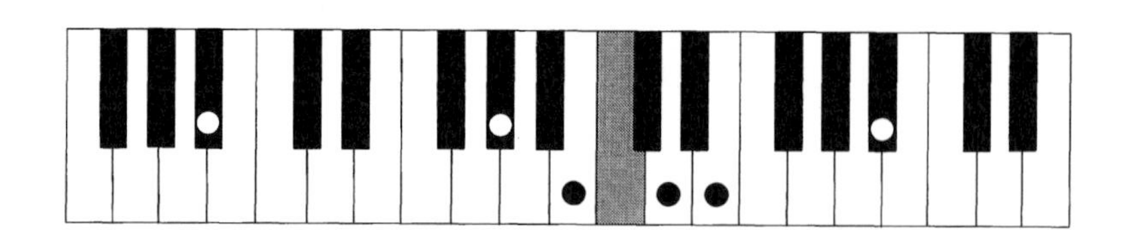

B♭ dominant 7th with sharpened 9th - B♭7(♯9)

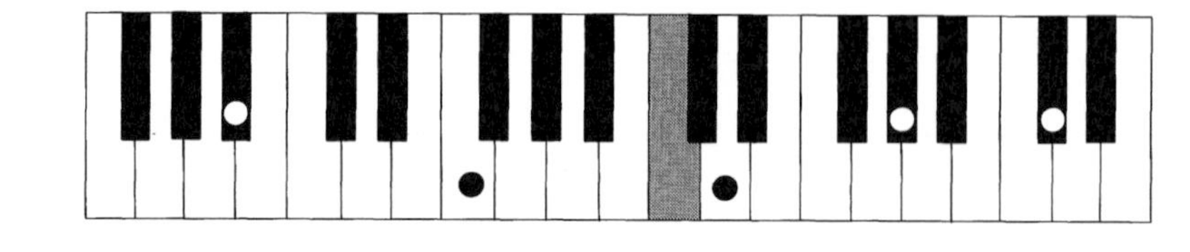

B♭ added 9th - B♭add9

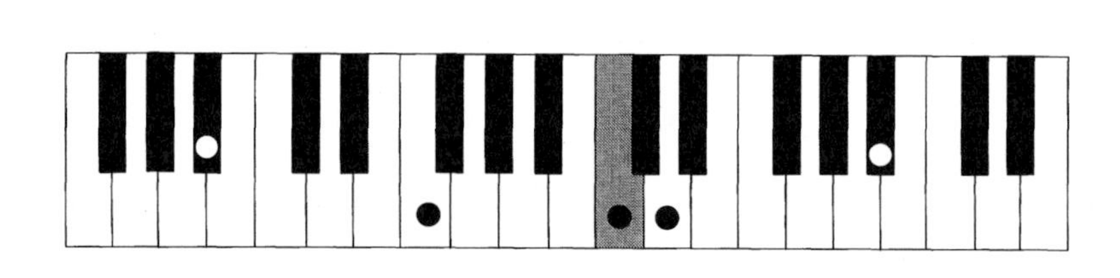

B♭ major 9th - B♭maj9

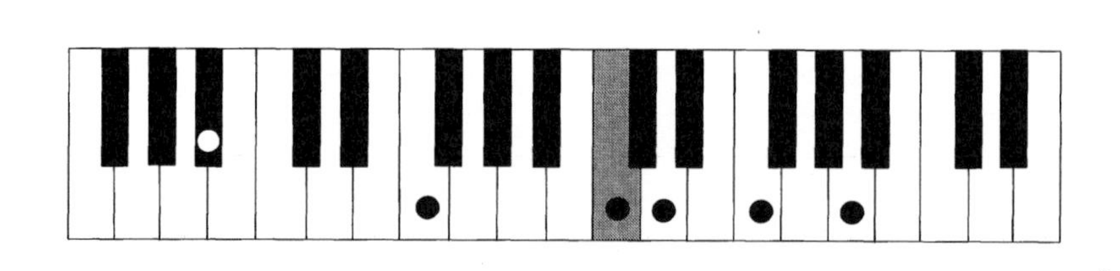

The B♭ Collection

B♭ dominant 9th - B♭9

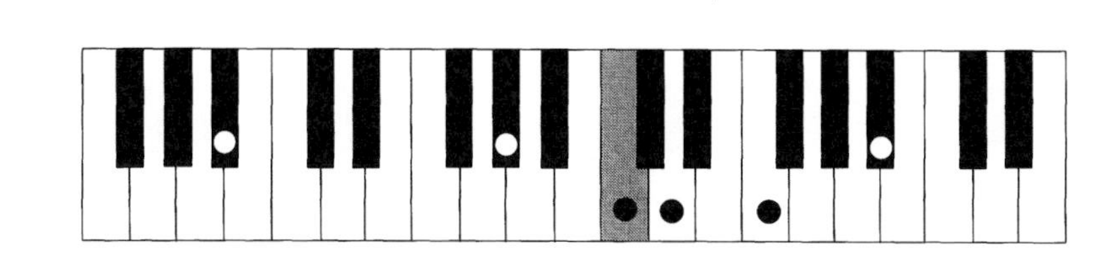

B♭ dominant 9th with suspended 4th - B♭9sus or B♭9sus4

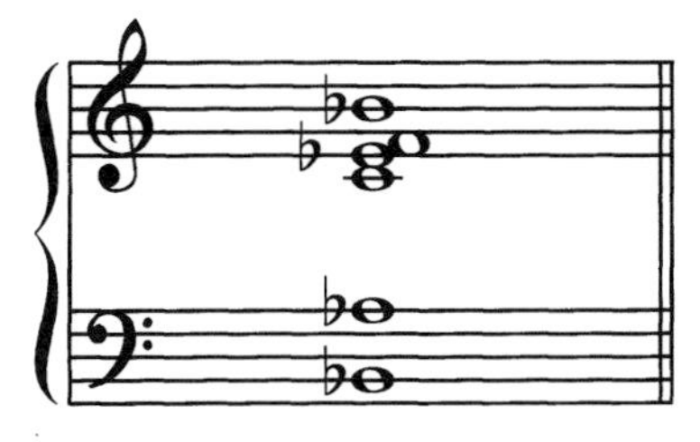

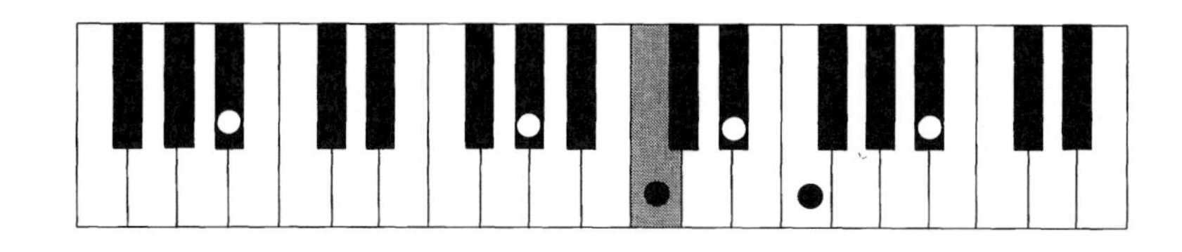

B♭ dominant 9th with augmented 5th - B♭9+ or B♭9aug

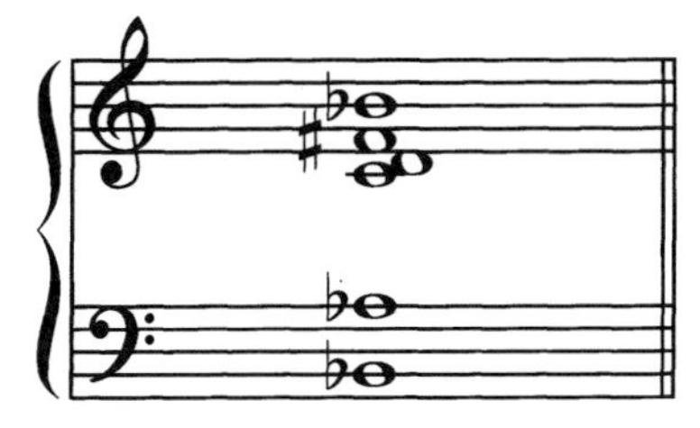

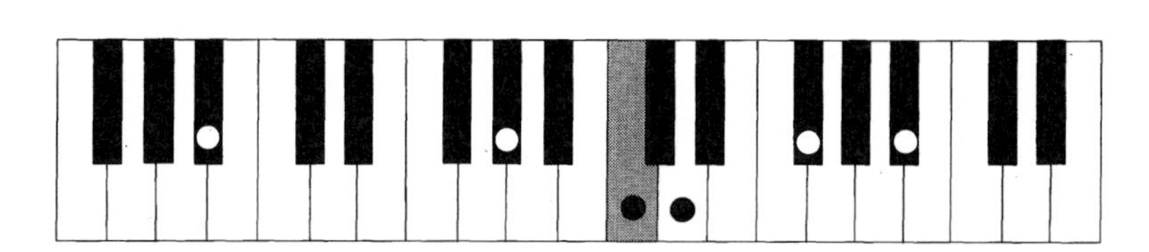

B♭ dominant 9th with sharpened 11th - B♭9(♯11)
with flattened 5th - B♭9(♭5)

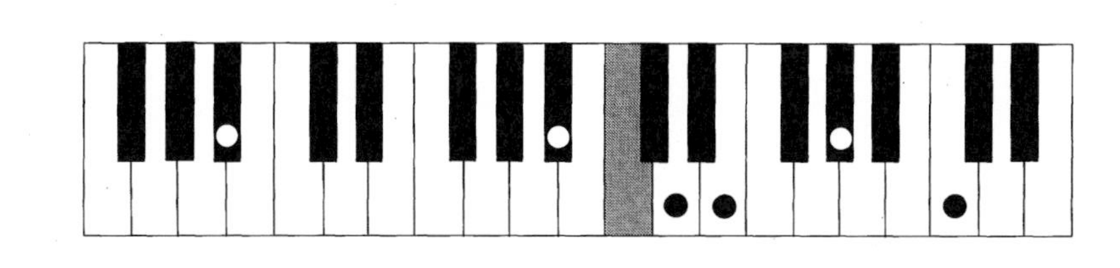

B♭ dominant 11th - B♭11

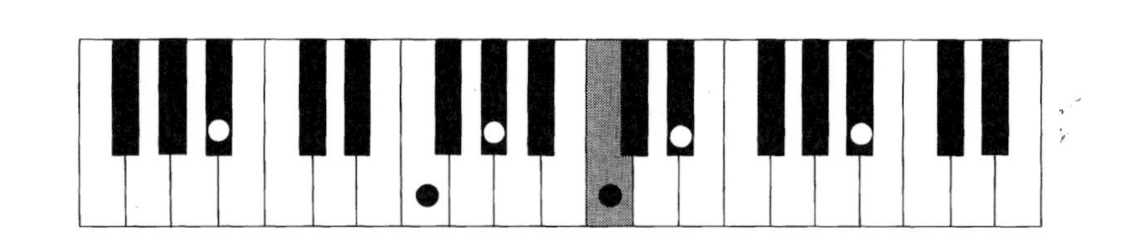

The B♭ Collection

B♭ dominant 11th with flattened 9th - B♭11(♭9)

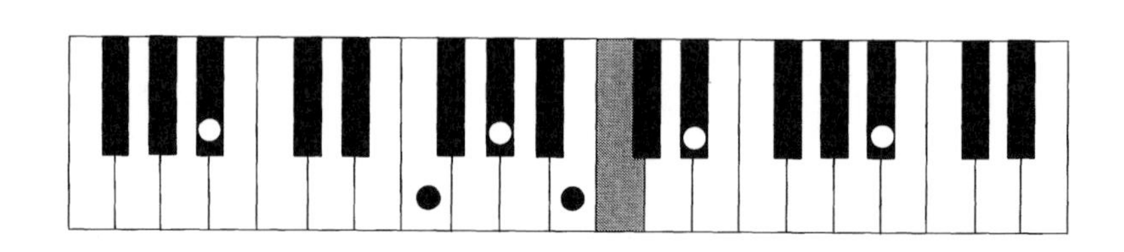

B♭ dominant 13th - B♭13

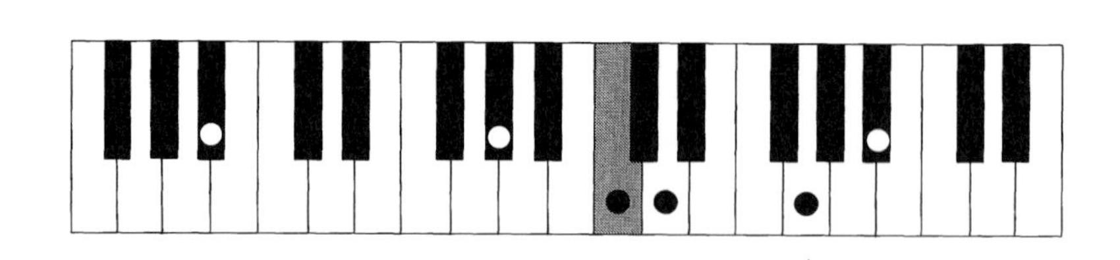

B♭ dominant 13th with flattened 9th - B♭13(♭9)

B♭ minor - B♭m

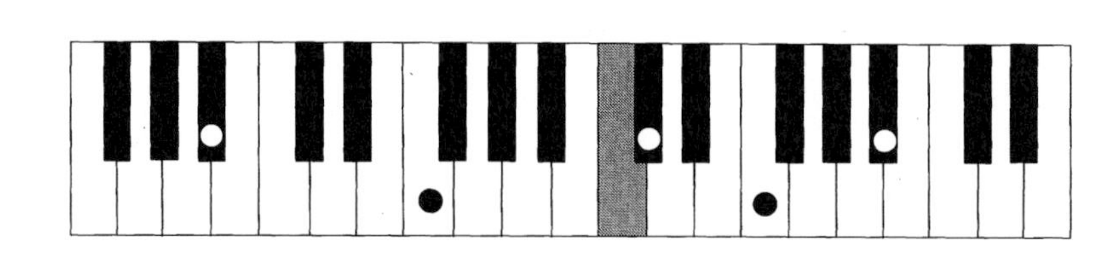

B♭ diminished - B♭° or B♭dim

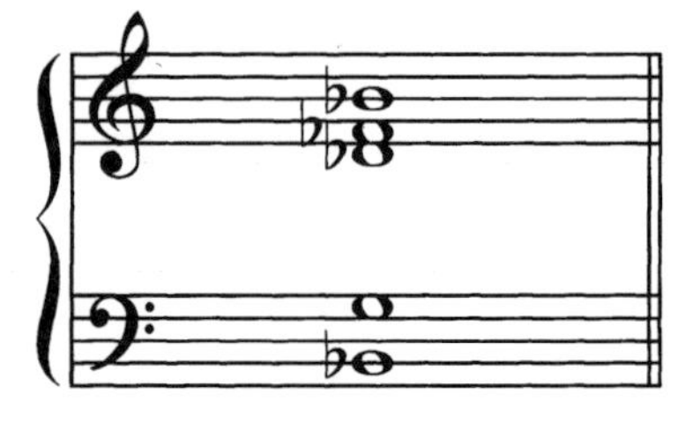

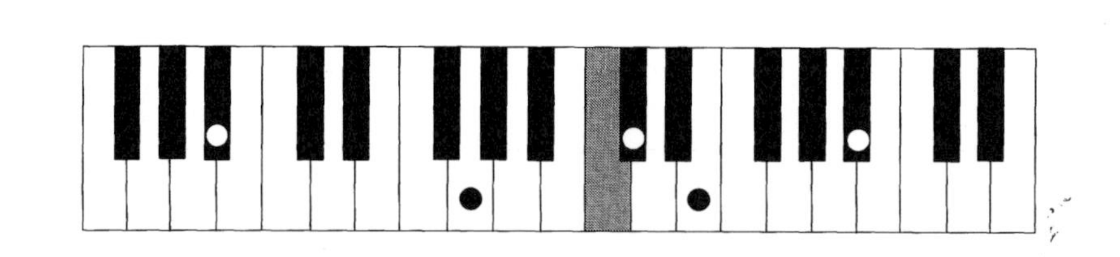

The B♭ Collection

B♭ minor added 6th - B♭m6

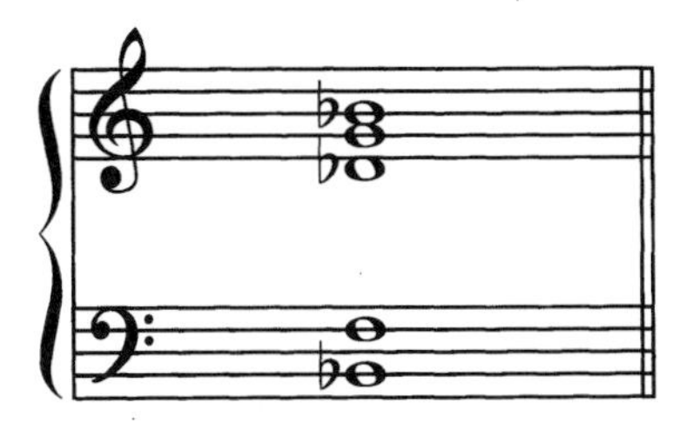

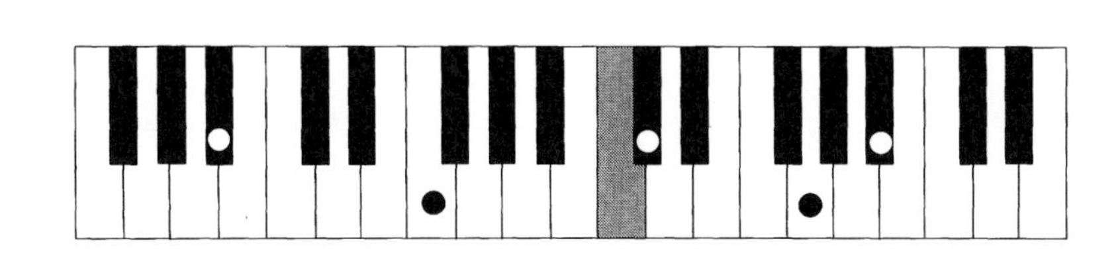

B♭ minor 7th - B♭m7

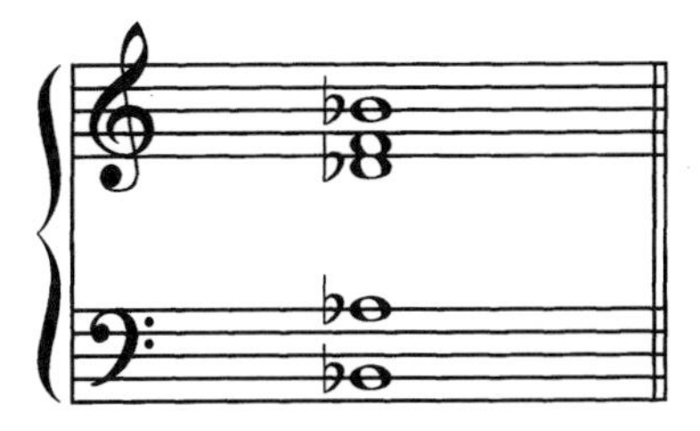

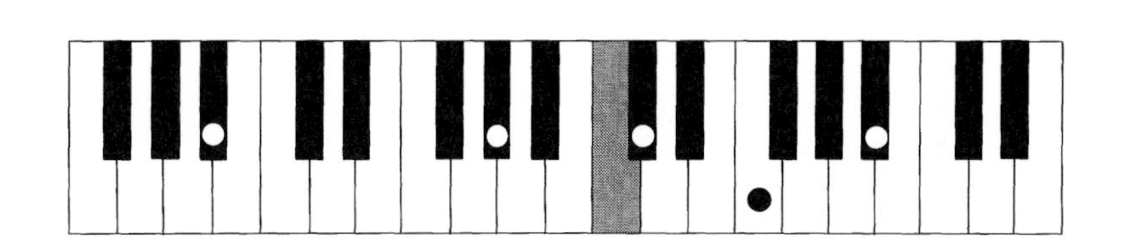

B♭ minor 7th with flattened 5th - B♭m7(♭5)

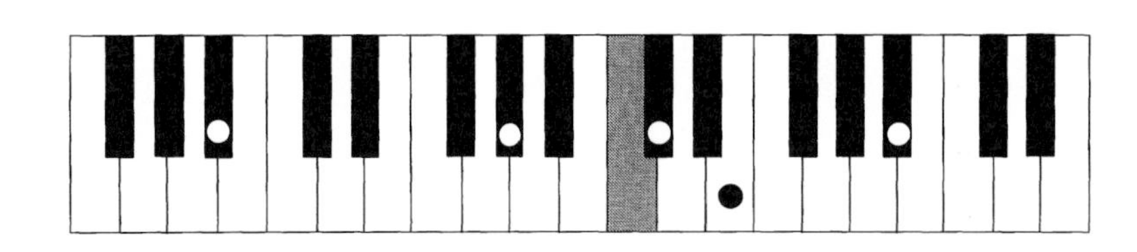

B♭ minor added major 7th - B♭m(maj7)

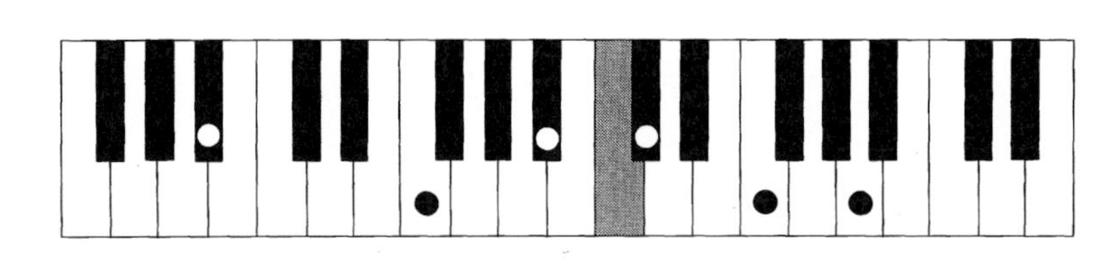

B♭ minor 9th - B♭m9

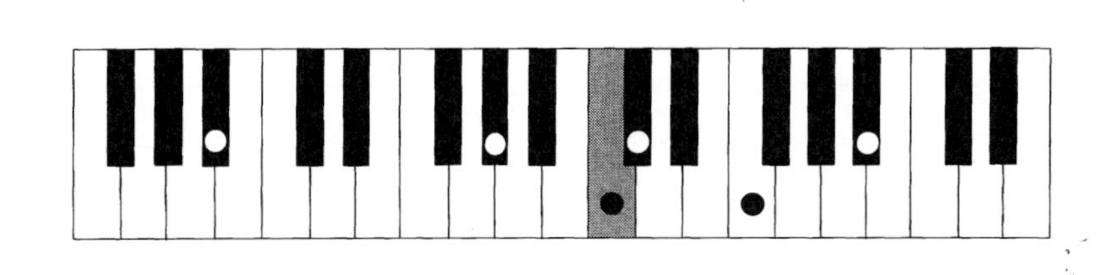

The B Collection

B major - B

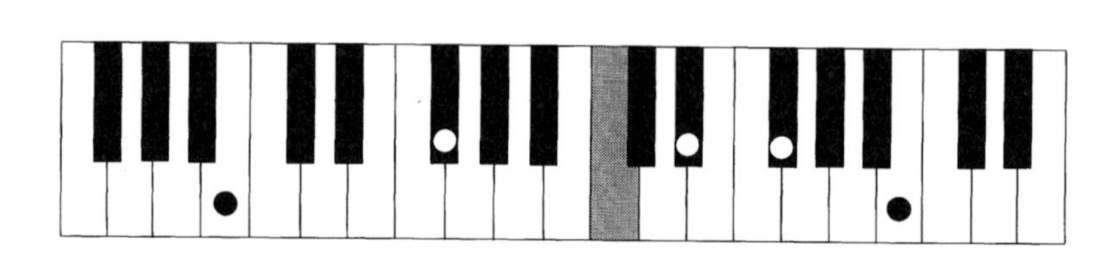

B suspended 4th - Bsus or Bsus4

B augmented 5th - B+ or Baug

B added 6th - B6

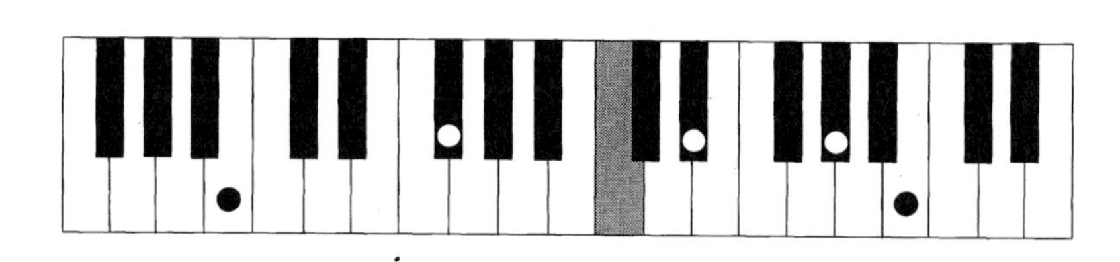

B added 6th and 9th - B6/9

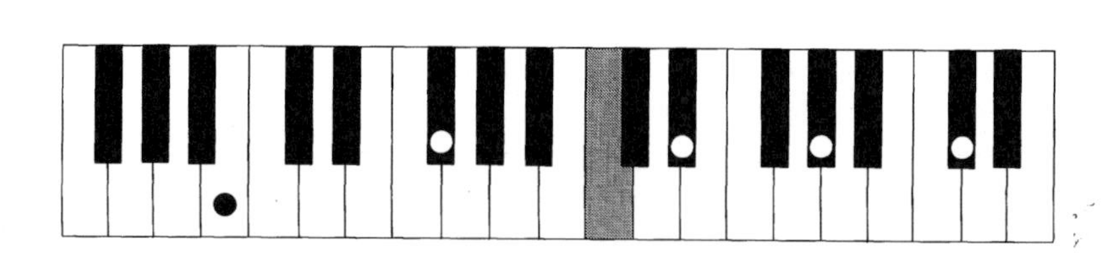

The B Collection

B major 7th - Bmaj7

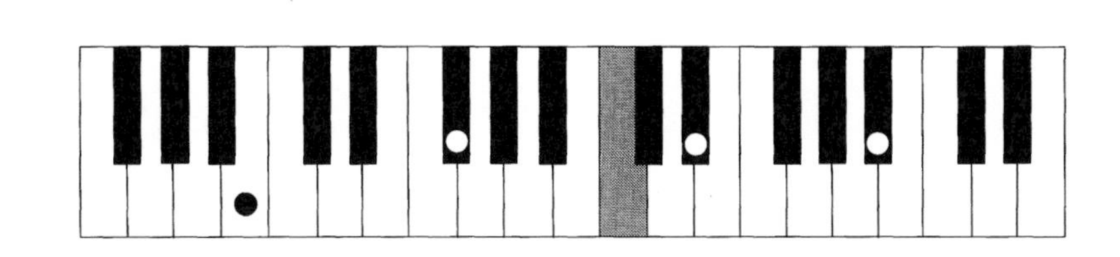

B dominant 7th - B7

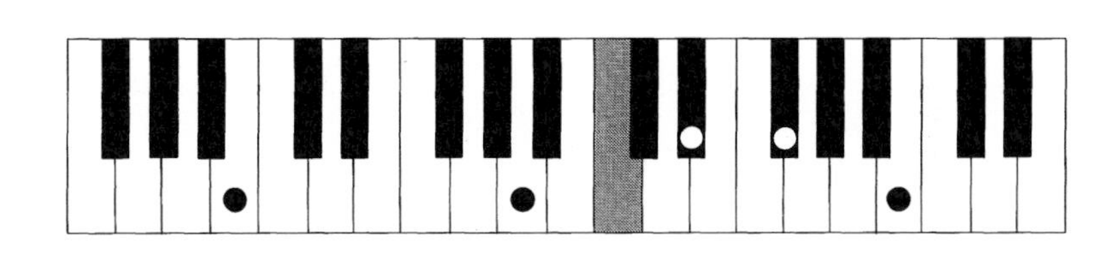

B dominant 7th with suspended 4th - B7sus or B7sus4

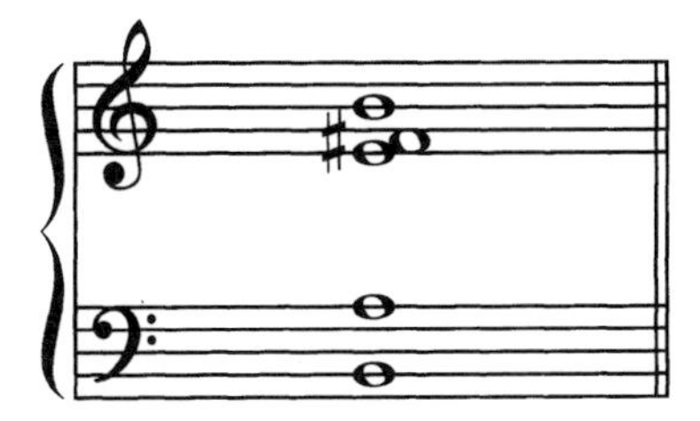

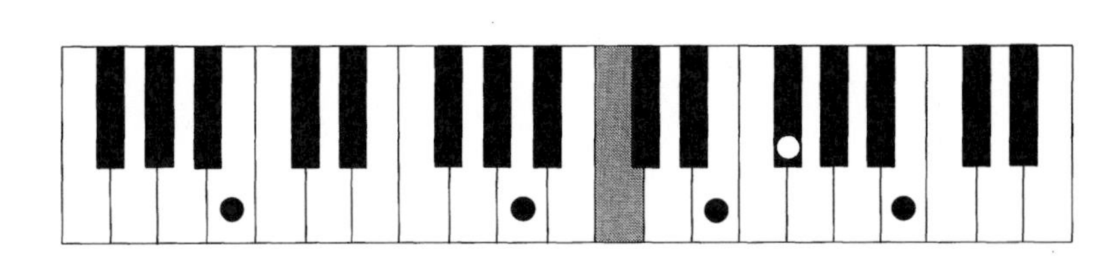

B dominant 7th with flattened 5th - B7(♭5)

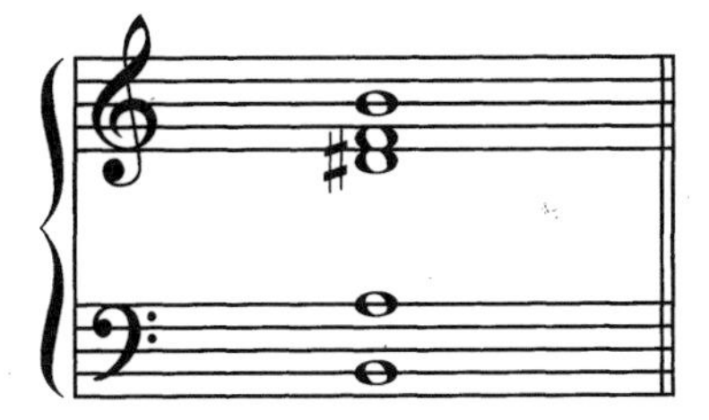

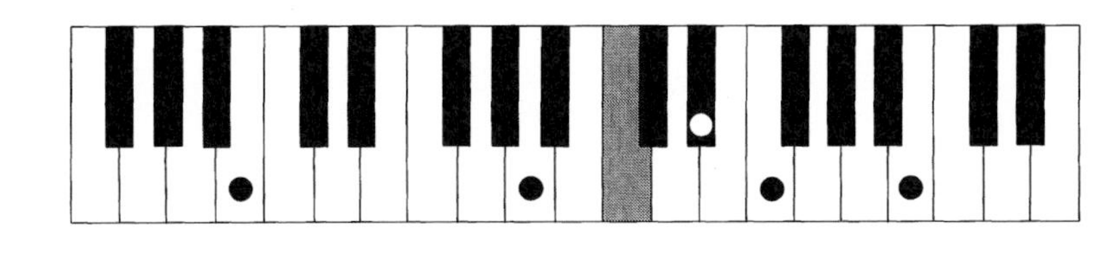

B dominant 7th with augmented 5th - B7+ or B7aug

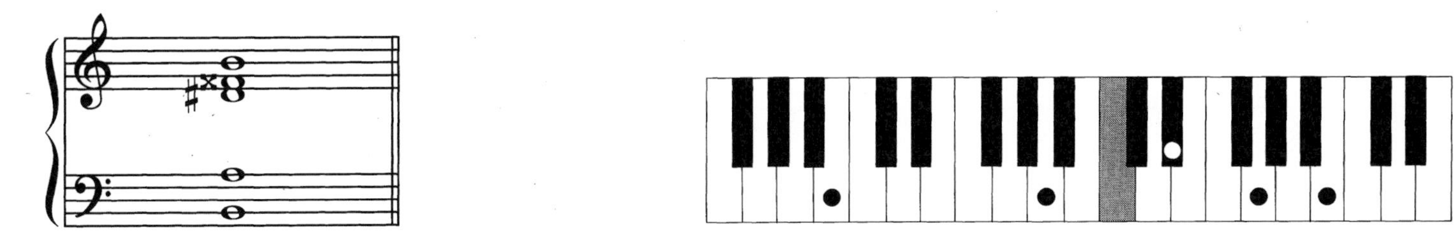

The B Collection

B dominant 7th with flattened 9th - B7(♭9)

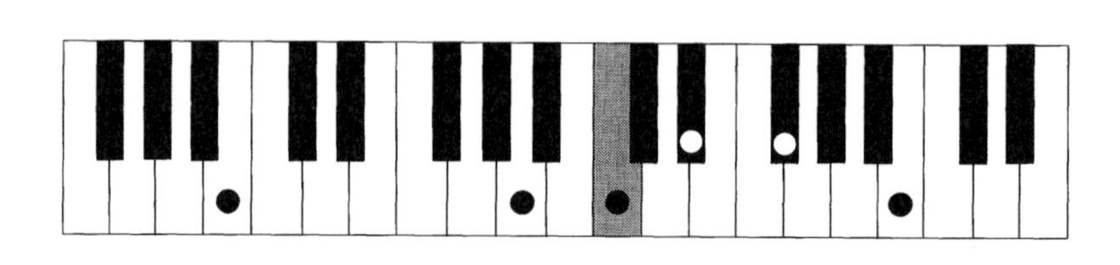

B dominant 7th with flattened 9th and 5th - B7(♭9/♭5)

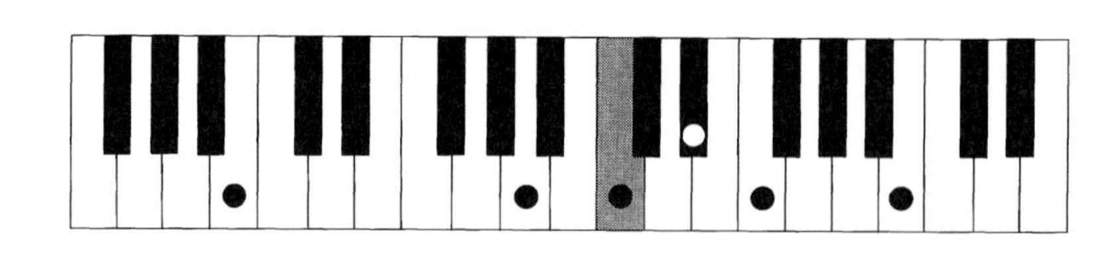

B dominant 7th with sharpened 9th - B7(♯9)

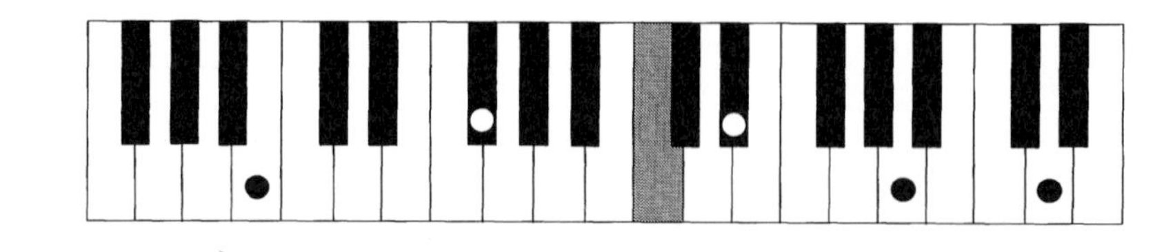

B added 9th - Badd9

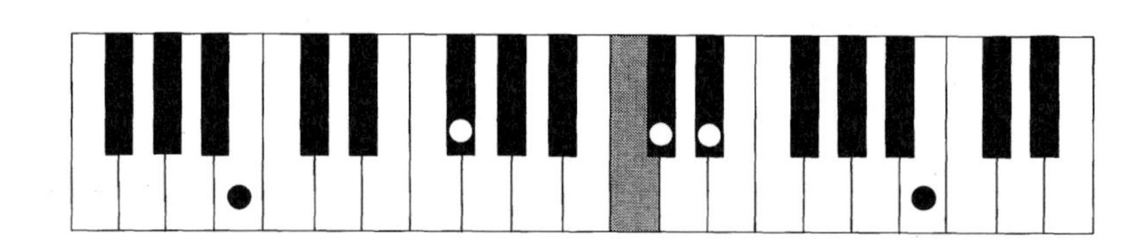

B major 9th - Bmaj9

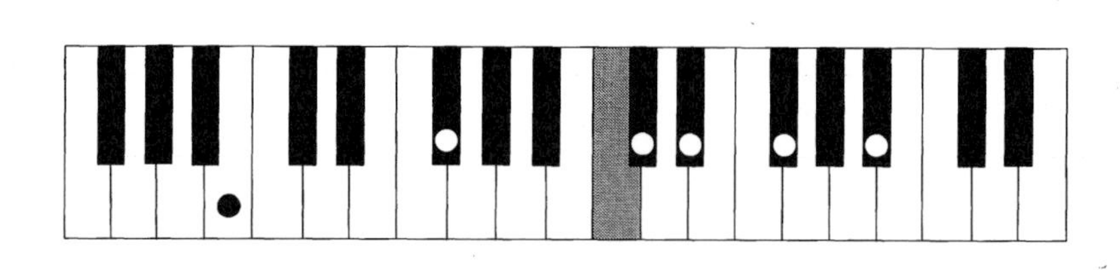

The B Collection

B dominant 9th - B9

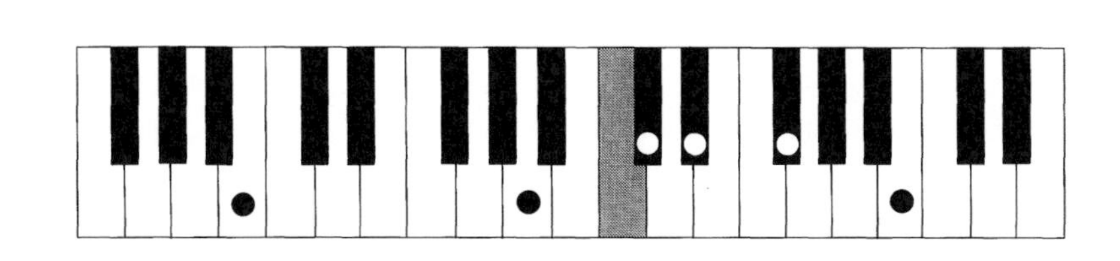

B dominant 9th with suspended 4th - B9sus or B9sus4

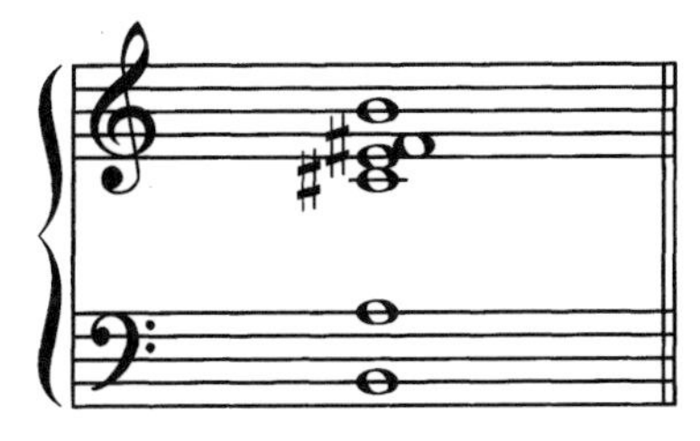

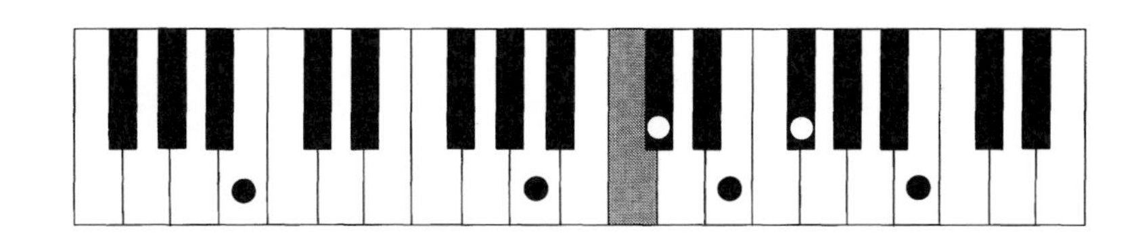

B dominant 9th with augmented 5th - B9+ or B9aug

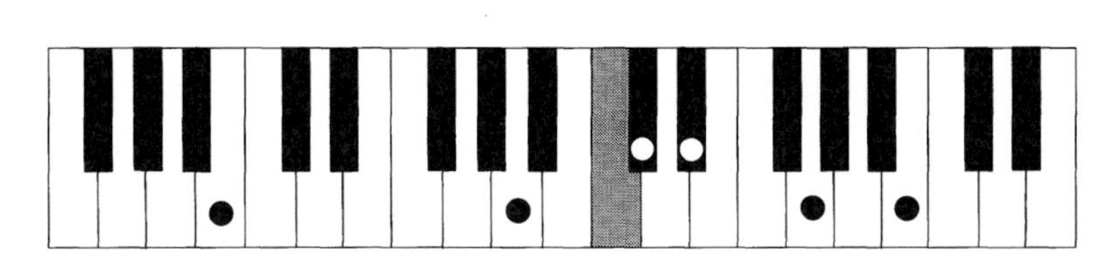

B dominant 9th with sharpened 11th - B9(♯11)
with flattened 5th - B9(♭5)

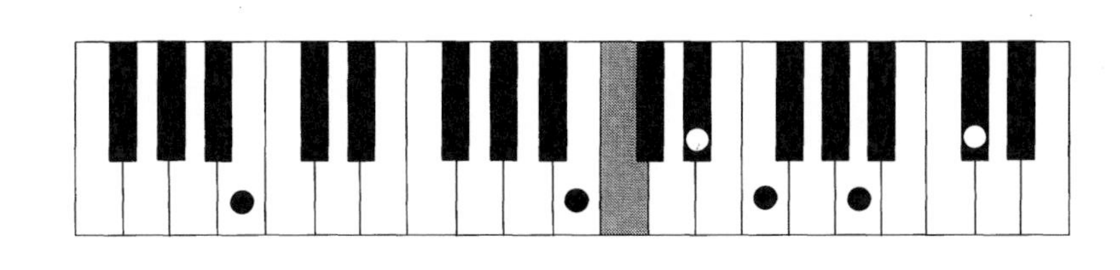

B dominant 11th - B11

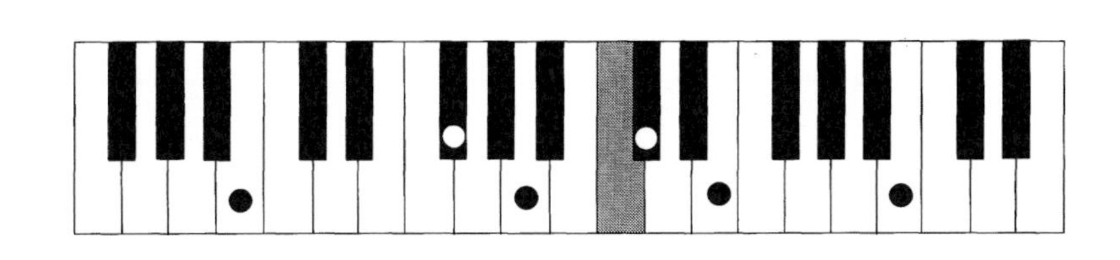

The B Collection

B dominant 11th with flattened 9th - B11(♭9)

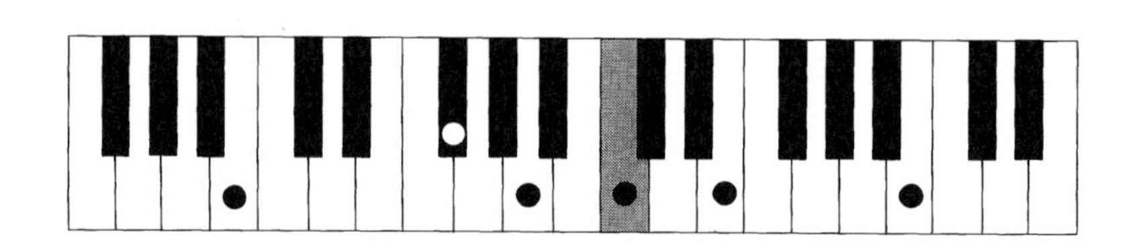

B dominant 13th - B13

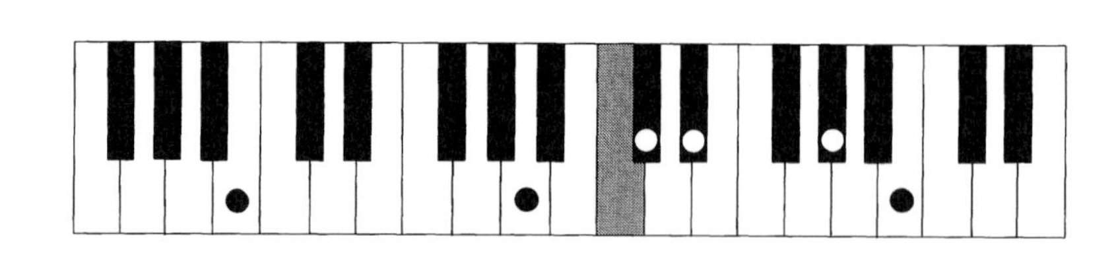

B dominant 13th with flattened 9th - B13(♭9)

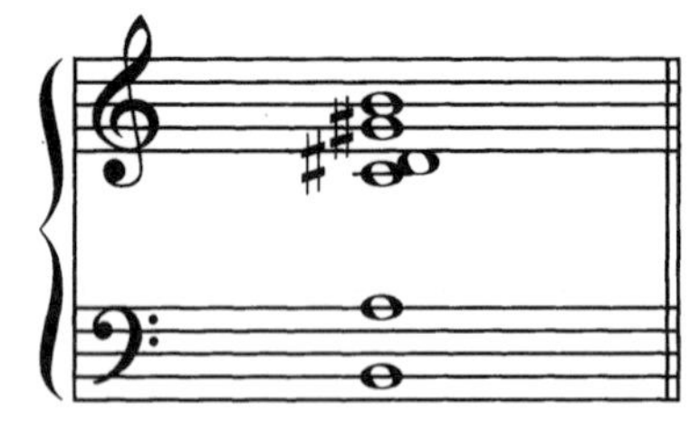

B minor - Bm

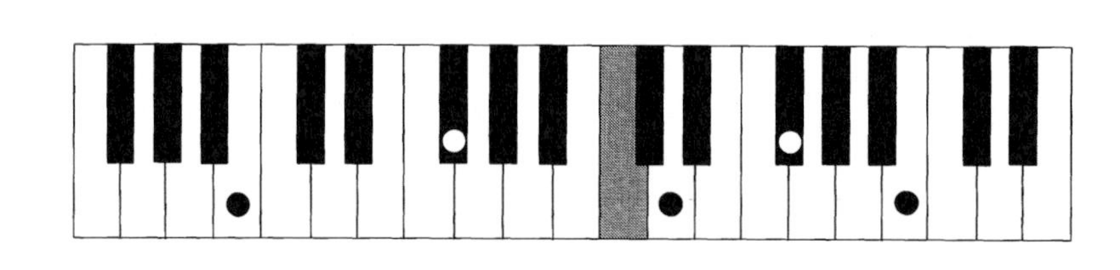

B diminished - B° or Bdim

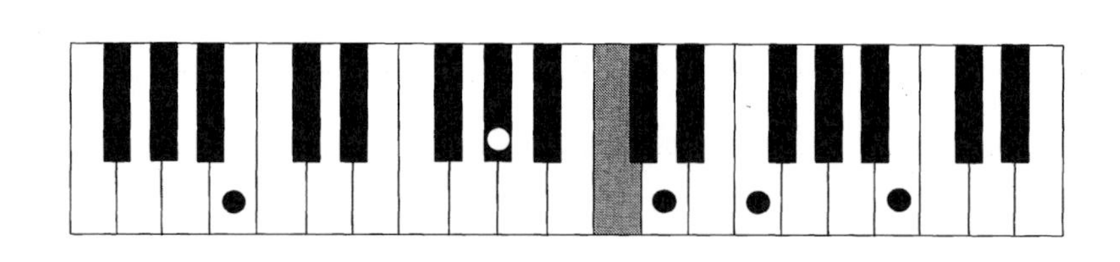

The B Collection

B minor added 6th - Bm6

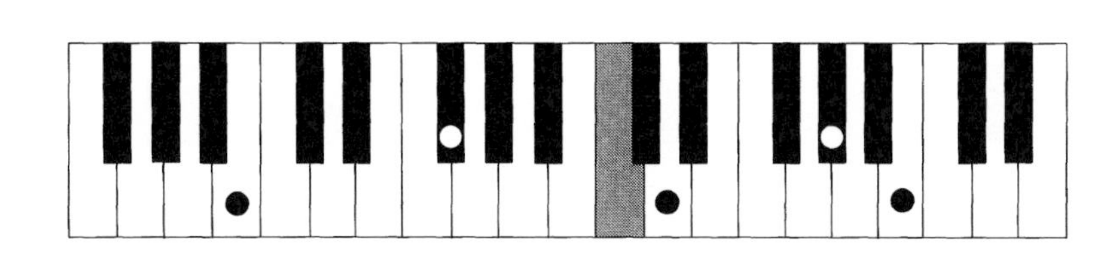

B minor 7th - Bm7

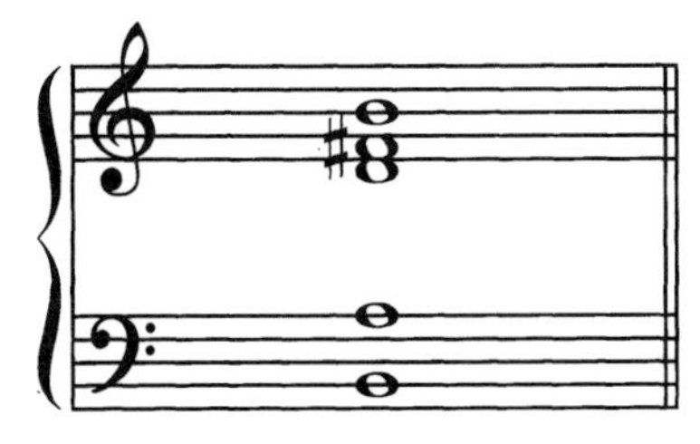

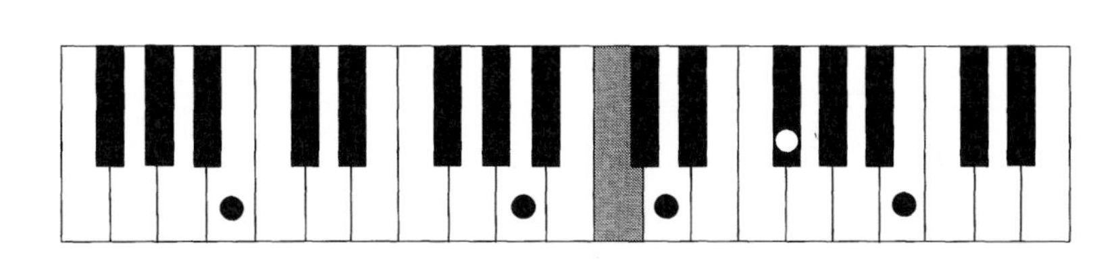

B minor 7th with flattened 5th - Bm7(♭5)

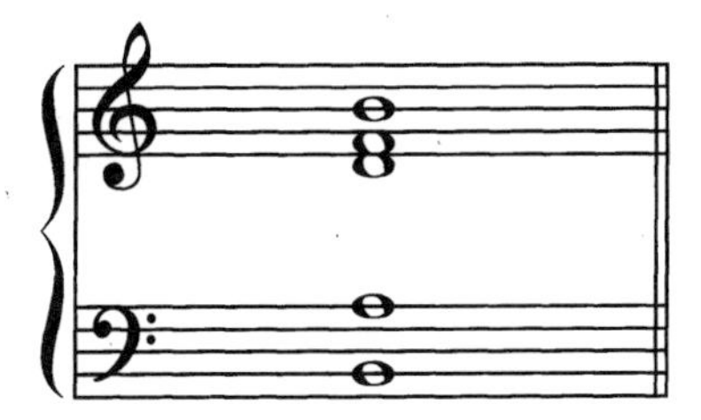

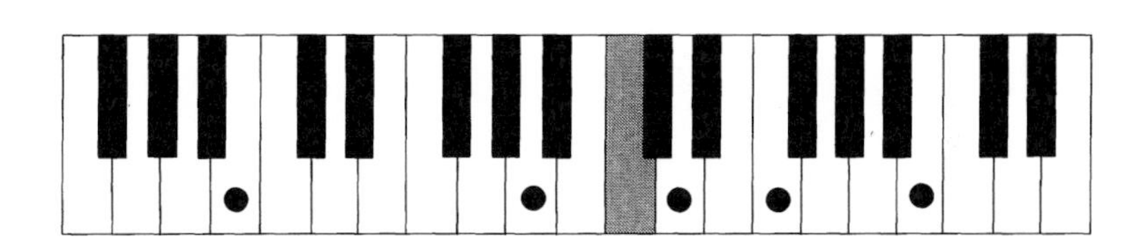

B minor added major 7th - Bm(maj7)

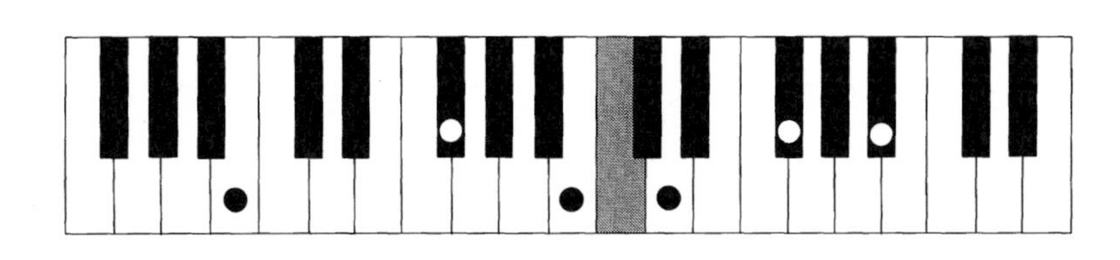

B minor 9th - Bm9

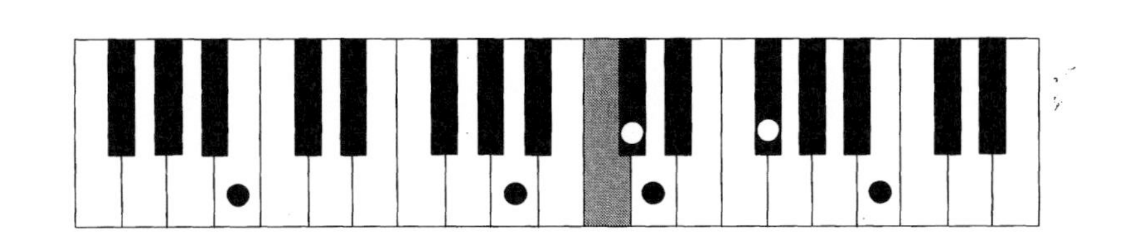

Your Own Collection

Why not use the charts below to notate your favourite chord voicings?

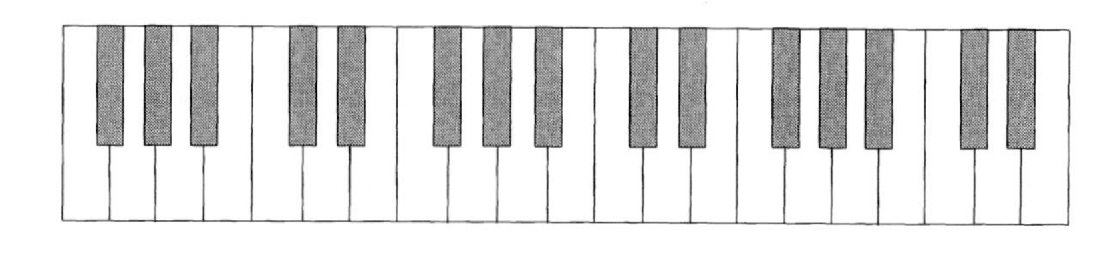

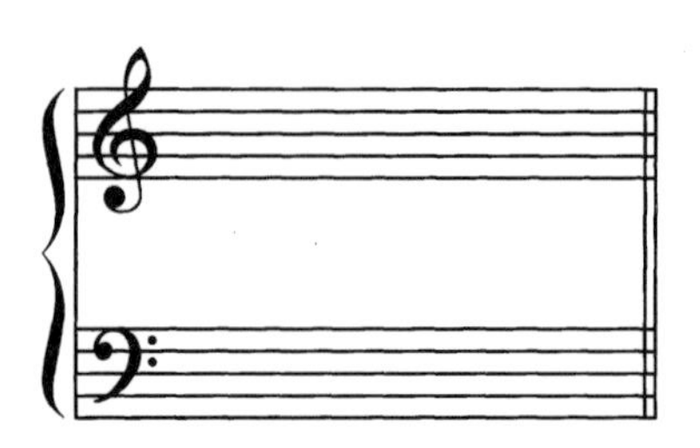
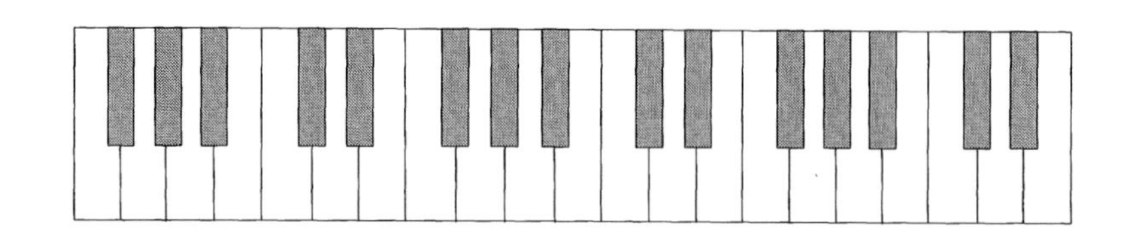

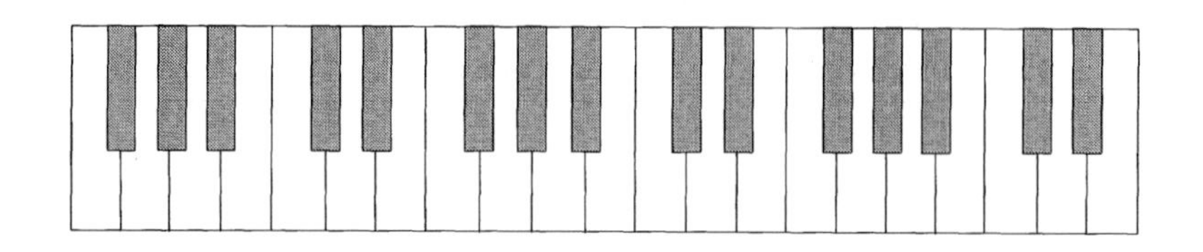

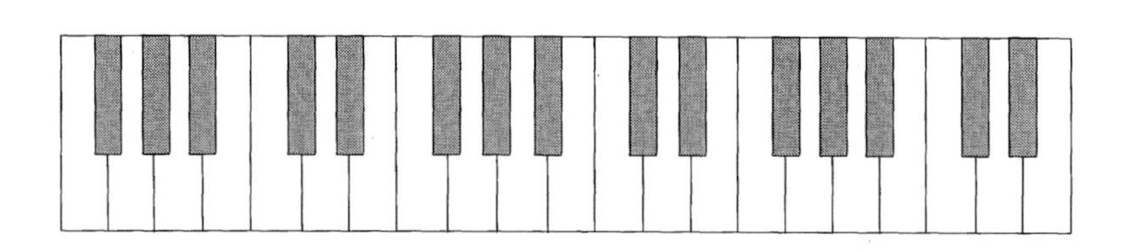

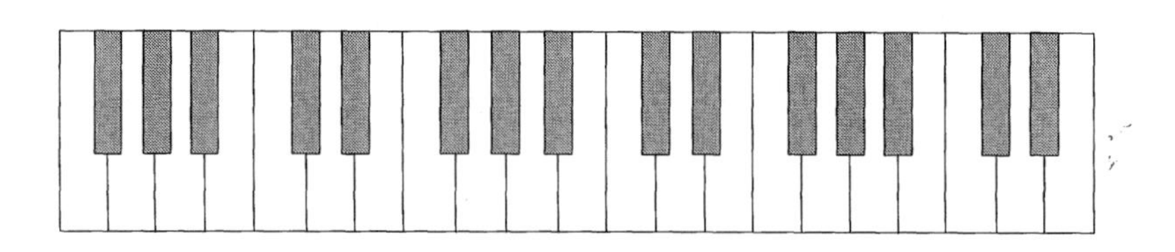

Your Own Collection

Why not use the charts below to notate your favourite chord voicings?

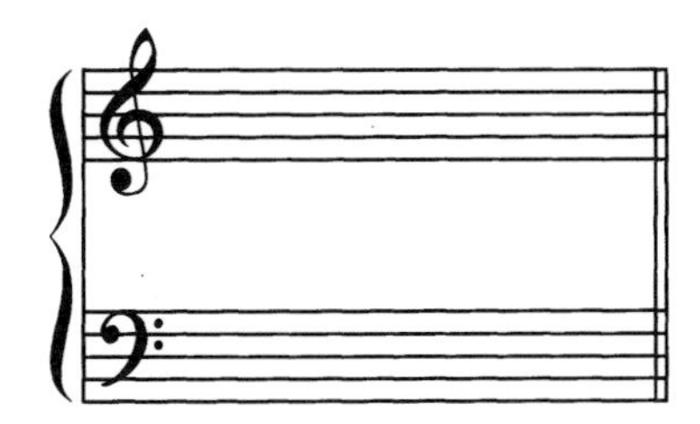
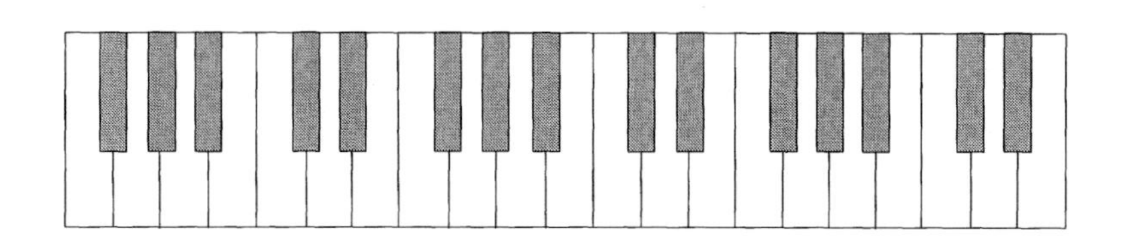

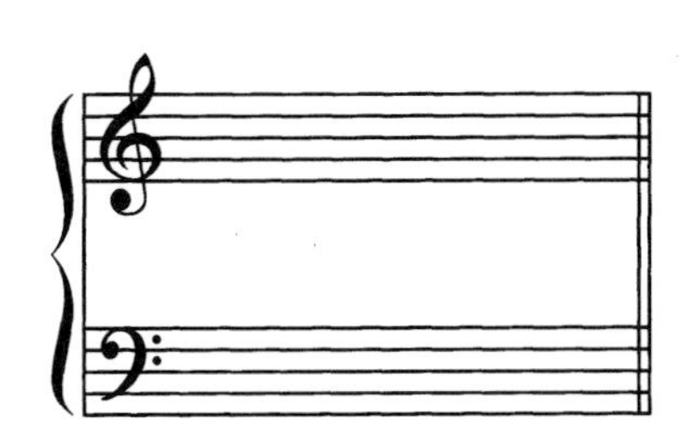
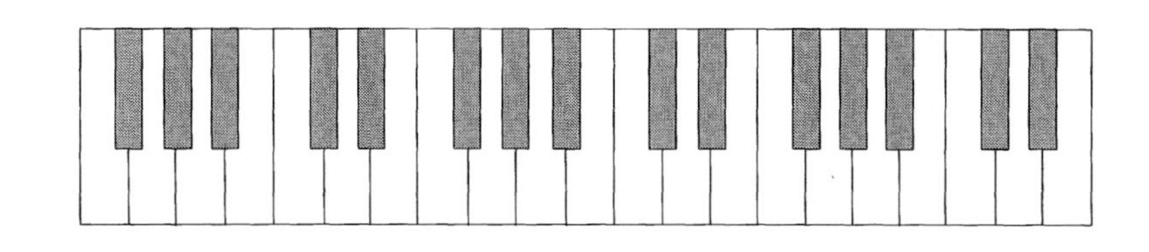

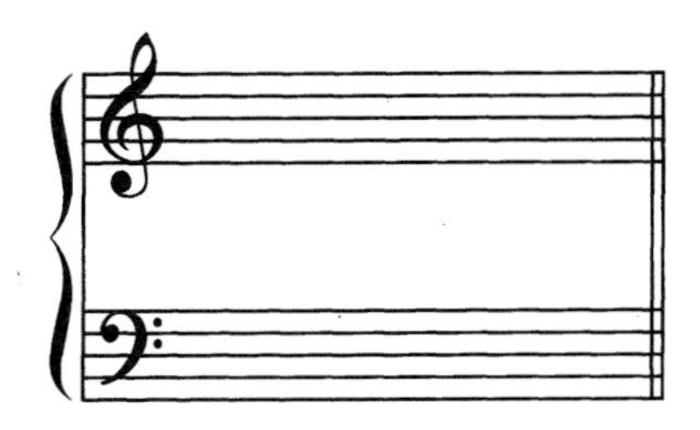
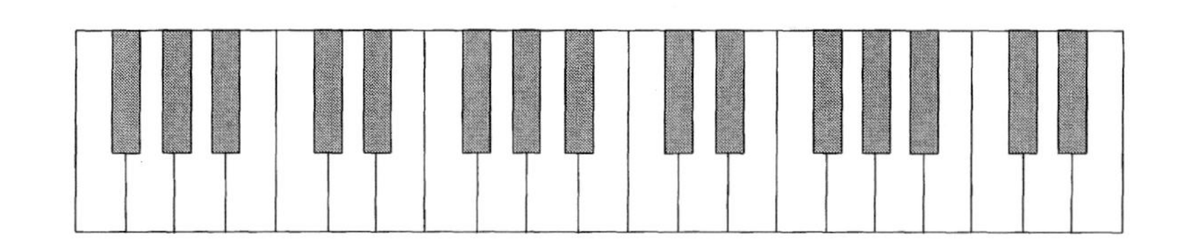

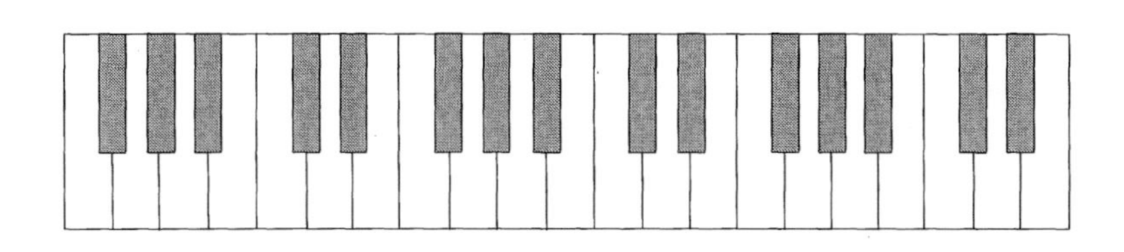

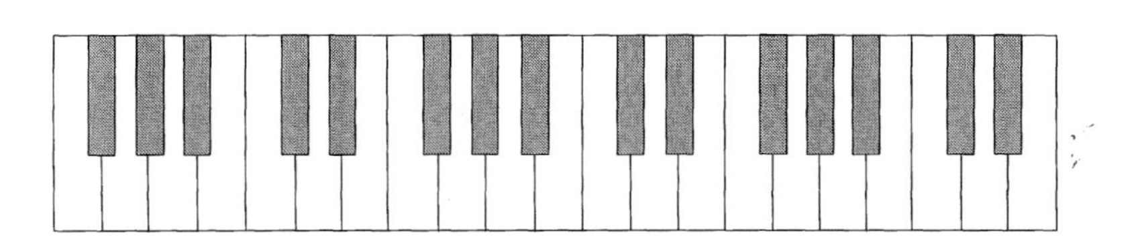

Your Own Collection

Why not use the charts below to notate your favourite chord voicings?

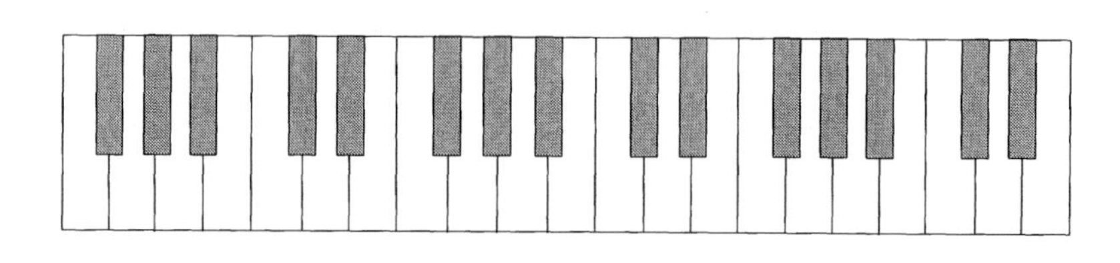

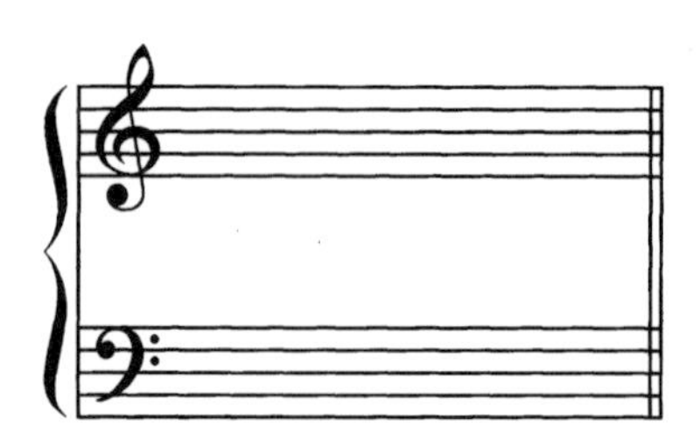

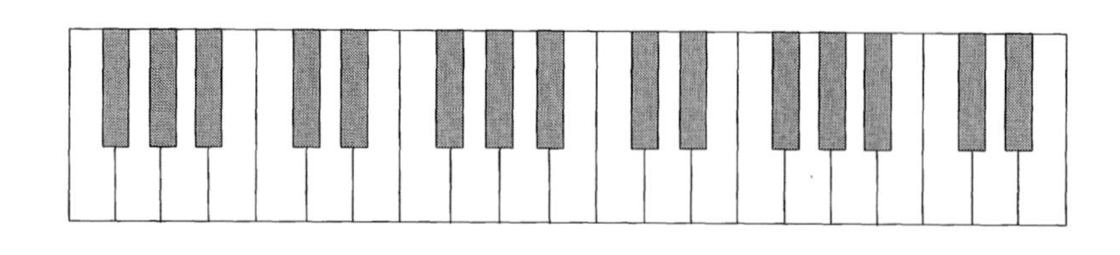

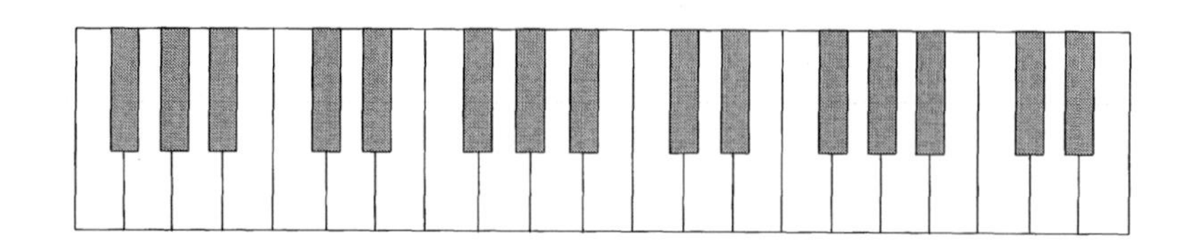

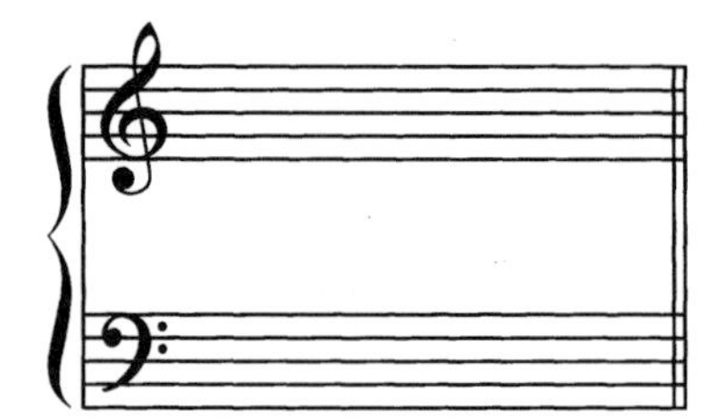

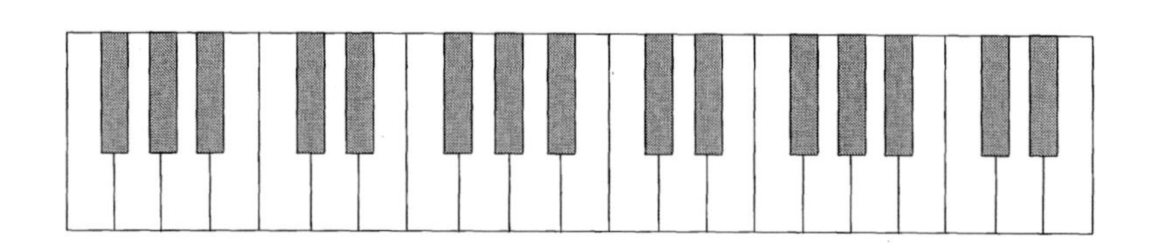

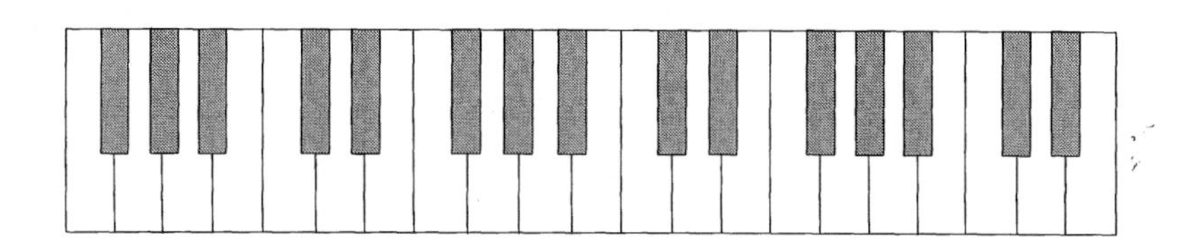

Your Own Collection

Why not use the charts below to notate your favourite chord voicings?

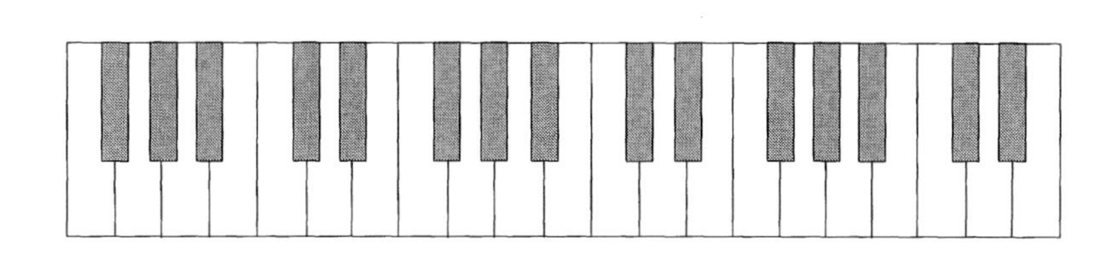

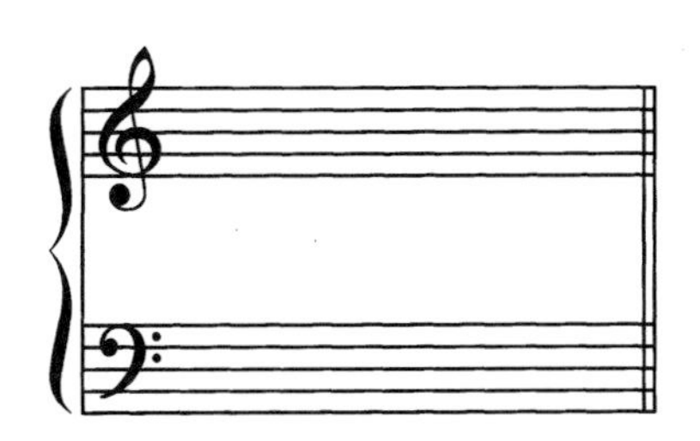

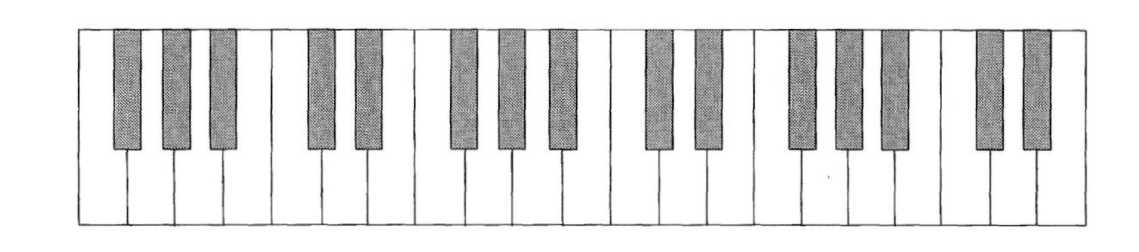

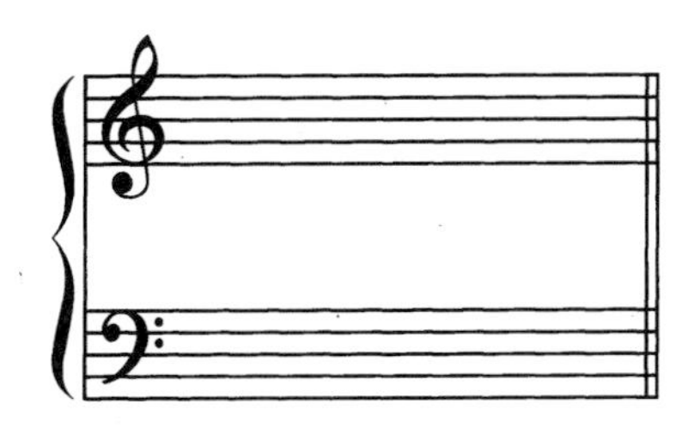

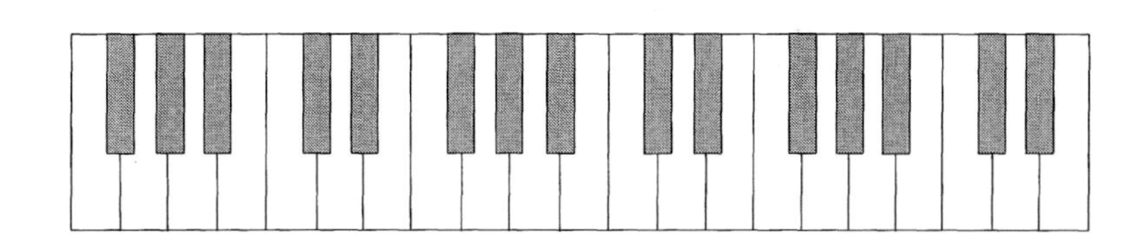

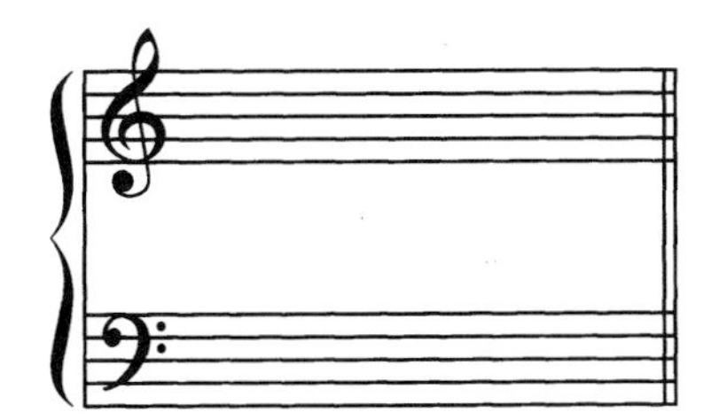

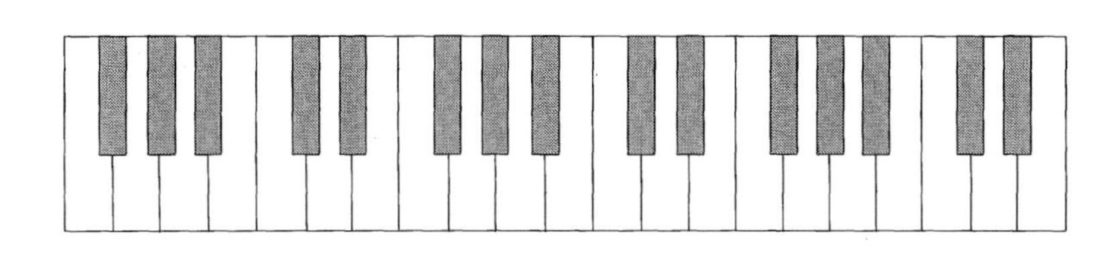

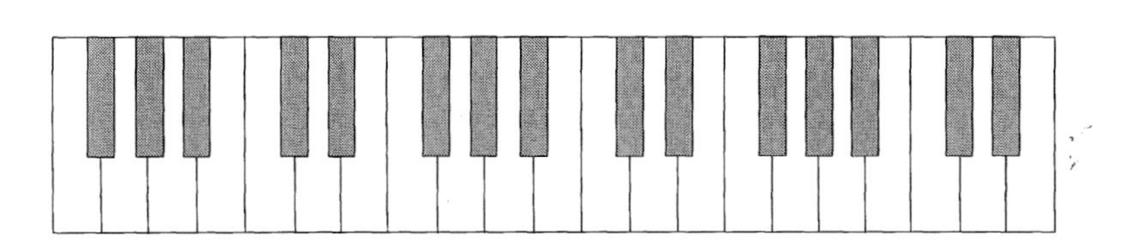

Your Own Collection

Why not use the charts below to notate your favourite chord voicings?

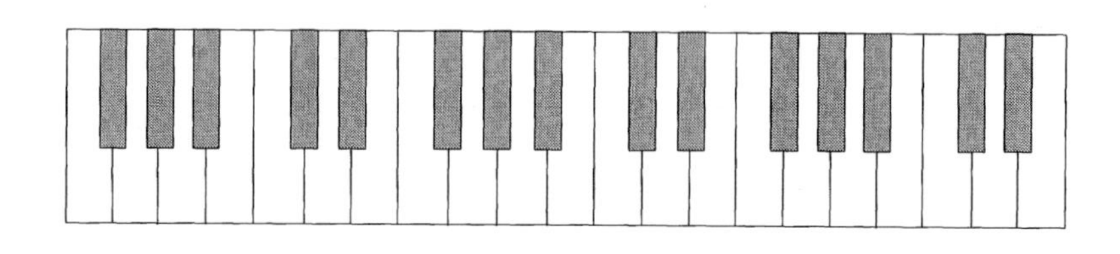

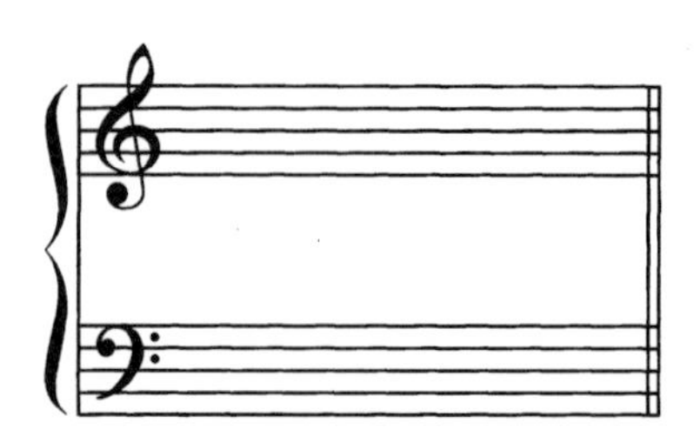
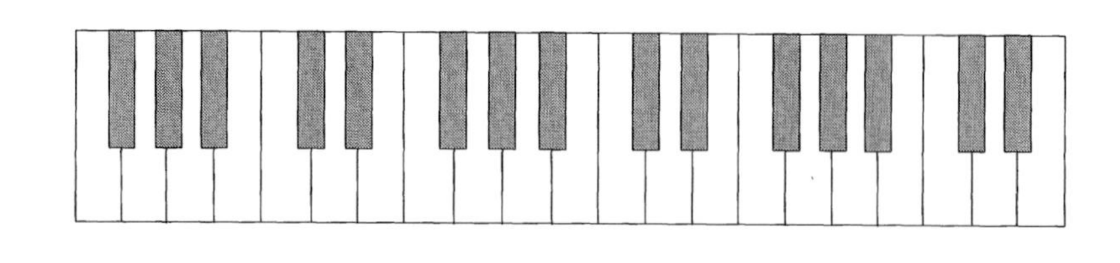

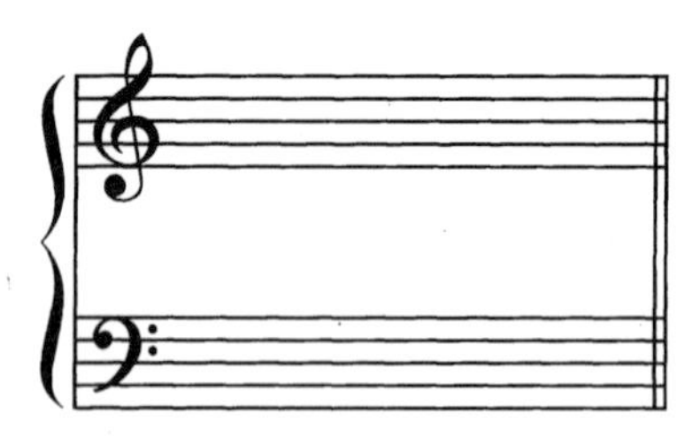
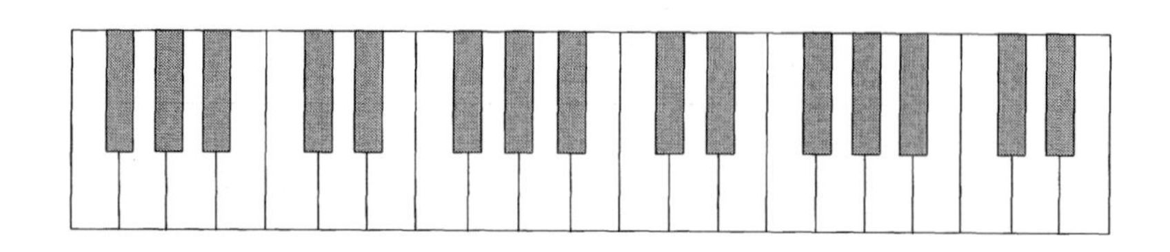

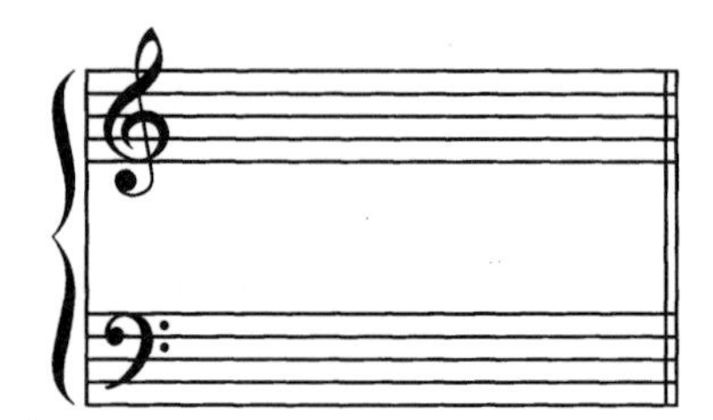
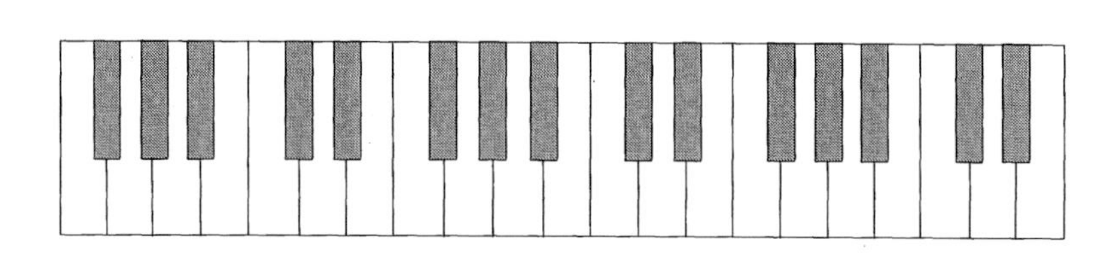

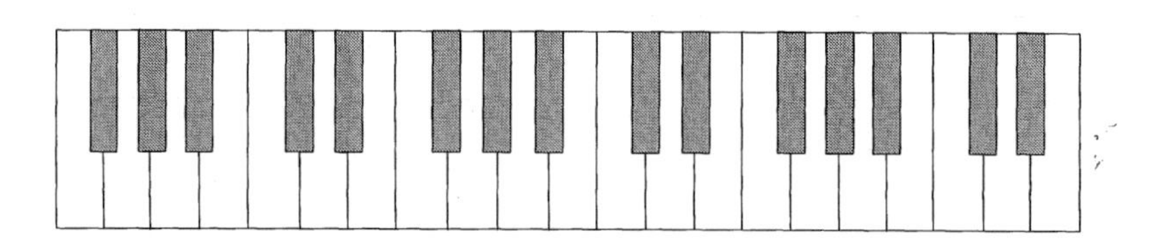

Your Own Collection

Why not use the charts below to notate your favourite chord voicings?

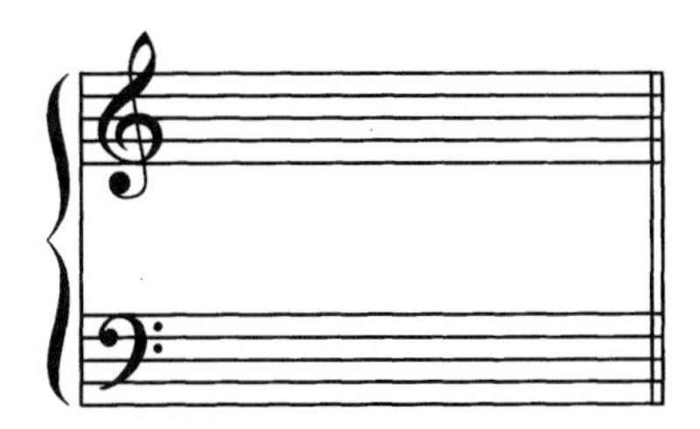
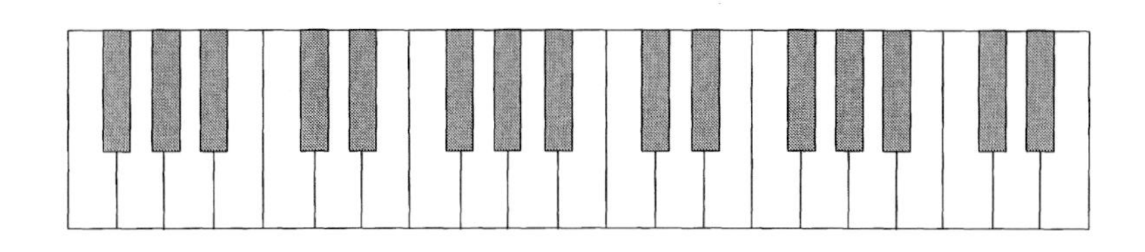

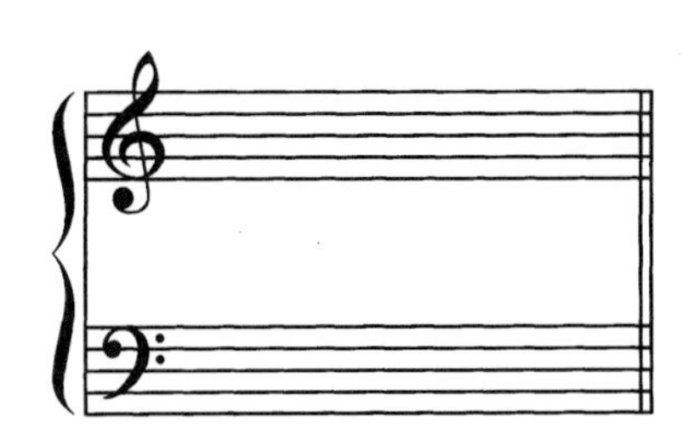
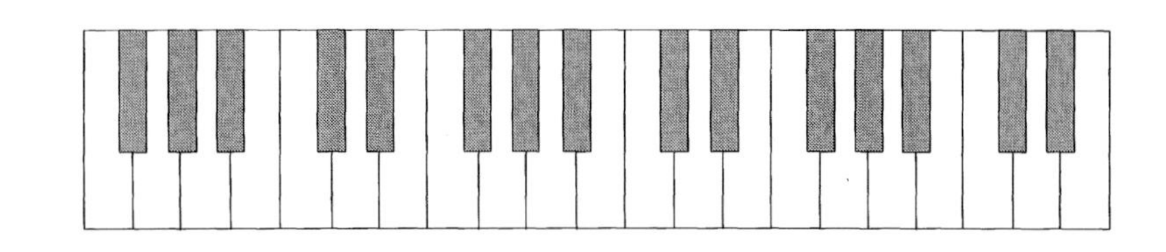

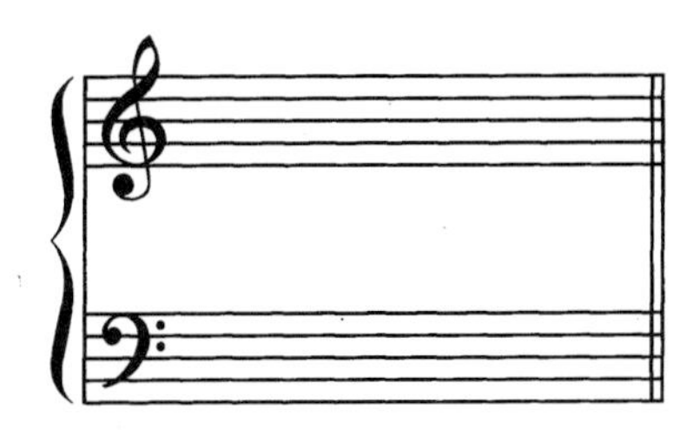
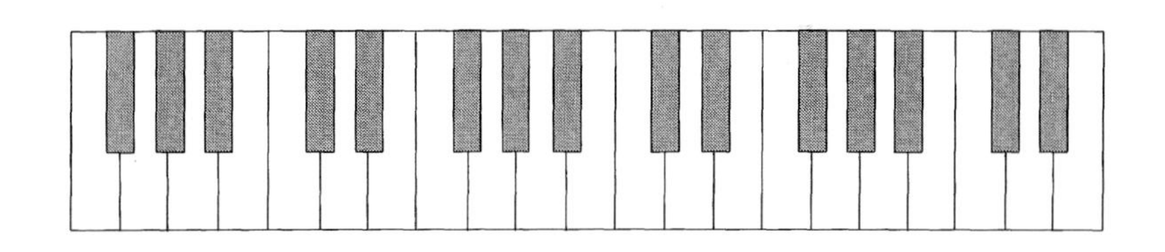

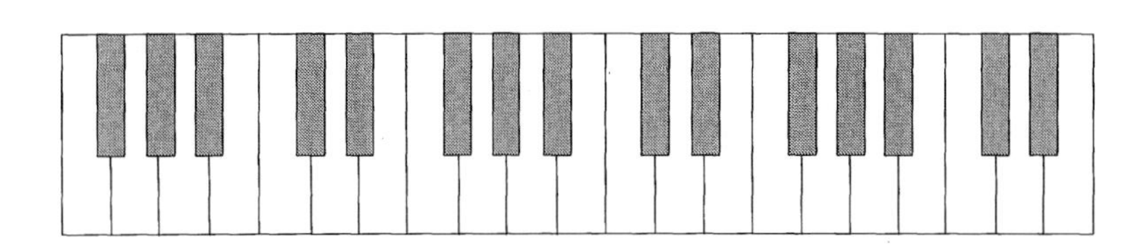

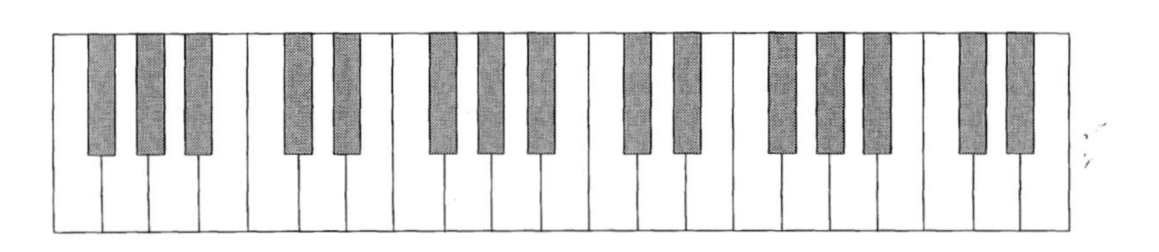

INDEX OF CHORDS

(in ascending order within the scale of C)

CHORD	PAGE
C	6
Csus4	6
Caug(C+)	6
C6	6
C6/9	6
Cmaj7	7
C7	7
C7sus4	7
C7(♭5)	7
C7aug(C7+)	7
C7(♭9)	8
C7(♭9/♭5)	8
C7(♯9)	8
Cadd9	8
Cmaj9	8
C9	9
C9sus4	9
C9aug(C9+)	9
C9(♯11)	9
C11	9
C11(♭9)	10
C13	10
C13(♭9)	10
Cm	10
Cdim(C°)	10
Cm6	11
Cm7	11
Cm7(♭5)	11
Cm(maj7)	11
Cm9	11
C♯	12
C♯sus4	12
C♯aug(C♯+)	12
C♯6	12
C♯6/9	12
C♯maj7	14
C♯7	14
C♯7sus4	14
C♯7(♭5)	14
C♯7aug(C♯7+)	14
C♯7(♭9)	16
C♯7(♭9/♭5)	16
C♯7(♯9)	16
C♯add9	16
C♯maj9	16
C♯9	18
C♯9sus4	18
C♯9aug(C♯9+)	18
C♯9(♯11)	18
C♯11	18
C♯11(♭9)	20
C♯13	20
C♯13(♭9)	20
C♯m	20
C♯dim(C♯°)	20
C♯m6	22
C♯m7	22
C♯m7(♭5)	22
C♯m(maj7)	22
C♯m9	22
D♭	13
D♭sus4	13
D♭aug(D♭+)	13
D♭6	13
D♭6/9	13
D♭maj7	15
D♭7	15
D♭7sus4	15
D♭7(♭5)	15
D♭7aug(D♭7+)	15
D♭7(♭9)	17
D♭7(♭9/♭5)	17
D♭7(♯9)	17
D♭add9	17
D♭maj9	17
D♭9	19
D♭9sus4	19
D♭9aug(D♭9+)	19
D♭9(♯11)	19
D♭11	19
D♭11(♭9)	21
D♭13	21
D♭13(♭9)	21
D♭m	21
D♭dim(D♭°)	21
D♭m6	23
D♭m7	23
D♭m7(♭5)	23
D♭m(maj7)	23
D♭m9	23
D	24
Dsus4	24
Daug(D+)	24
D6	24
D6/9	24
Dmaj7	25
D7	25
D7sus4	25
D7(♭5)	25
D7aug(D7+)	25
D7(♭9)	26
D7(♭9/♭5)	26
D7(♯9)	26
Dadd9	26
Dmaj9	26
D9	27
D9sus4	27
D9aug(D9+)	27
D9(♯11)	27
D11	27
D11(♭9)	28
D13	28
D13(♭9)	28
Dm	28
Ddim(D°)	28
Dm6	29
Dm7	29
Dm7(♭5)	29
Dm(maj7)	29
Dm9	29
D♯	30
D♯sus4	30
D♯aug(D♯+)	30
D♯6	30
D♯6/9	30
D♯maj7	32
D♯7	32
D♯7sus4	32
D♯7(♭5)	32
D♯7aug(D♯7+)	32
D♯7(♭9)	34
D♯7(♭9/♭5)	34
D♯7(♯9)	34
D♯add9	34
D♯maj9	34
D♯9	36
D♯9sus4	36
D♯9aug(D♯9+)	36
D♯9(♯11)	36
D♯11	36
D♯11(♭9)	38
D♯13	38
D♯13(♭9)	38
D♯m	38
D♯dim(D♯°)	38
D♯m6	40
D♯m7	40
D♯m7(♭5)	40
D♯m(maj7)	40
D♯m9	40
E♭	31
E♭sus4	31
E♭aug(E♭+)	31
E♭6	31
E♭6/9	31
E♭maj7	33
E♭7	33
E♭7sus4	33
E♭7(♭5)	33
E♭7aug(E♭7+)	33
E♭7(♭9)	35
E♭7(♭9/♭5)	35
E♭7(♯9)	35
E♭add9	35
E♭maj9	35
E♭9	37
E♭9sus4	37
E♭9aug(E♭9+)	37
E♭9(♯11)	37
E♭11	37
E♭11(♭9)	39
E♭13	39
E♭13(♭9)	39
E♭m	39
E♭dim(E♭°)	39
E♭m6	41
E♭m7	41
E♭m7(♭5)	41
E♭m(maj7)	41
E♭m9	41
E	42
Esus4	42
Eaug(E+)	42
E6	42
E6/9	42
Emaj7	43
E7	43
E7sus4	43
E7(♭5)	43
E7aug(E7+)	43
E7(♭9)	44
E7(♭9/♭5)	44
E7(♯9)	44
Eadd9	44
Emaj9	44
E9	45
E9sus4	45
E9aug(E9+)	45
E9(♯11)	45
E11	45
E11(♭9)	46
E13	46
E13(♭9)	46
Em	46
Edim(E°)	46
Em6	47
Em7	47
Em7(♭5)	47
Em(maj7)	47
Em9	47
F	48
Fsus4	48
Faug(F+)	48
F6	48
F6/9	48
Fmaj7	49
F7	49
F7sus4	49
F7(♭5)	49
F7aug(F7+)	49
F7(♭9)	50
F7(♭9/♭5)	50
F7(♯9)	50
Fadd9	50
Fmaj9	50
F9	51
F9sus4	51
F9aug(F9+)	51
F9(♯11)	51
F11	51
F11(♭9)	52
F13	52
F13(♭9)	52
Fm	52
Fdim(F°)	52
Fm6	53
Fm7	53
Fm7(♭5)	53
Fm(maj7)	53
Fm9	53

CHORD	PAGE
F♯	54
F♯sus4	54
F♯aug(F♯+)	54
F♯6	54
F♯6/9	54
F♯maj7	56
F♯7	56
F♯7sus4	56
F♯7(♭5)	56
F♯7aug(F♯7+)	56
F♯7(♭9)	58
F♯7(♭9/♭5)	58
F♯7(♯9)	58
F♯add9	58
F♯maj9	58
F♯9	60
F♯9sus4	60
F♯9aug(F♯9+)	60
F♯9(♯11)	60
F♯11	60
F♯11(♭9)	62
F♯13	62
F♯13(♭9)	62
F♯m	62
F♯dim(F♯°)	62
F♯m6	64
F♯m7	64
F♯m7(♭5)	64
F♯m(maj7)	64
F♯m9	64
G♭	55
G♭sus4	55
G♭aug(G♭+)	55
G♭6	55
G♭6/9	55
G♭maj7	57
G♭7	57
G♭7sus4	57
G♭7(♭5)	57
G♭7aug(G♭7+)	57
G♭7(♭9)	59
G♭7(♭9/♭5)	59
G♭7(♯9)	59
G♭add9	59
G♭maj9	59
G♭9	61
G♭9sus4	61
G♭9aug(G♭9+)	61
G♭9(♯11)	61
G♭11	61
G♭11(♭9)	63
G♭13	63
G♭13(♭9)	63

CHORD	PAGE
G♭m	63
G♭dim(G♭°)	63
G♭m6	65
G♭m7	65
G♭m7(♭5)	65
G♭m(maj7)	65
G♭m9	65
G	66
Gsus4	66
Gaug(G+)	66
G6	66
G6/9	66
Gmaj7	67
G7	67
G7sus4	67
G7(♭5)	67
G7aug(G7+)	67
G7(♭9)	68
G7(♭9/♭5)	68
G7(♯9)	68
Gadd9	68
Gmaj9	68
G9	69
G9sus4	69
G9aug(G9+)	69
G9(♯11)	69
G11	69
G11(♭9)	70
G13	70
G13(♭9)	70
Gm	70
Gdim(G°)	70
Gm6	71
Gm7	71
Gm7(♭5)	71
Gm(maj7)	71
Gm9	71
G♯	72
G♯sus4	72
G♯aug(G♯+)	72
G♯6	72
G♯6/9	72
G♯maj7	74
G♯7	74
G♯7sus4	74
G♯7(♭5)	74
G♯7aug(G♯7+)	74
G♯7(♭9)	76
G♯7(♭9/♭5)	76
G♯7(♯9)	76
G♯add9	76
G♯maj9	76
G♯9	78

CHORD	PAGE
G♯9sus4	78
G♯9aug(G♯9+)	78
G♯9(♯11)	78
G♯11	78
G♯11(♭9)	80
G♯13	80
G♯13(♭9)	80
G♯m	80
G♯dim(G♯°)	80
G♯m6	82
G♯m7	82
G♯m7(♭5)	82
G♯m(maj7)	82
G♯m9	82
A♭	73
A♭sus4	73
A♭aug(A♭+)	73
A♭6	73
A♭6/9	73
A♭maj7	75
A♭7	75
A♭7sus4	75
A♭7(♭5)	75
A♭7aug(A♭7+)	75
A♭7(♭9)	77
A♭7(♭9/♭5)	77
A♭7(♯9)	77
A♭add9	77
A♭maj9	77
A♭9	79
A♭9sus4	79
A♭9aug(A♭9+)	79
A♭9(♯11)	79
A♭11	79
A♭11(♭9)	81
A♭13	81
A♭13(♭9)	81
A♭m	81
A♭dim(A♭°)	81
A♭m6	83
A♭m7	83
A♭m7(♭5)	83
A♭m(maj7)	83
A♭m9	83
A	84
Asus4	84
Aaug(A+)	84
A6	84
A6/9	84
Amaj7	85
A7	85
A7sus4	85
A7(♭5)	85

CHORD	PAGE
A7aug(A7+)	85
A7(♭9)	86
A7(♭9/♭5)	86
A7(♯9)	86
Aadd9	86
Amaj9	86
A9	87
A9sus4	87
A9aug(A9+)	87
A9(♯11)	87
A11	87
A11(♭9)	88
A13	88
A13(♭9)	88
Am	88
Adim(A°)	88
Am6	89
Am7	89
Am7(♭5)	89
Am(maj7)	89
Am9	89
B♭	90
B♭sus4	90
B♭aug(B♭+)	90
B♭6	90
B♭6/9	90
B♭maj7	91
B♭7	91
B♭7sus4	91
B♭7(♭5)	91
B♭7aug(B♭7+)	91
B♭7(♭9)	92
B♭7(♭9/♭5)	92
B♭7(♯9)	92
B♭add9	92
B♭maj9	92
B♭9	93
B♭9sus4	93
B♭9aug(B♭9+)	93
B♭9(♯11)	93
B♭11	93
B♭11(♭9)	94
B♭13	94
B♭13(♭9)	94
B♭m	94
B♭dim(B♭°)	94
B♭m6	95
B♭m7	95
B♭m7(♭5)	95
B♭m(maj7)	95
B♭m9	95
B	96
Bsus4	96

CHORD	PAGE
Baug(B+)	96
B6	96
B6/9	96
Bmaj7	97
B7	97
B7sus4	97
B7(♭5)	97
B7aug(B7+)	97
B7(♭9)	98
B7(♭9/♭5)	98
B7(♯9)	98
Badd9	98
Bmaj9	98
B9	99
B9sus4	99
B9aug(B9+)	99
B9(♯11)	99
B11	99
B11(♭9)	100
B13	100
B13(♭9)	100
Bm	100
Bdim(B°)	100
Bm6	101
Bm7	101
Bm7(♭5)	101
Bm(maj7)	101
Bm9	101